Compositions Book 2

Music for
Chorus and Piano

by
Ken Langer

Compositions Book 2

Music for
sChorus and Piano

by
Ken Langer

Compositions Book 2
Music for Chorus and Piano
by Ken Langer

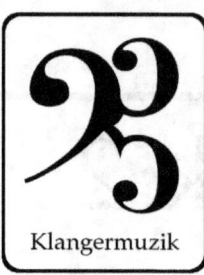

Klangermuzik
http://www.klangermuzik.com

First Edition (Softcover)

Copyright © 2013, Ken Langer

ISBN: 978-1-300-67425-2

Produced in the United States of America

The author may be contacted at ken@kenlanger.com.

Table of Contents

Introduction

I have been involved as a performer, composer, and director of choral ensembles since my high school band director asked me to join the choir because they had no tenors. Alas, being a high tenor got me invitations to join a lot of choirs and singing in those groups made me want to conduct and compose for them as well. When I became a full-time director of a Unitarian-Universalist music program I had the opportunity to compose quite a few numbers for them. Many of those works are in this collection and reflect a spiritual overtone to them reflective of U-U values. Since one of those values is a respect for all religious traditions, many of these works are suitable for many different kinds of choirs.

Some of the works are published by Yelton Rhodes Music (those marked with an asterisk in the Table of Contents above). Individual copies for those pieces can be obtained through that publisher. Other works can be obtained directly through me.

For more information and to hear recordings and transcriptions of music in this and all the other collections please visit http://klangermuzik.com.

All The Best

Ken Langer

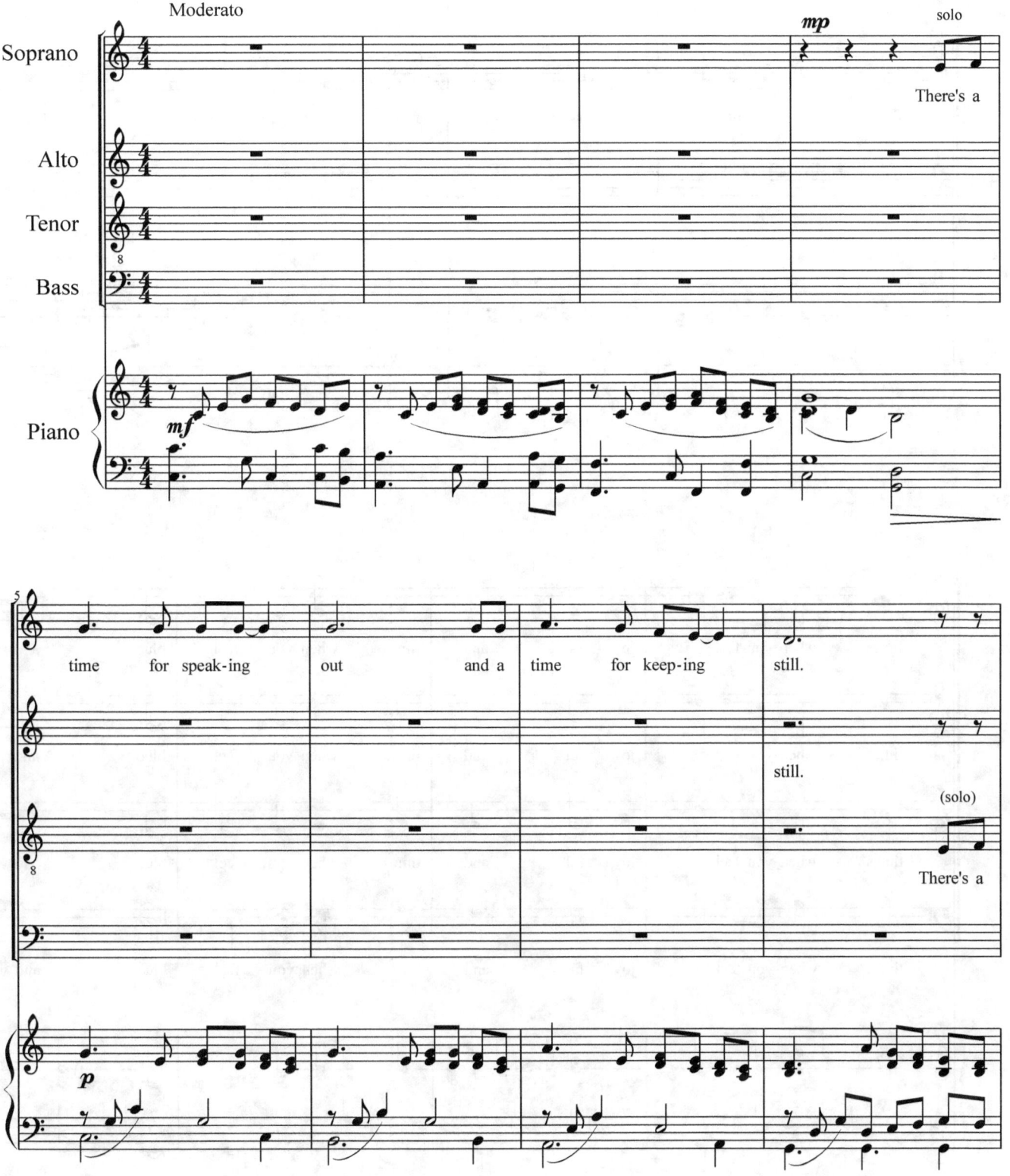

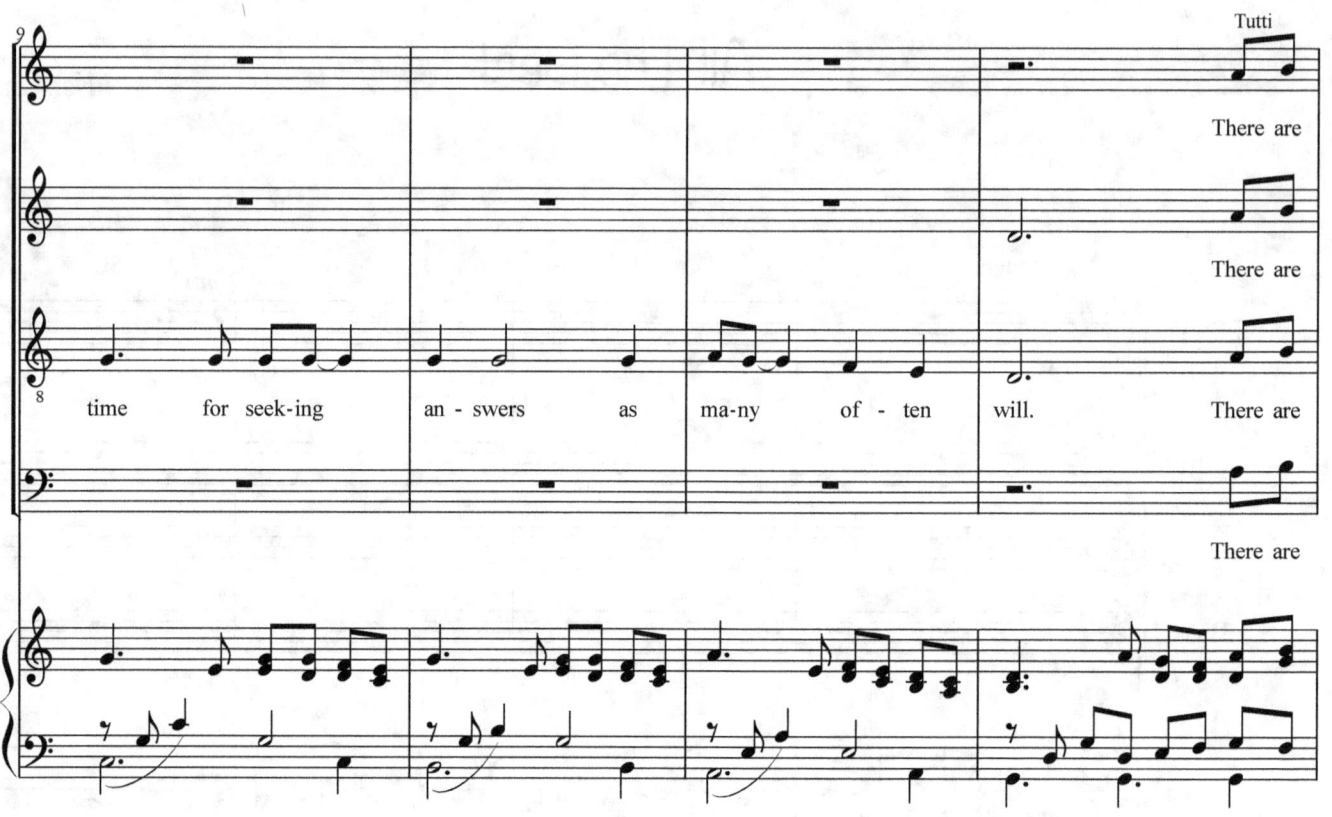

There are

There are

time for seek-ing an - swers as ma-ny of - ten will. There are

There are

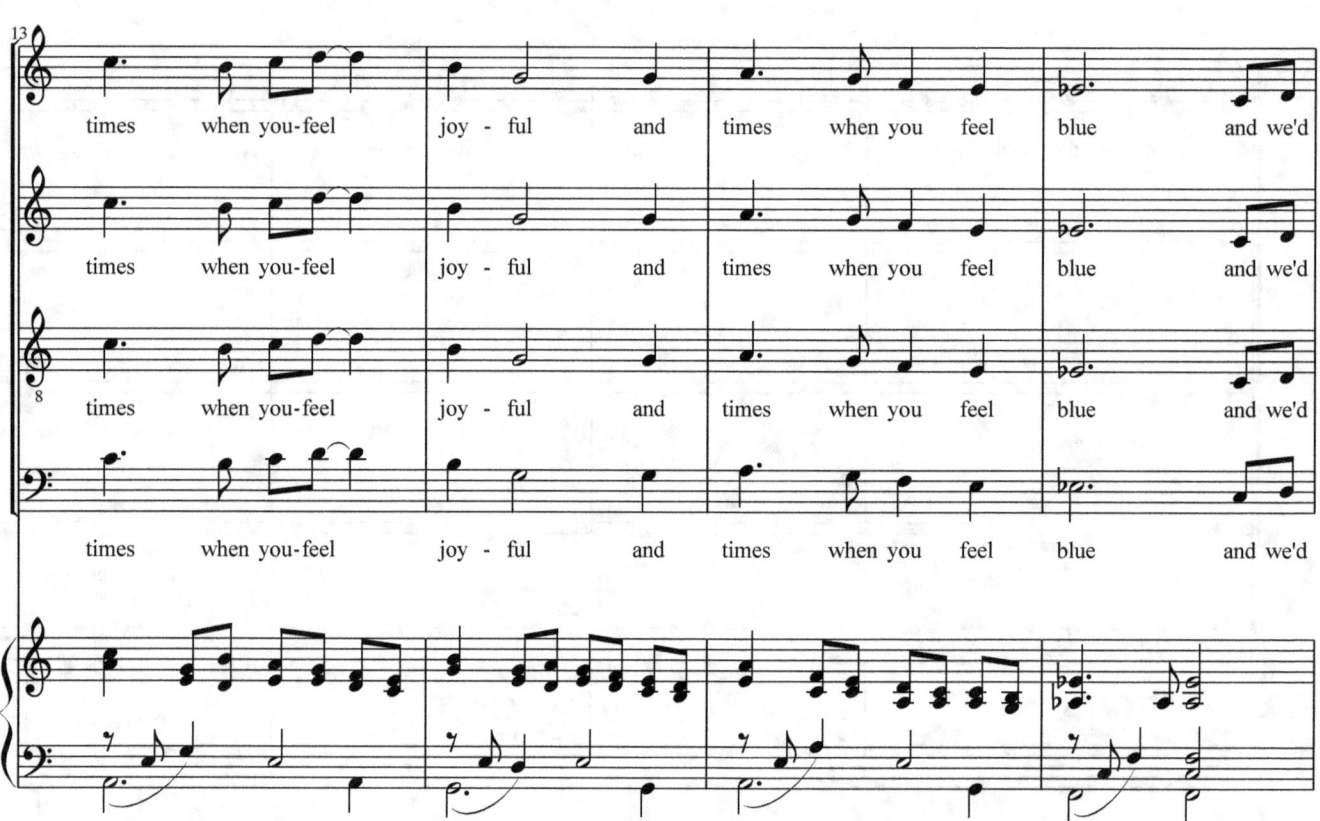

times when you-feel joy - ful and times when you feel blue and we'd

times when you-feel joy - ful and times when you feel blue and we'd

times when you-feel joy - ful and times when you feel blue and we'd

times when you-feel joy - ful and times when you feel blue and we'd

10

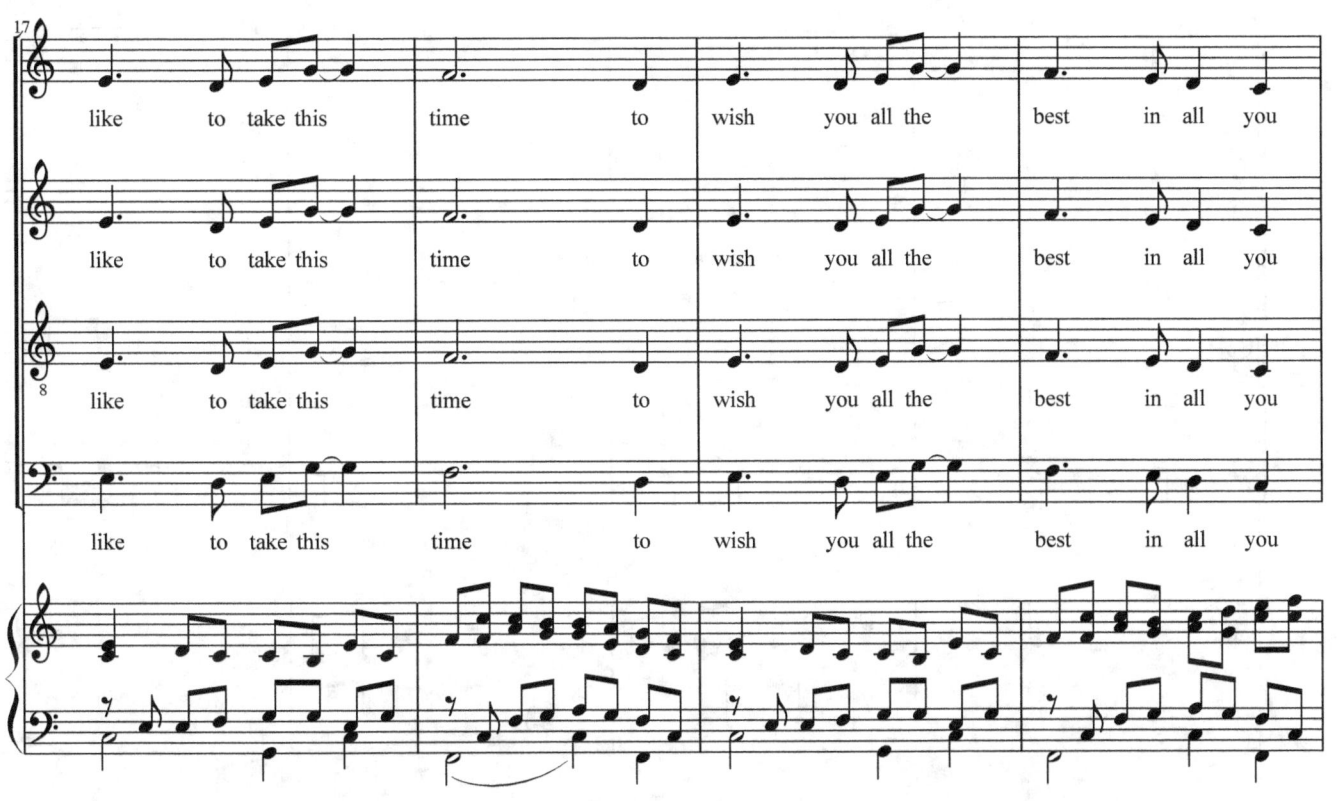

like to take this time to wish you all the best in all you

like to take this time to wish you all the best in all you

like to take this time to wish you all the best in all you

like to take this time to wish you all the best in all you

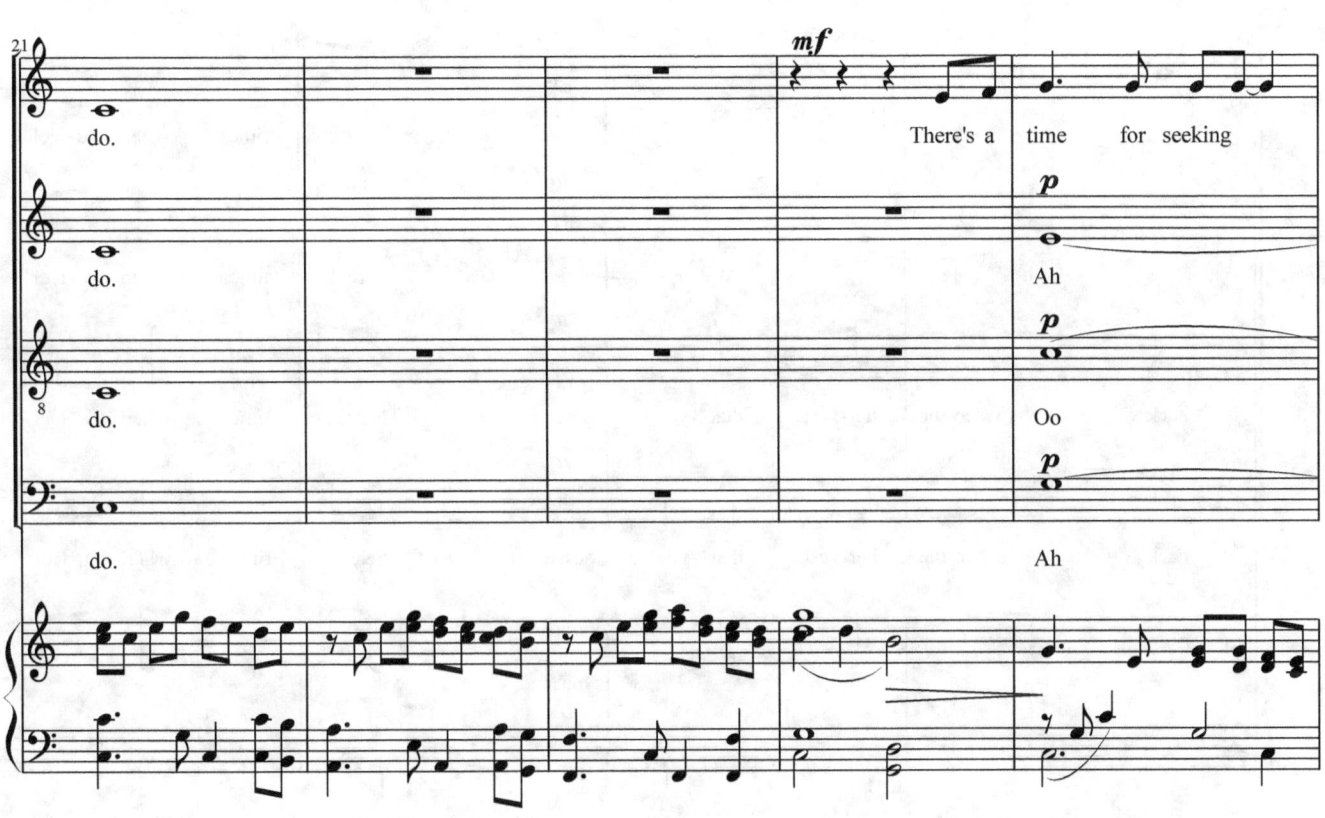

do.

There's a time for seeking

do.

Ah

do.

Oo

do.

Ah

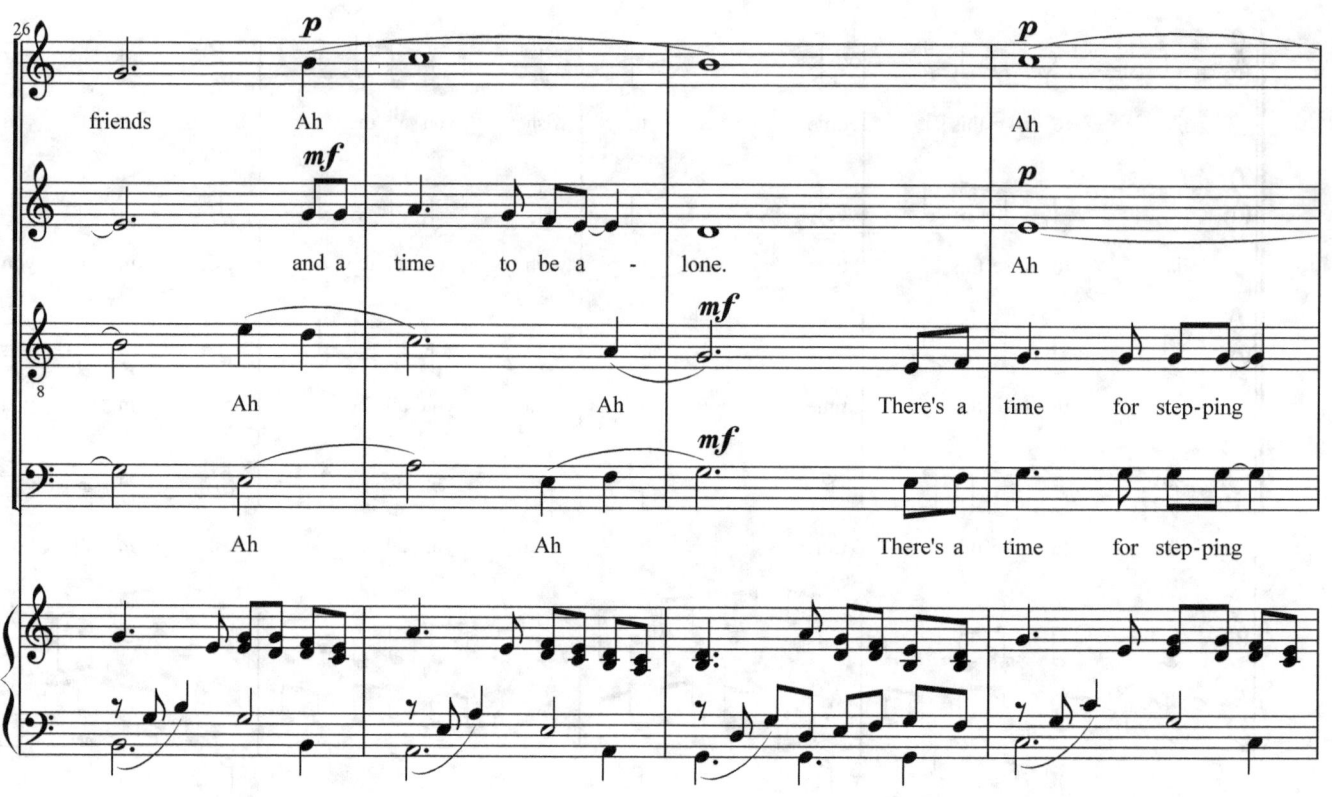

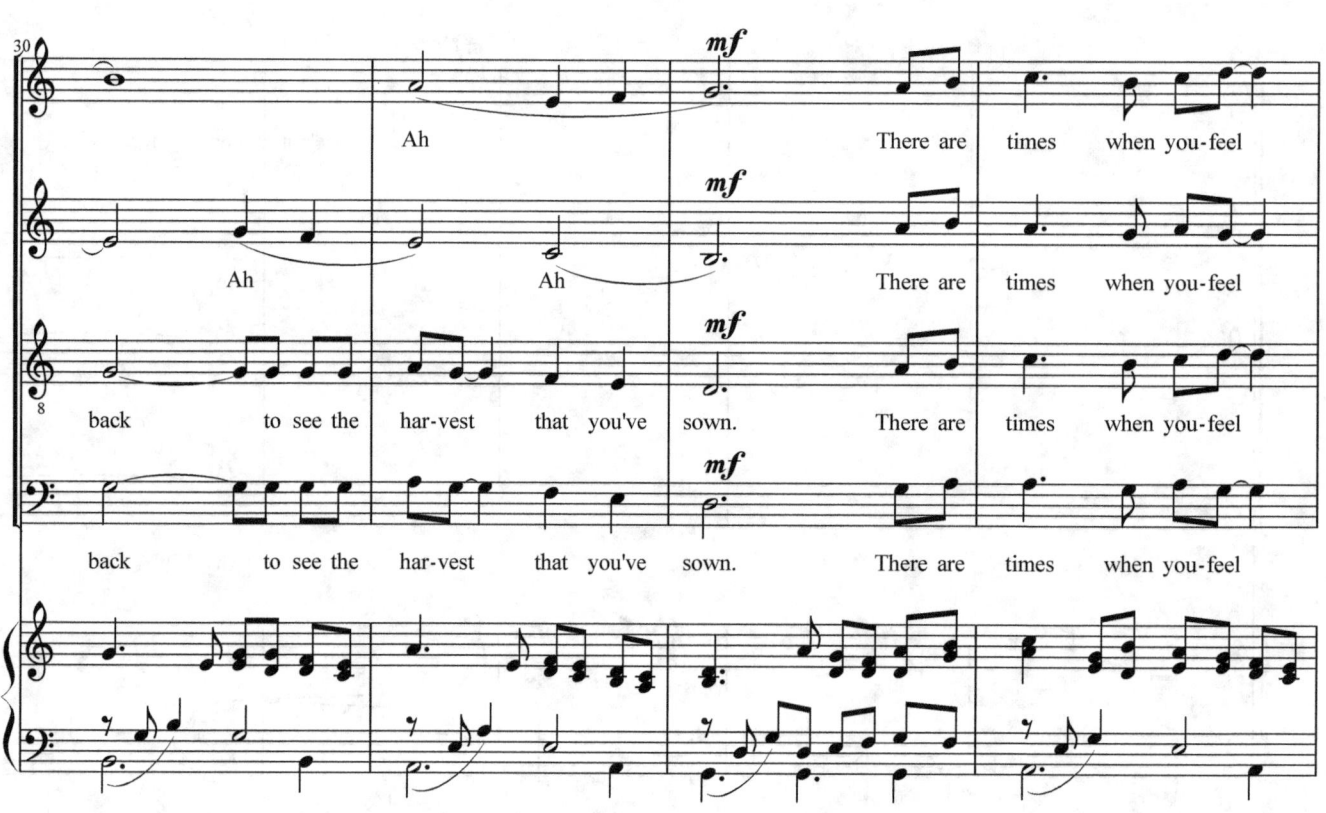

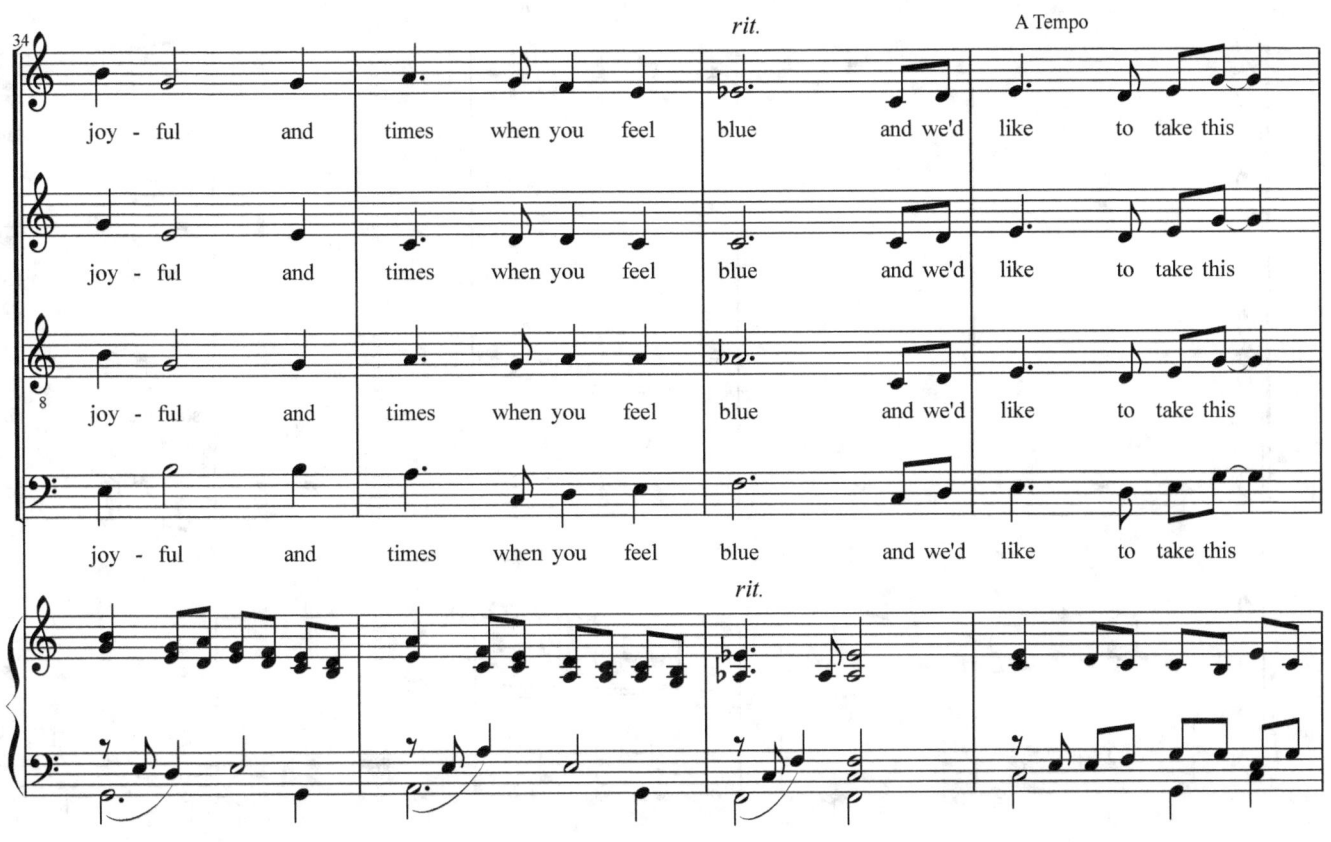

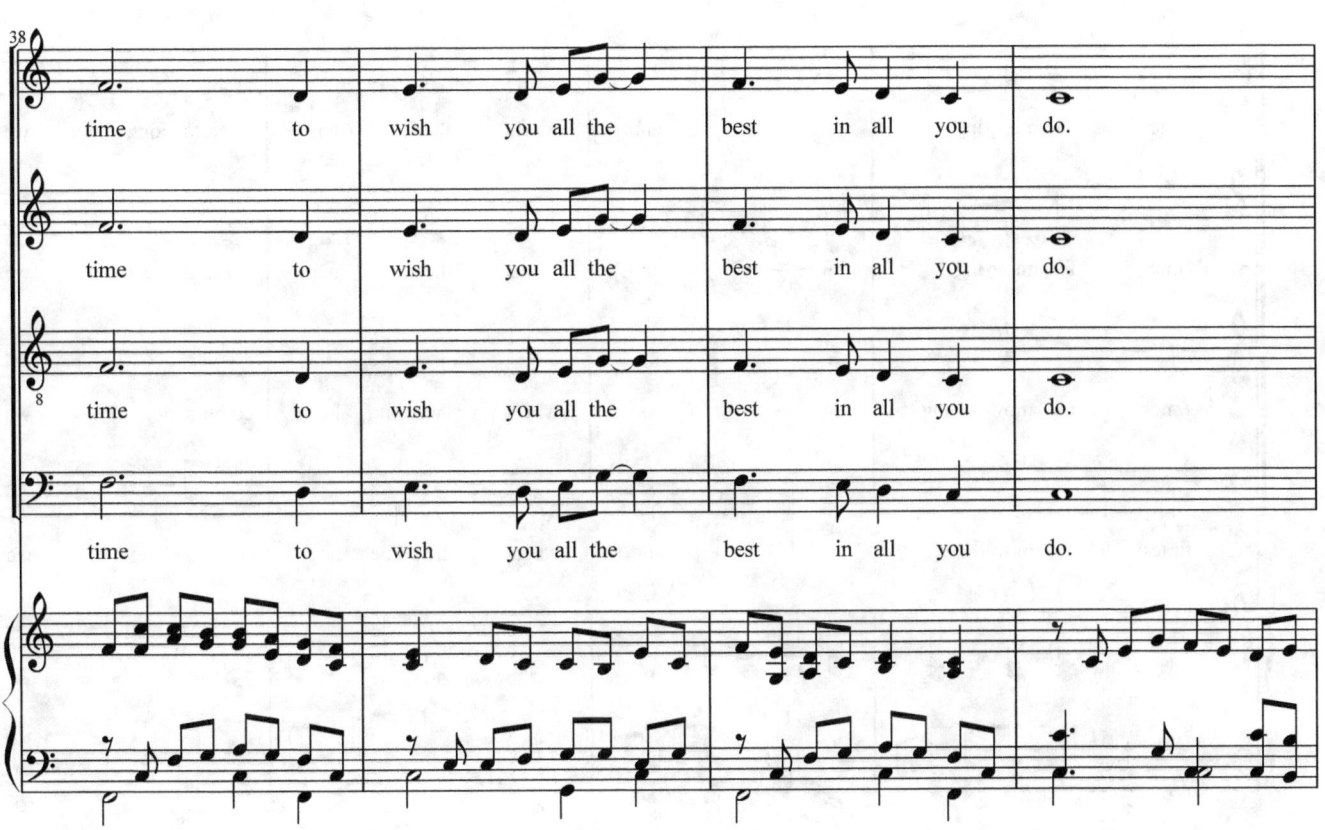

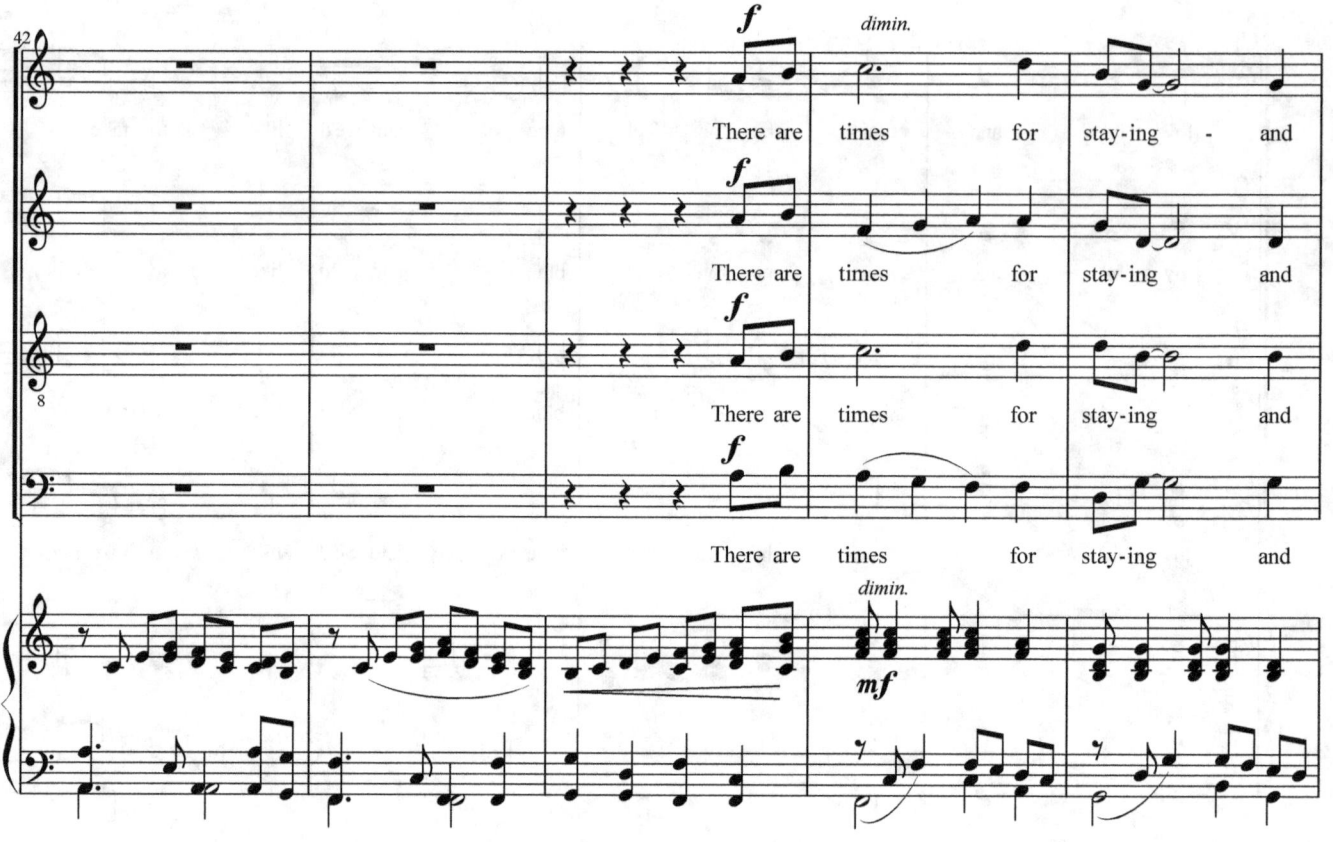

There are times for stay-ing - and
There are times for stay-ing and
There are times for stay-ing and
There are times for stay-ing and

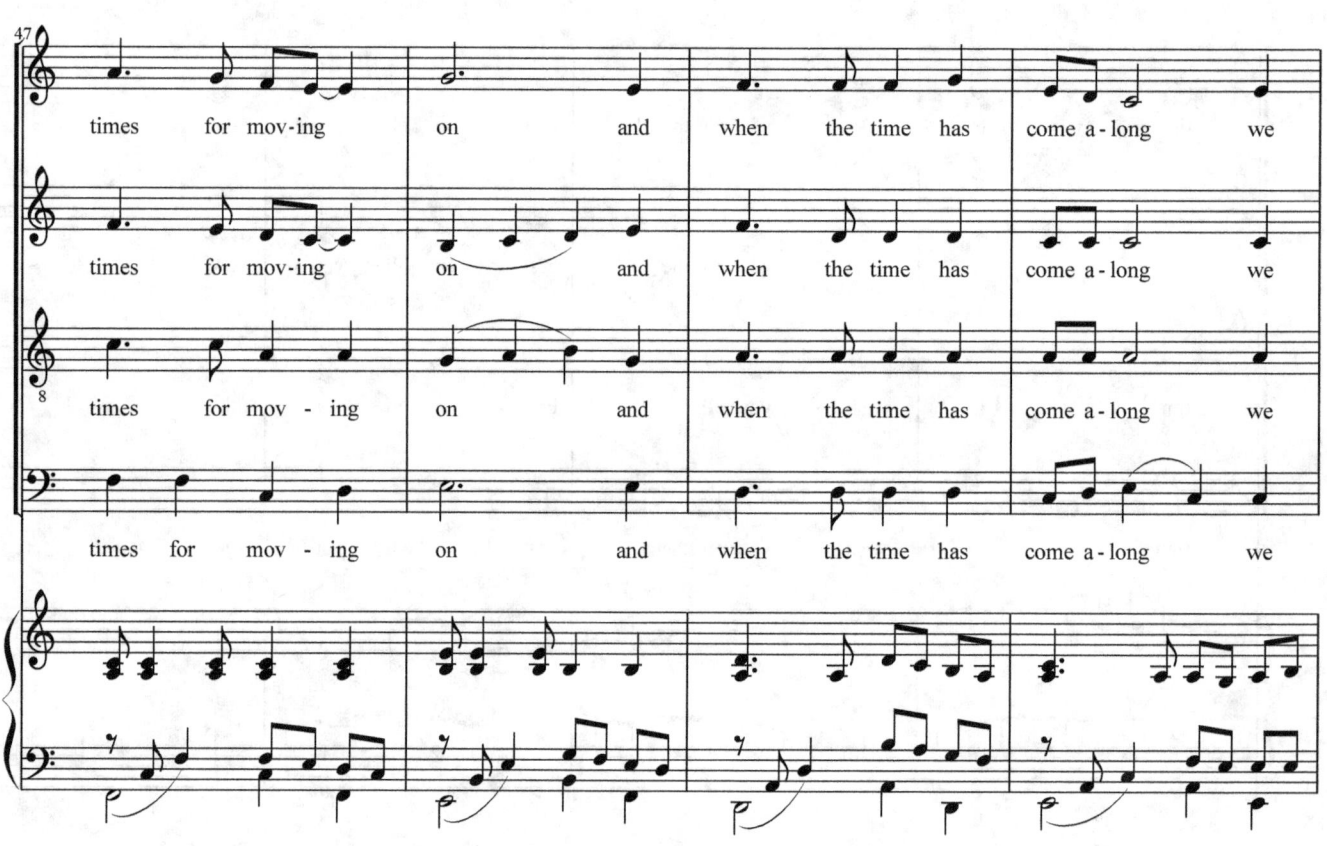

times for mov-ing on and when the time has come a-long we
times for mov-ing on and when the time has come a-long we
times for mov - ing on and when the time has come a-long we
times for mov - ing on and when the time has come a-long we

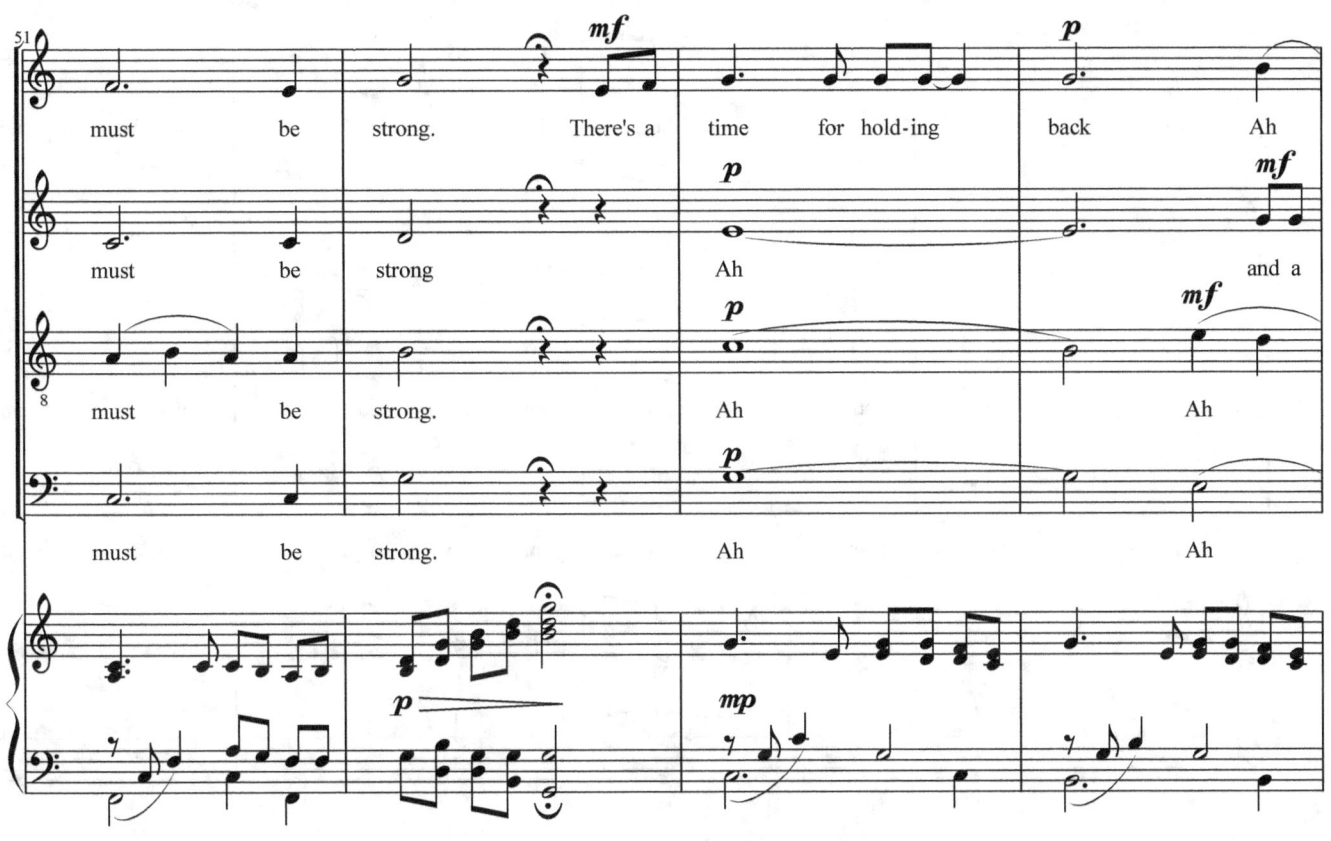

must be strong. There's a time for hold-ing back Ah

must be strong Ah and a

must be strong. Ah Ah

must be strong. Ah Ah

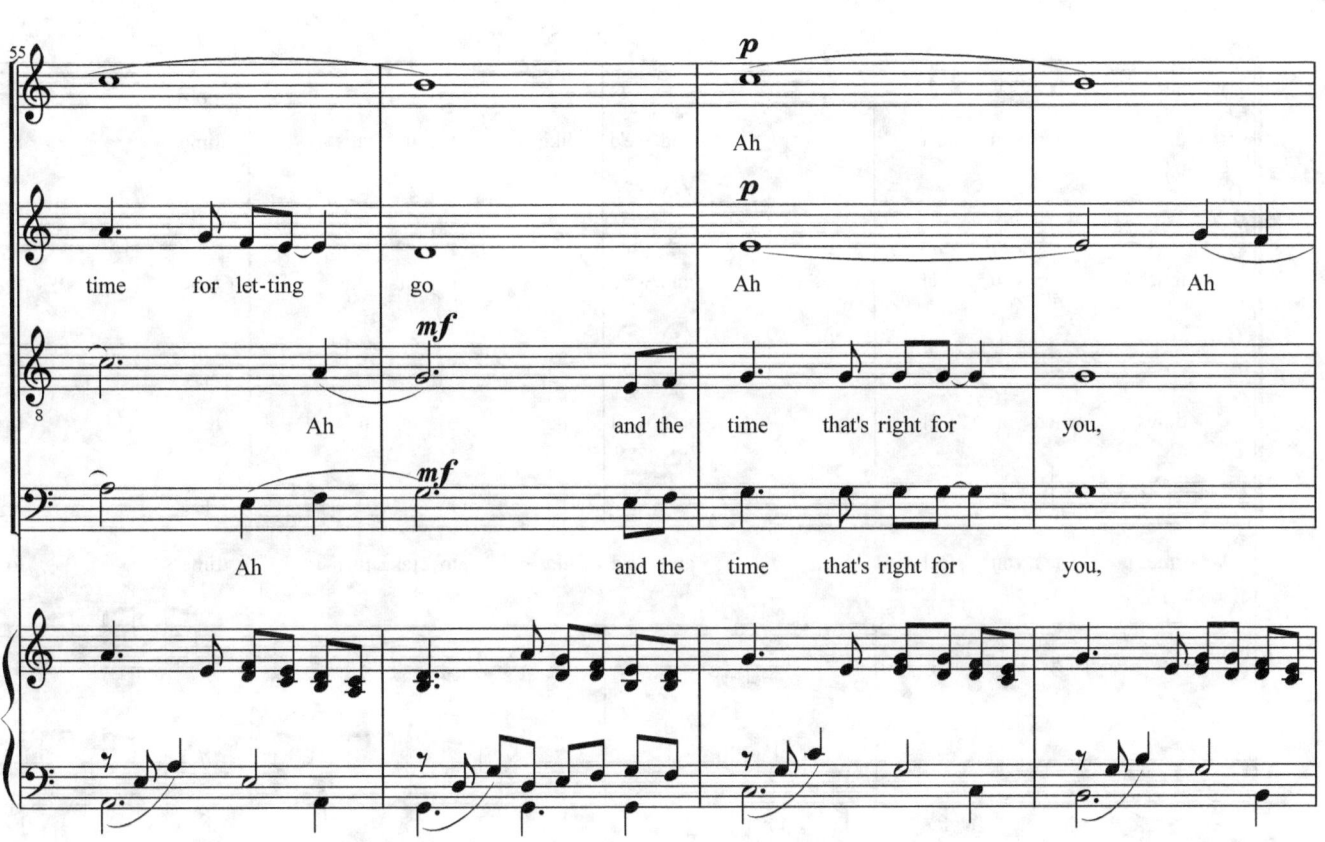

time for let-ting go Ah Ah

Ah and the time that's right for you,

Ah and the time that's right for you,

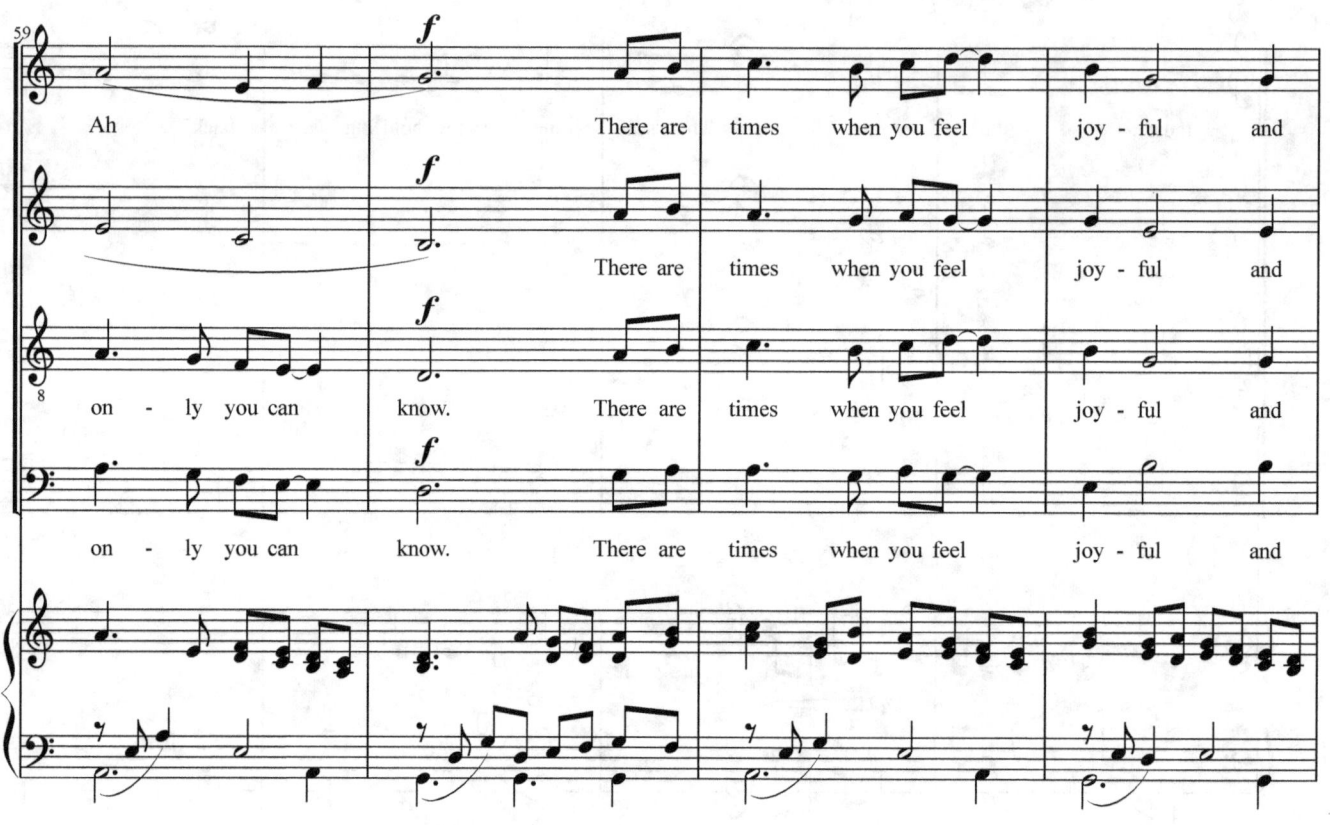

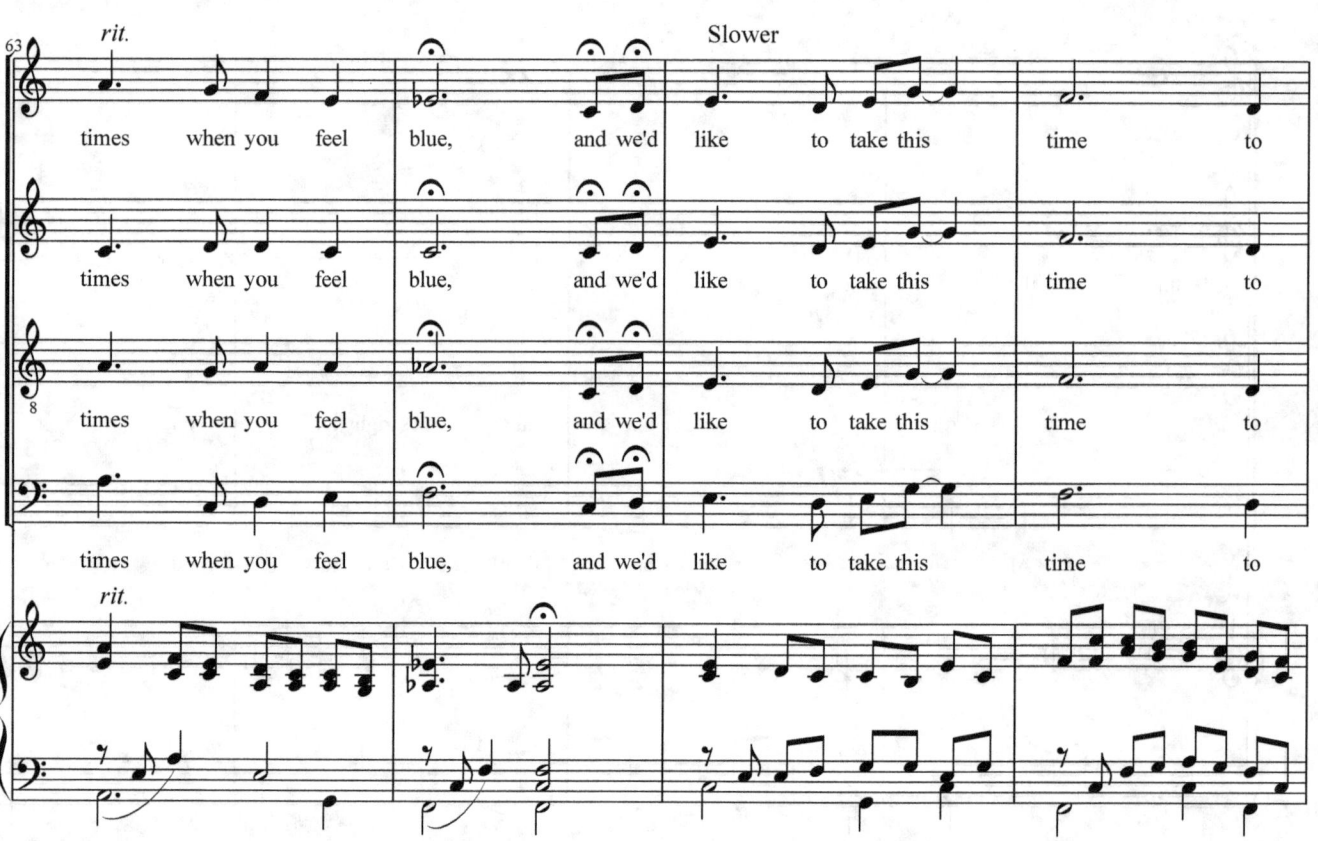

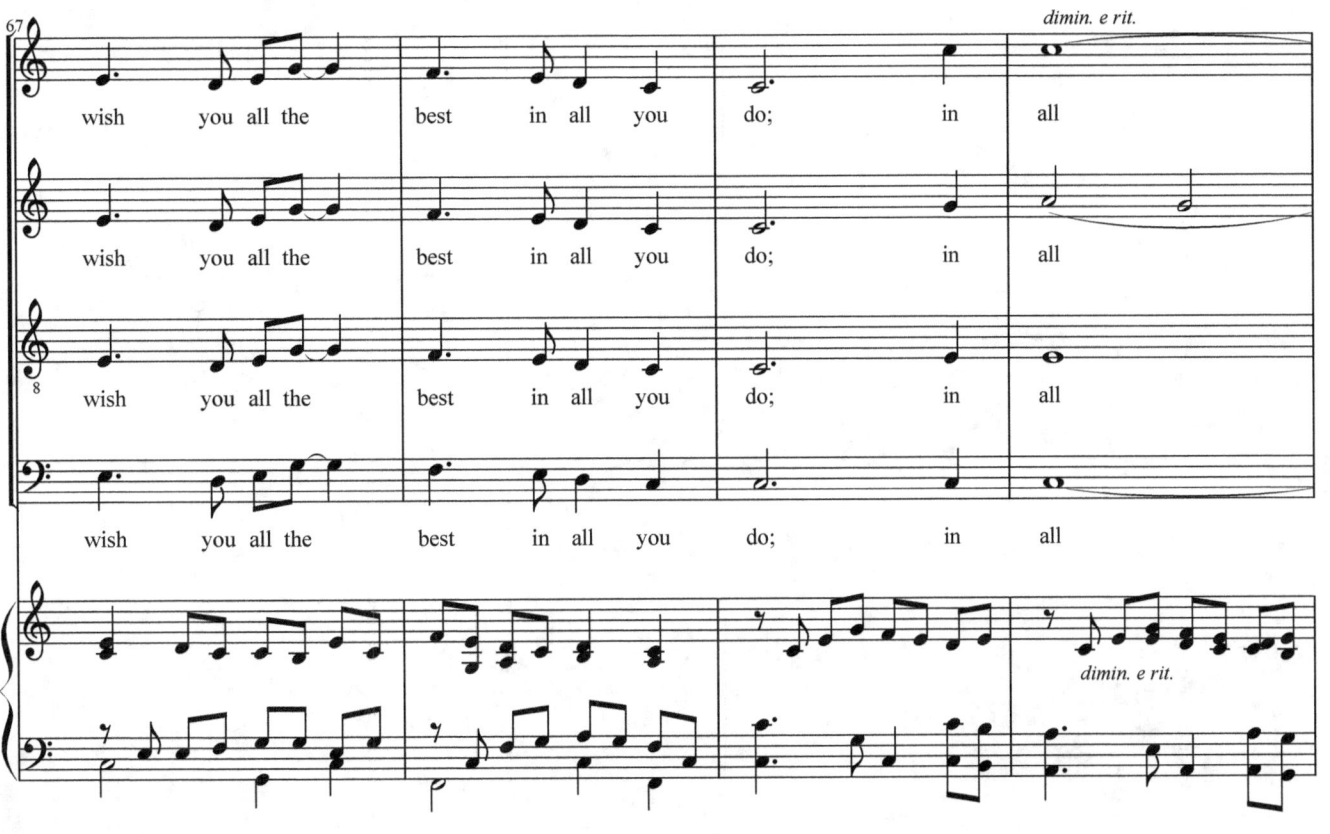

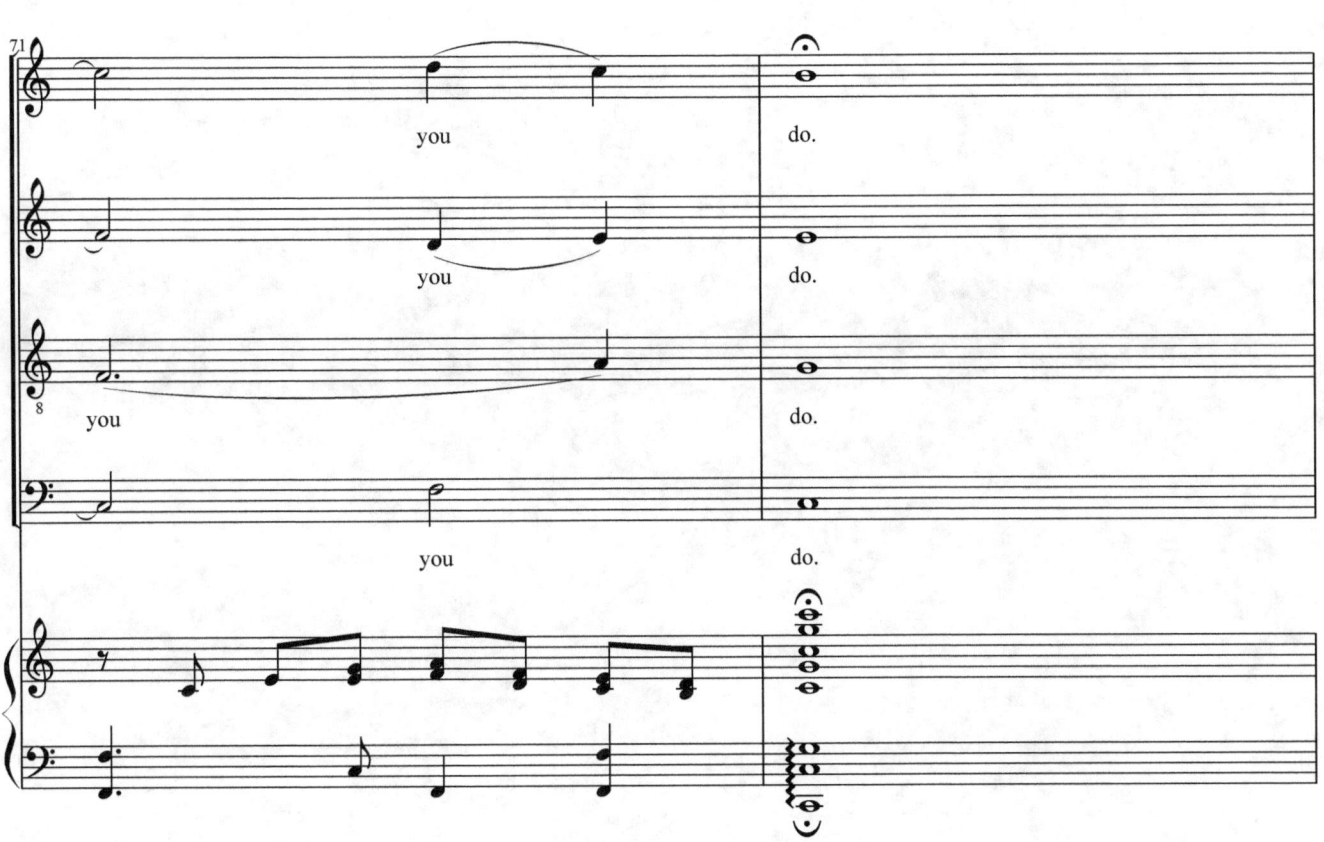

17

A Time of Jubilation

Ken Langer

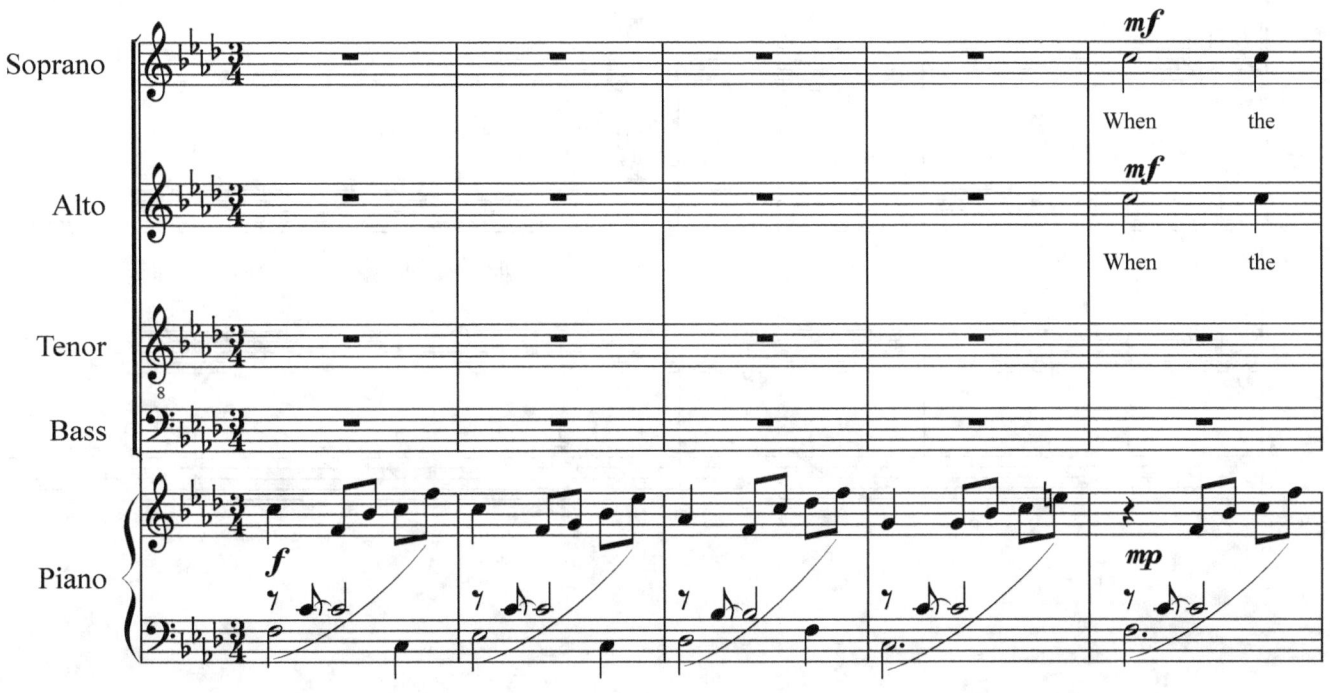

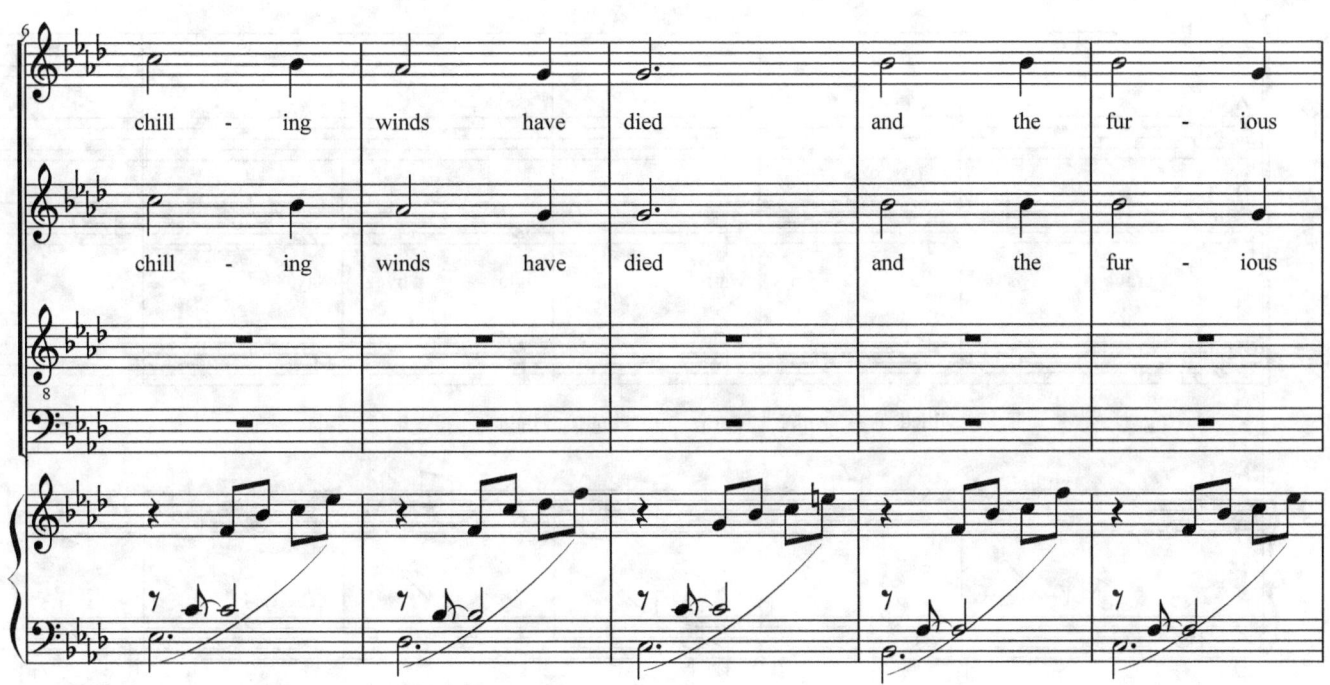

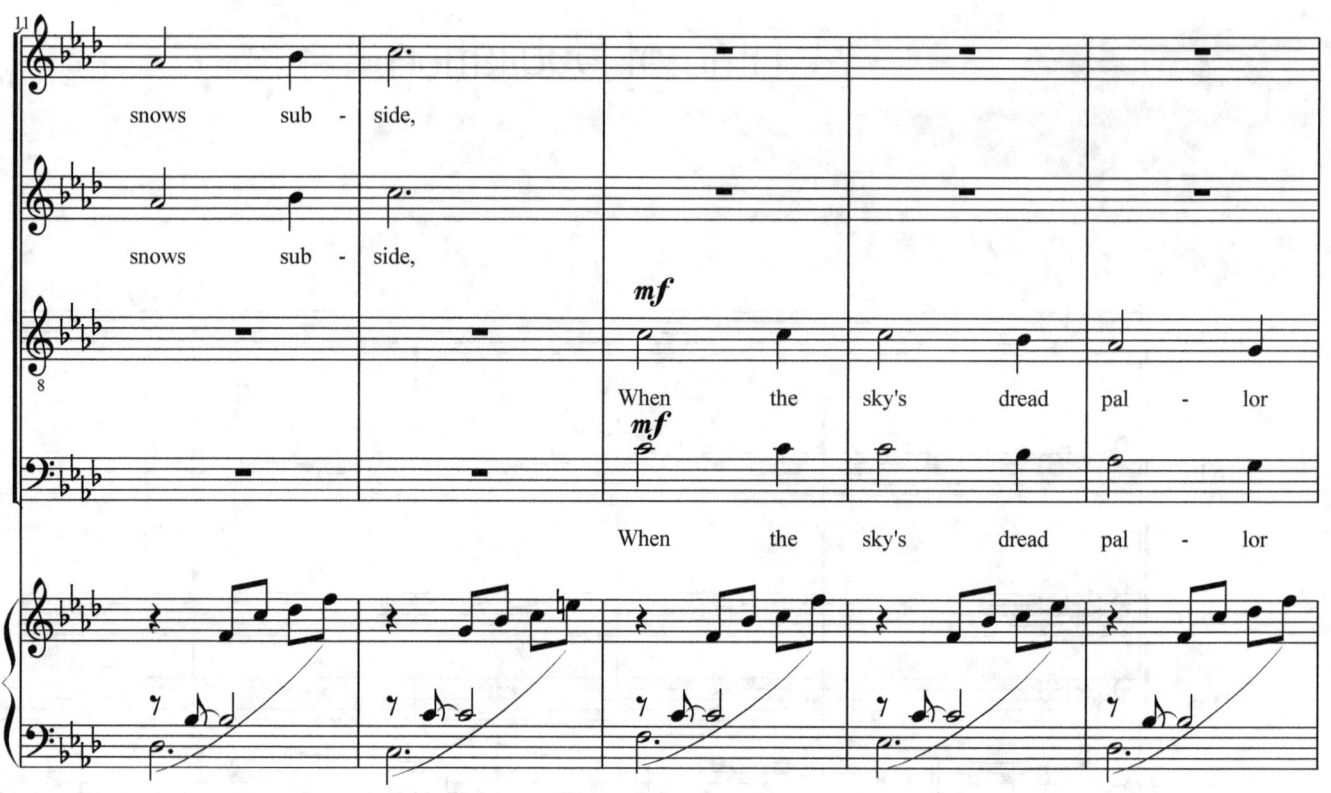

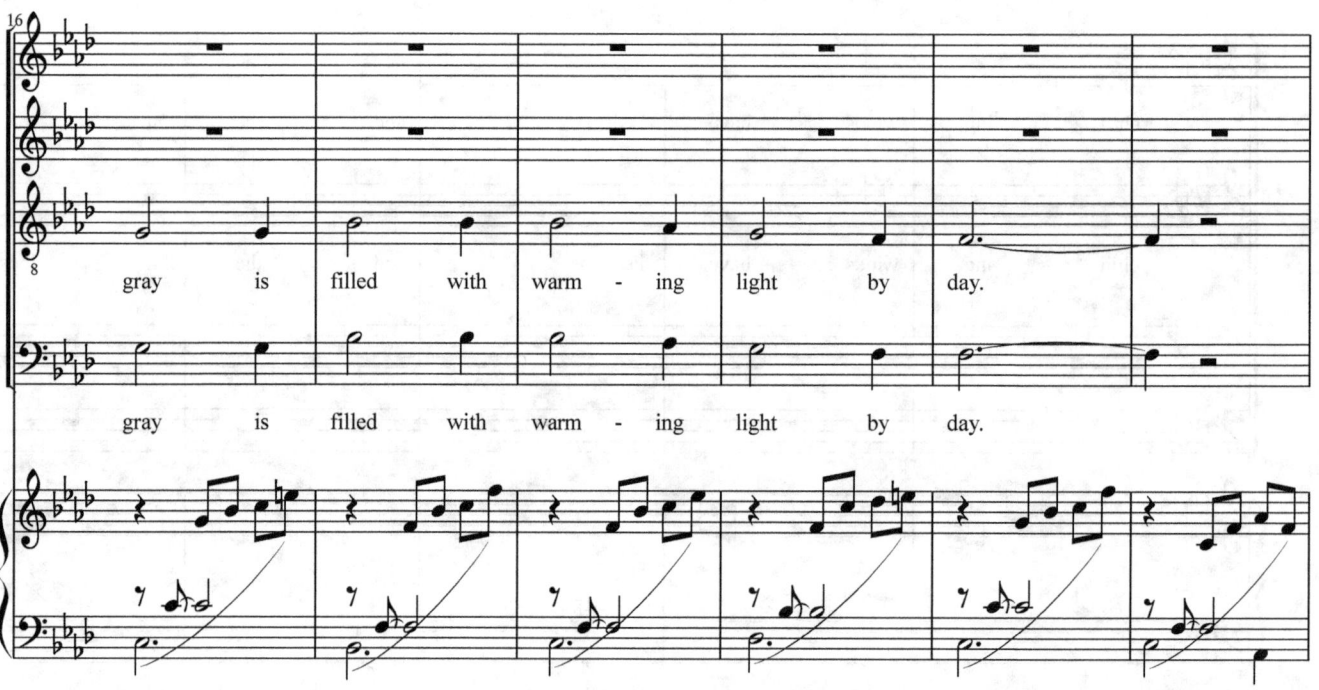

20

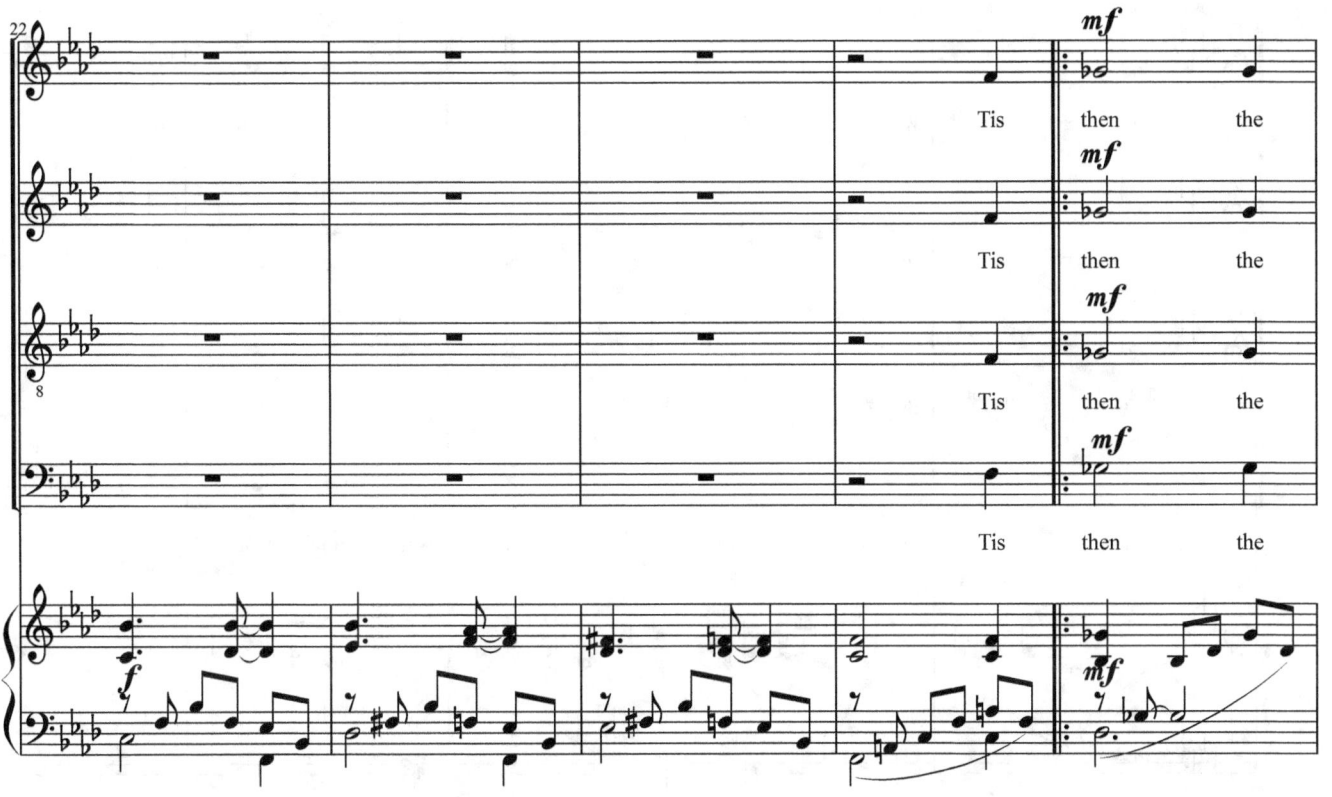

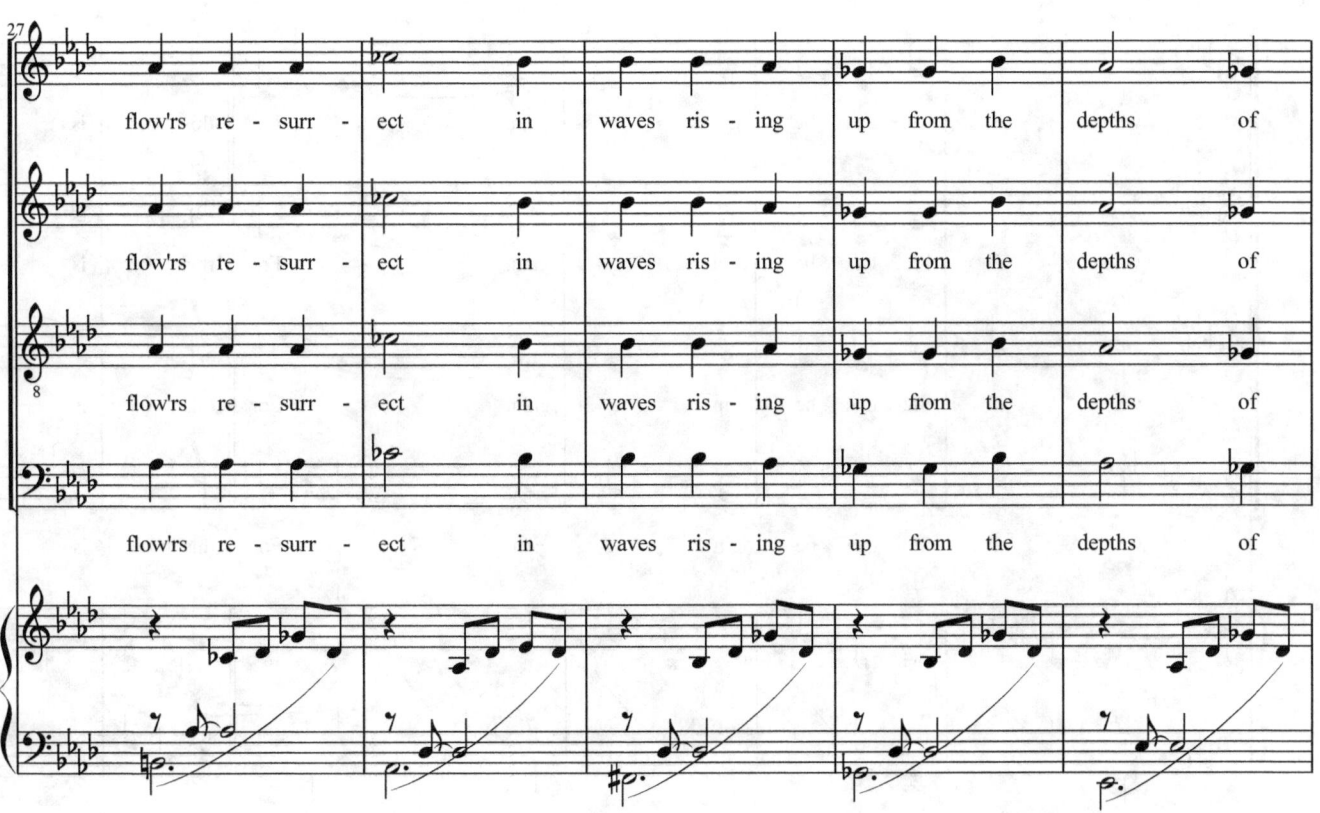

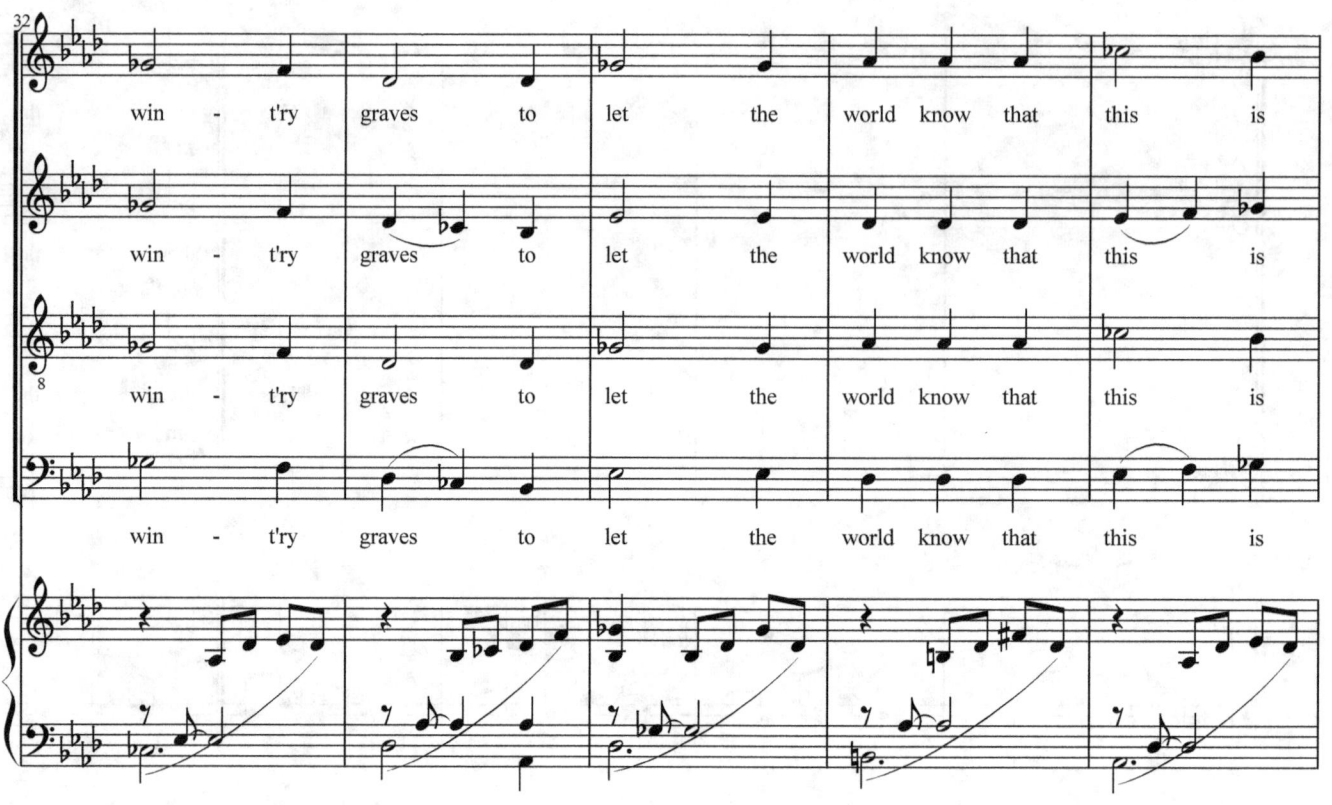

win - t'ry graves to let the world know that this is

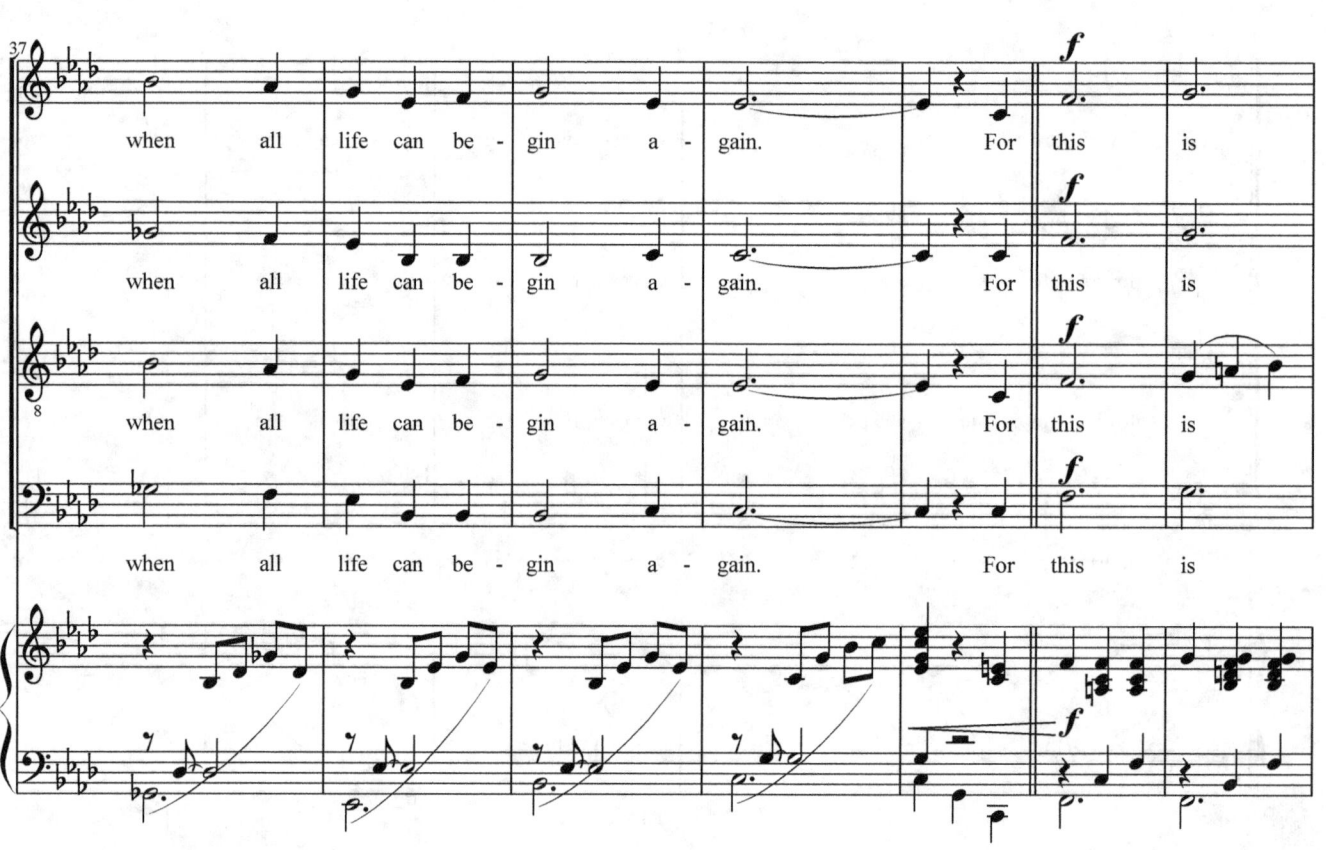

when all life can be - gin a - gain. For this is

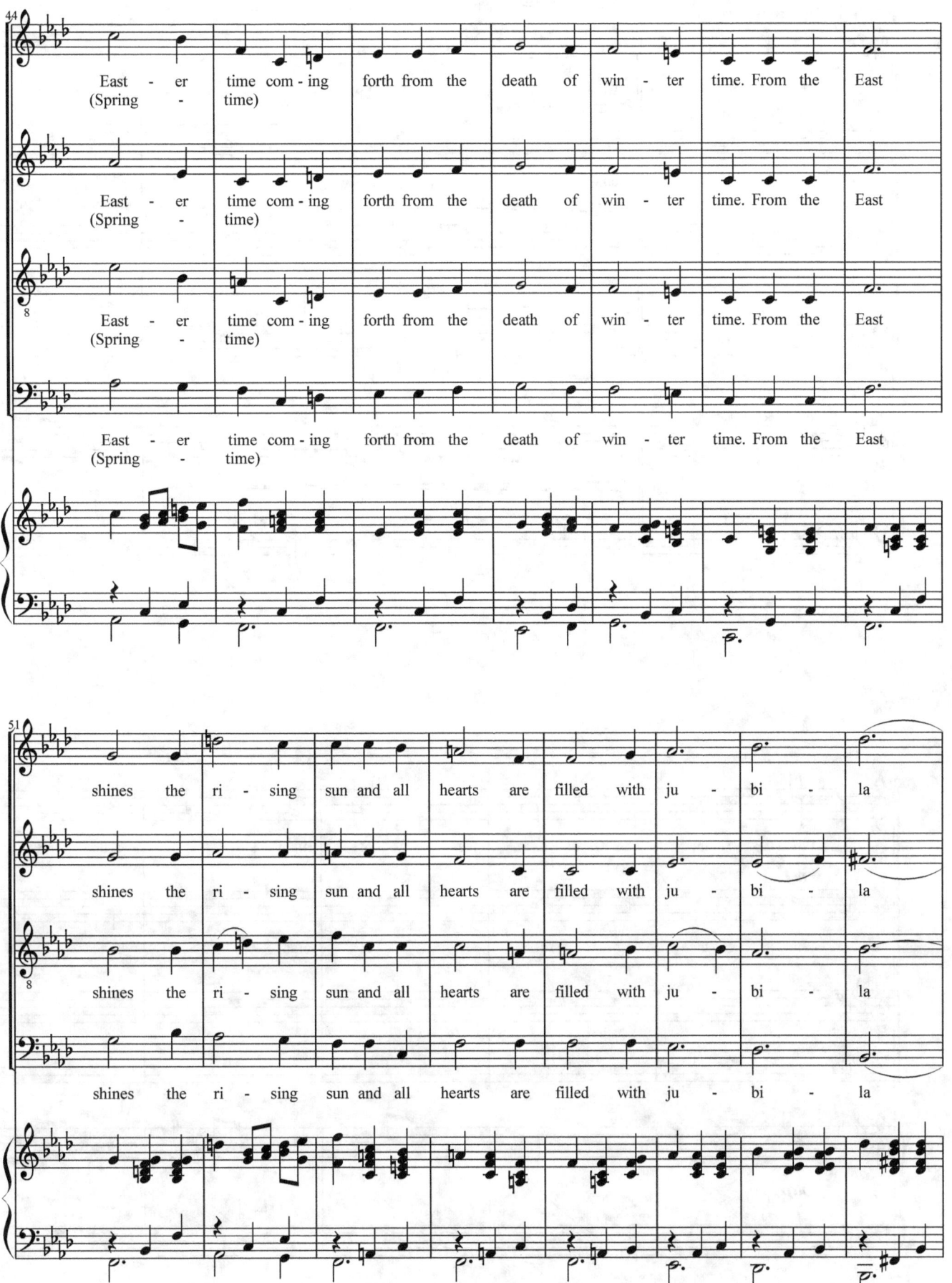

East - er time com - ing forth from the death of win - ter time. From the East
(Spring - time)

shines the ri - sing sun and all hearts are filled with ju - bi - la

23

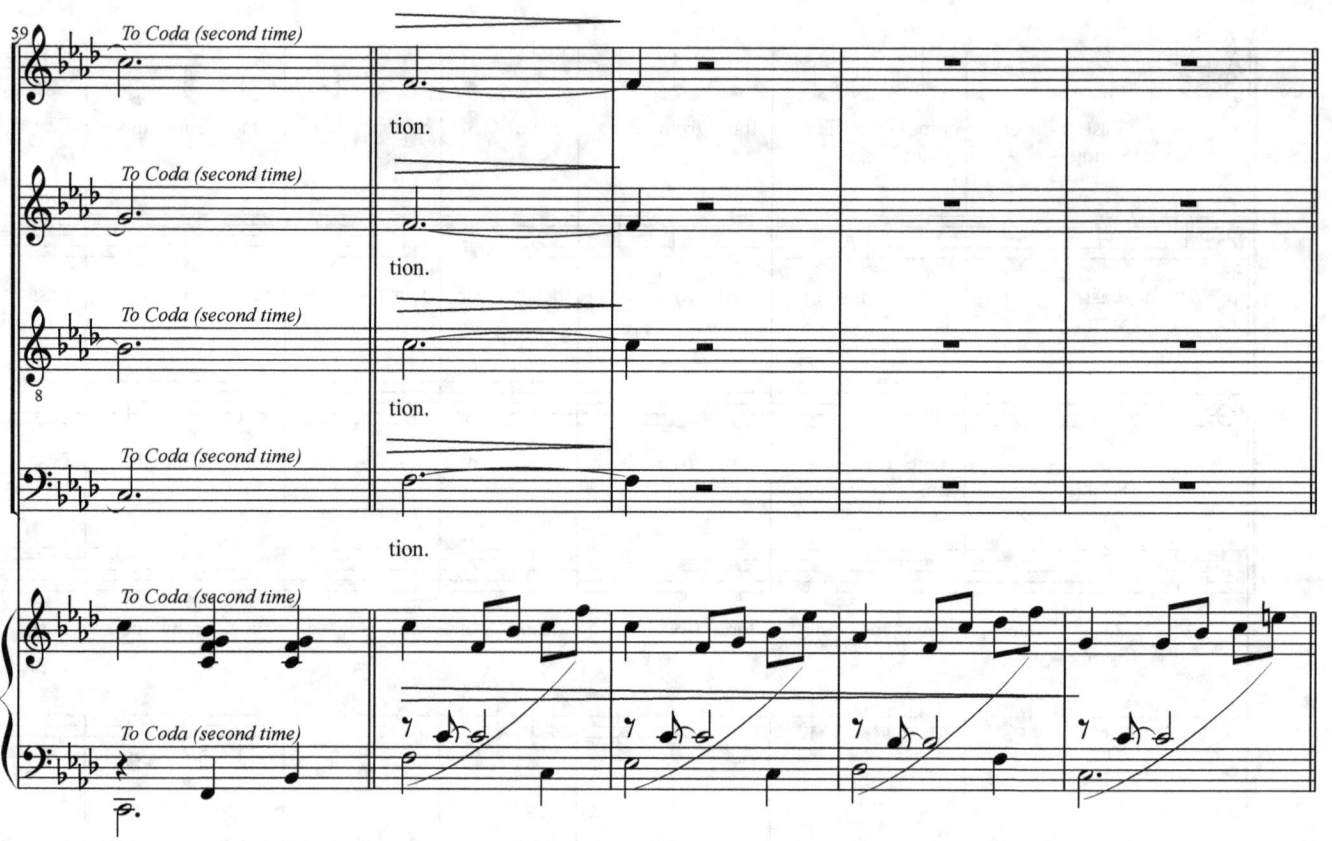

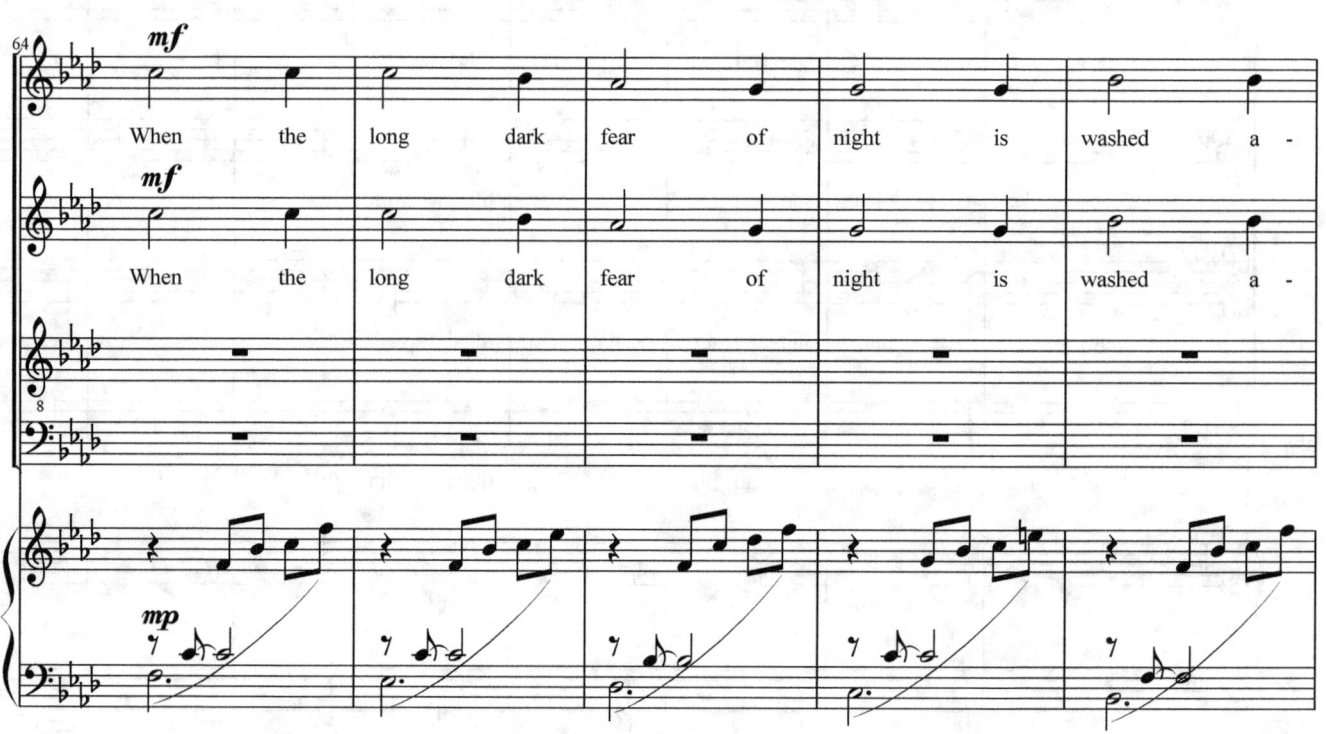

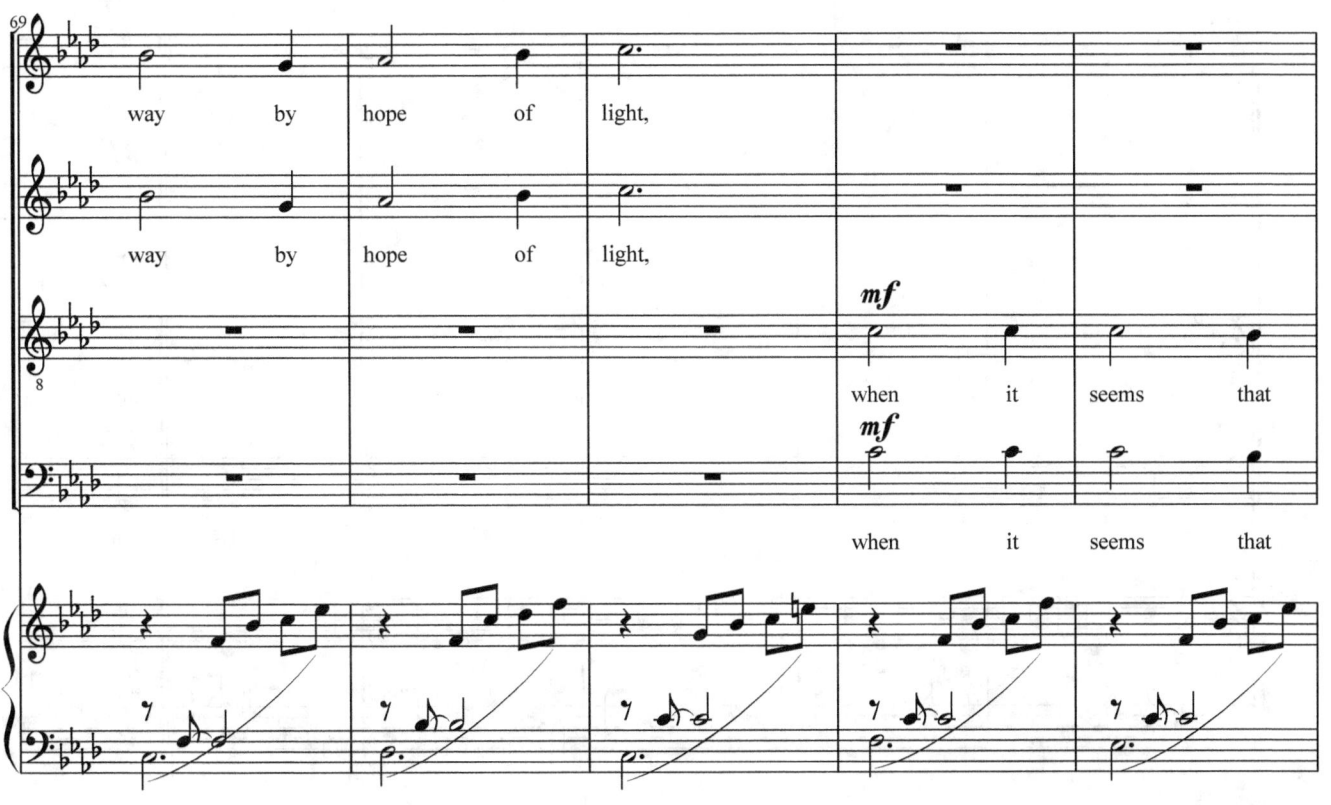

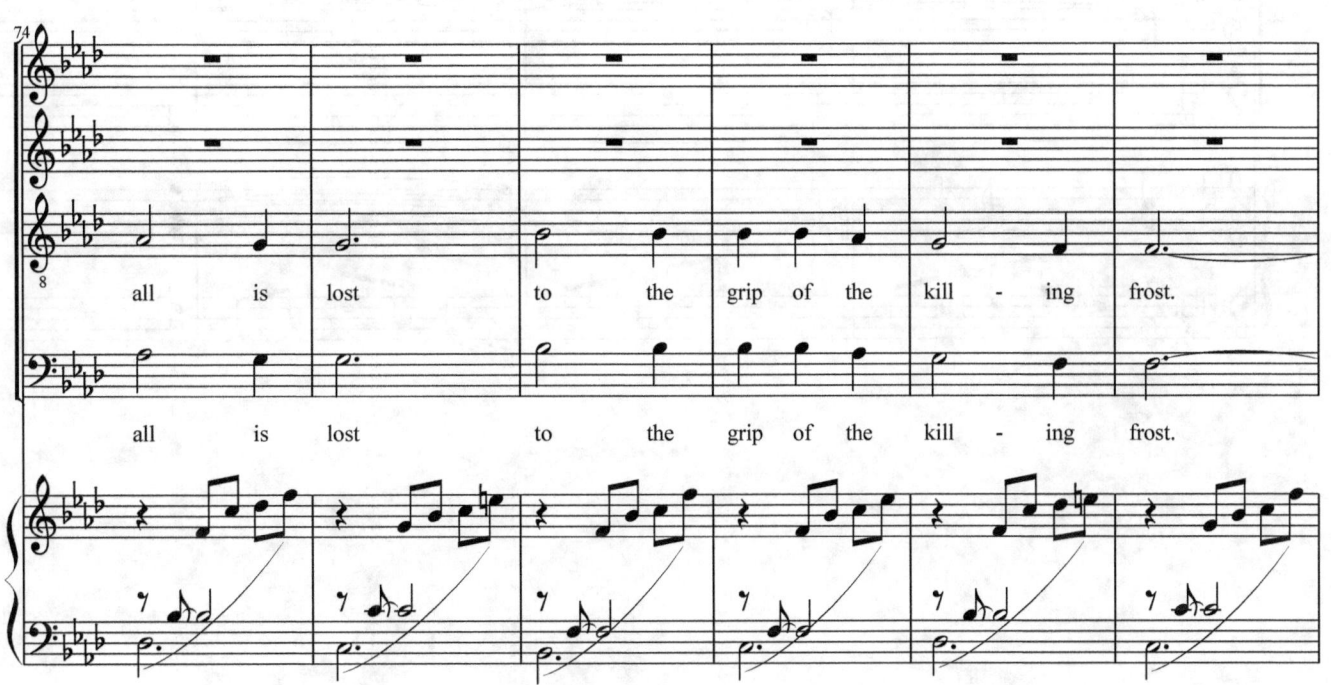

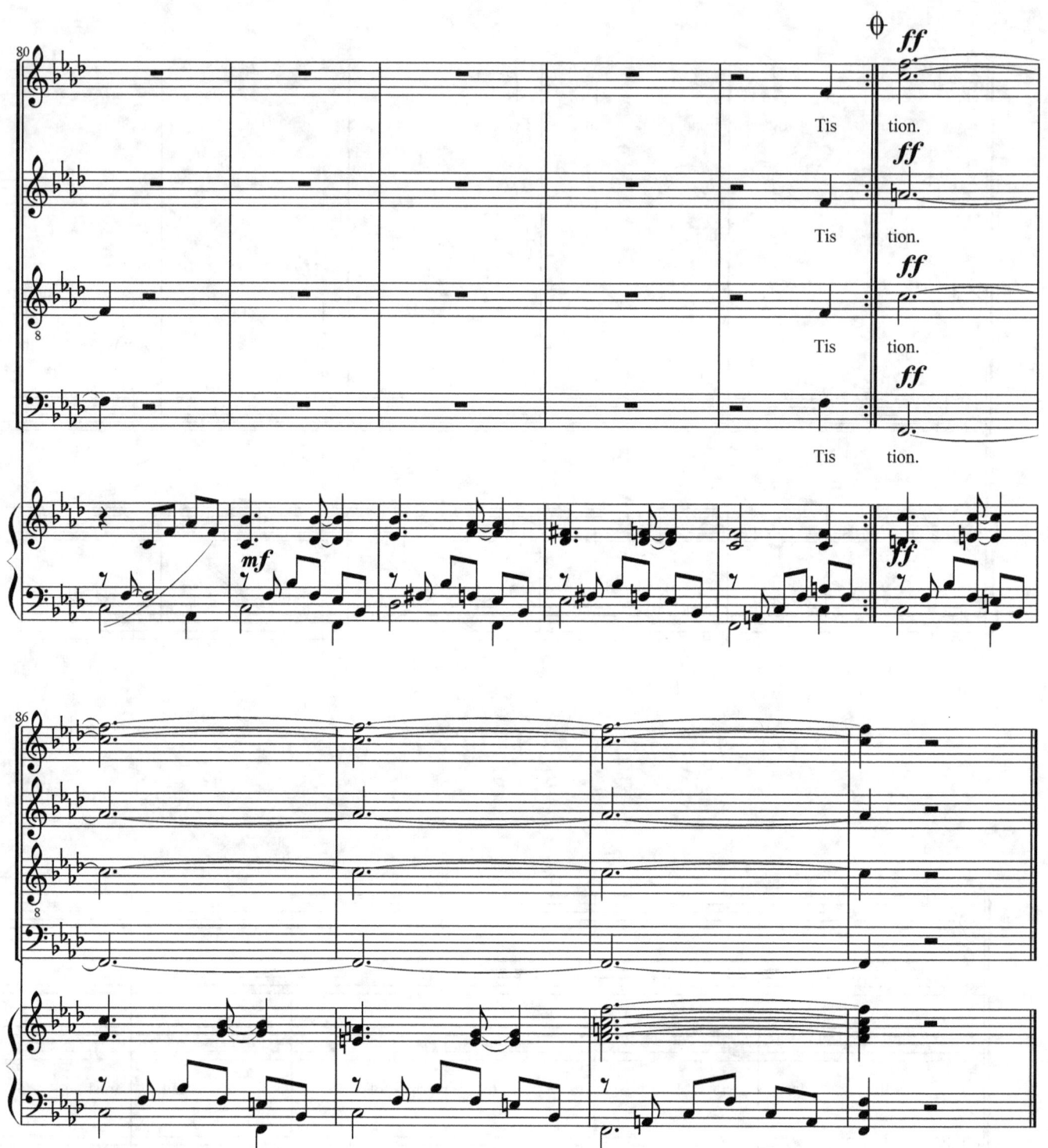

Tis — tion.

Tis — tion.

Tis — tion.

Tis — tion.

Come Now

Ken Langer

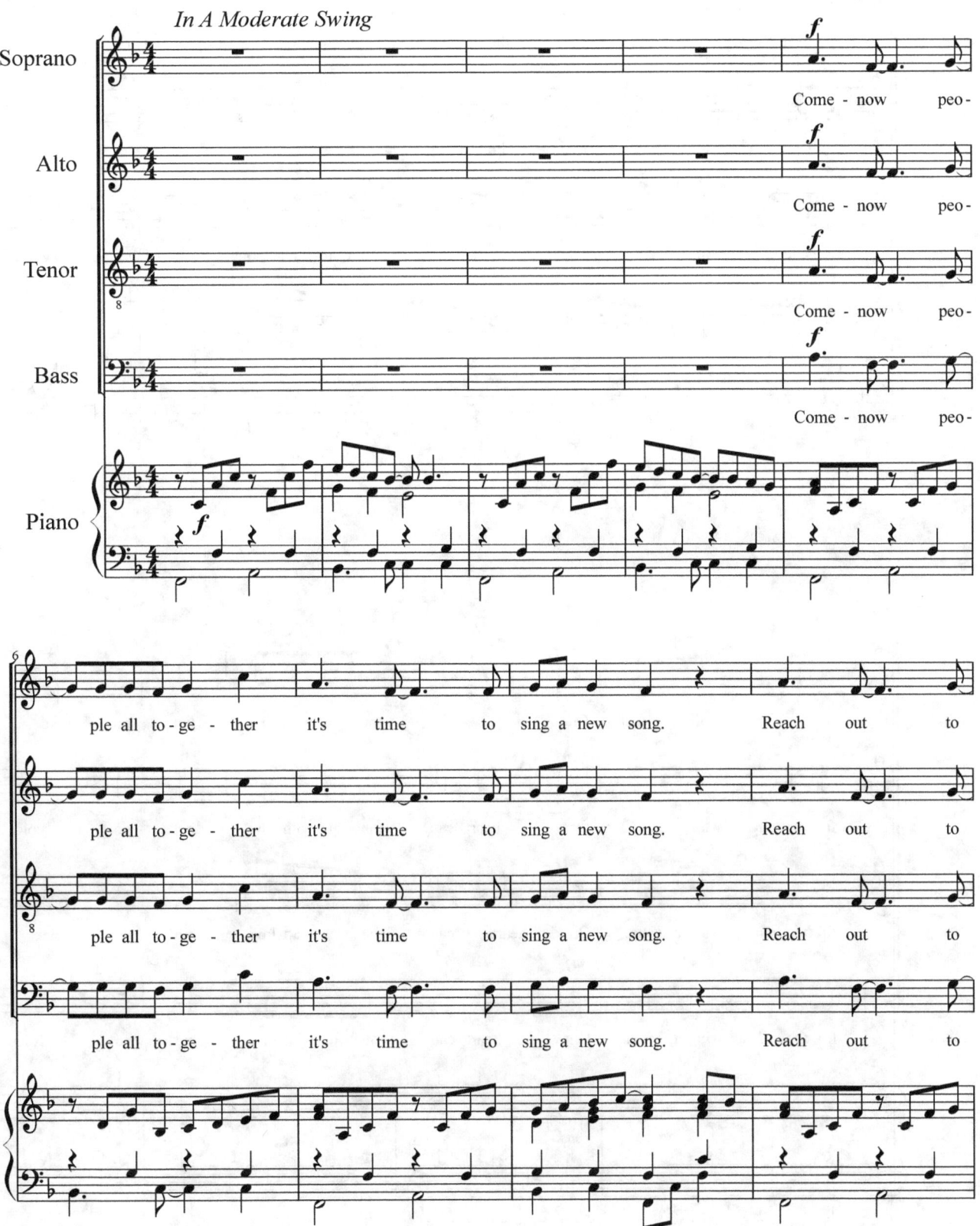

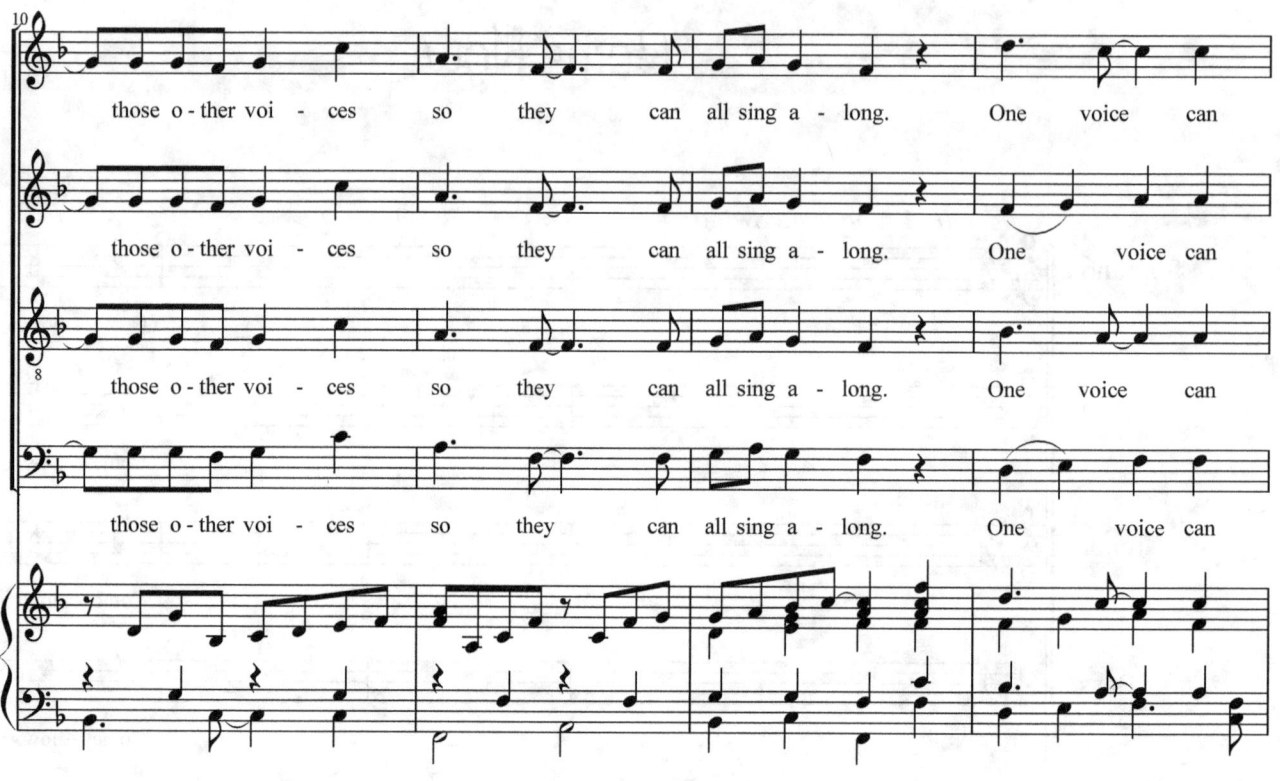

those o-ther voi - ces so they can all sing a - long. One voice can

those o-ther voi - ces so they can all sing a - long. One voice can

those o-ther voi - ces so they can all sing a - long. One voice can

those o-ther voi - ces so they can all sing a - long. One voice can

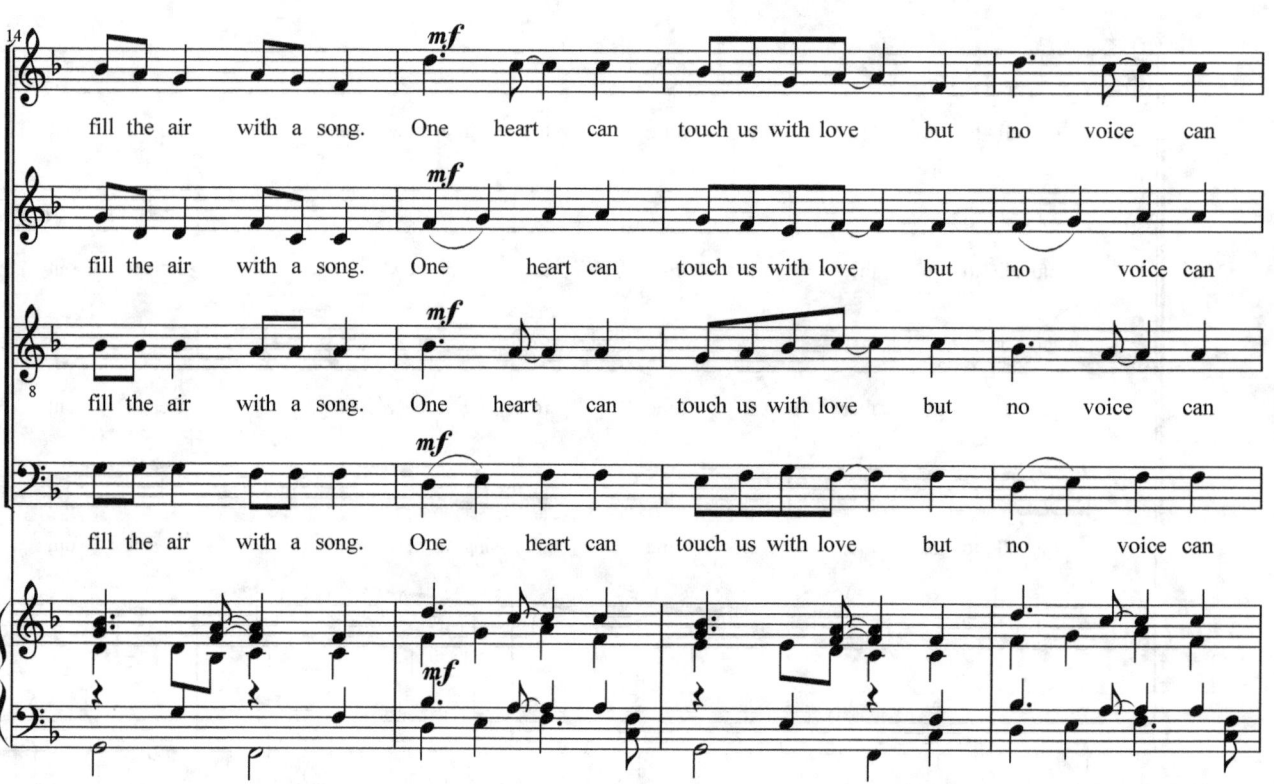

fill the air with a song. One heart can touch us with love but no voice can

fill the air with a song. One heart can touch us with love but no voice can

fill the air with a song. One heart can touch us with love but no voice can

fill the air with a song. One heart can touch us with love but no voice can

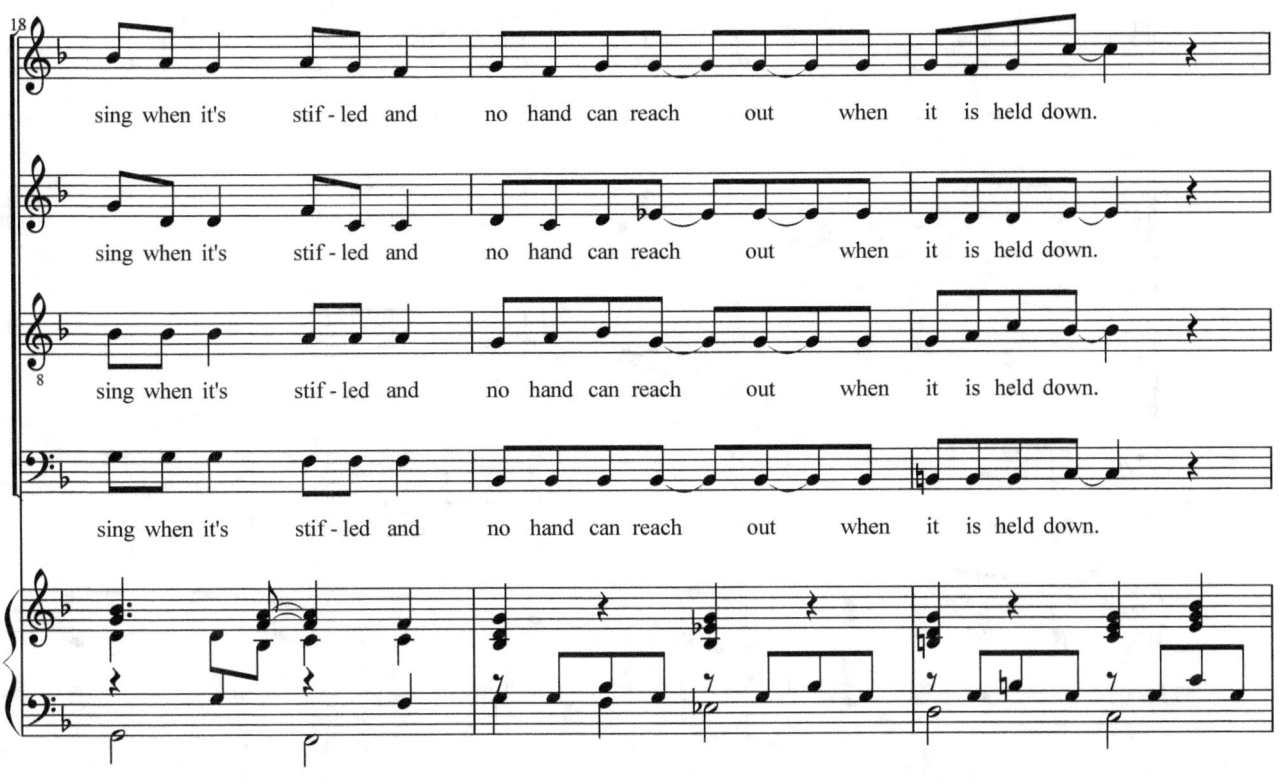

sing when it's stif - led and no hand can reach out when it is held down.

sing when it's stif - led and no hand can reach out when it is held down.

sing when it's stif - led and no hand can reach out when it is held down.

sing when it's stif - led and no hand can reach out when it is held down.

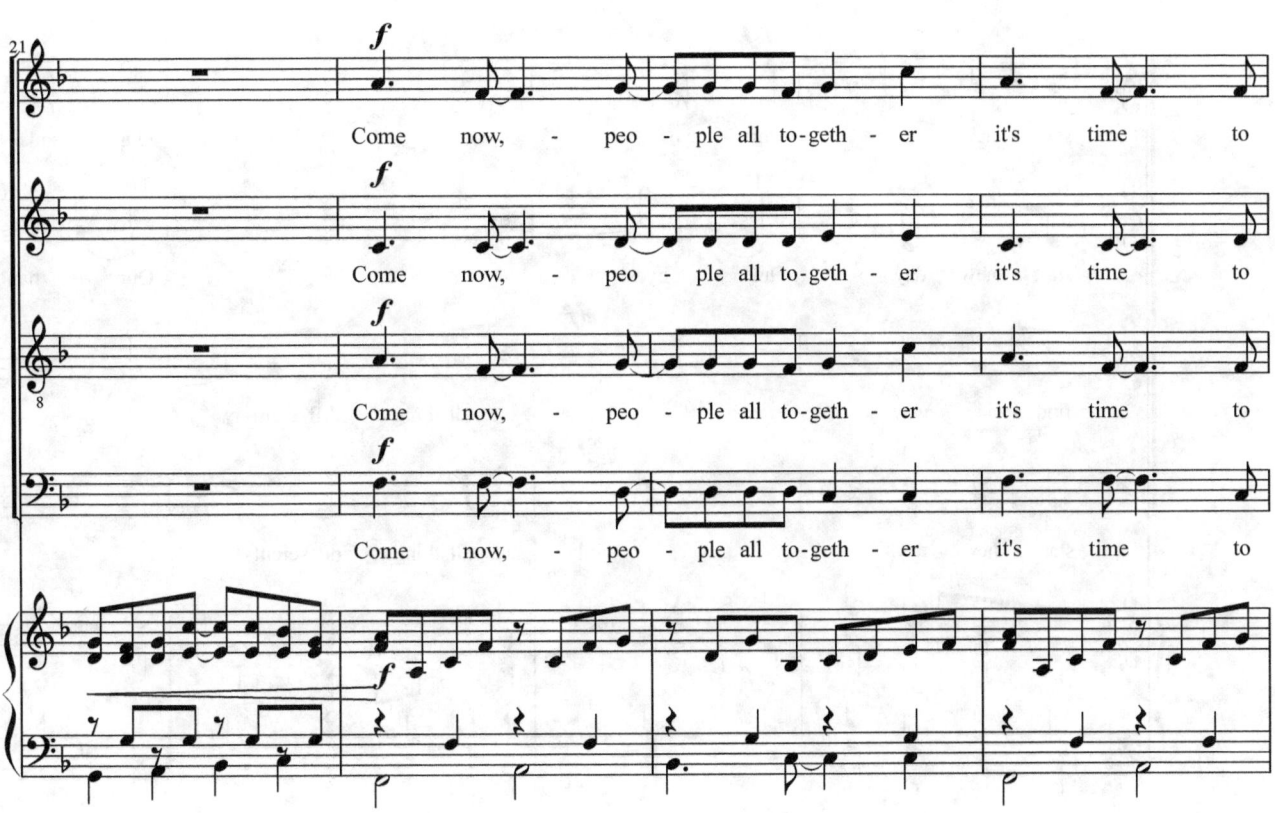

Come now, - peo - ple all to-geth - er it's time to

Come now, - peo - ple all to-geth - er it's time to

Come now, - peo - ple all to-geth - er it's time to

Come now, - peo - ple all to-geth - er it's time to

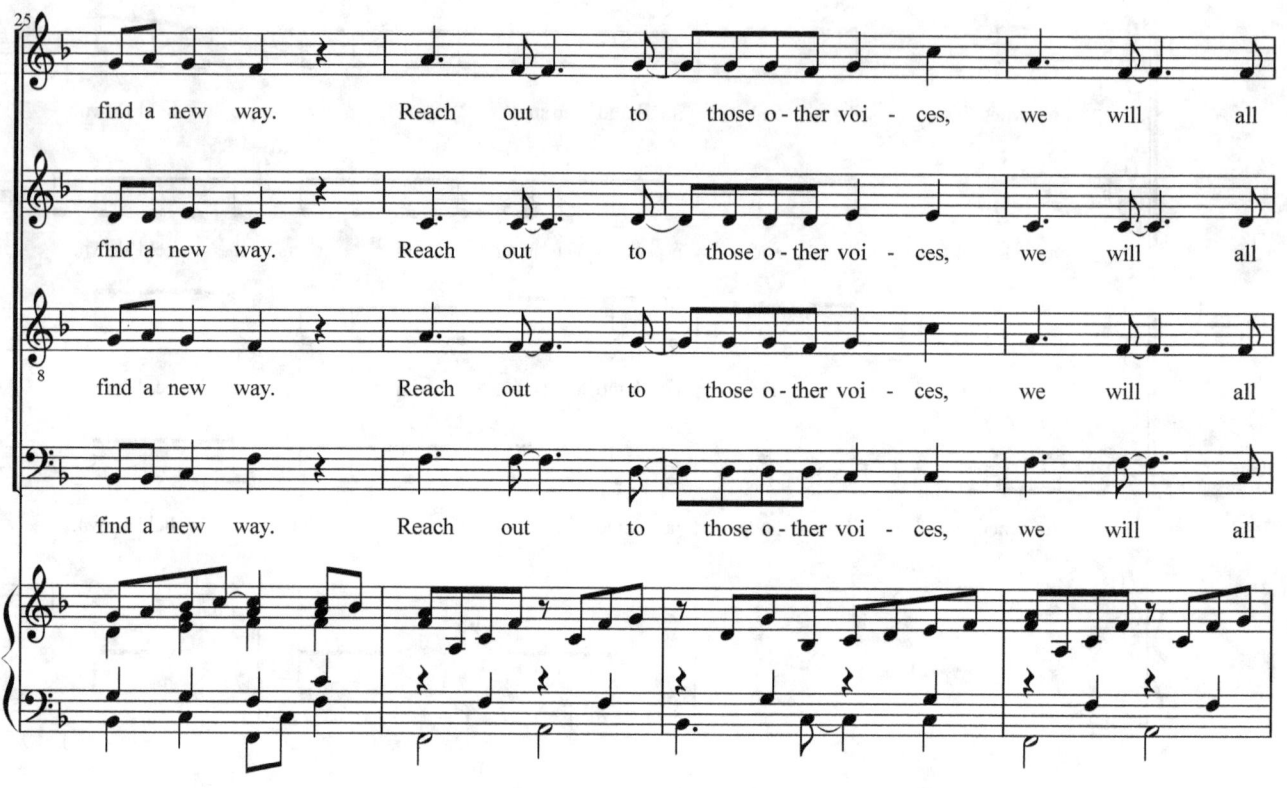

find a new way. Reach out to those o-ther voi - ces, we will all

find a new way. Reach out to those o-ther voi - ces, we will all

find a new way. Reach out to those o-ther voi - ces, we will all

find a new way. Reach out to those o-ther voi - ces, we will all

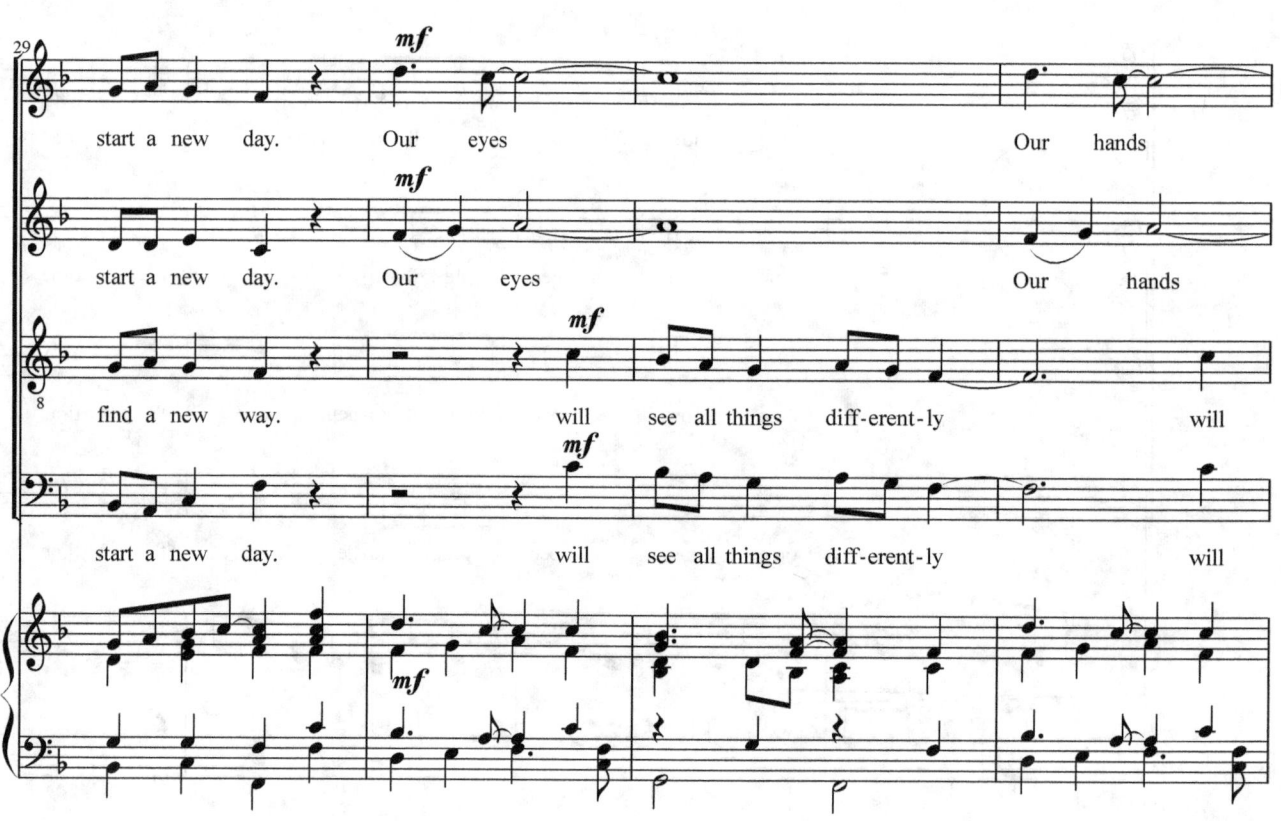

start a new day. Our eyes Our hands

start a new day. Our eyes Our hands

find a new way. will see all things diff-erent-ly will

start a new day. will see all things diff-erent-ly will

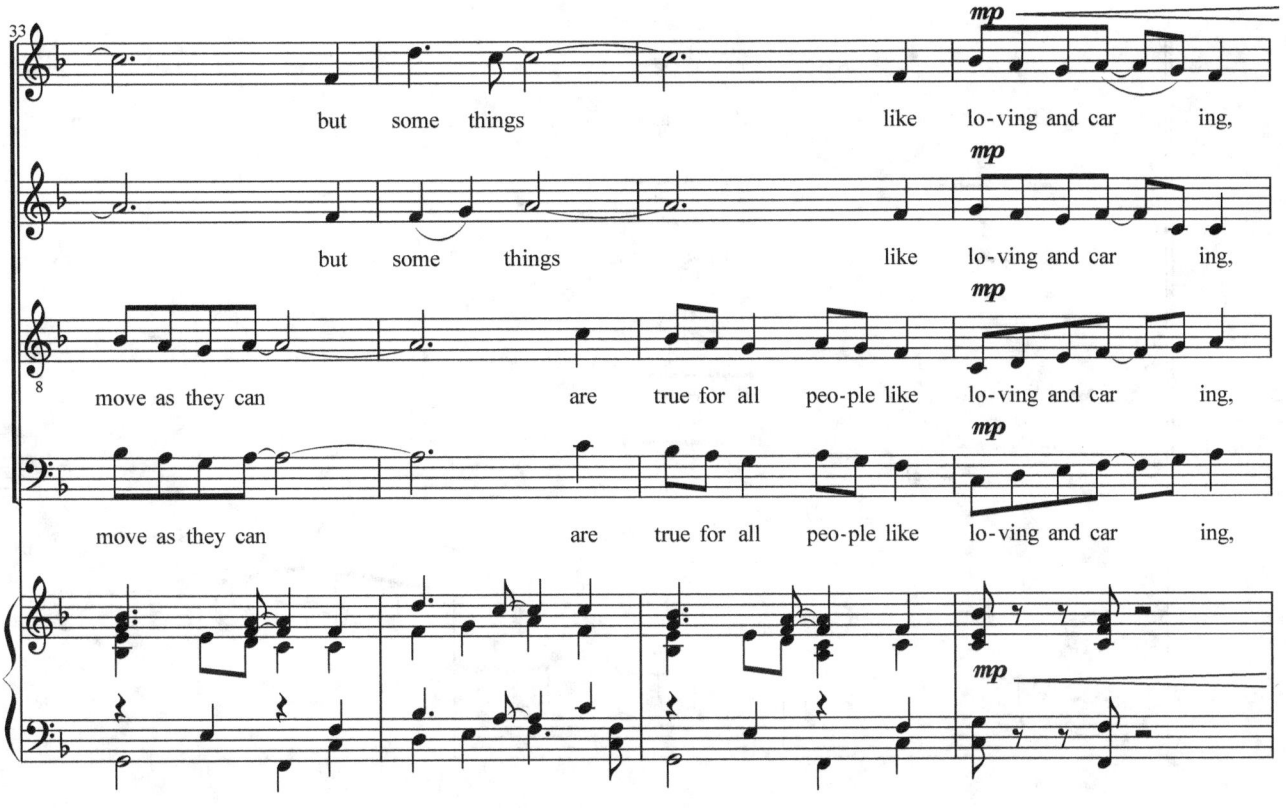

but some things like lo-ving and car ing,

but some things like lo-ving and car ing,

move as they can are true for all peo-ple like lo-ving and car ing,

move as they can are true for all peo-ple like lo-ving and car ing,

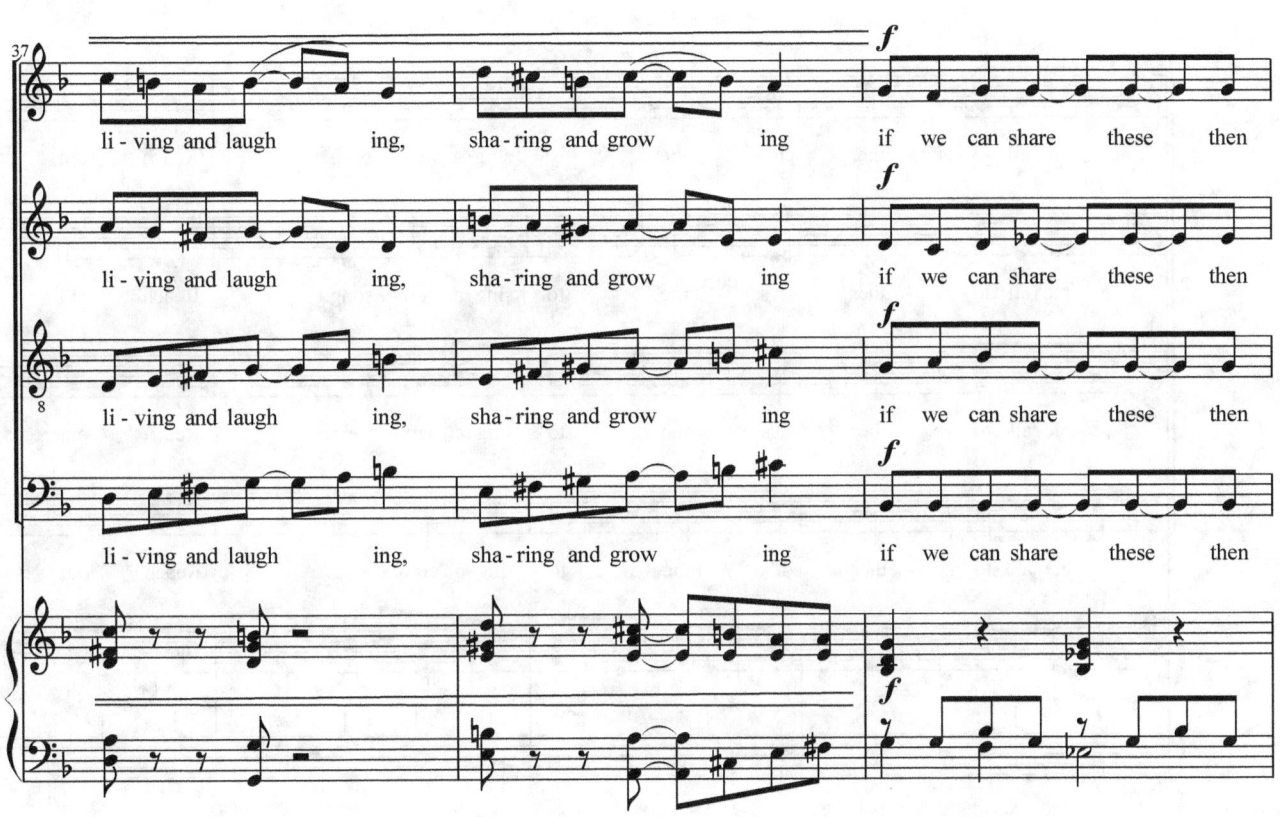

li - ving and laugh ing, sha - ring and grow ing if we can share these then

li - ving and laugh ing, sha - ring and grow ing if we can share these then

li - ving and laugh ing, sha - ring and grow ing if we can share these then

li - ving and laugh ing, sha - ring and grow ing if we can share these then

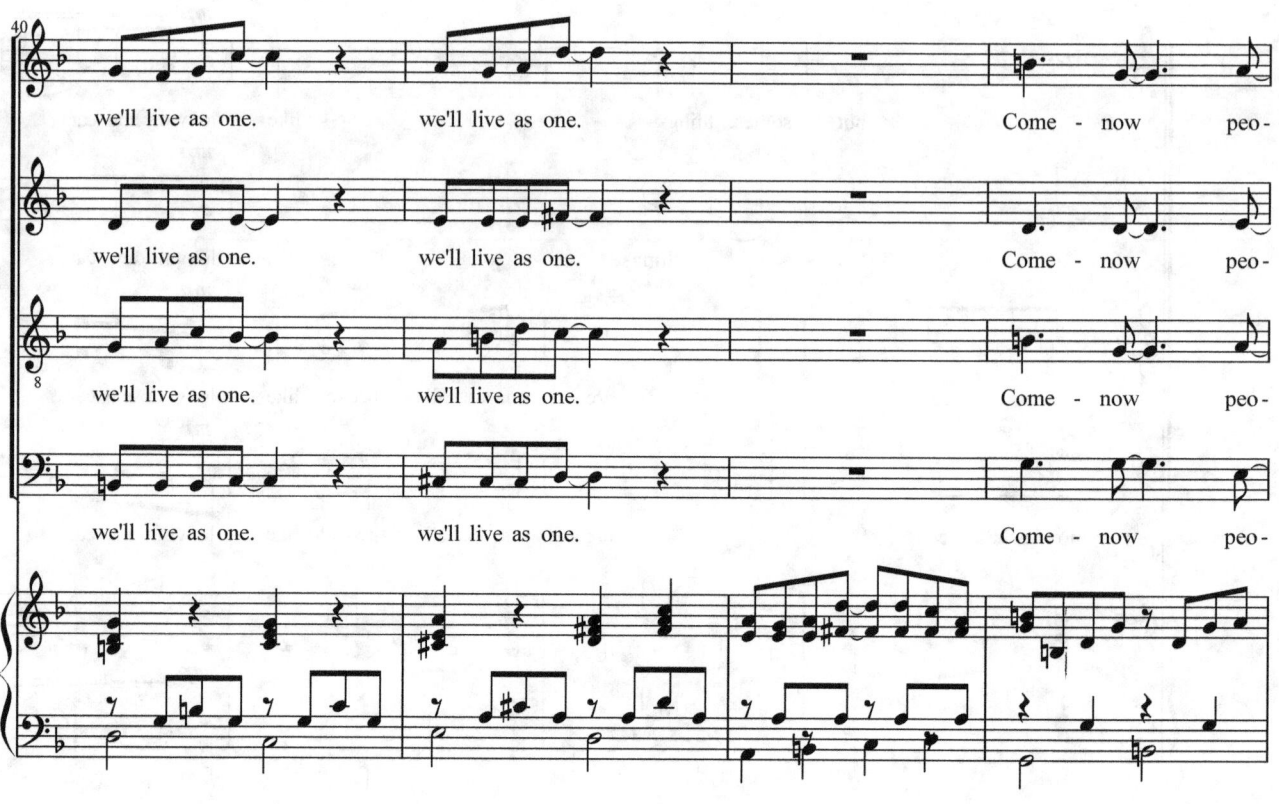

we'll live as one.   we'll live as one.   Come - now   peo-

we'll live as one.   we'll live as one.   Come - now   peo-

we'll live as one.   we'll live as one.   Come - now   peo-

we'll live as one.   we'll live as one.   Come - now   peo-

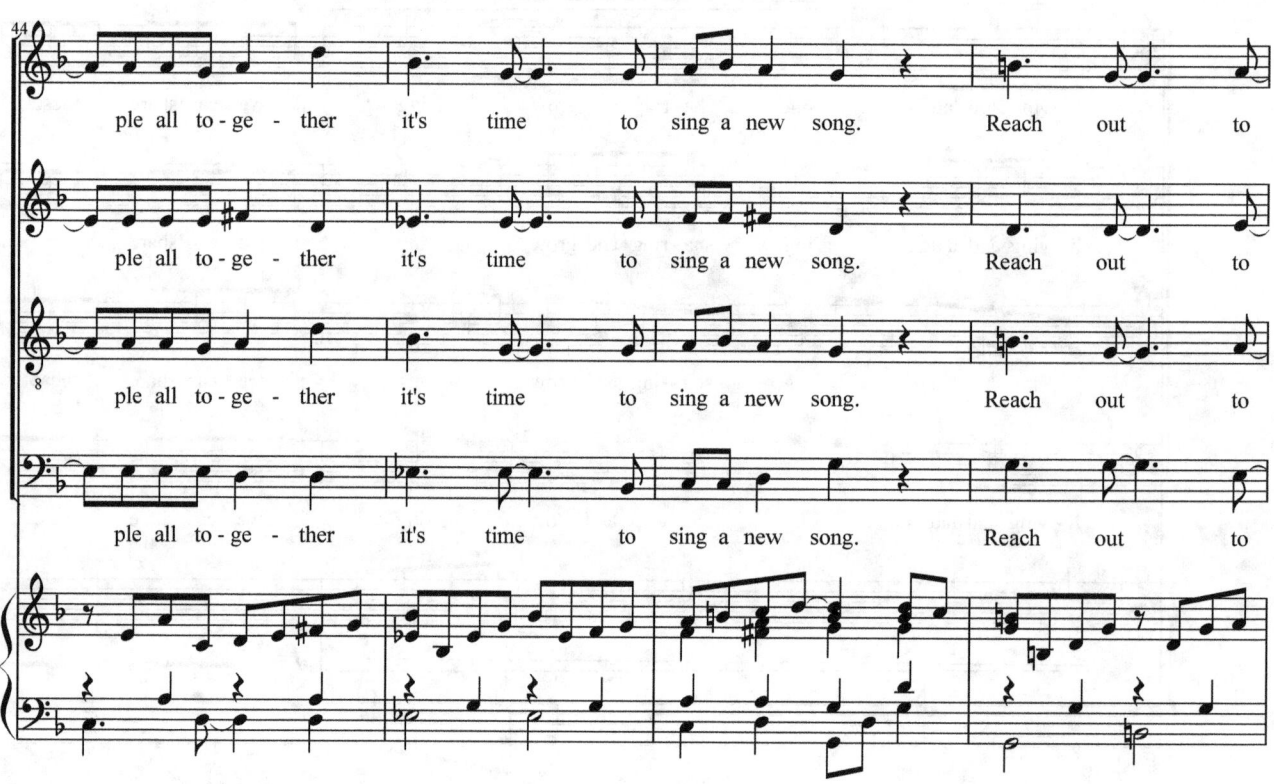

ple all to - ge - ther   it's time   to sing a new song.   Reach out   to

ple all to - ge - ther   it's time   to sing a new song.   Reach out   to

ple all to - ge - ther   it's time   to sing a new song.   Reach out   to

ple all to - ge - ther   it's time   to sing a new song.   Reach out   to

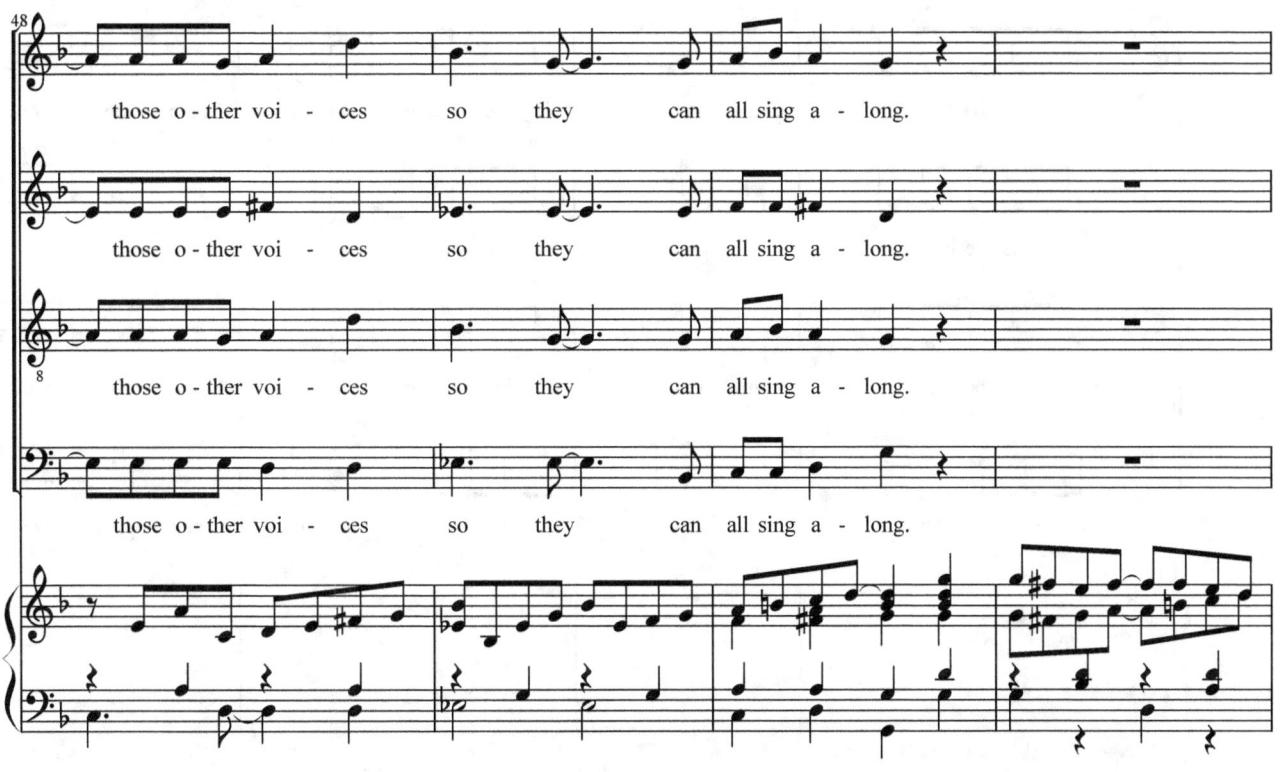

those o - ther voi - ces   so   they   can all sing a - long.

those o - ther voi - ces   so   they   can all sing a - long.

those o - ther voi - ces   so   they   can all sing a - long.

those o - ther voi - ces   so   they   can all sing a - long.

(choir encourages audience or congregation to join in)
(begin clapping on 2 and 4)

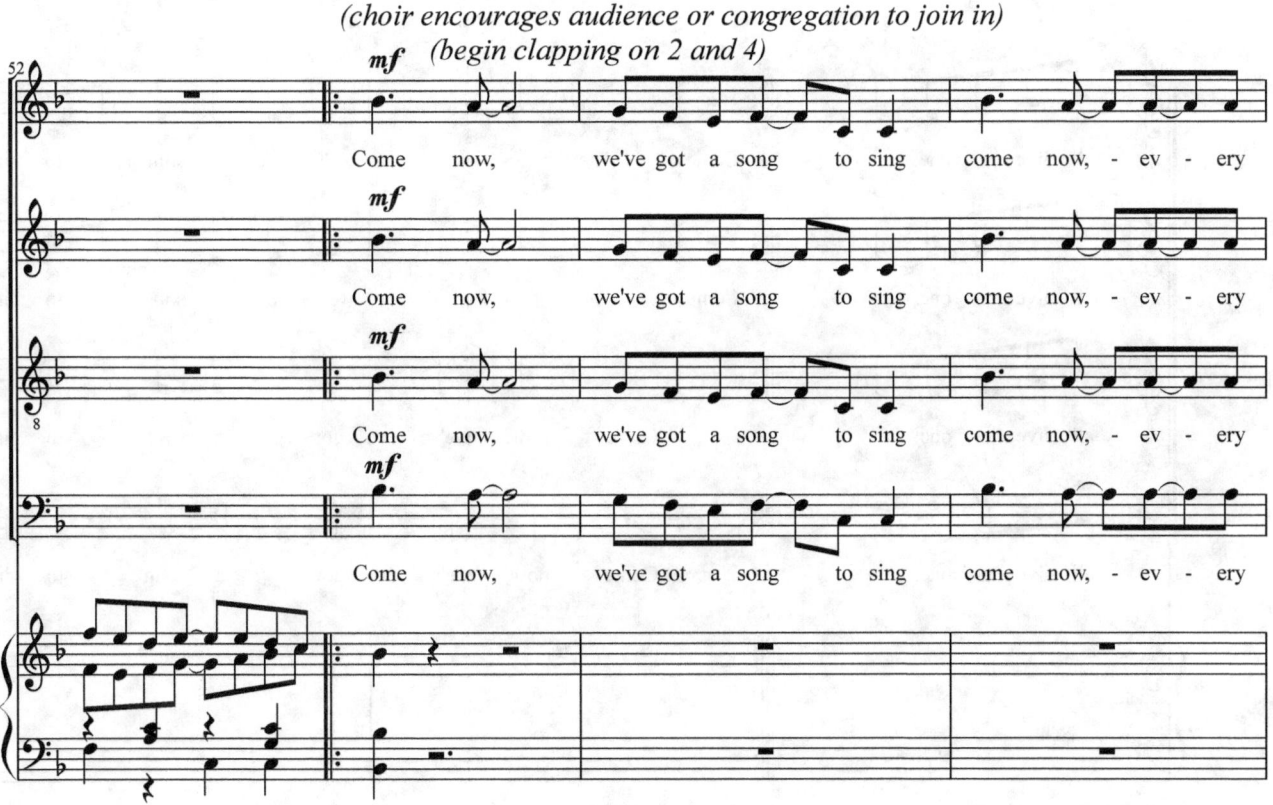

Come   now,   we've got a song   to sing   come now, - ev - ery

Come   now,   we've got a song   to sing   come now, - ev - ery

Come   now,   we've got a song   to sing   come now, - ev - ery

Come   now,   we've got a song   to sing   come now, - ev - ery

33

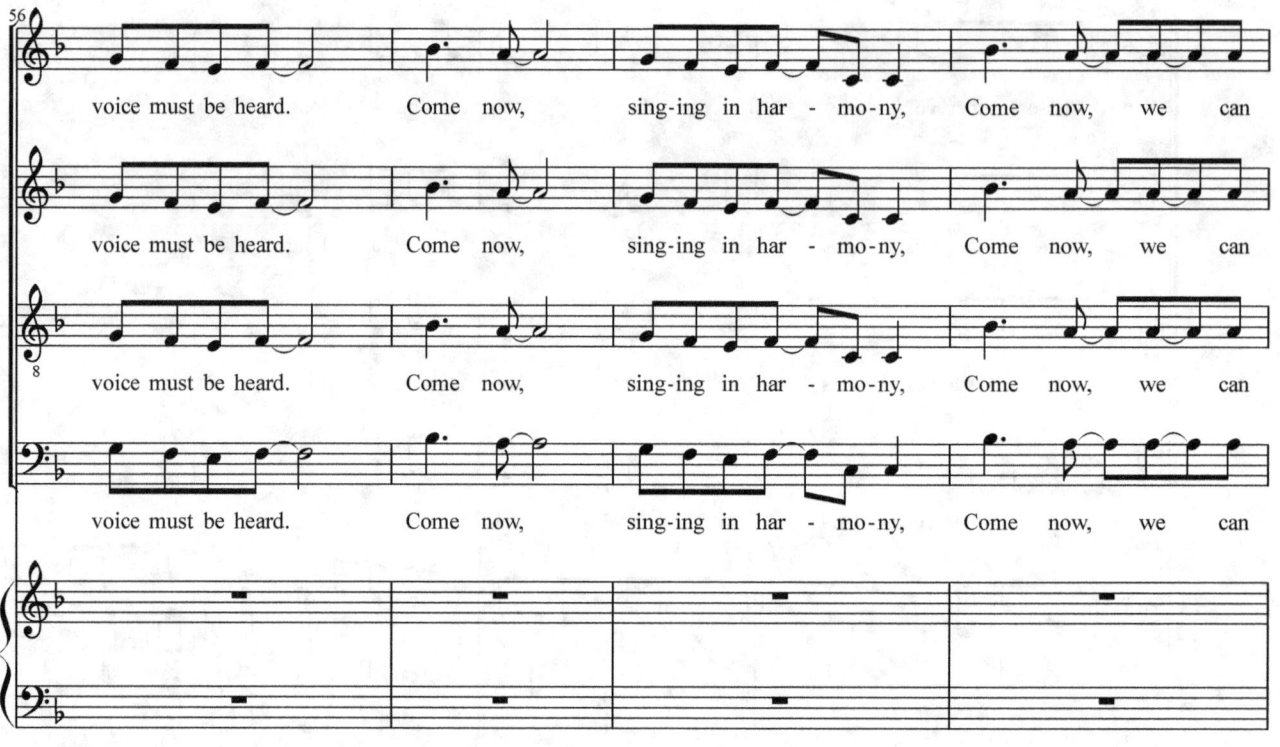

voice must be heard. Come now, sing-ing in har - mo-ny, Come now, we can

voice must be heard. Come now, sing-ing in har - mo-ny, Come now, we can

voice must be heard. Come now, sing-ing in har - mo-ny, Come now, we can

voice must be heard. Come now, sing-ing in har - mo-ny, Come now, we can

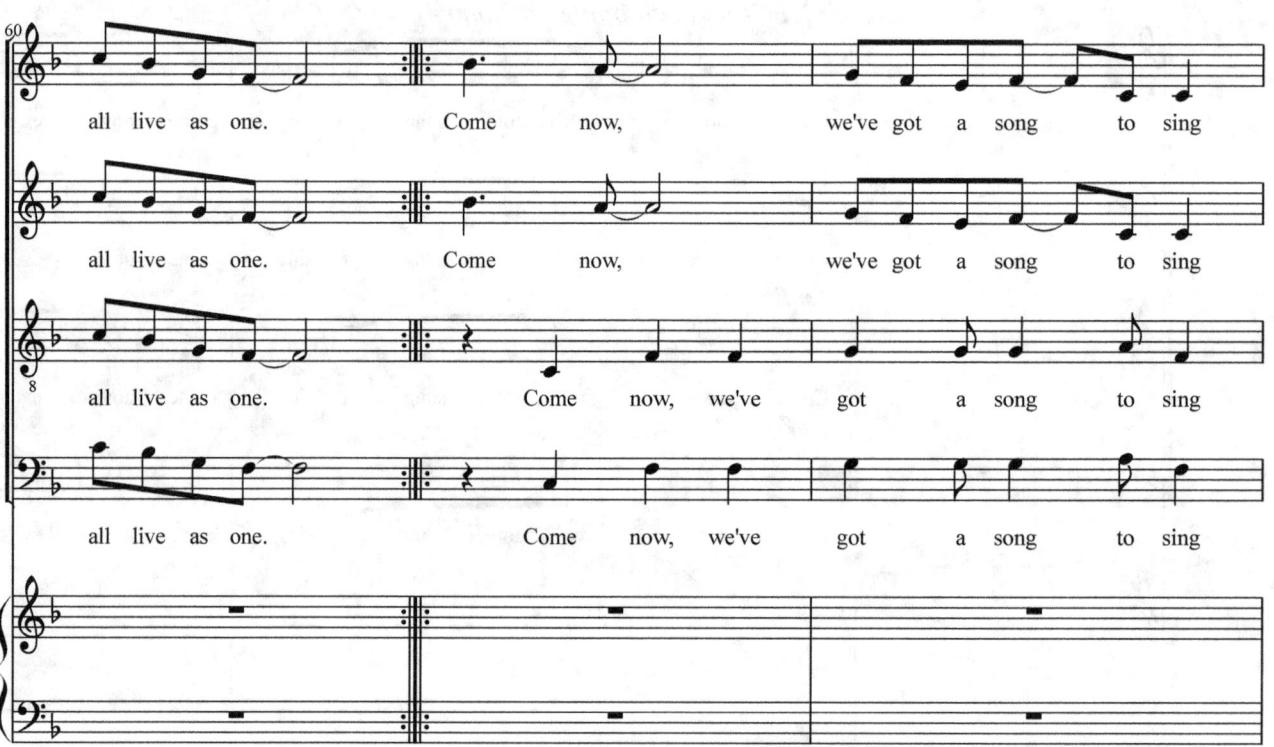

all live as one. Come now, we've got a song to sing

all live as one. Come now, we've got a song to sing

all live as one. Come now, we've got a song to sing

all live as one. Come now, we've got a song to sing

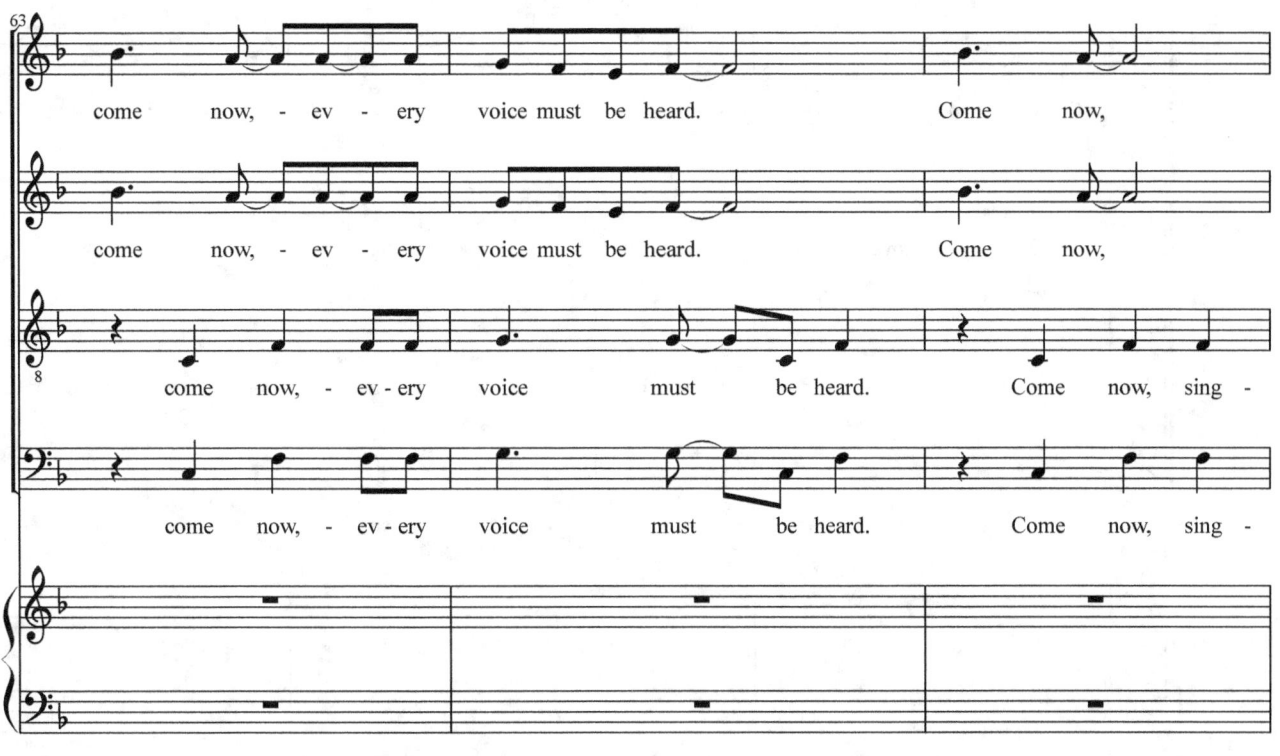

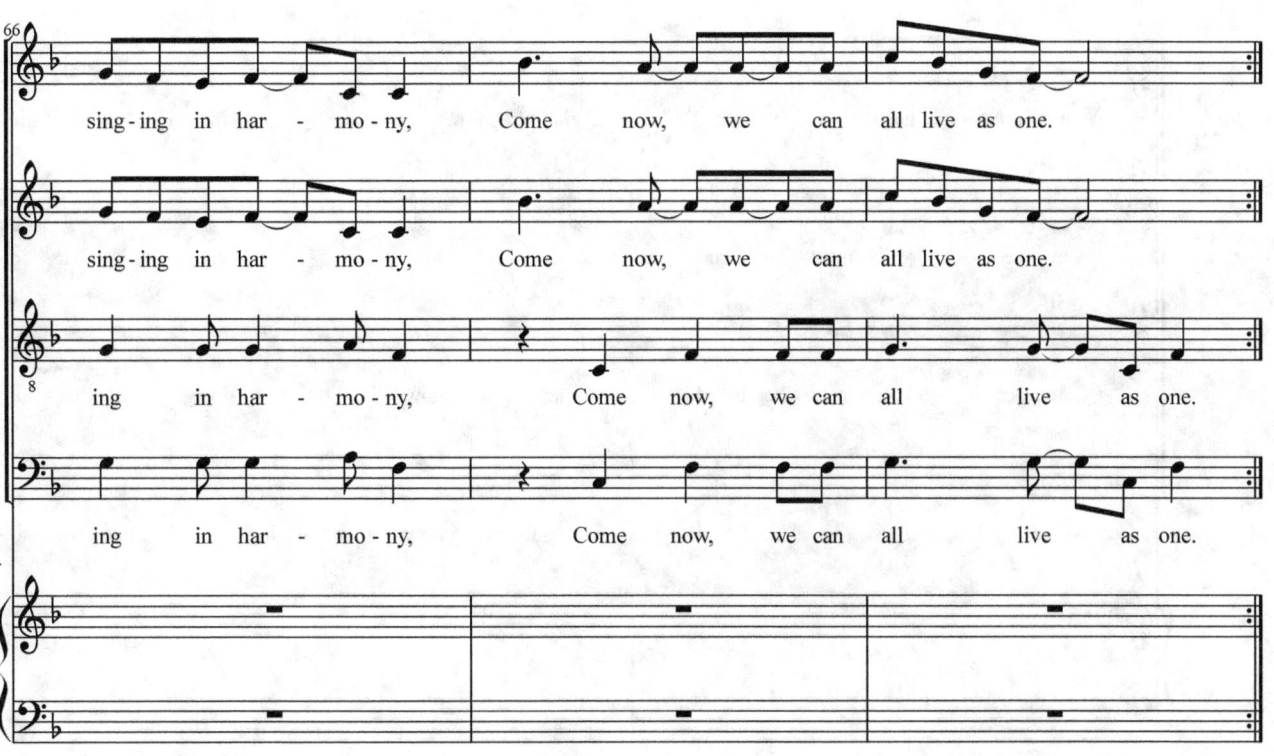

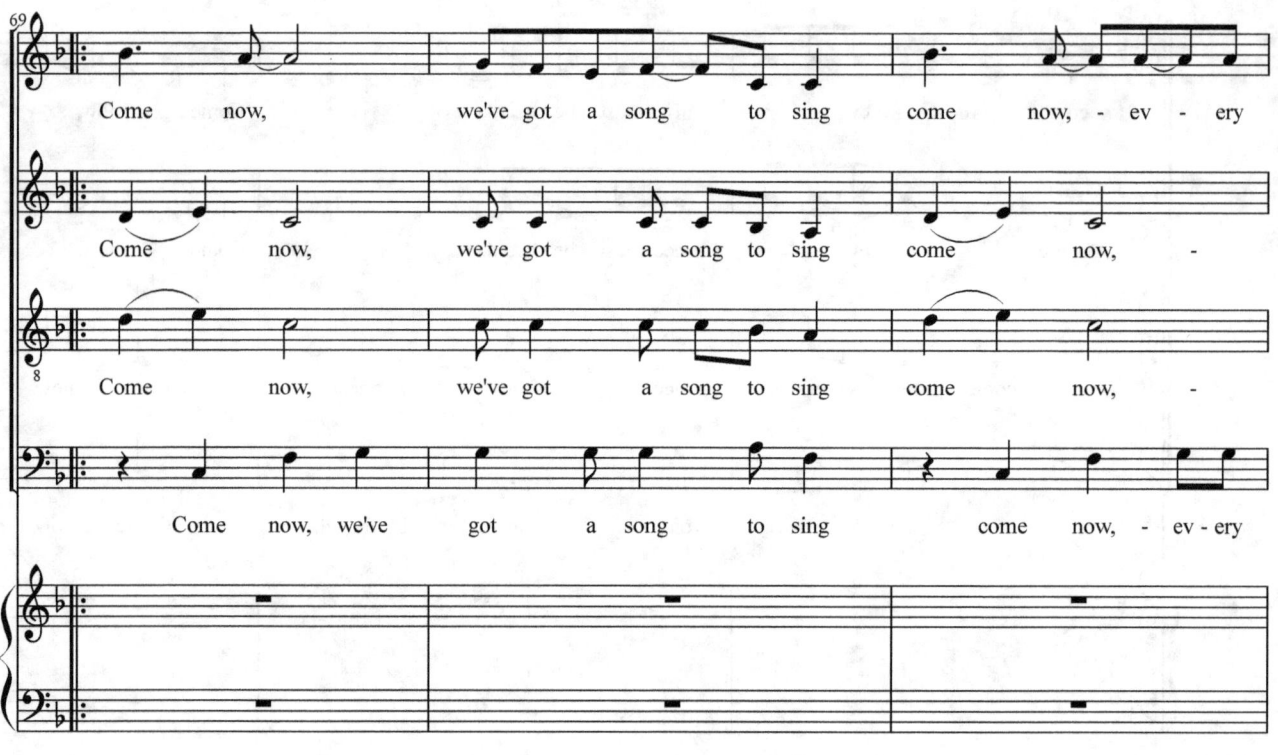

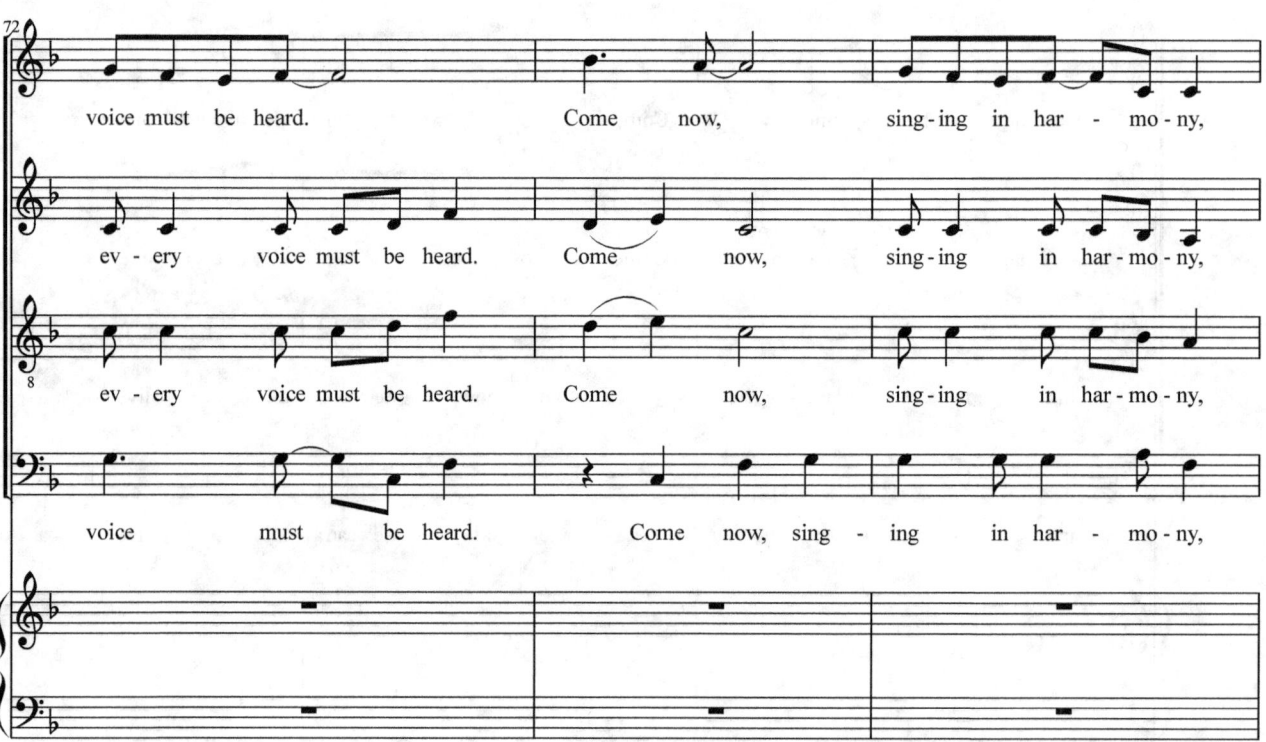

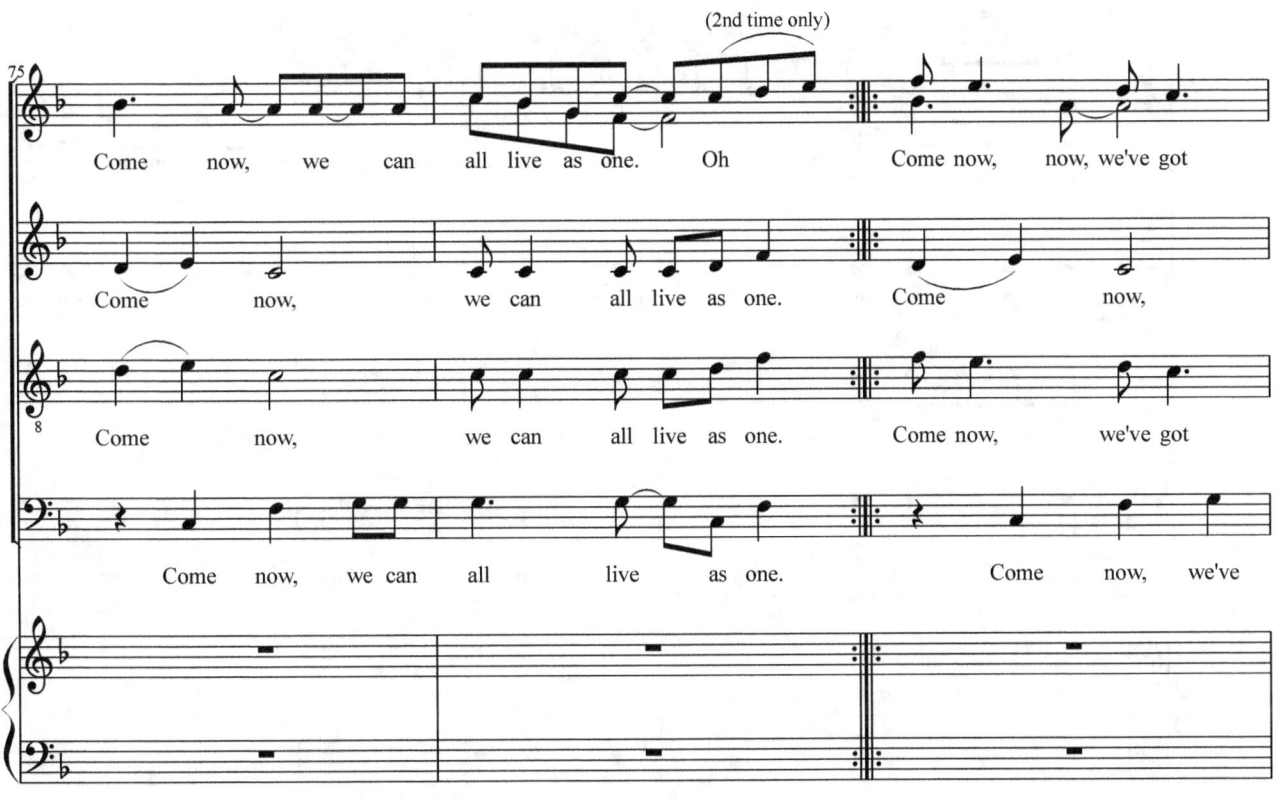

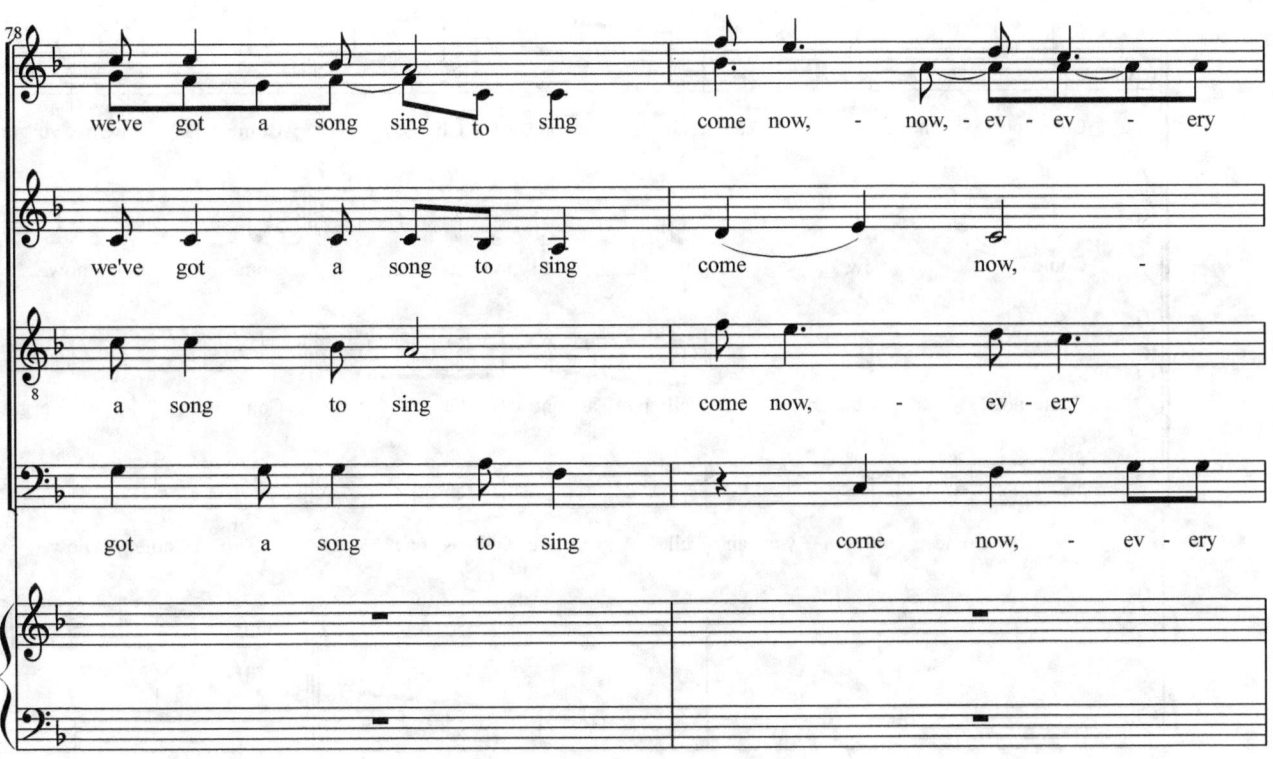

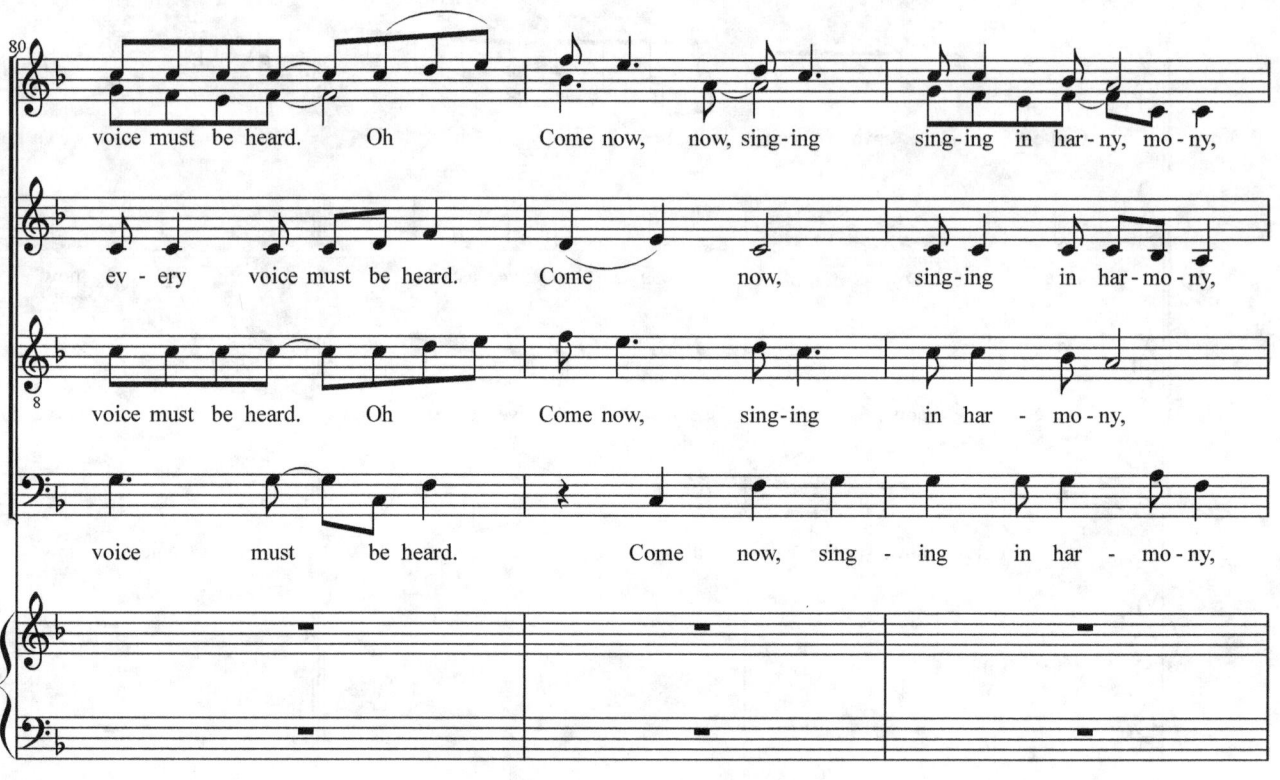

voice must be heard. Oh Come now, now, sing-ing singing in har-ny, mo-ny,

ev - ery voice must be heard. Come now, sing-ing in har-mo-ny,

voice must be heard. Oh Come now, sing-ing in har - mo-ny,

voice must be heard. Come now, sing-ing in har-mo-ny,

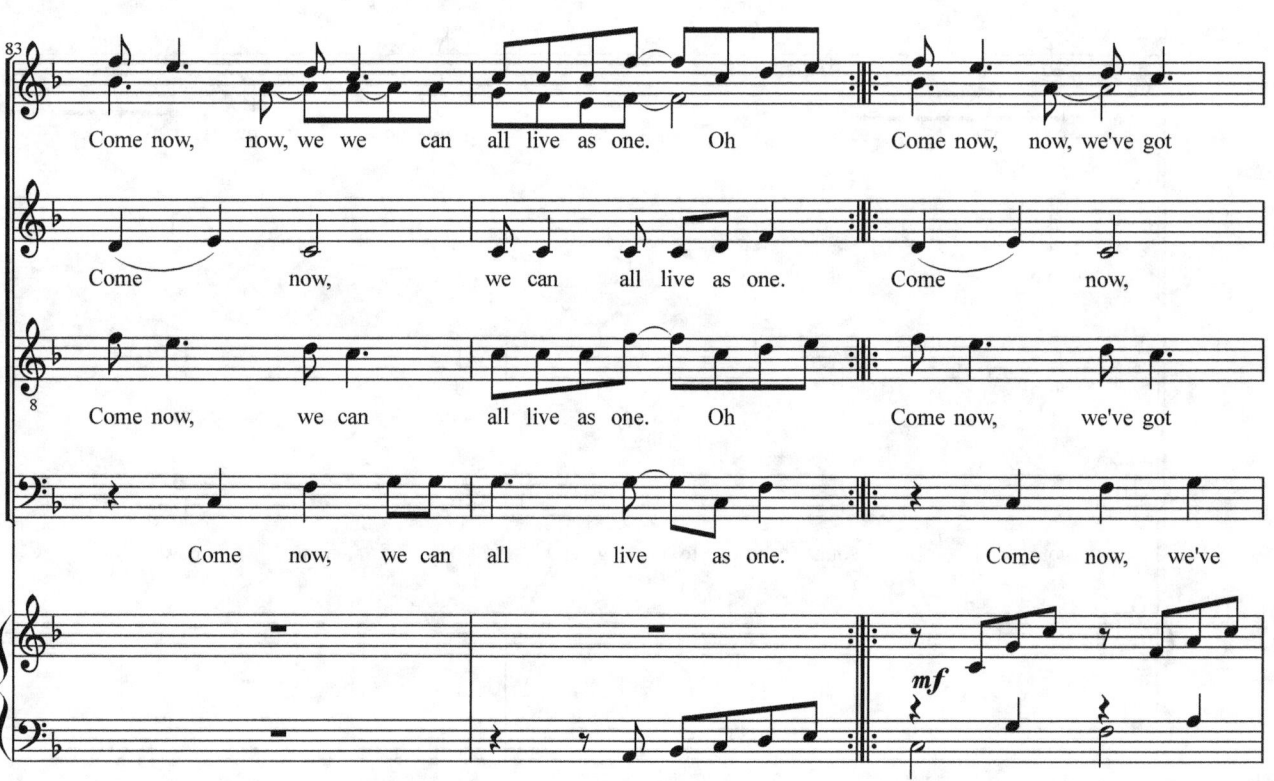

Come now, now, we we can all live as one. Oh Come now, now, we've got

Come now, we can all live as one. Come now,

Come now, we can all live as one. Oh Come now, we've got

Come now, we can all live as one. Come now, we've

mf

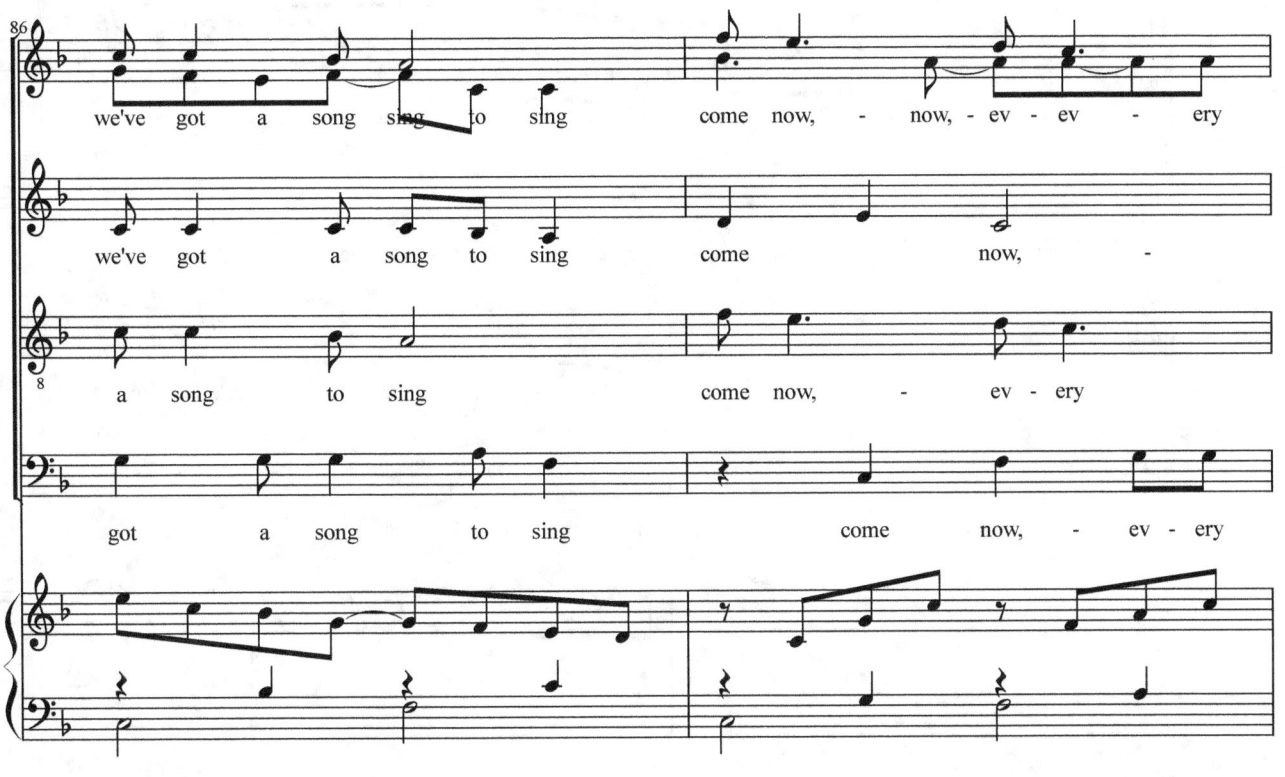

we've got a song sing to sing come now, - now, - ev - ery
we've got a song to sing come now, -
a song to sing come now, - ev - ery
got a song to sing come now, - ev - ery

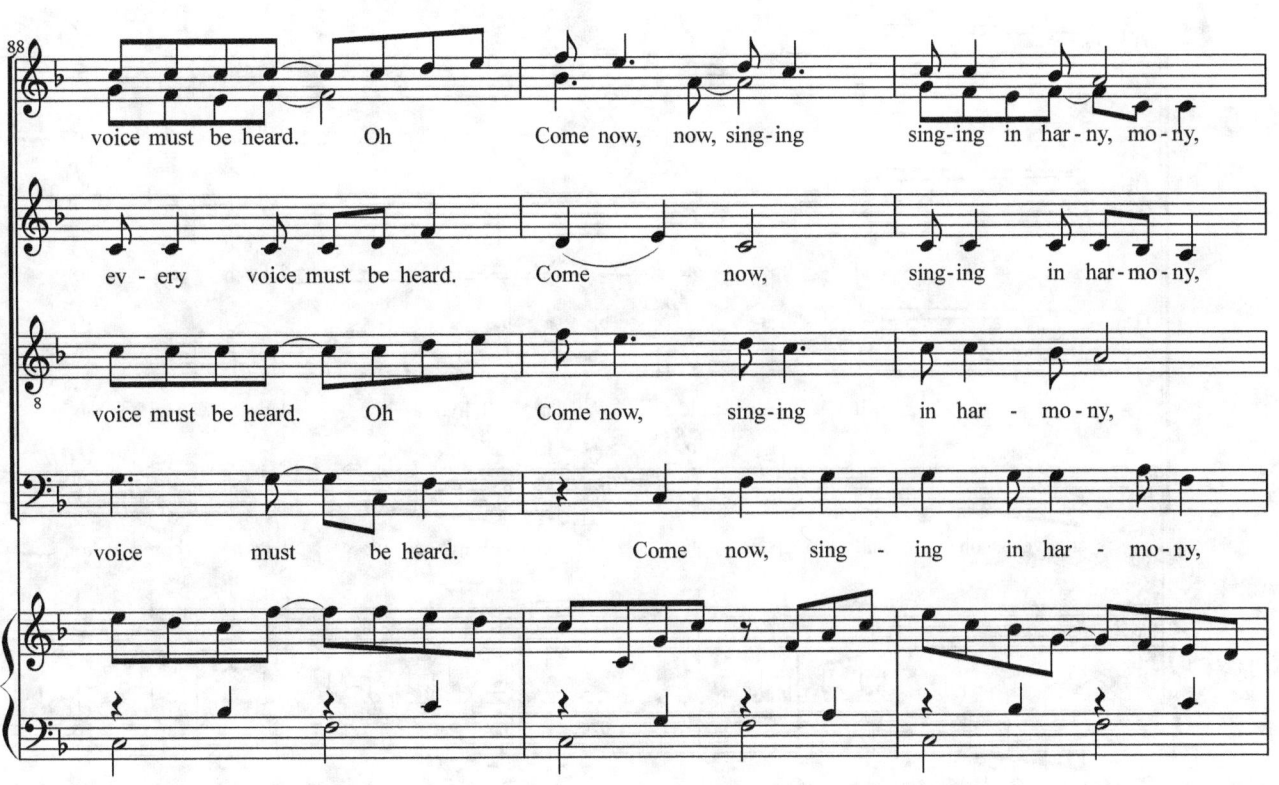

voice must be heard. Oh Come now, now, sing-ing sing-ing in har-ny, mo-ny,
ev - ery voice must be heard. Come now, sing-ing in har-mo-ny
voice must be heard. Oh Come now, sing-ing in har - mo-ny,
voice must be heard. Come now, sing - ing in har - mo-ny,

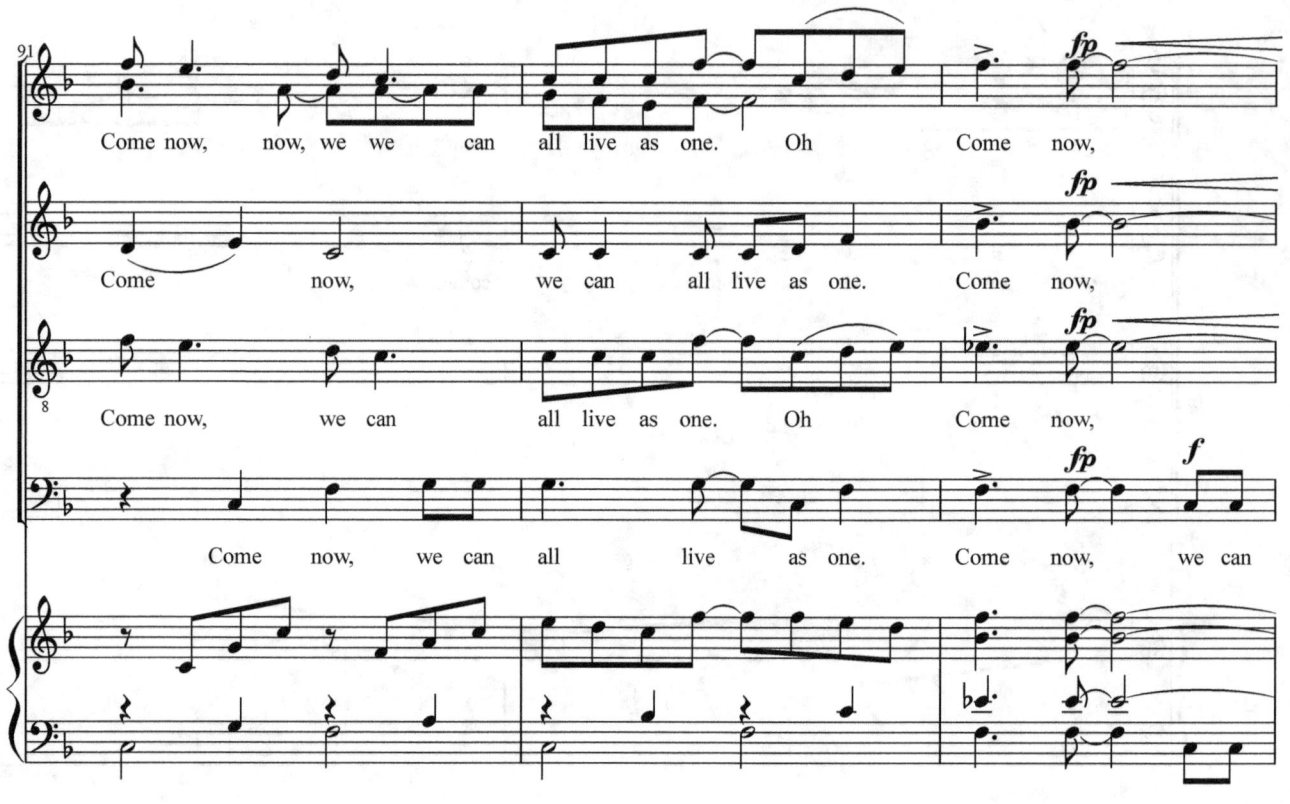

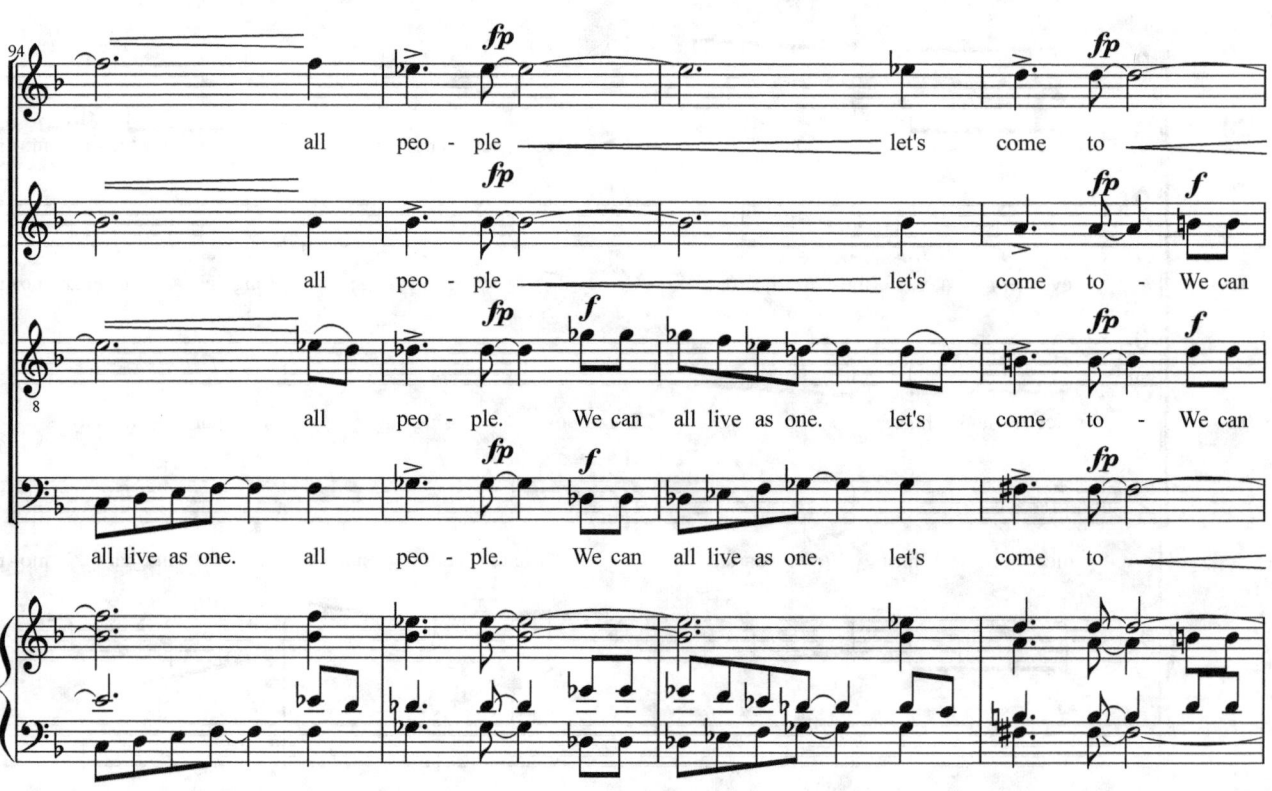

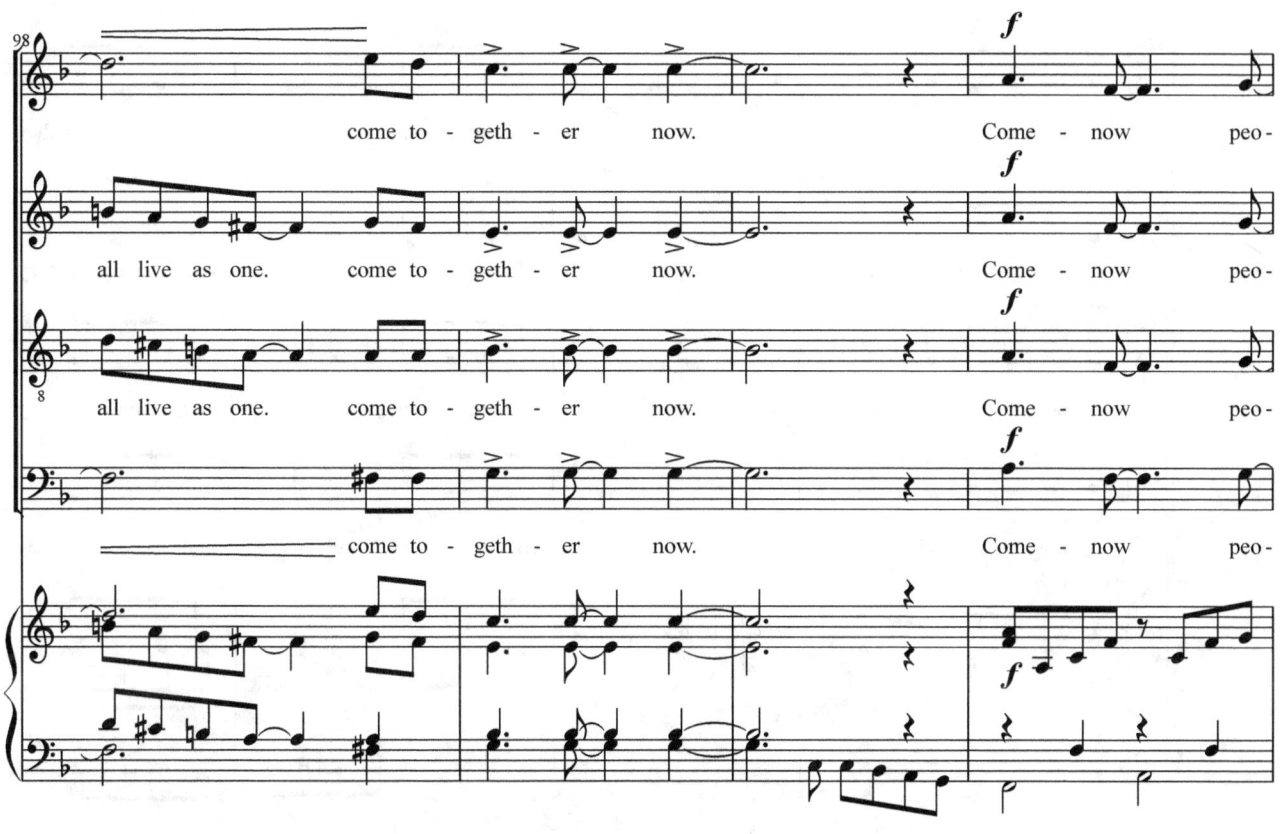

come to - geth - er now. Come now peo -
all live as one. come to - geth - er now. Come now peo -
all live as one. come to - geth - er now. Come now peo -
come to - geth - er now. Come now peo -

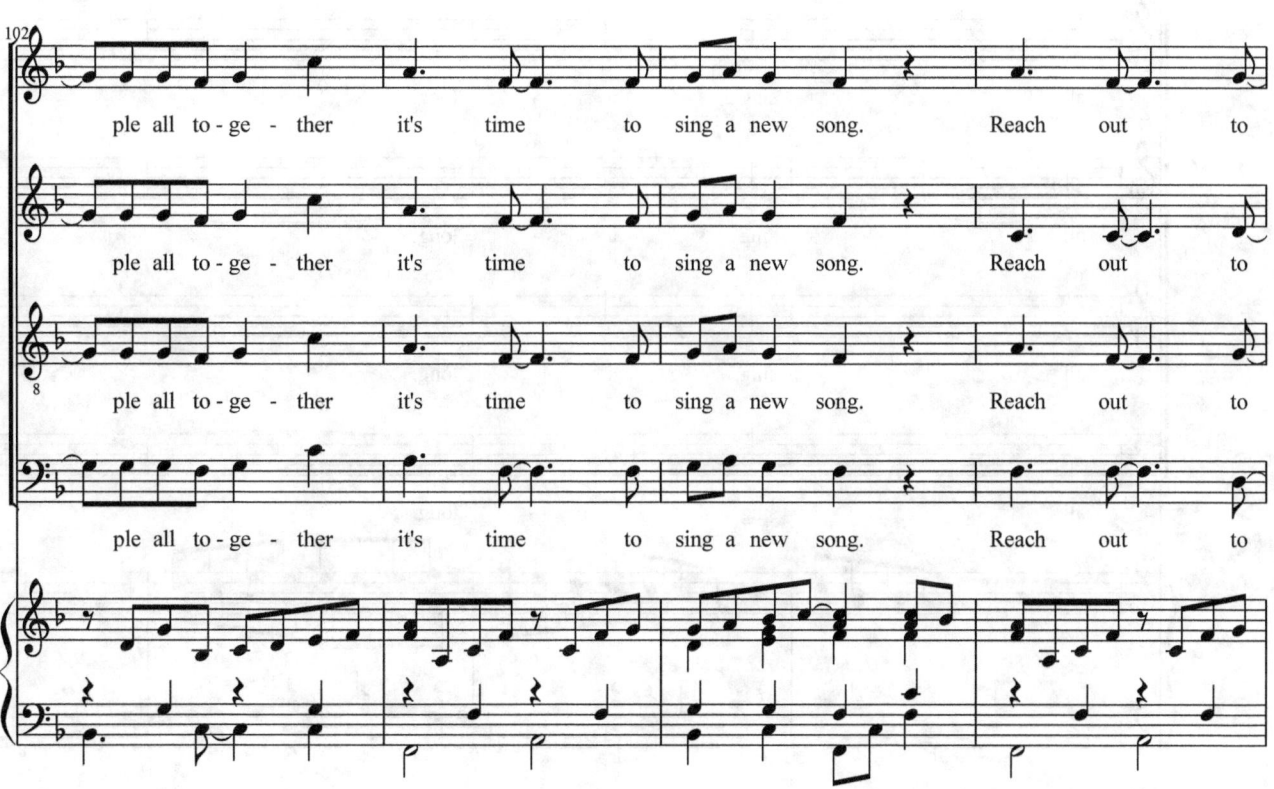

ple all to - ge - ther it's time to sing a new song. Reach out to
ple all to - ge - ther it's time to sing a new song. Reach out to
ple all to - ge - ther it's time to sing a new song. Reach out to
ple all to - ge - ther it's time to sing a new song. Reach out to

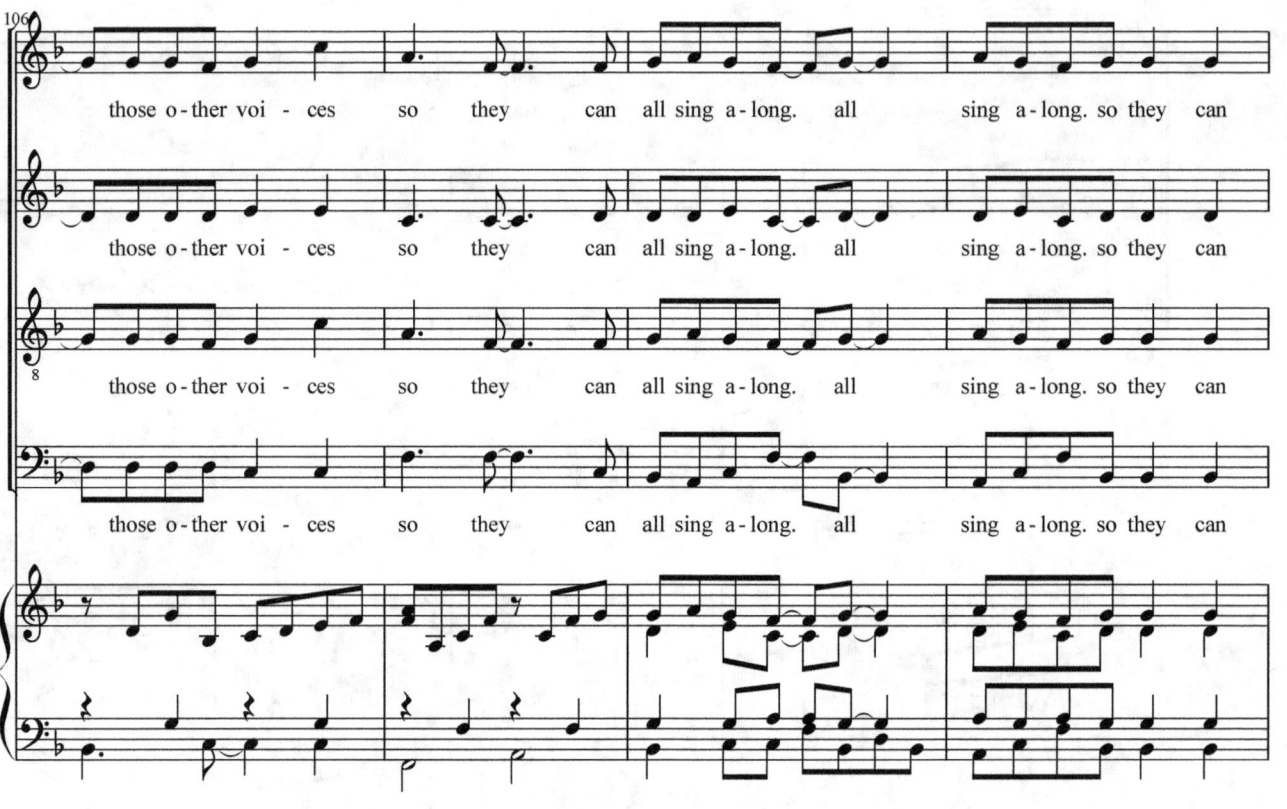

those o-ther voi - ces so they can all sing a-long. all sing a-long. so they can

those o-ther voi - ces so they can all sing a-long. all sing a-long. so they can

those o-ther voi - ces so they can all sing a-long. all sing a-long. so they can

those o-ther voi - ces so they can all sing a-long. all sing a-long. so they can

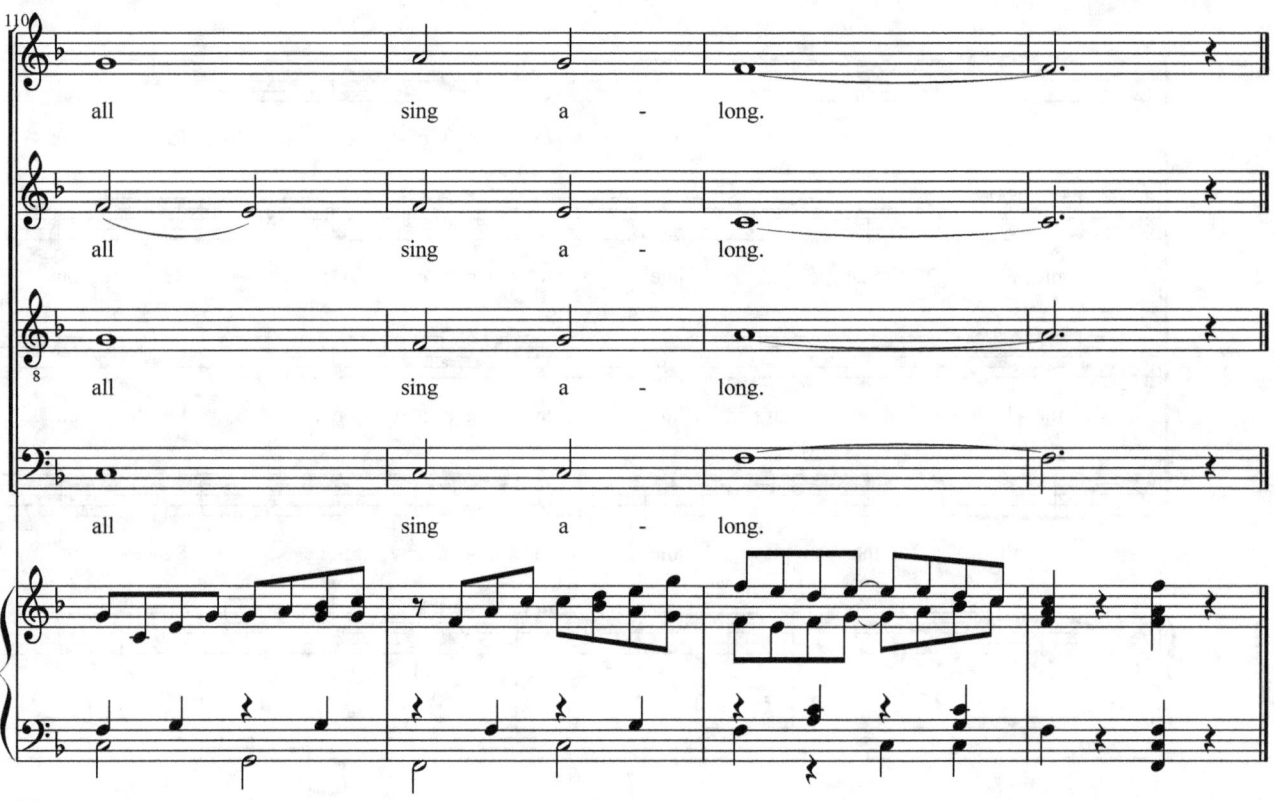

all sing a - long.

all sing a - long.

all sing a - long.

all sing a - long.

Oh Eternal Spirit

Text by Martha Kirby Capo

Music by Ken Langer

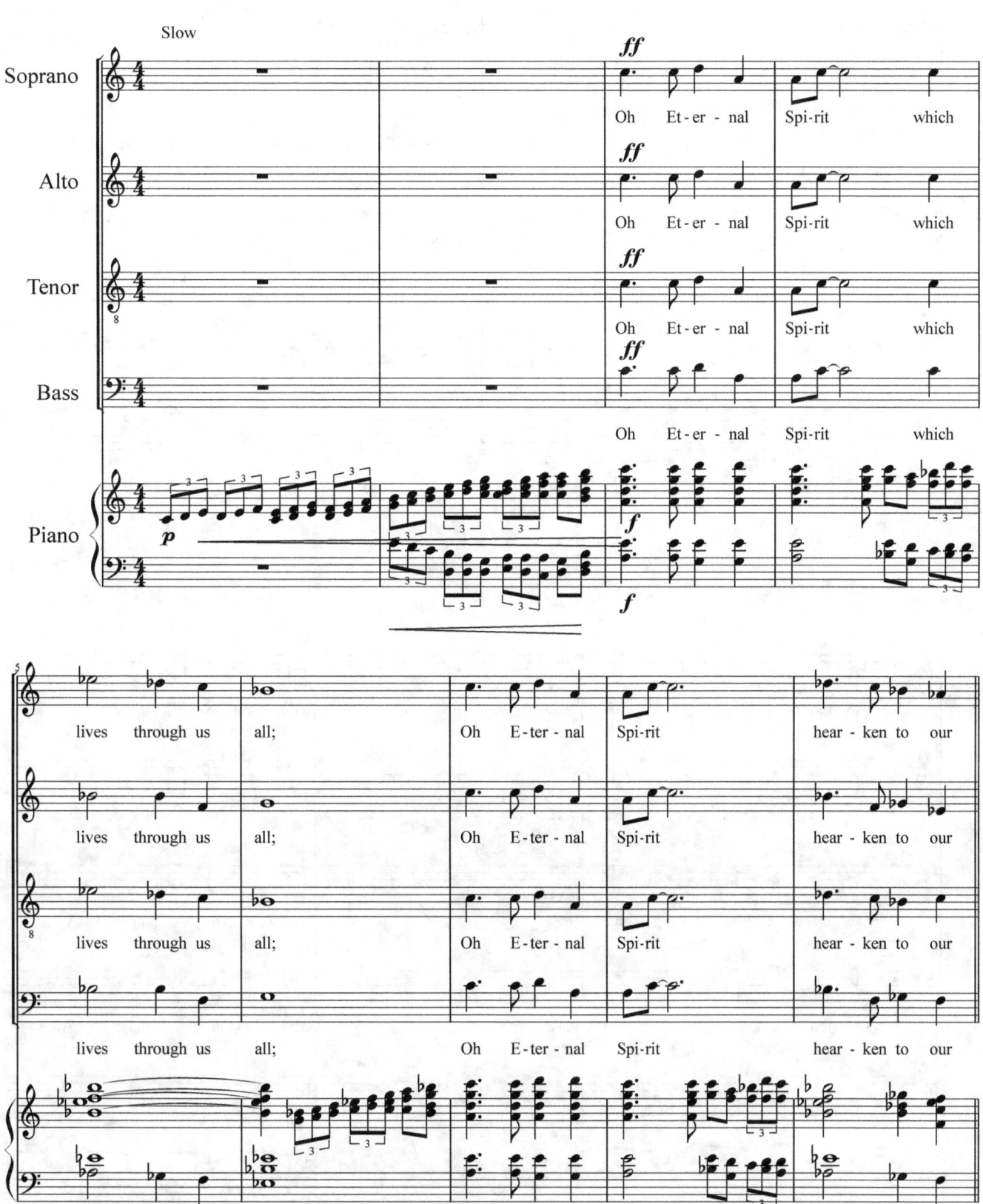

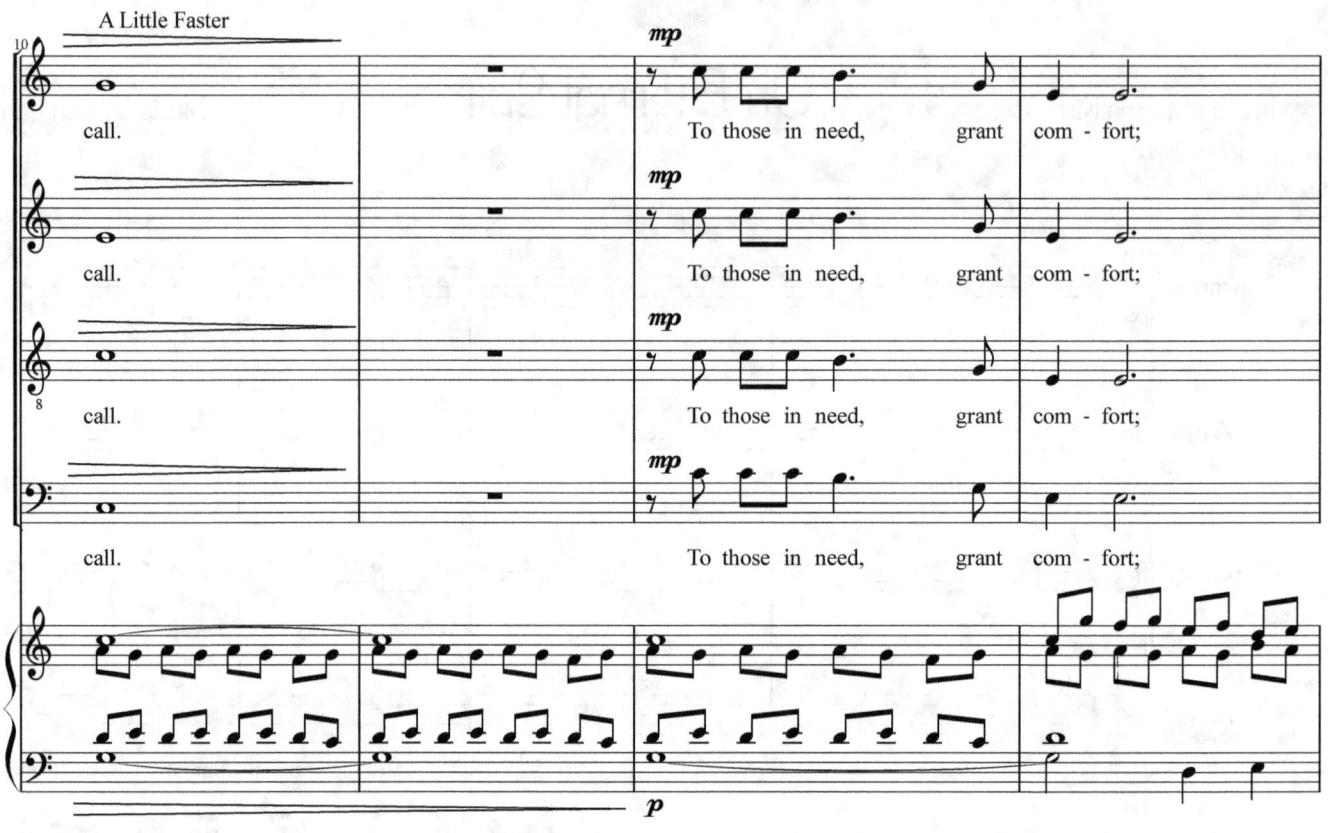

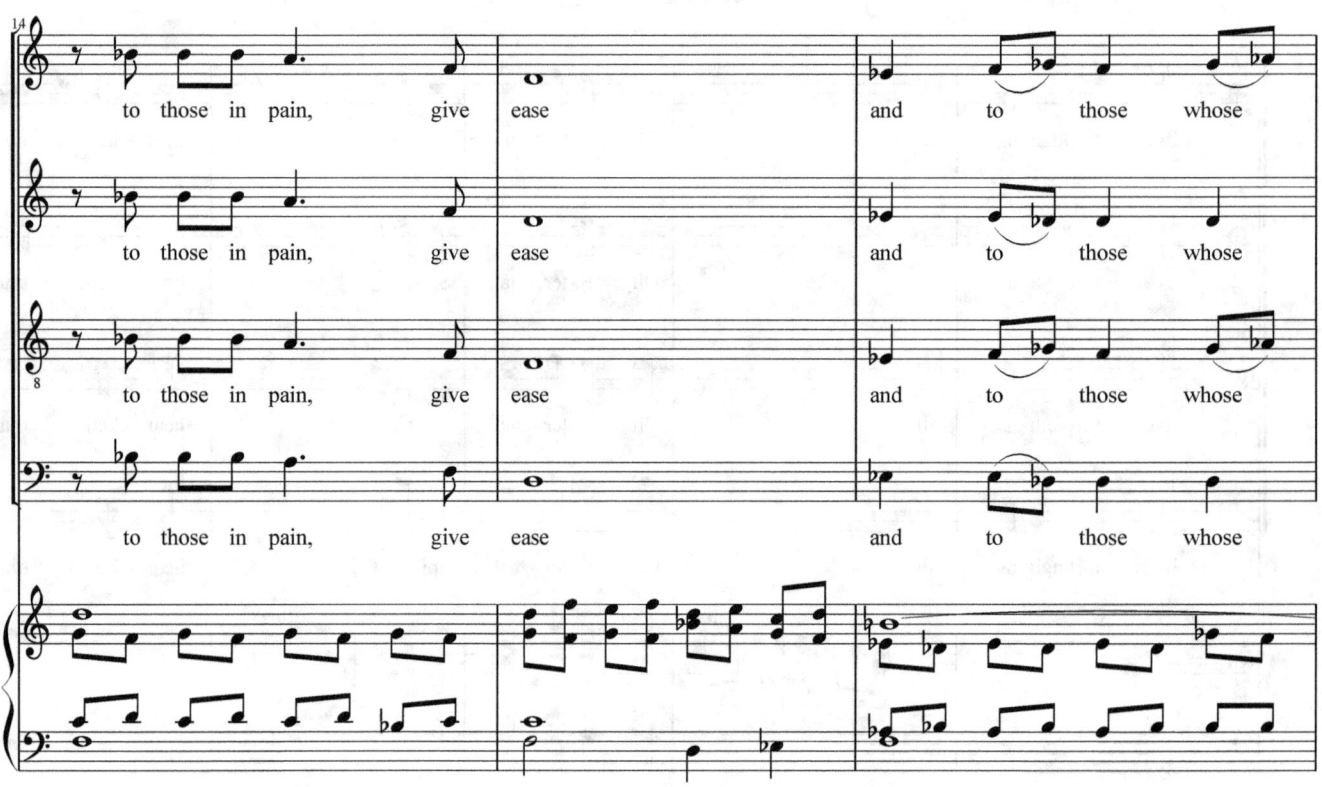

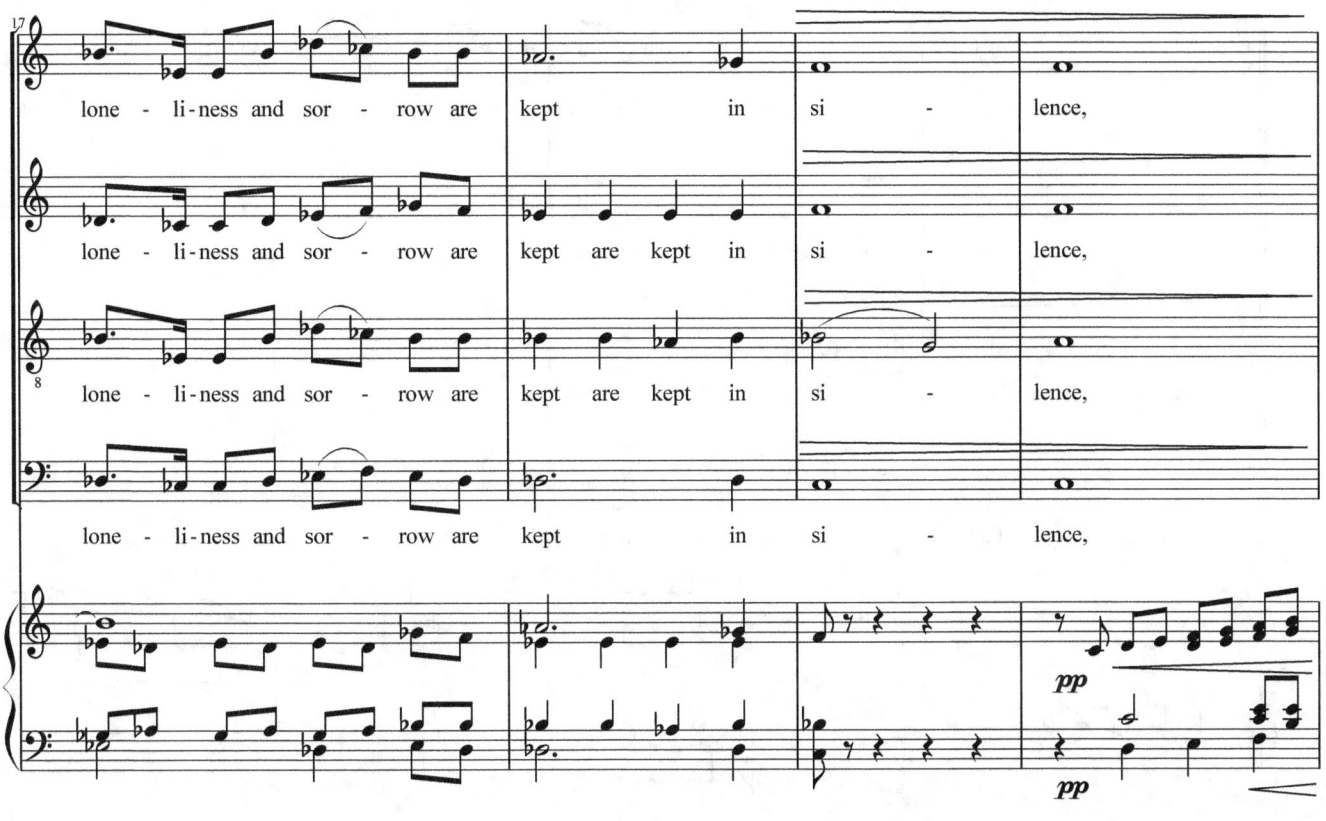

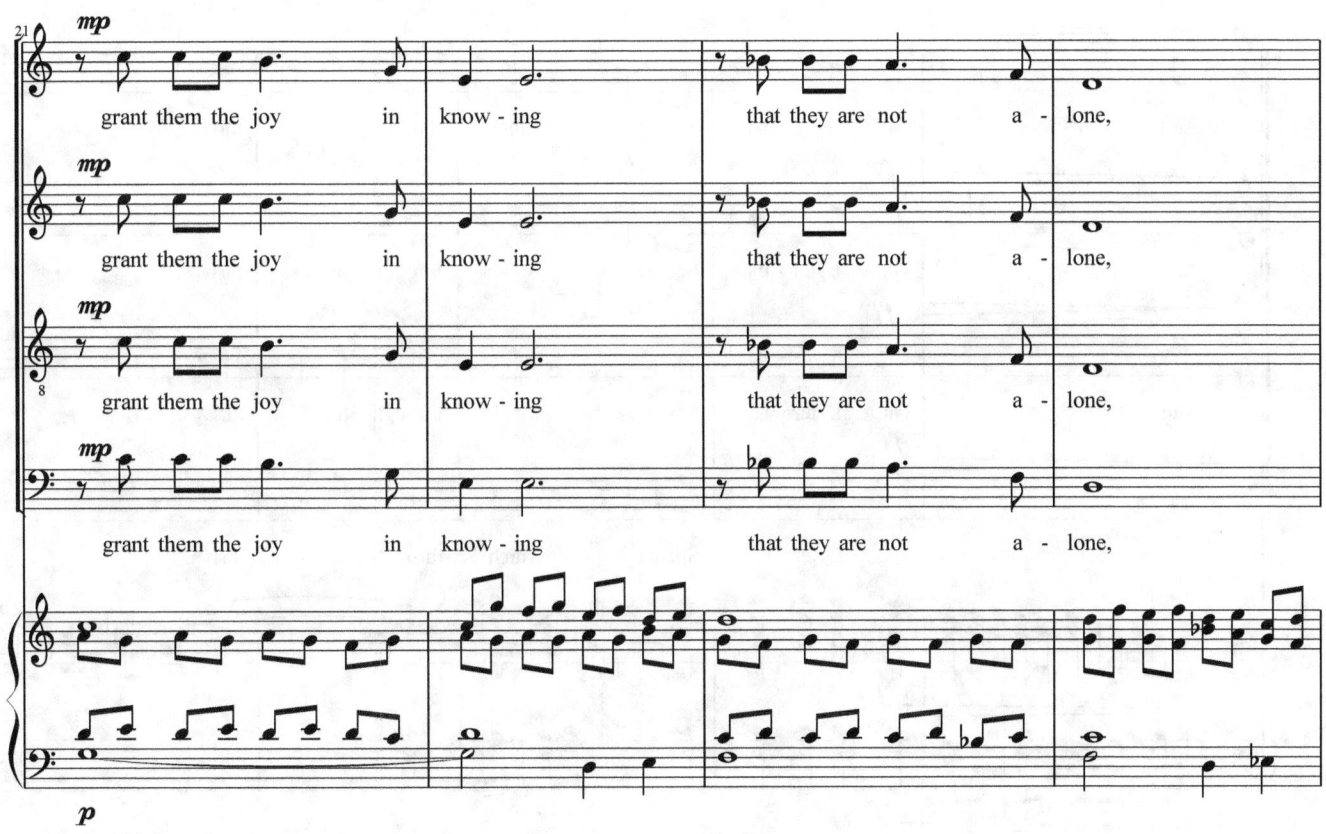

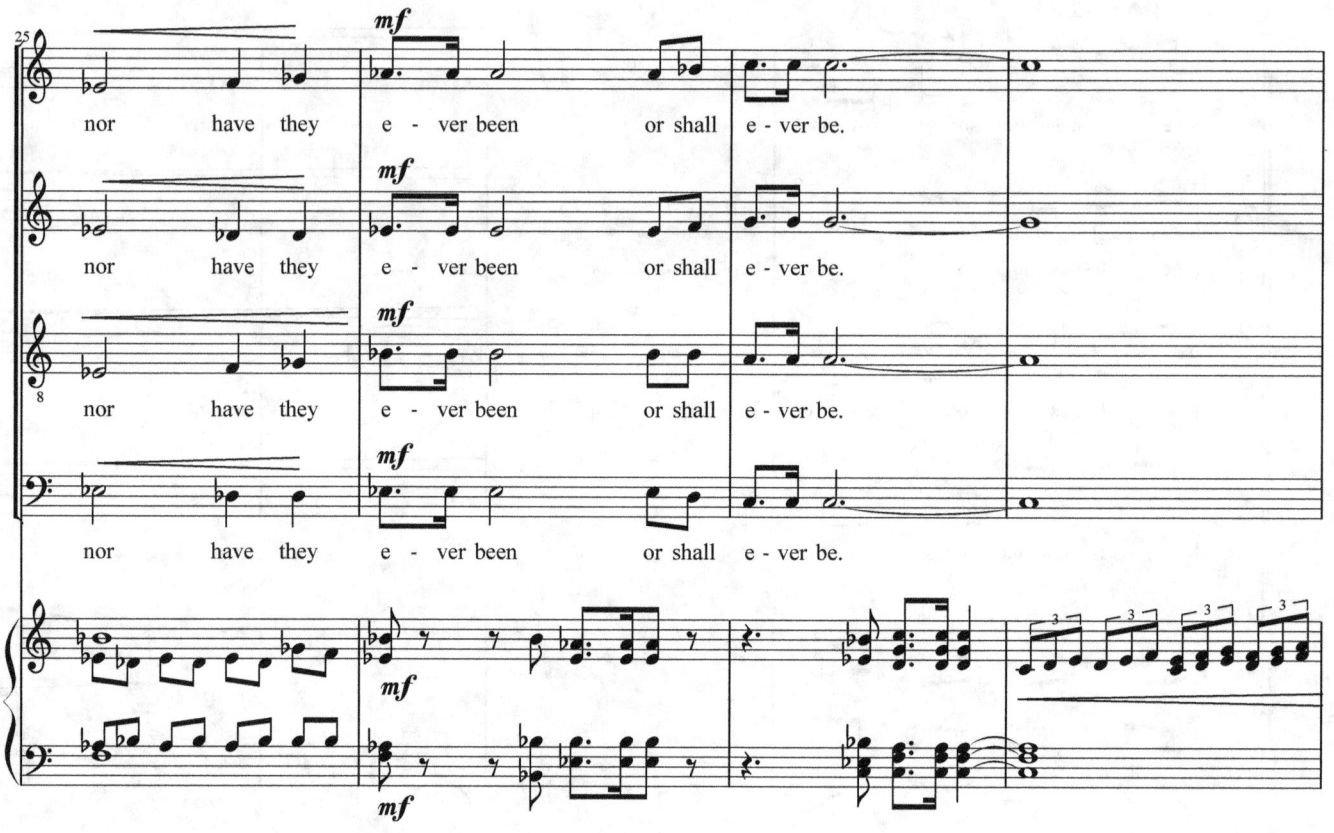

nor have they e - ver been or shall e - ver be.

nor have they e - ver been or shall e - ver be.

nor have they e - ver been or shall e - ver be.

nor have they e - ver been or shall e - ver be.

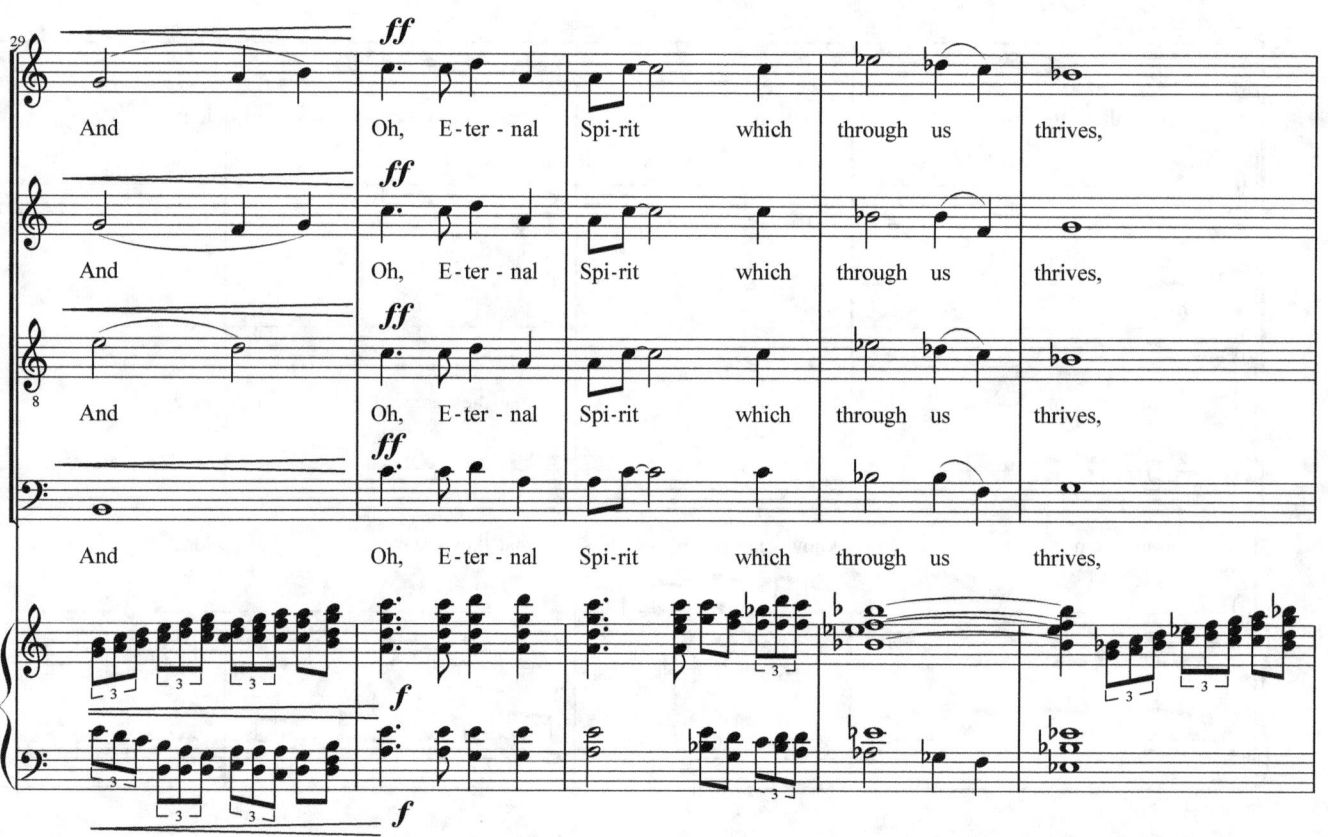

And Oh, E-ter - nal Spi - rit which through us thrives,

And Oh, E-ter - nal Spi - rit which through us thrives,

And Oh, E-ter - nal Spi - rit which through us thrives,

And Oh, E-ter - nal Spi - rit which through us thrives,

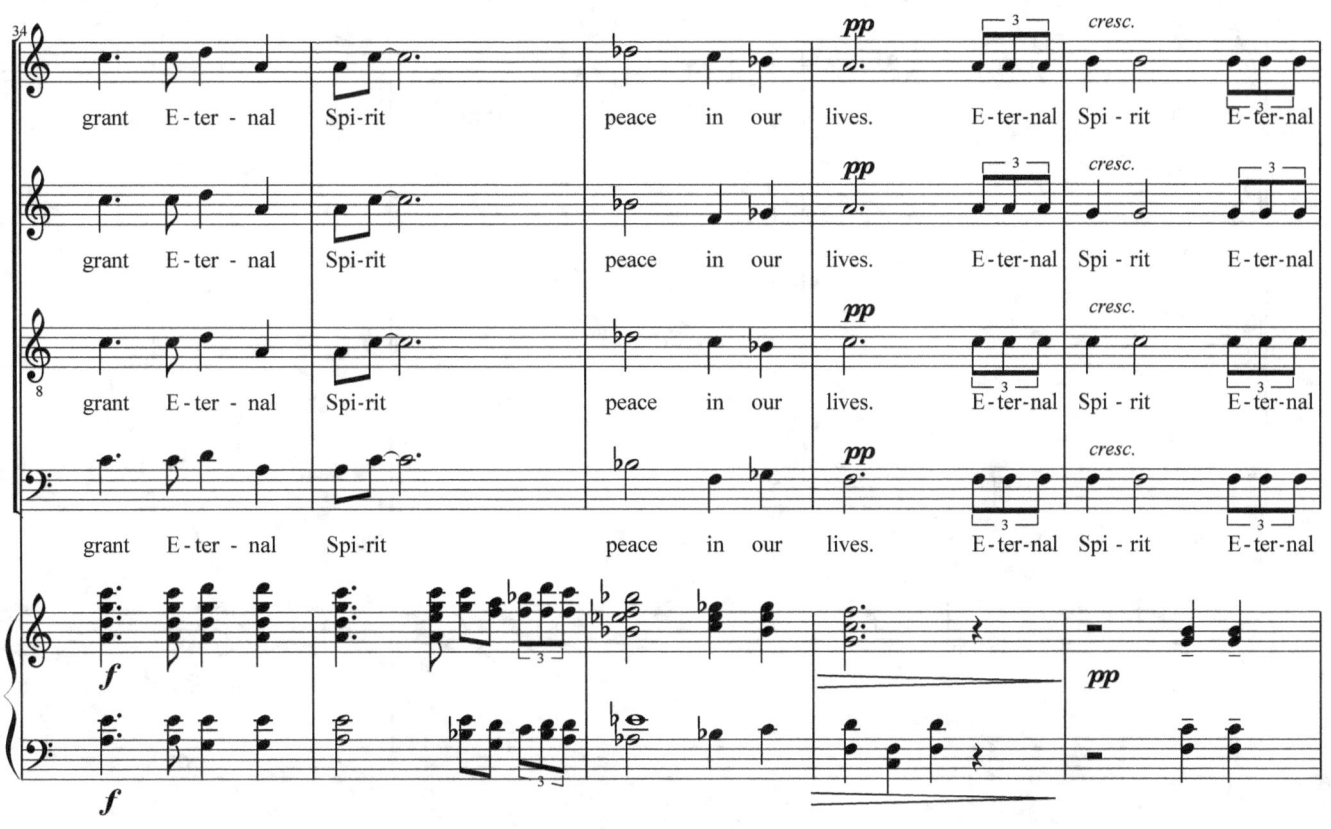

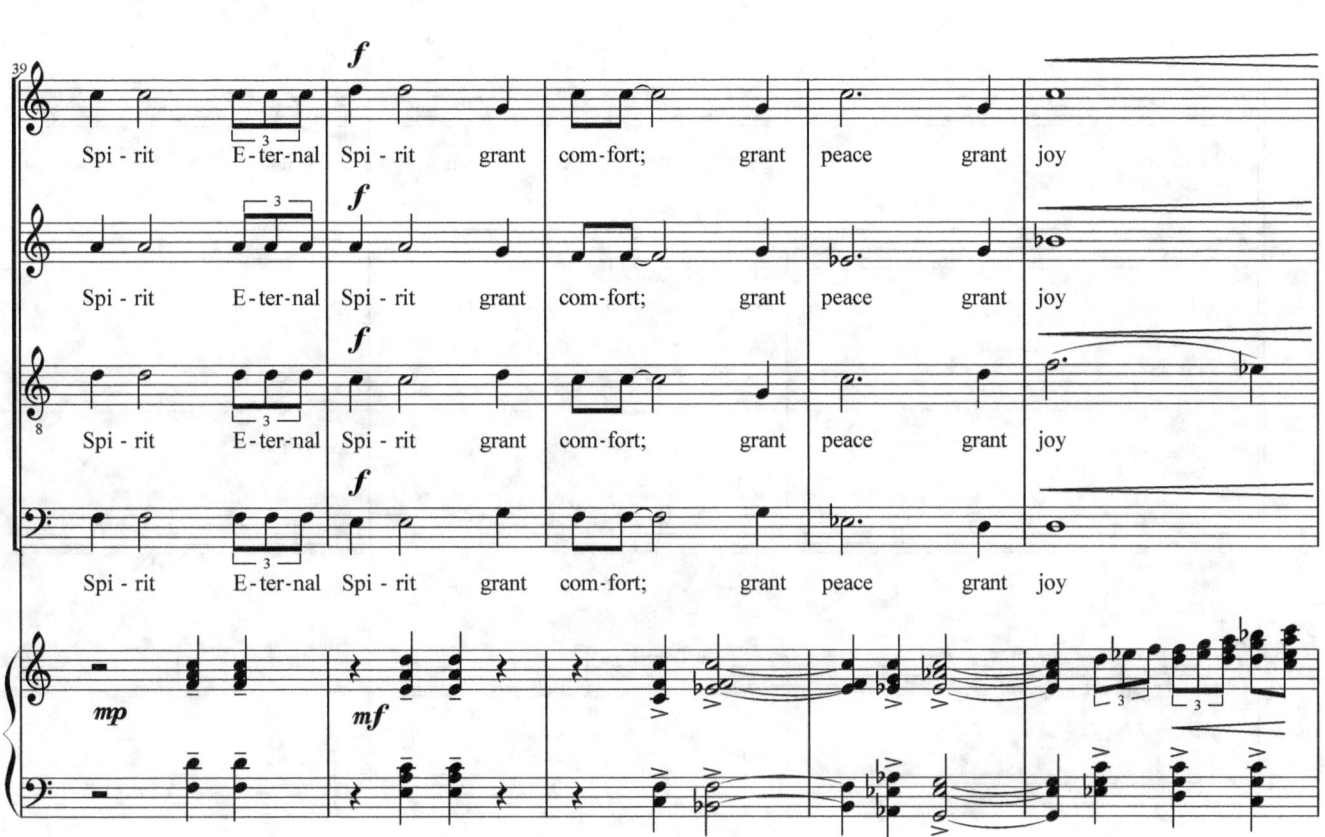

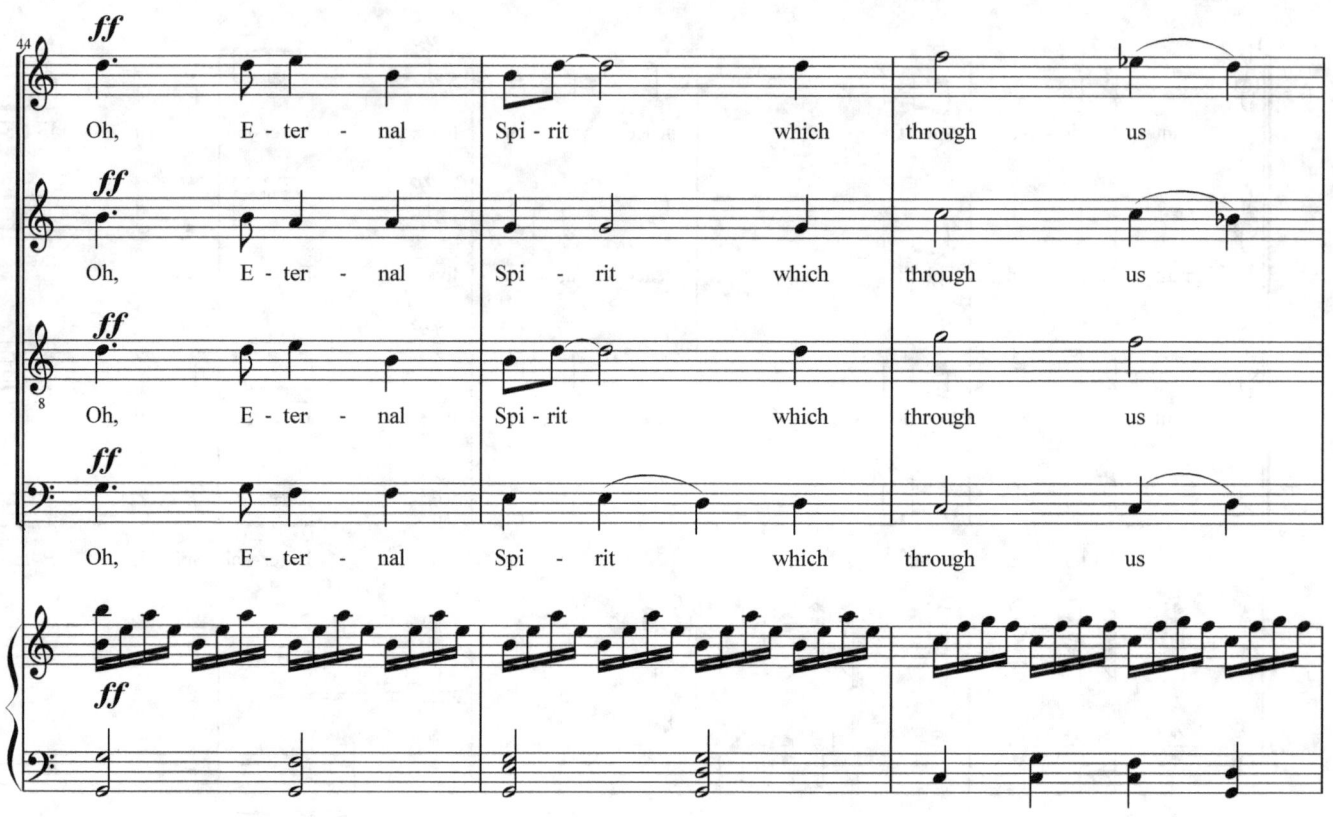

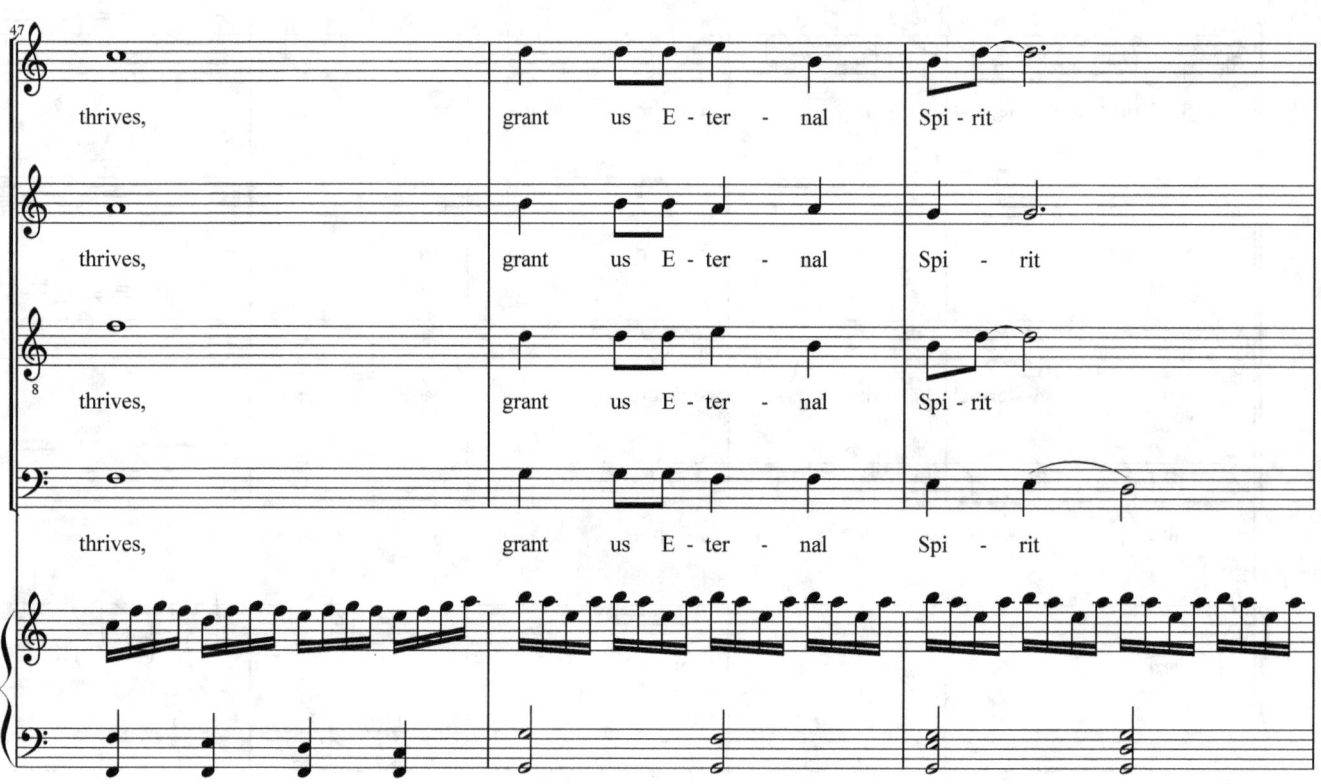

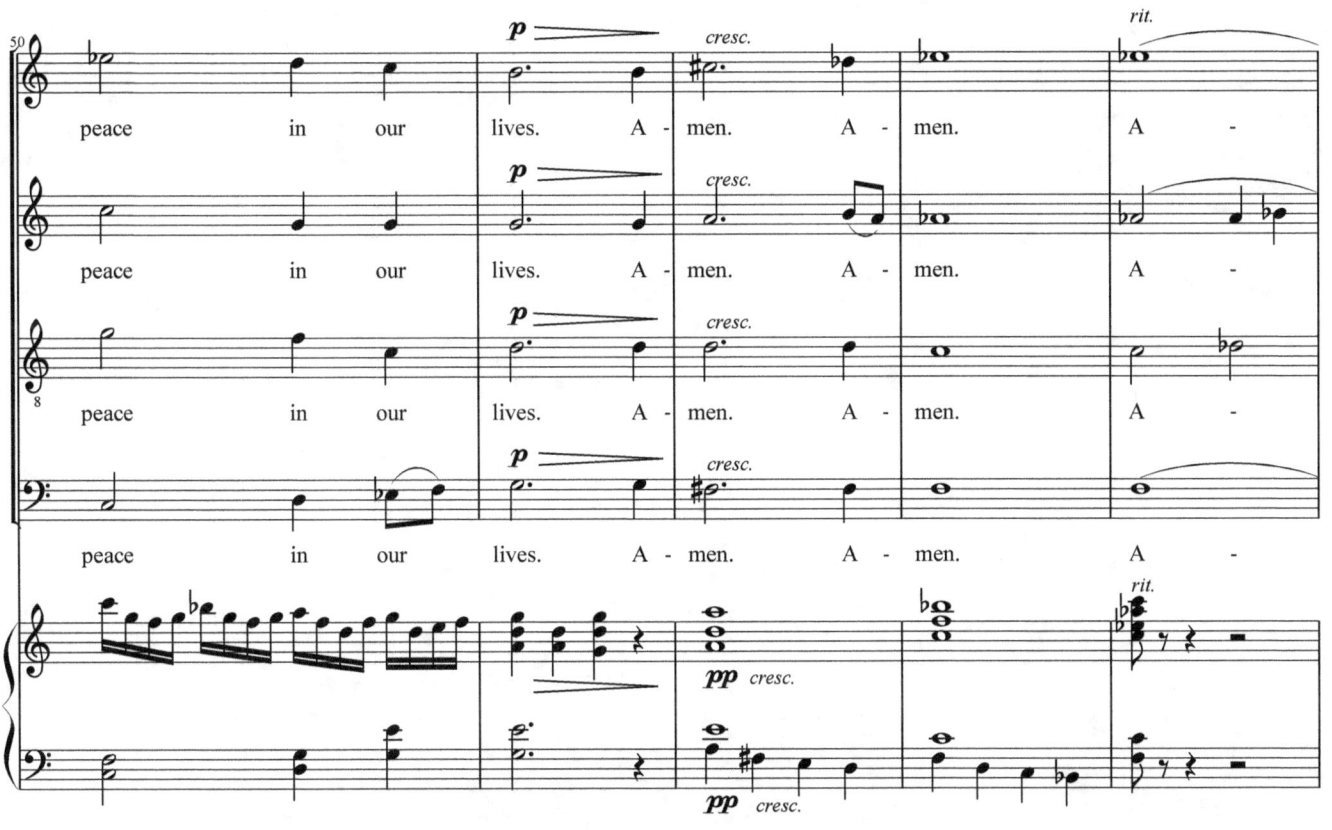

peace in our lives. A - men. A - men. A -

peace in our lives. A - men. A - men. A -

peace in our lives. A - men. A - men. A -

peace in our lives. A - men. A - men. A -

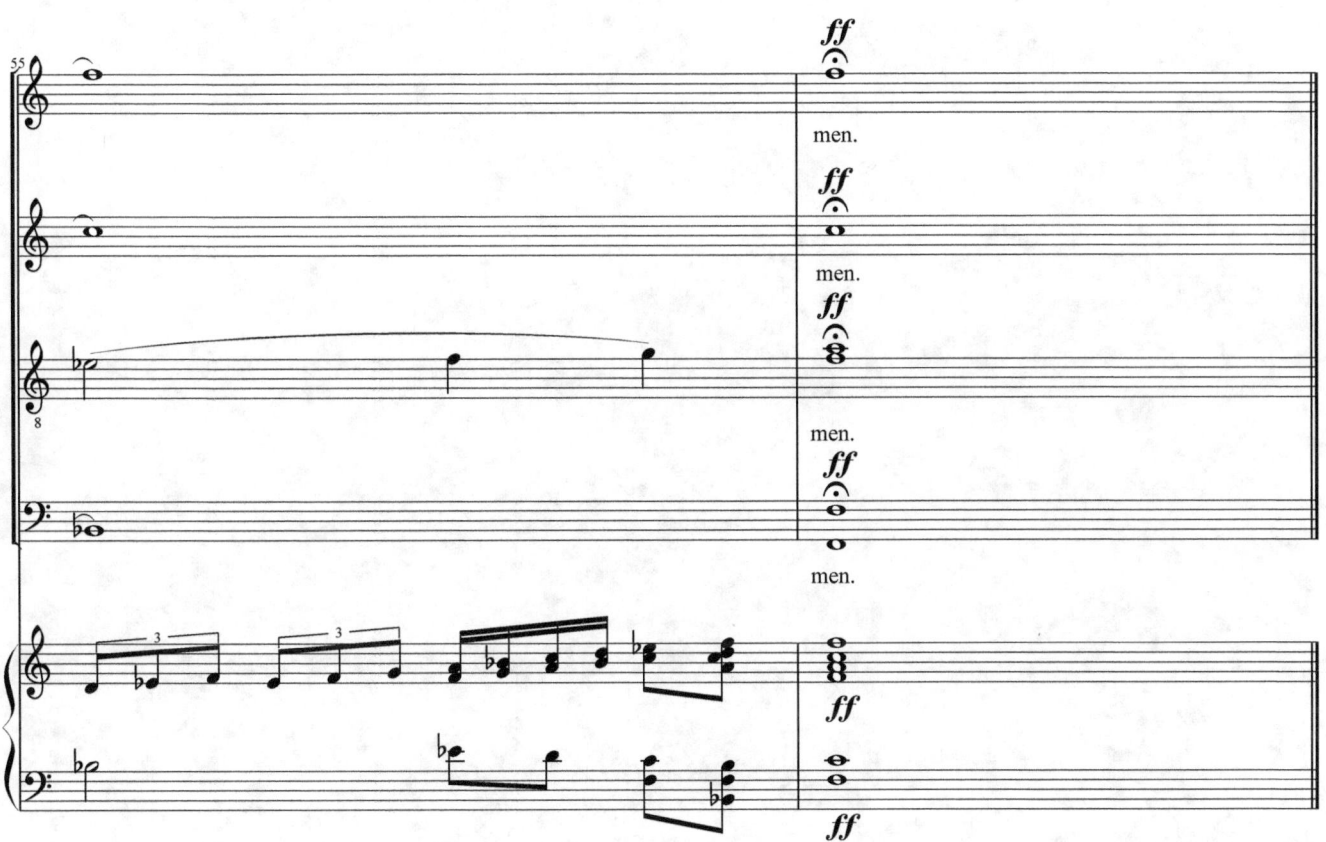

men.

men.

men.

men.

Go Now In Peace

Ken Langer

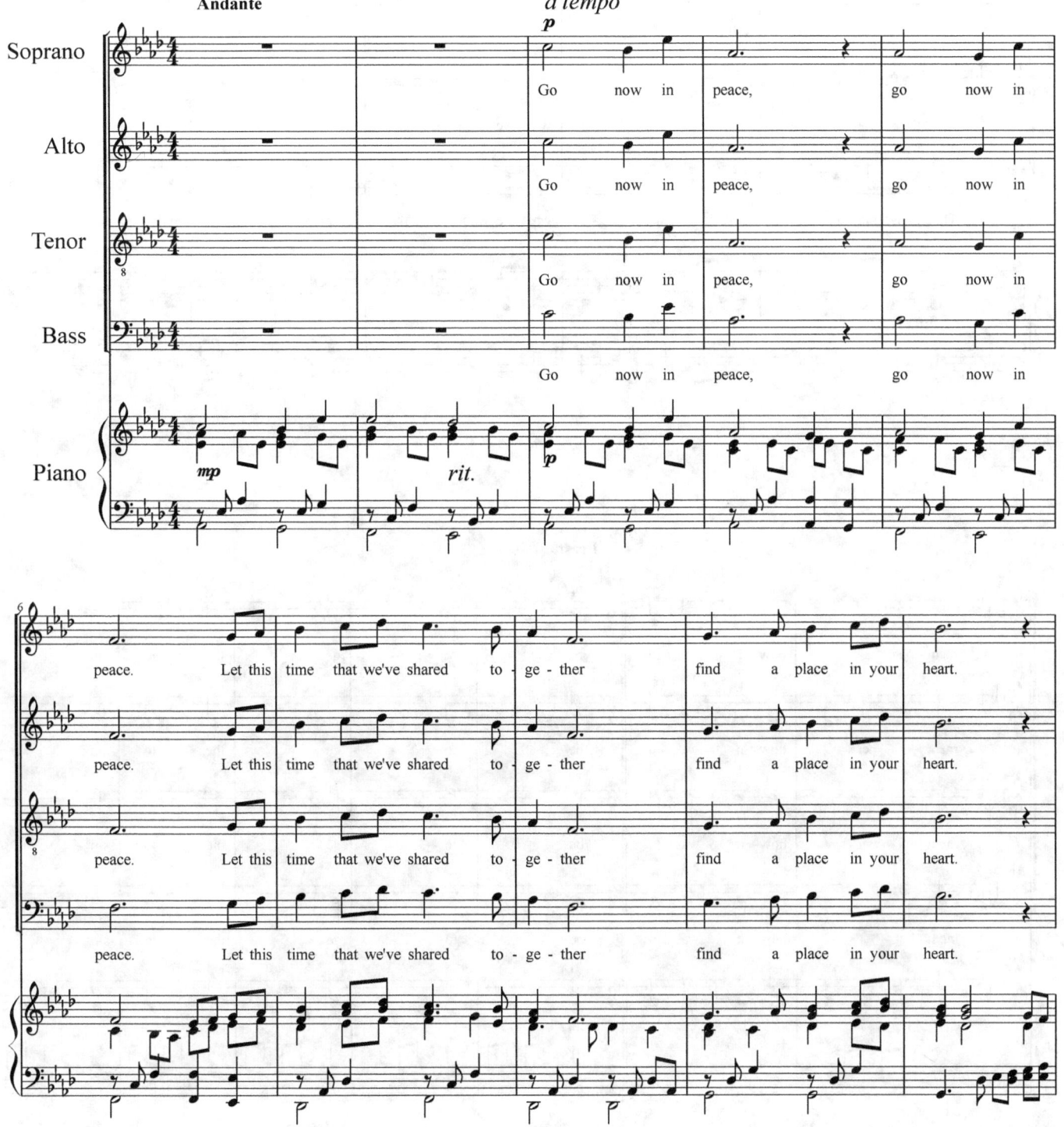

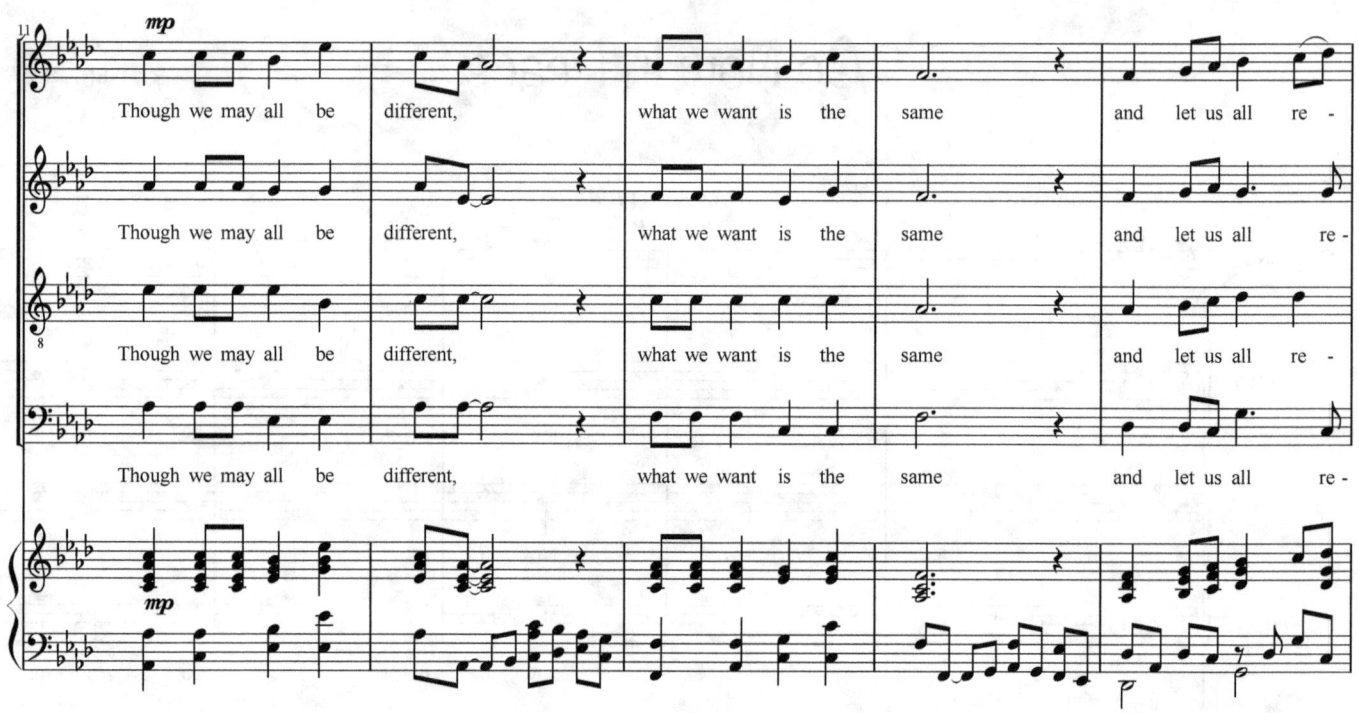

Presto (In one)

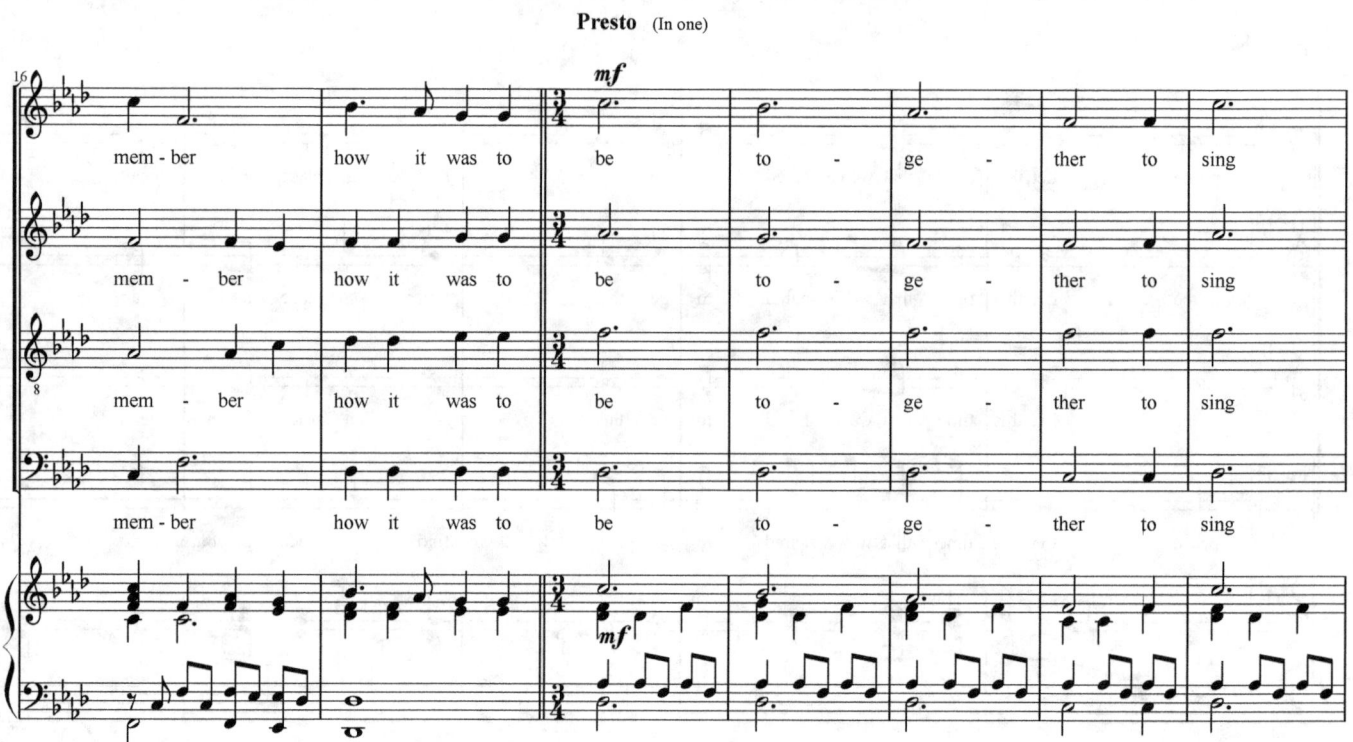

molto rit.

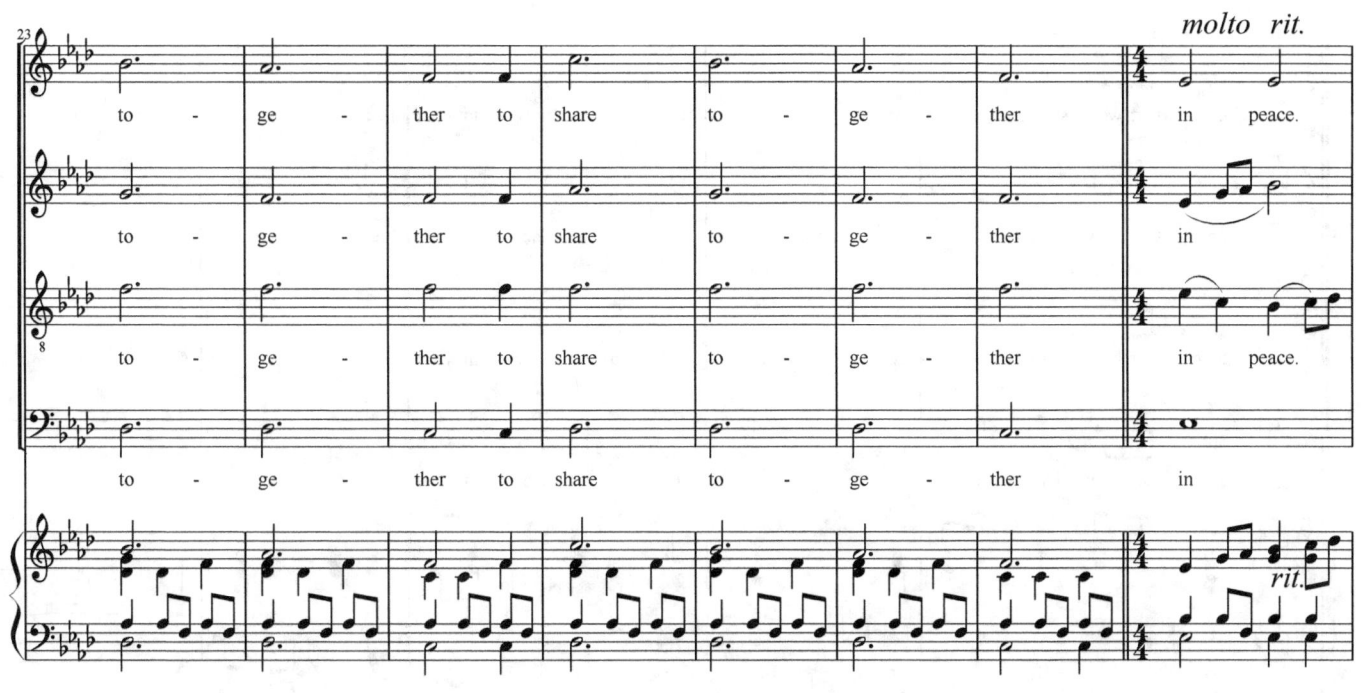

to - ge - ther to share to - ge - ther in peace.
to - ge - ther to share to - ge - ther in
to - ge - ther to share to - ge - ther in peace.
to - ge - ther to share to - ge - ther in

rit.

Andante _(a tempo)_

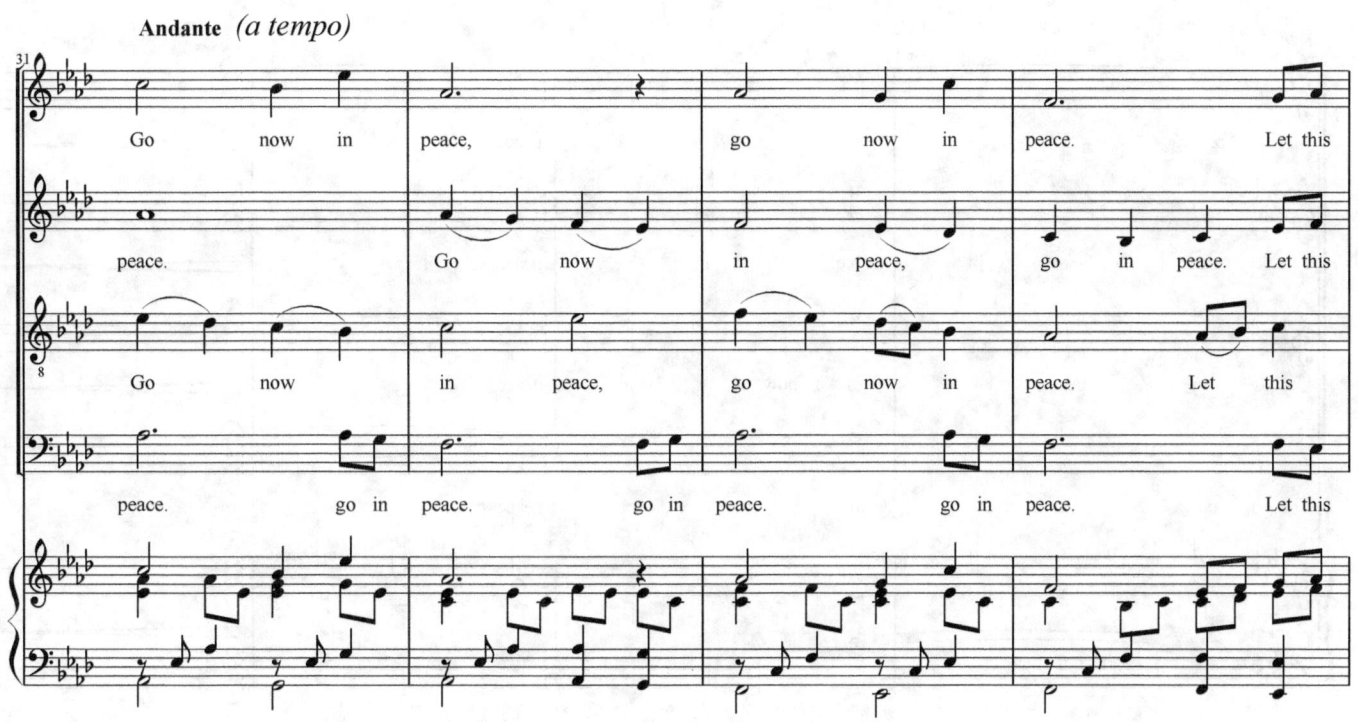

Go now in peace, go now in peace. Let this
peace. Go now in peace, go in peace. Let this
Go now in peace, go now in peace. Let this
peace. go in peace. go in peace. go in peace. Let this

53

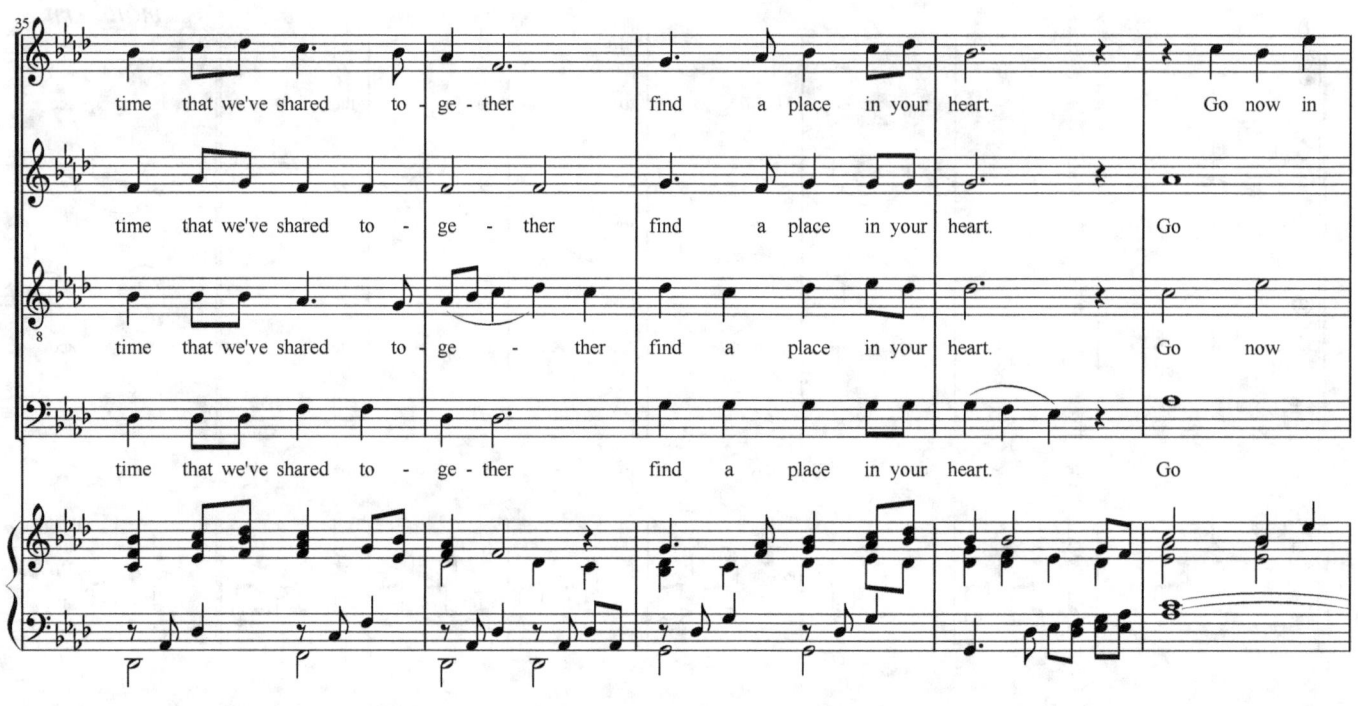

time that we've shared to-ge-ther find a place in your heart. Go now in

time that we've shared to-ge-ther find a place in your heart. Go

time that we've shared to-ge-ther find a place in your heart. Go now

time that we've shared to-ge-ther find a place in your heart. Go

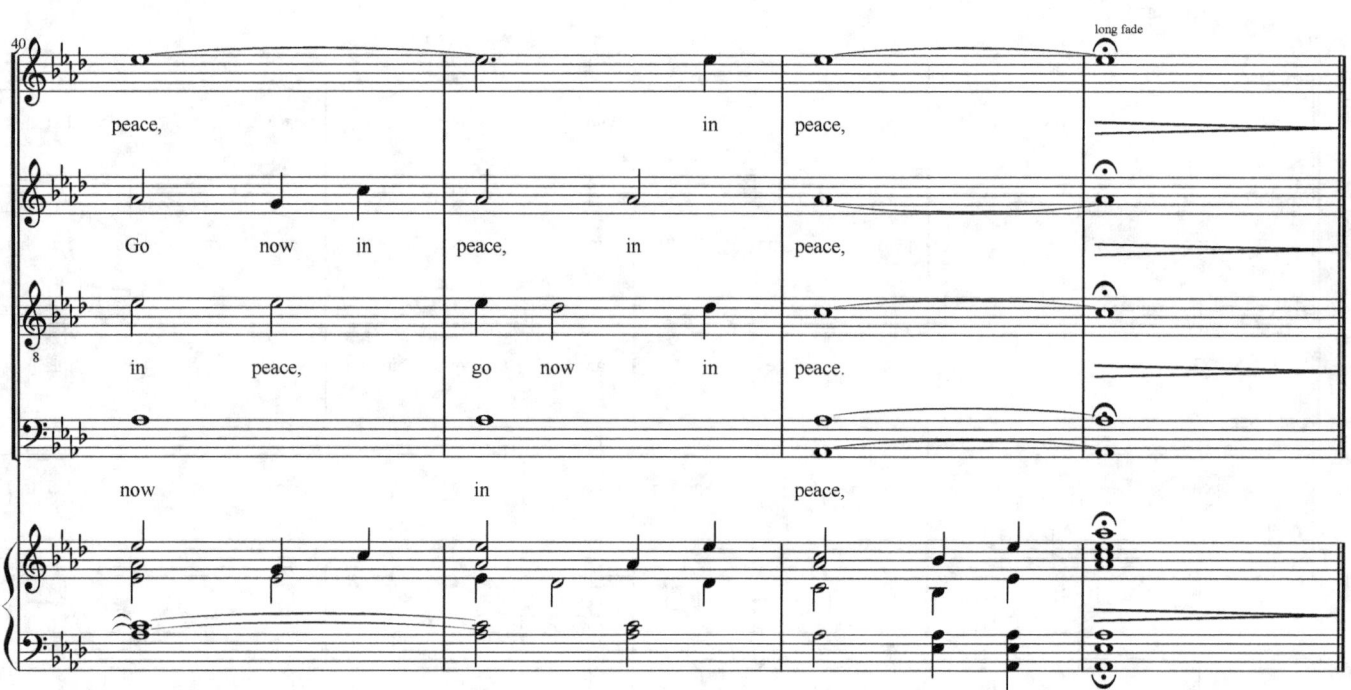

peace, in peace,

Go now in peace, in peace,

in peace, go now in peace.

now in peace,

Invocation
from "Wedding Music"

Ken Langer

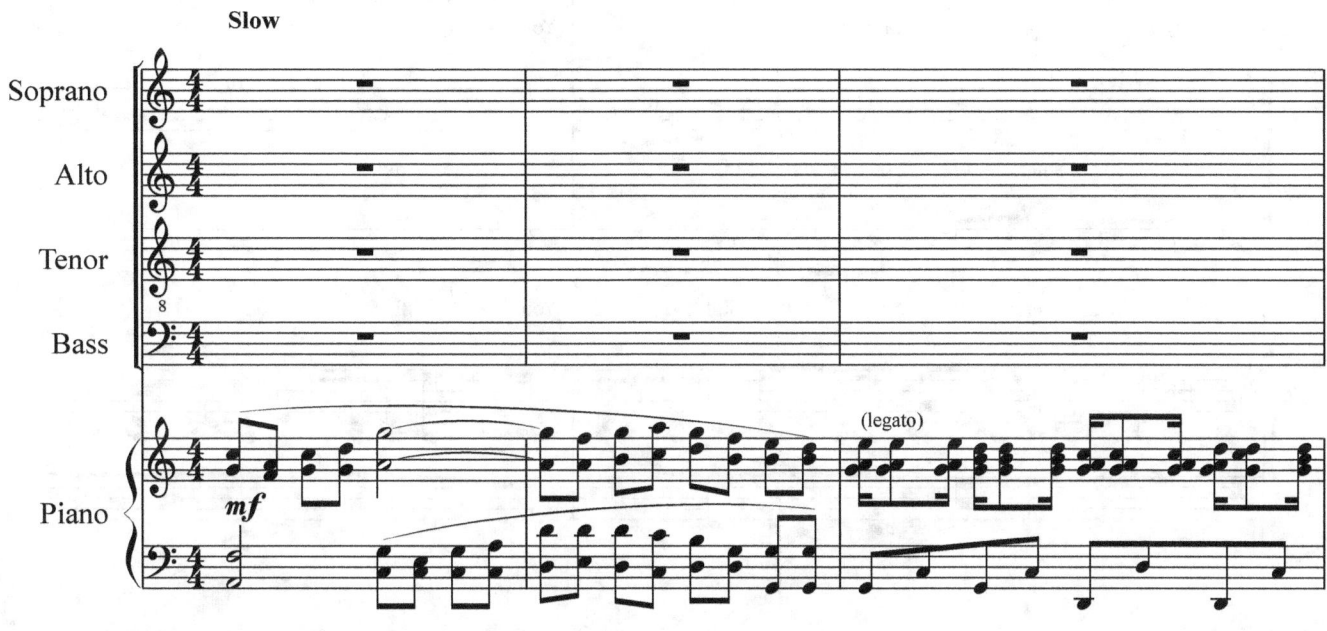

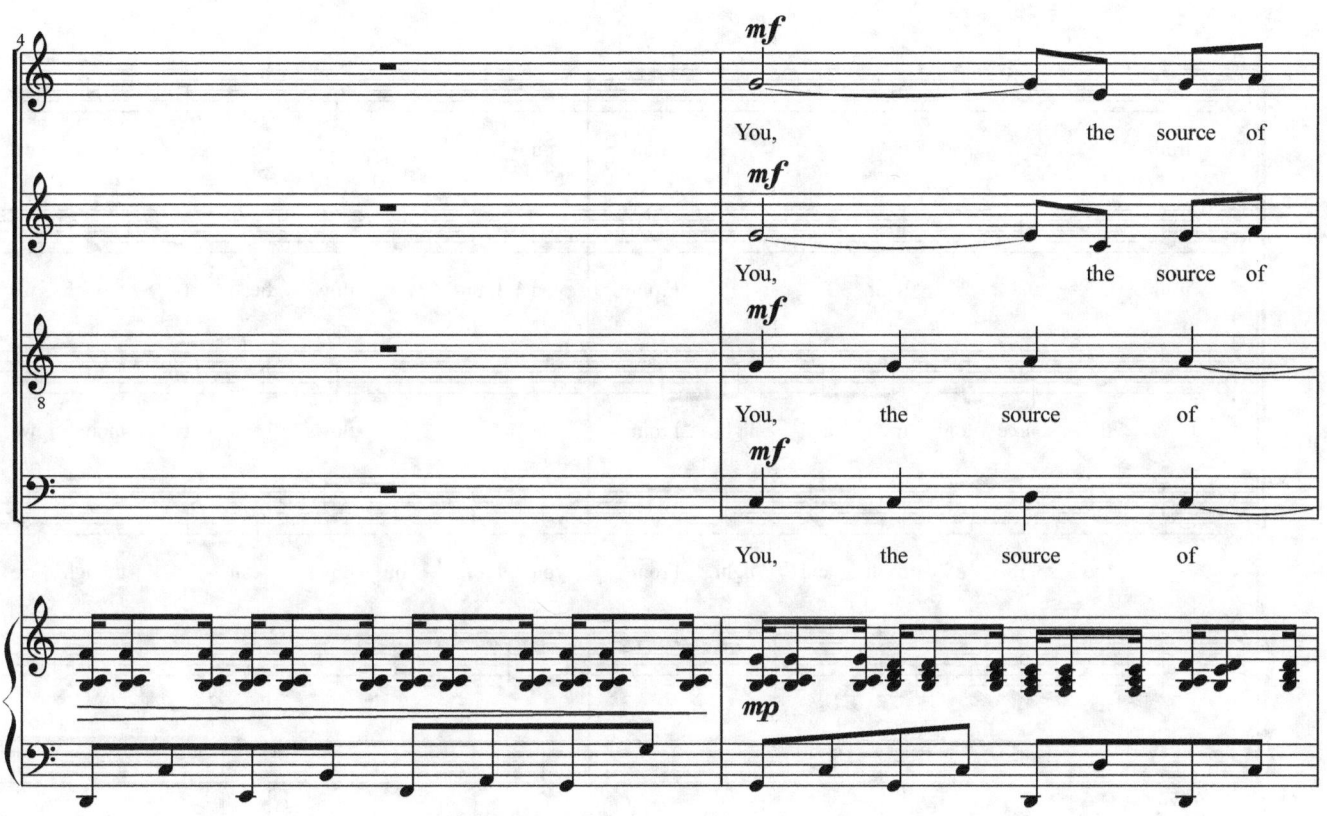

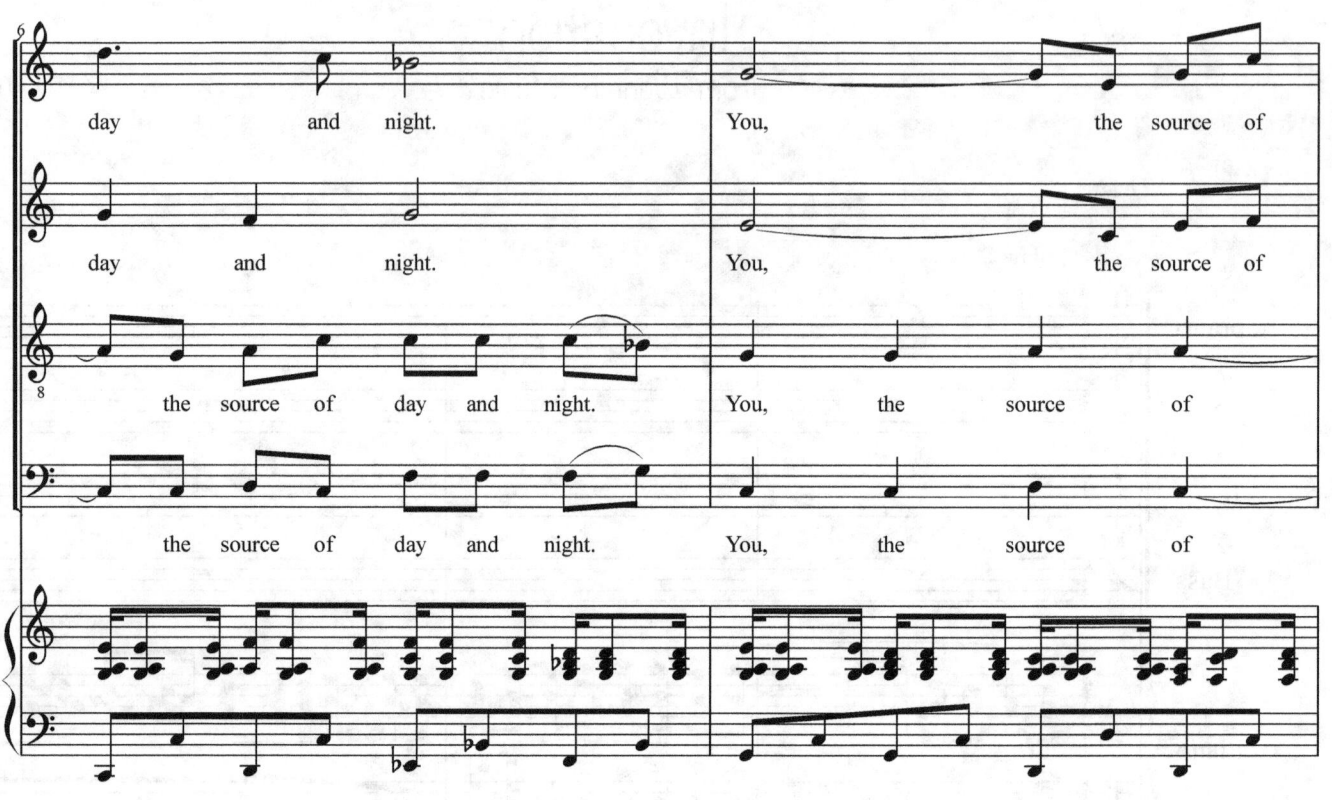

day and night. You, the source of

day and night. You, the source of

the source of day and night. You, the source of

the source of day and night. You, the source of

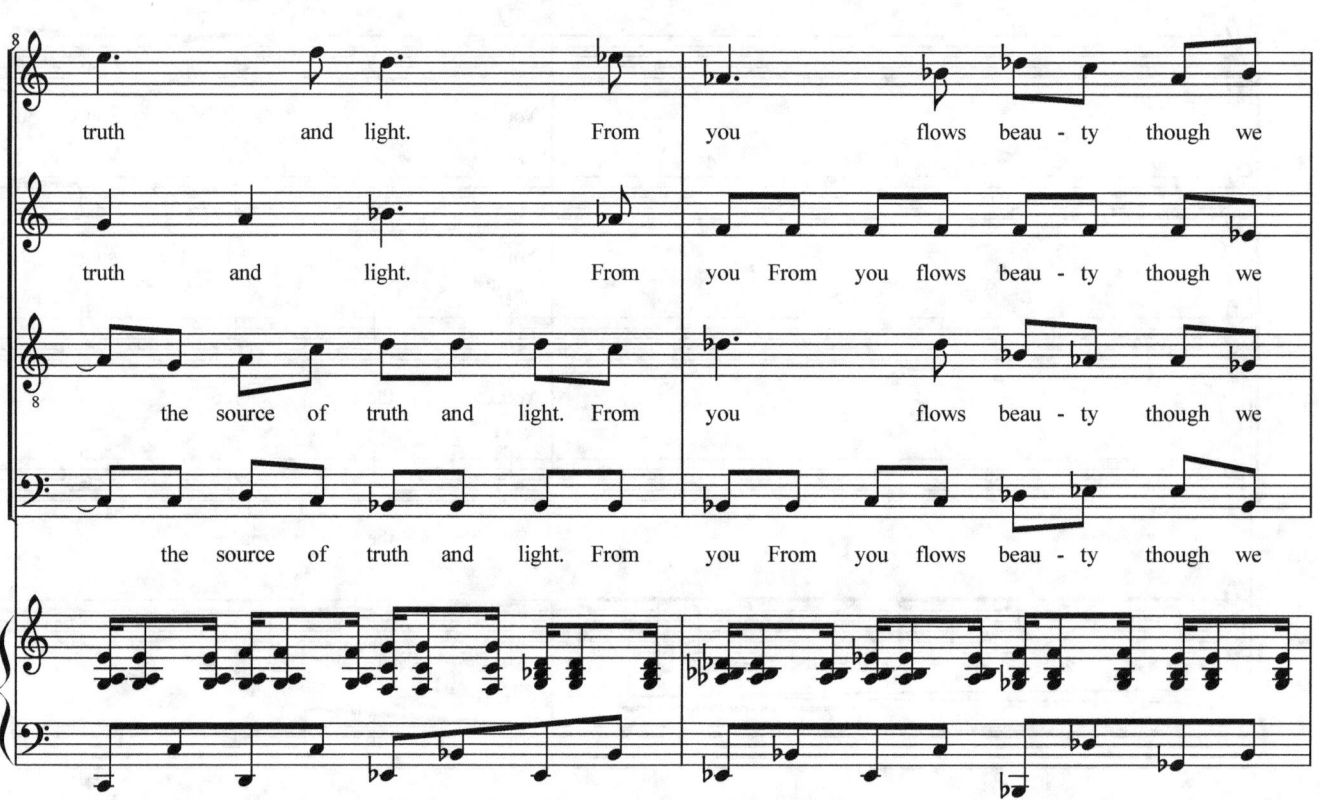

truth and light. From you flows beau - ty though we

truth and light. From you From you flows beau - ty though we

the source of truth and light. From you flows beau - ty though we

the source of truth and light. From you From you flows beau - ty though we

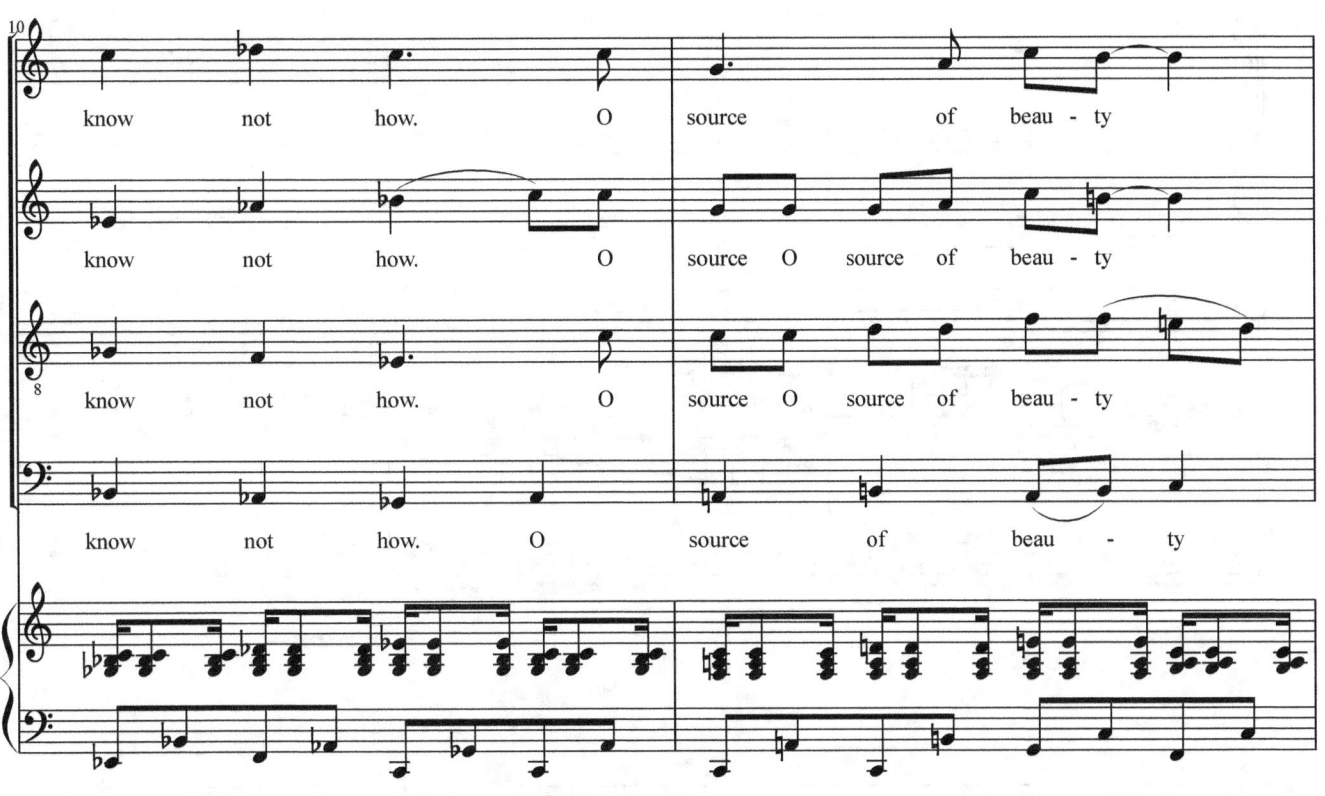

know   not   how.   O   source   of   beau - ty

know   not   how.   O   source   O   source   of   beau - ty

know   not   how.   O   source   O   source   of   beau - ty

know   not   how.   O   source   of   beau - ty

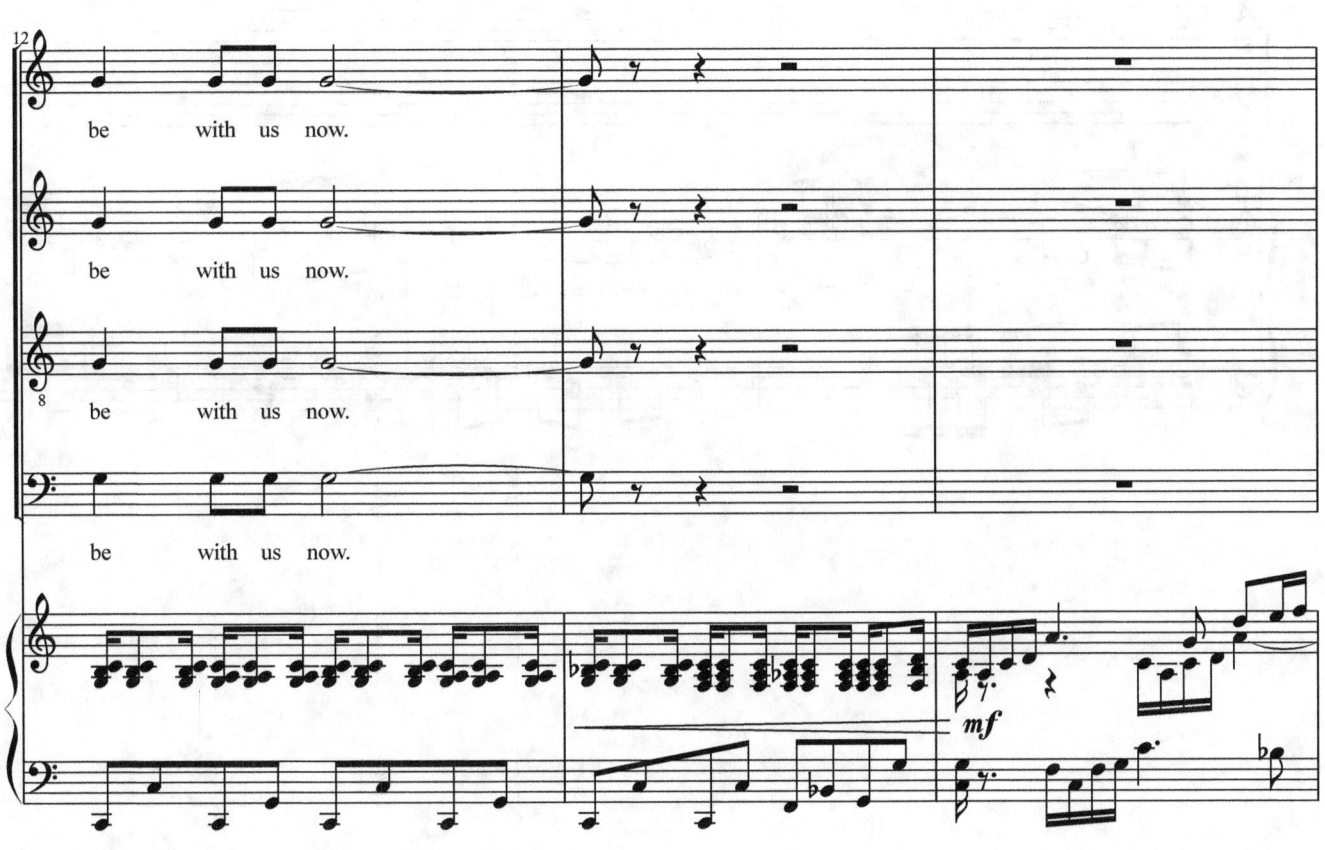

be   with   us   now.

be   with   us   now.

be   with   us   now.

be   with   us   now.

mf

57

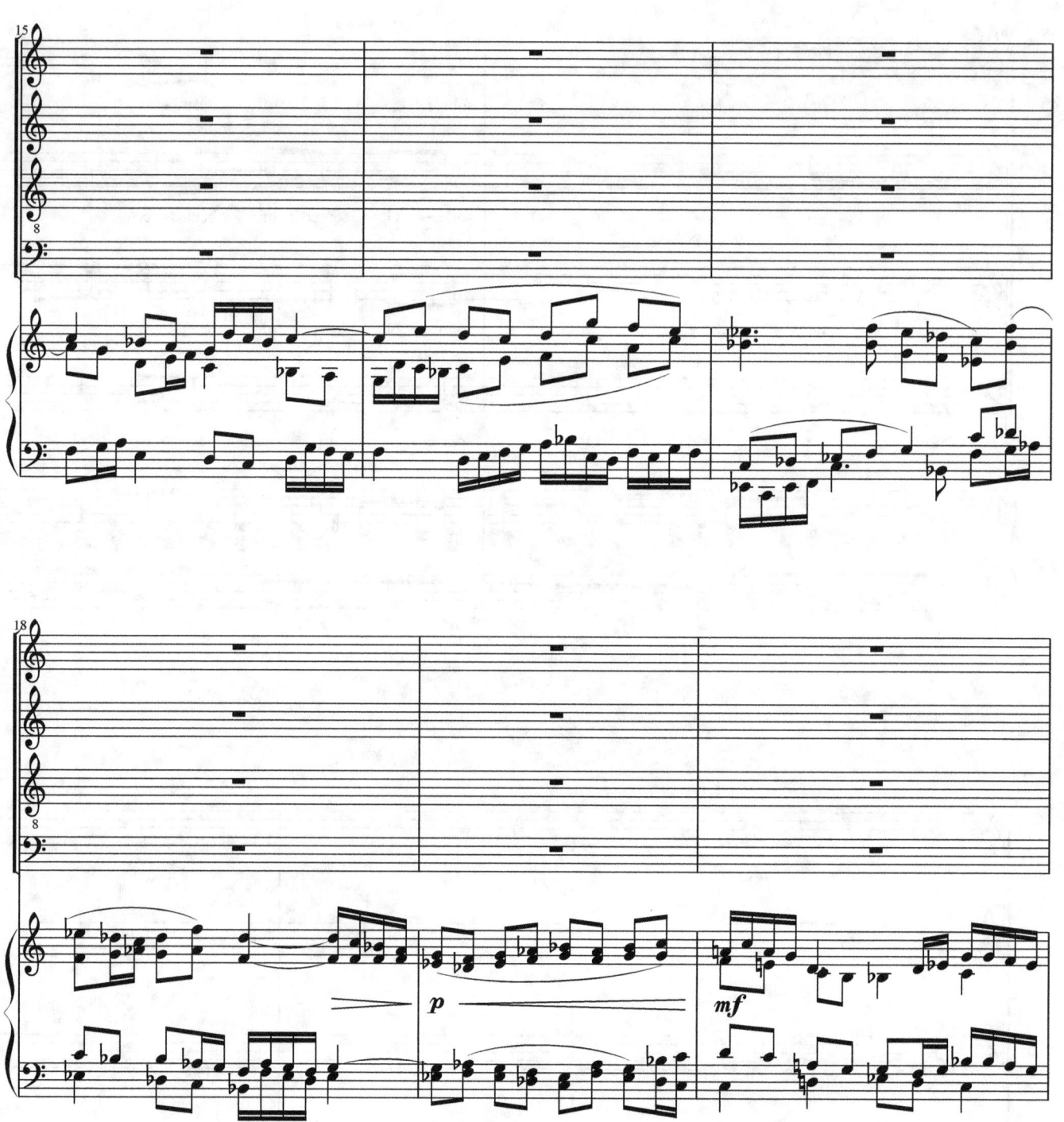

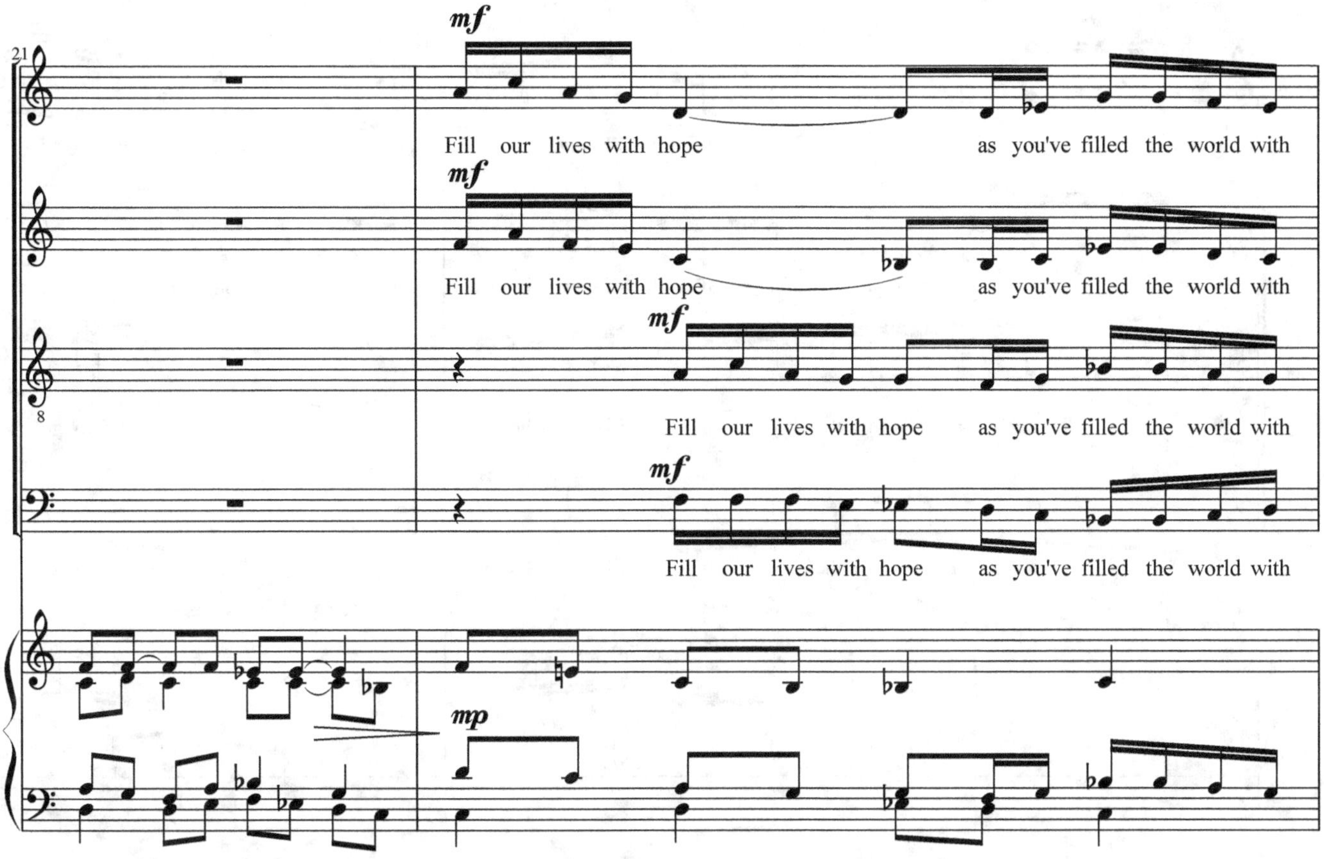

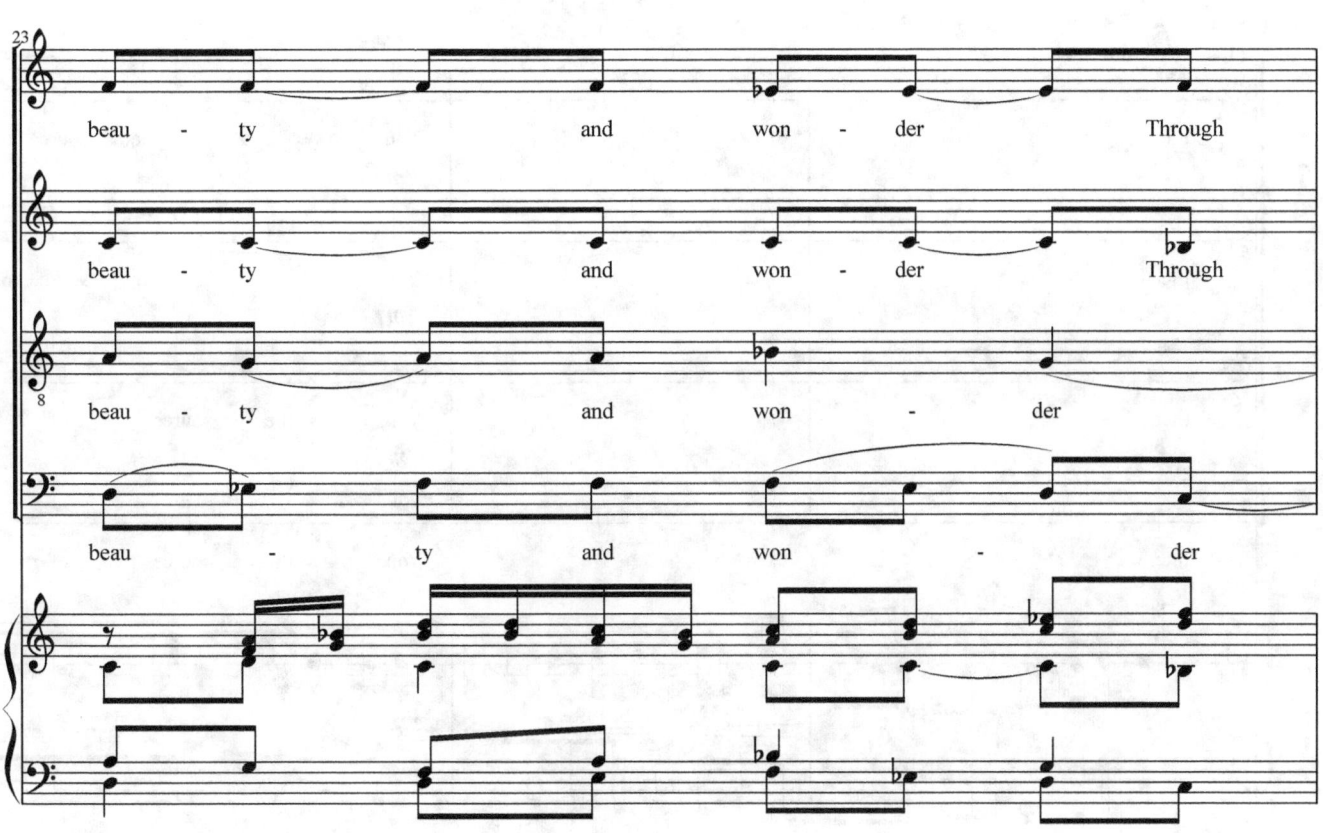

Fill our lives with hope as you've filled the world with
Fill our lives with hope as you've filled the world with
Fill our lives with hope as you've filled the world with
Fill our lives with hope as you've filled the world with

beau - ty and won - der Through
beau - ty and won - der Through
beau - ty and won - der
beau - ty and won - der

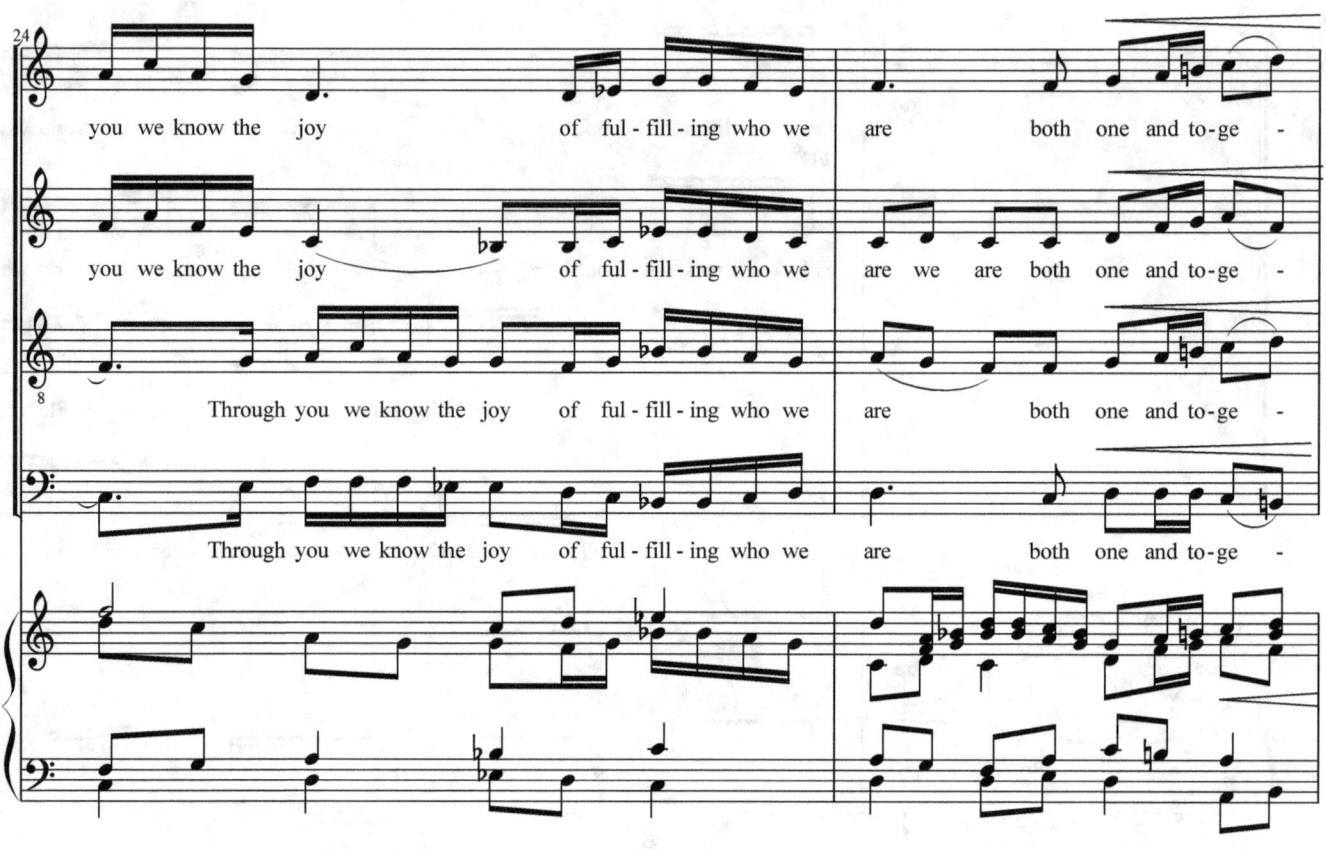

you we know the joy of ful-fill-ing who we are both one and to-ge -

you we know the joy of ful-fill-ing who we are we are both one and to-ge -

Through you we know the joy of ful-fill-ing who we are both one and to-ge -

Through you we know the joy of ful-fill-ing who we are both one and to-ge -

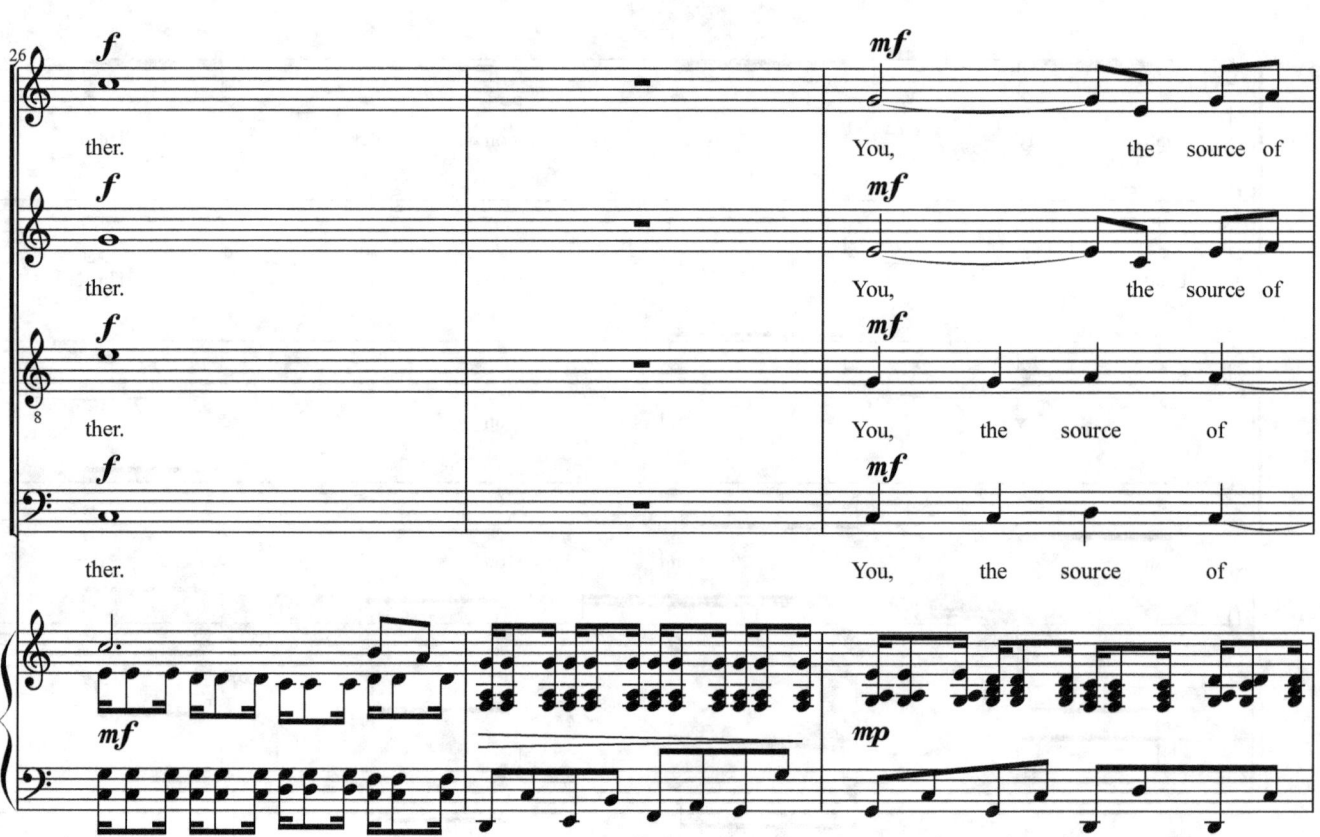

ther. You, the source of

ther. You, the source of

ther. You, the source of

ther. You, the source of

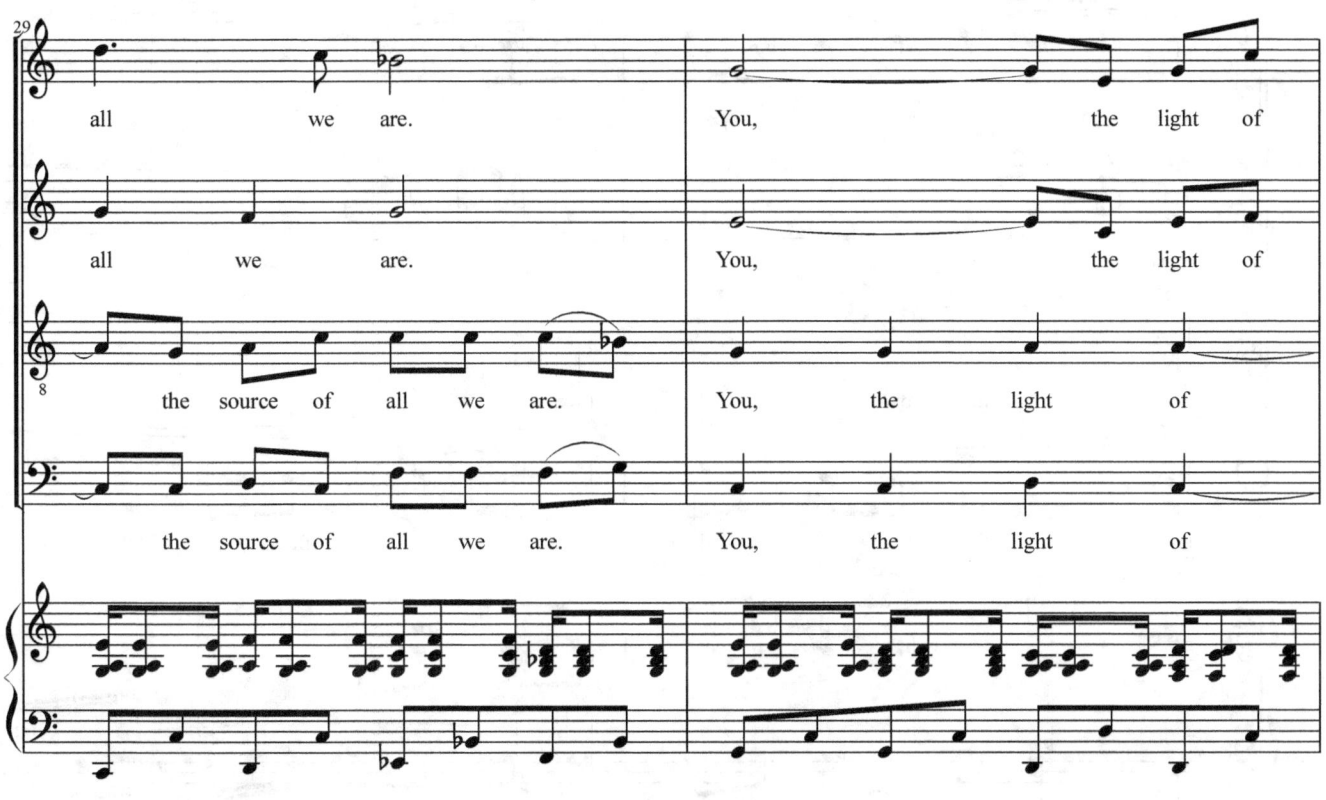

all we are. You, the light of

all we are. You, the light of

the source of all we are. You, the light of

the source of all we are. You, the light of

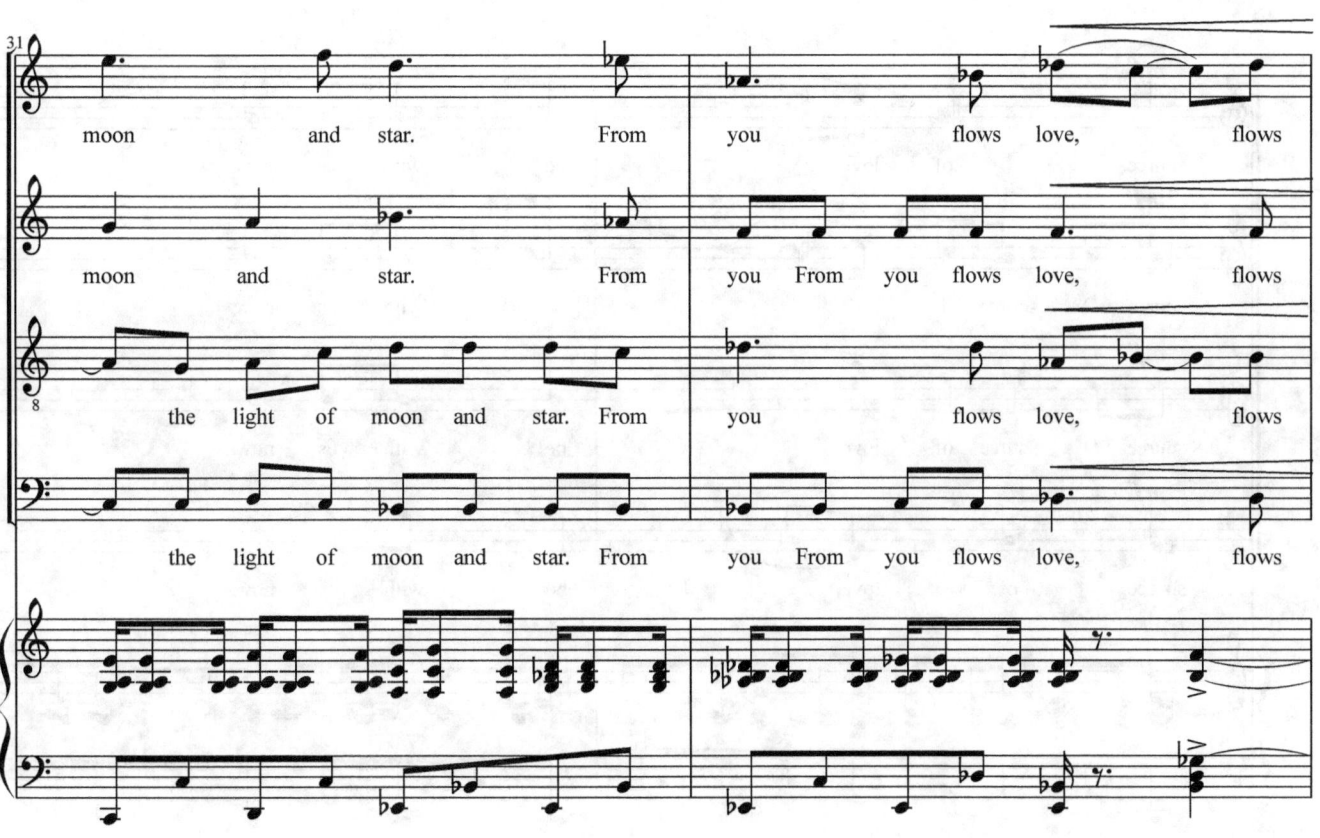

moon and star. From you flows love, flows

moon and star. From you From you flows love, flows

the light of moon and star. From you flows love, flows

the light of moon and star. From you From you flows love, flows

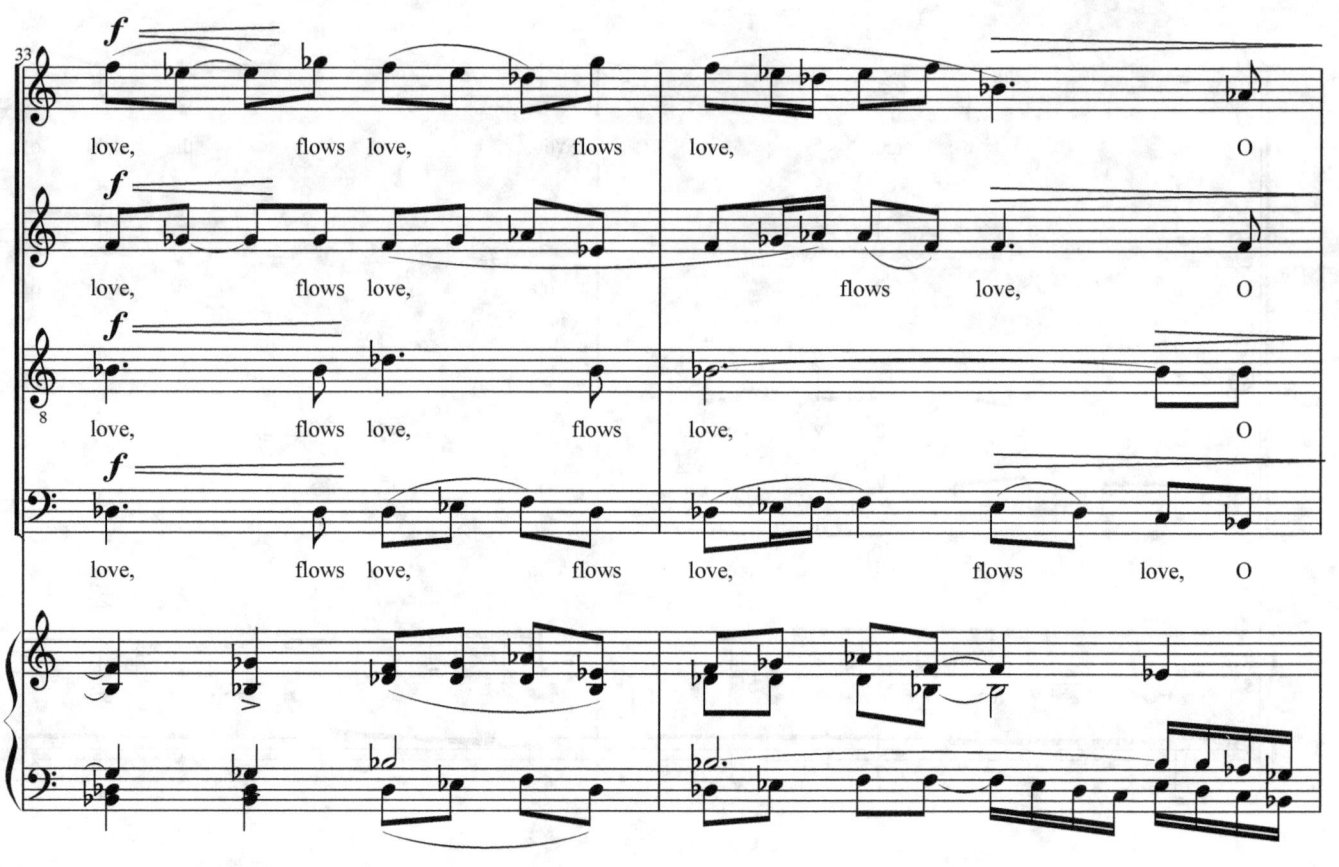

love, flows love, flows love, O

love, flows love, flows love, O

love, flows love, flows love, O

love, flows love, flows love, O

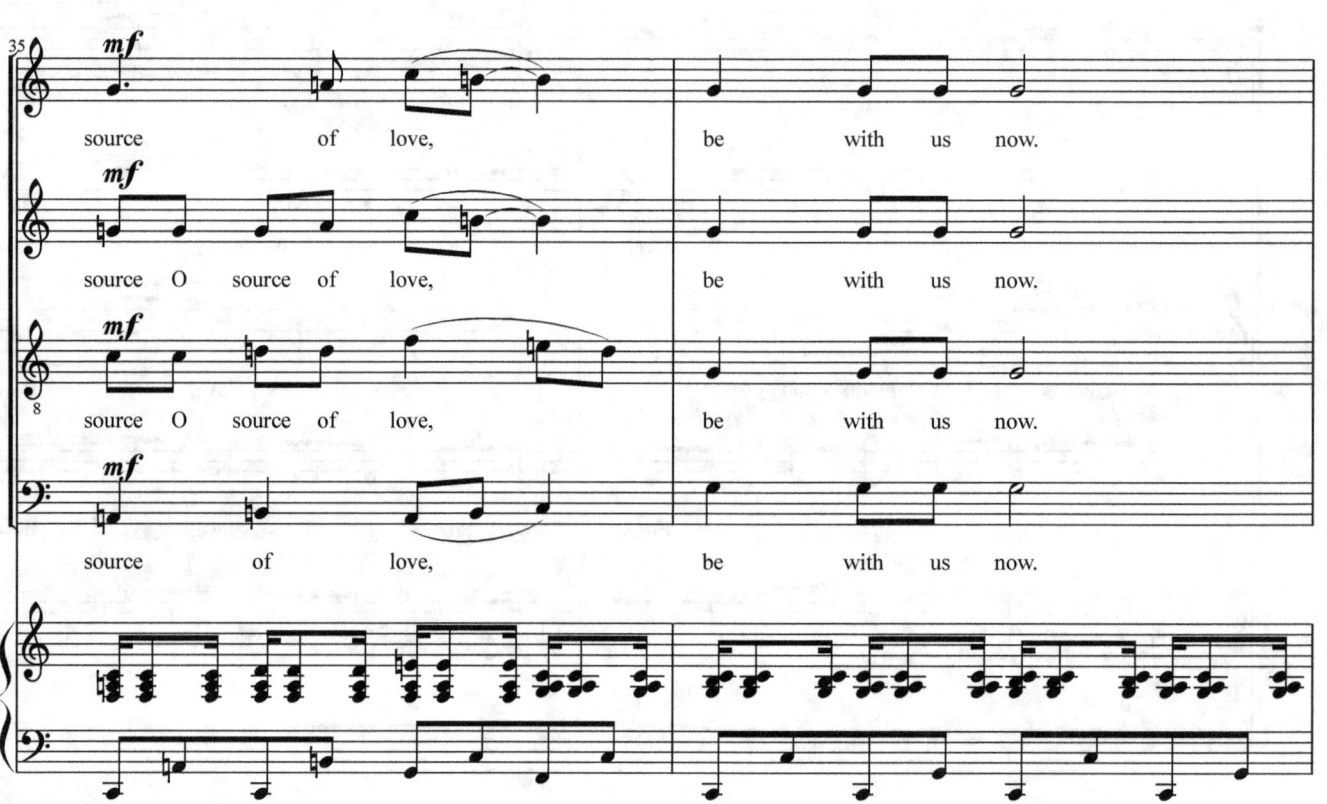

source of love, be with us now.

source O source of love, be with us now.

source O source of love, be with us now.

source of love, be with us now.

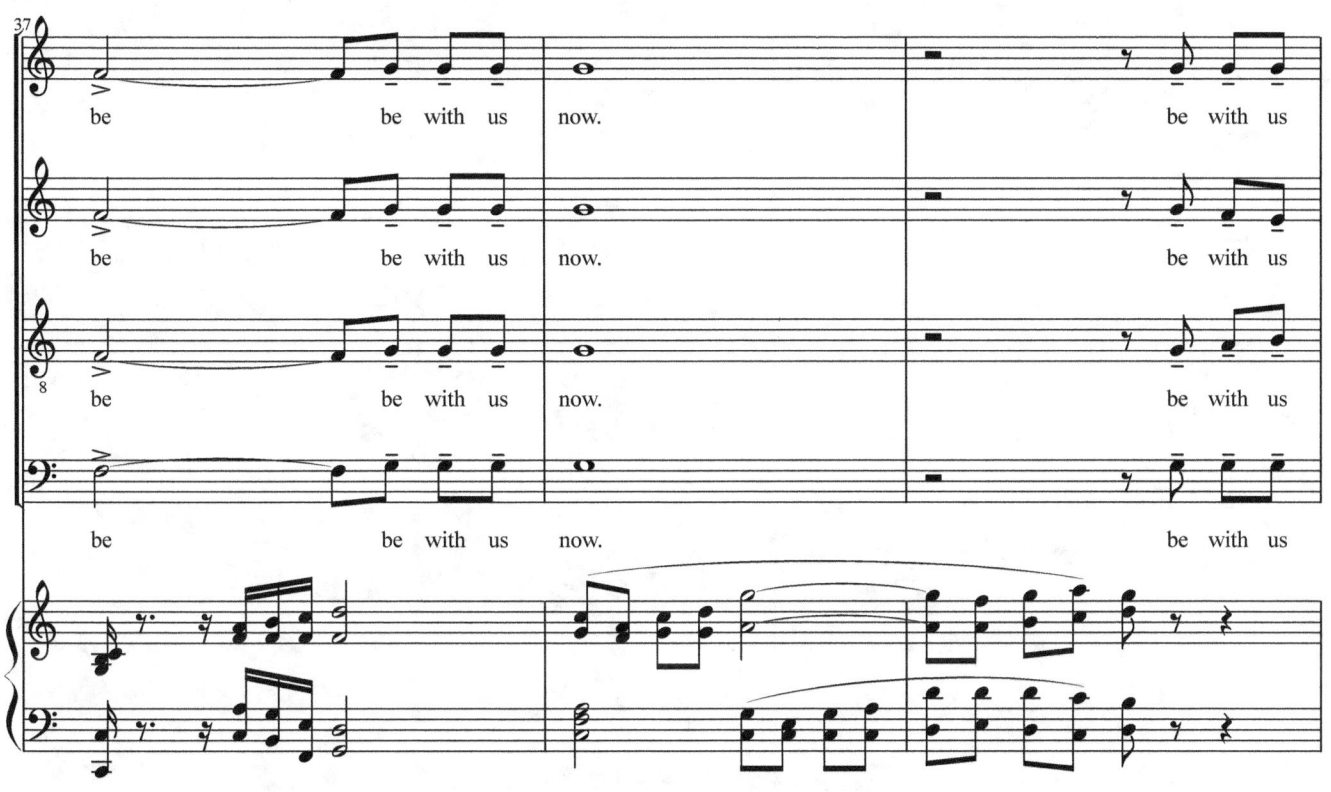

be   be with us   now.   be with us

be   be with us   now.   be with us

be   be with us   now.   be with us

be   be with us   now.   be with us

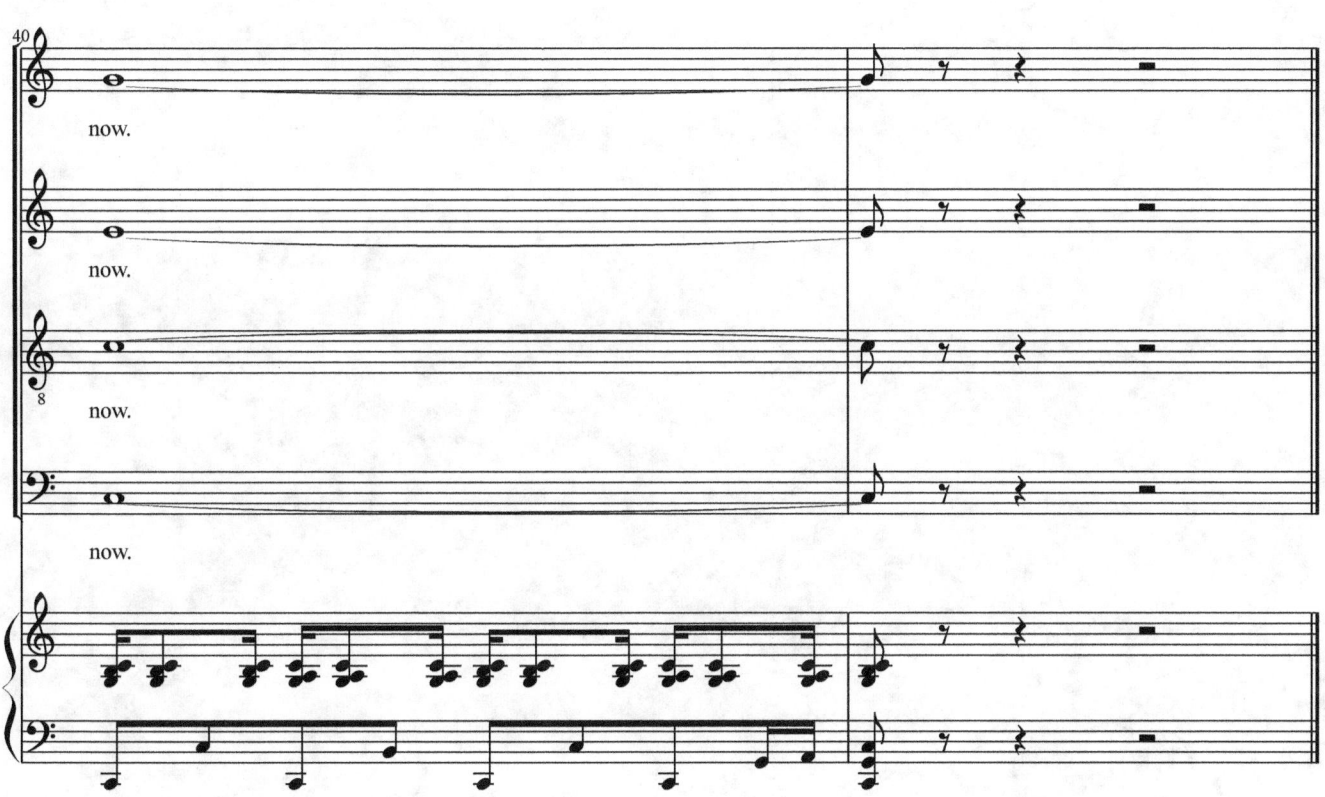

now.

now.

now.

now.

Live In Peace
from "Dona Nobis Pacem

Ken Langer

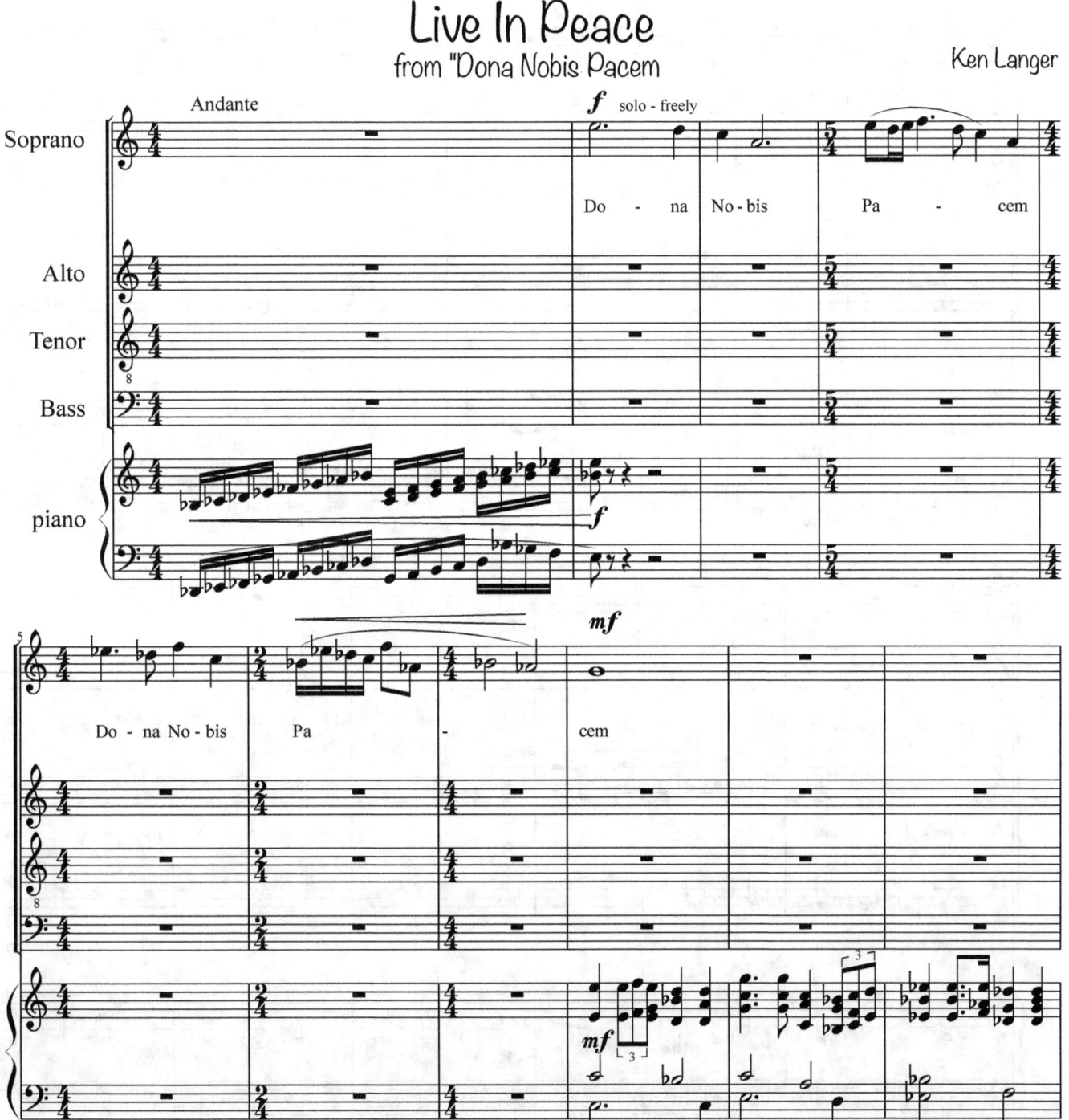

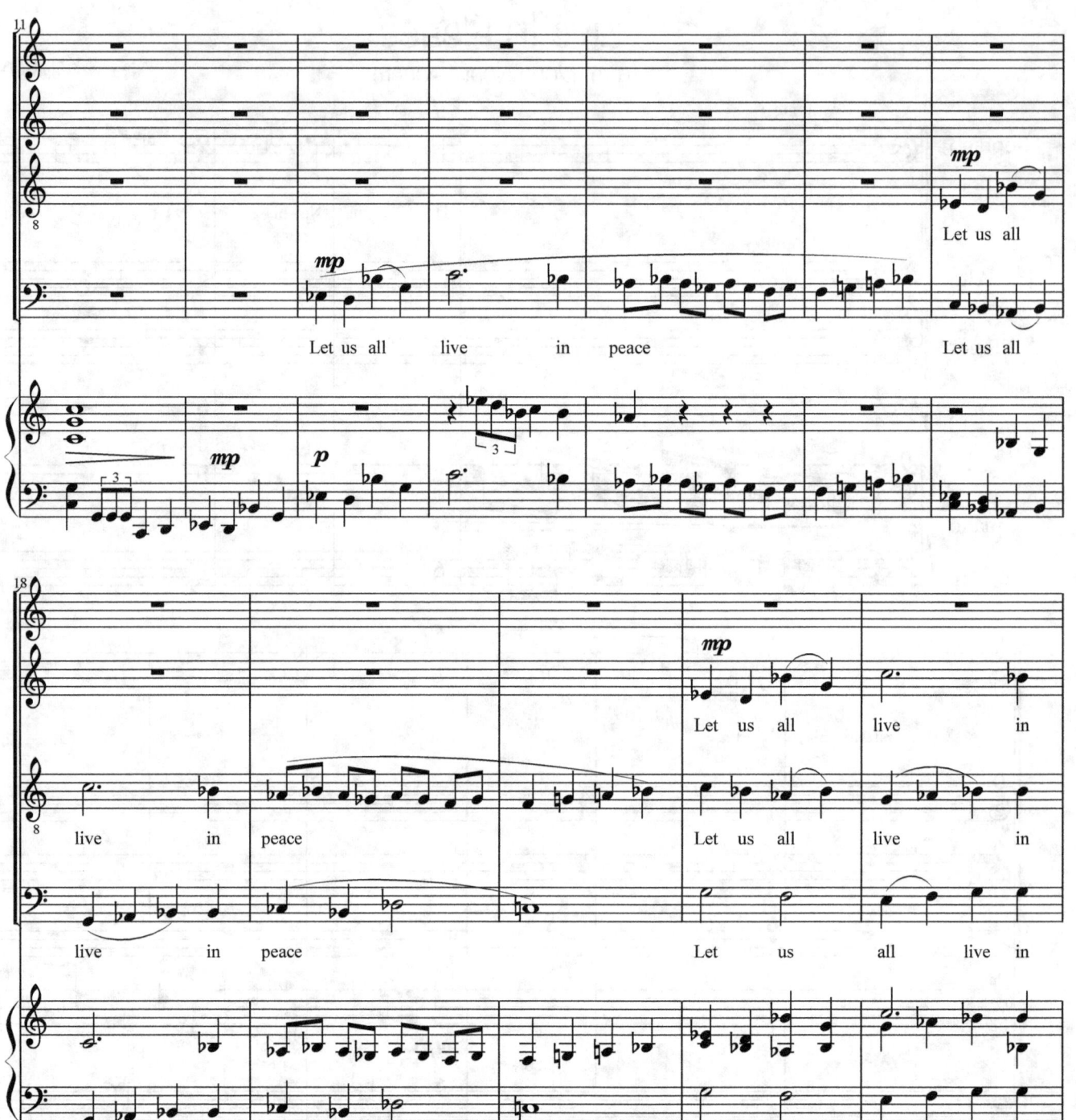

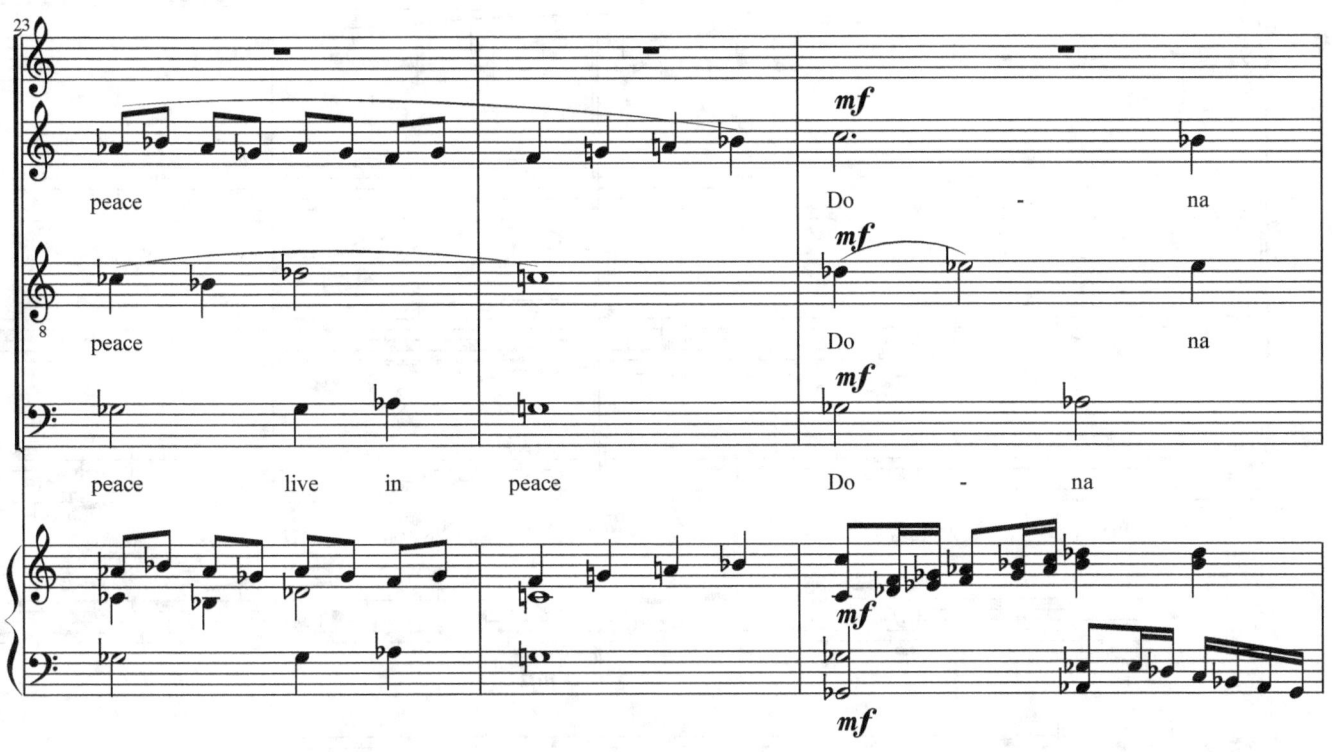

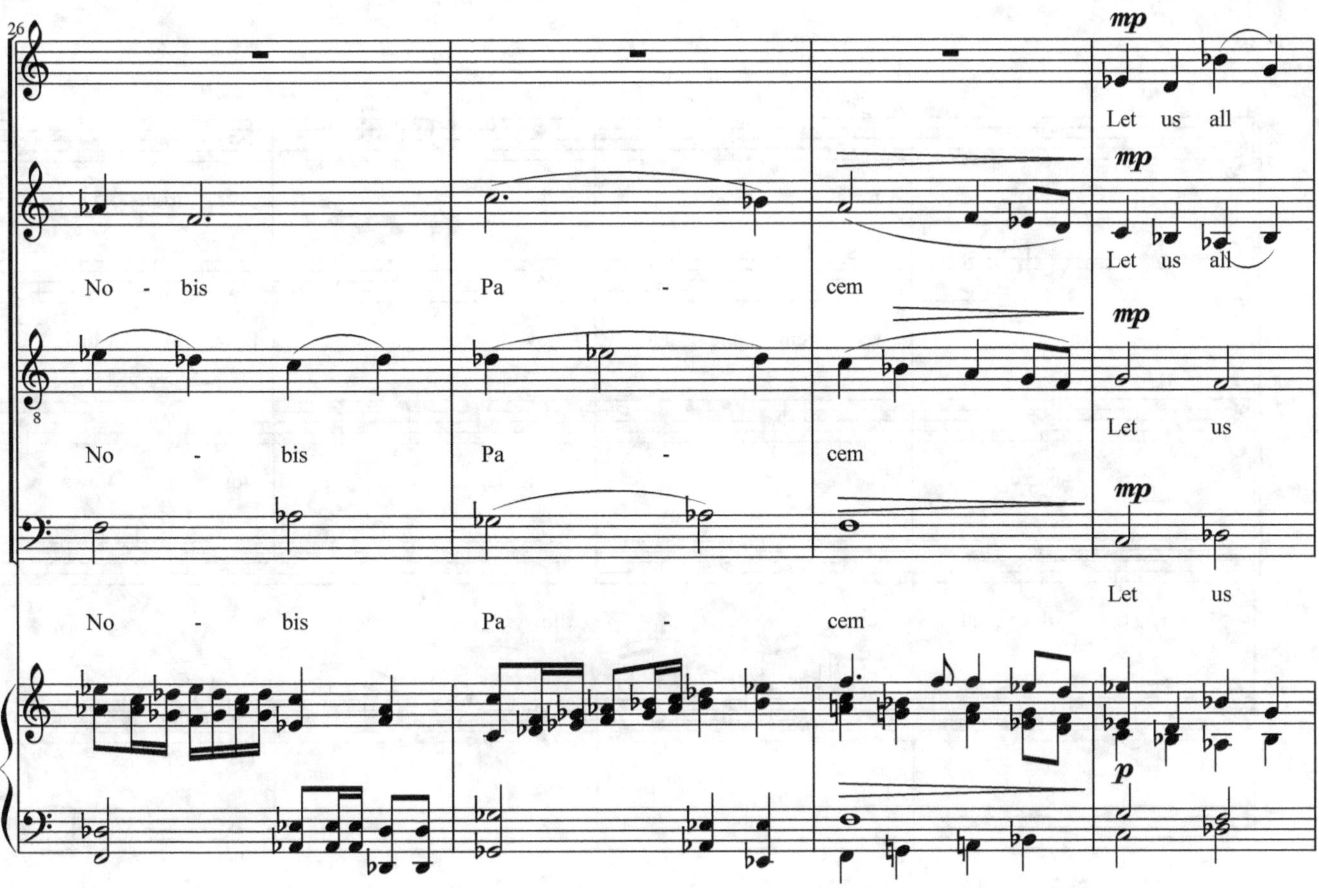

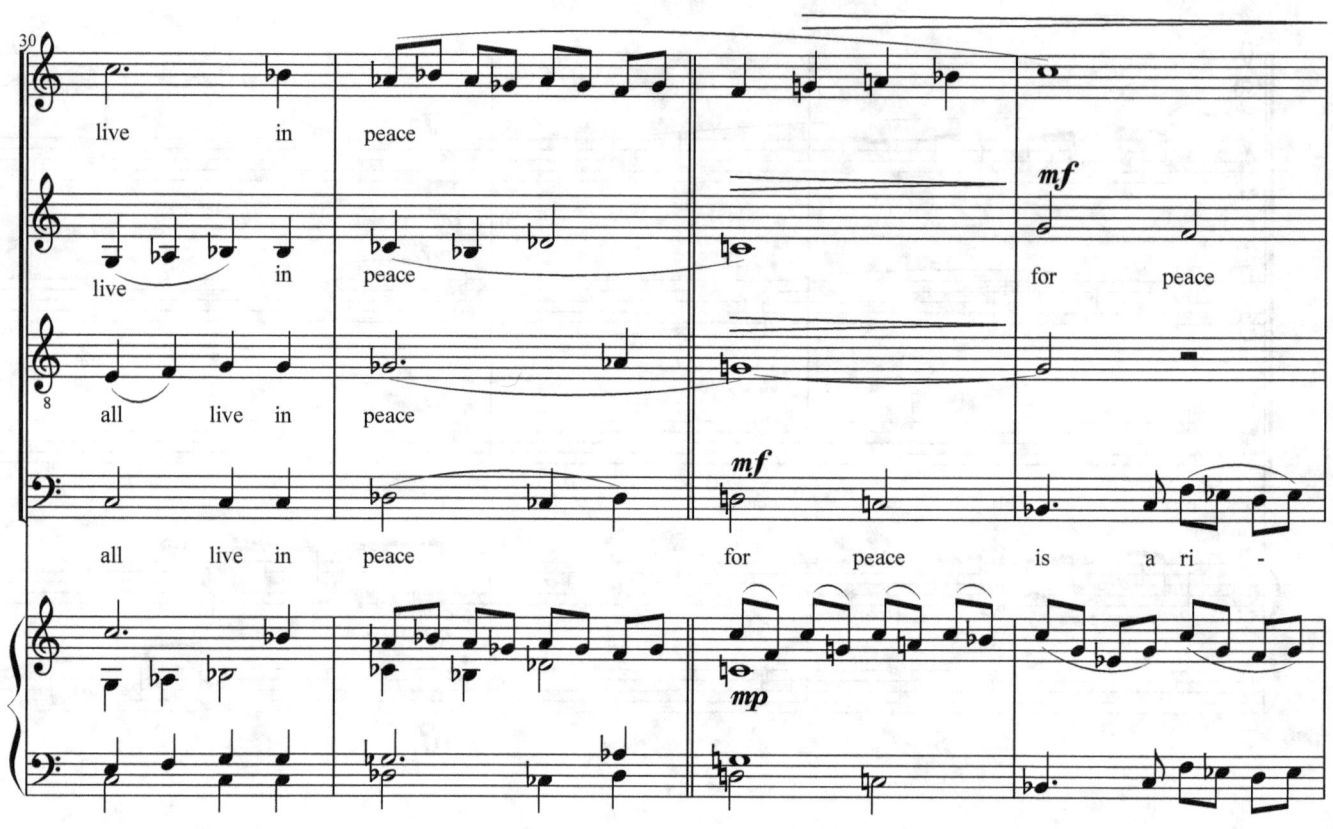

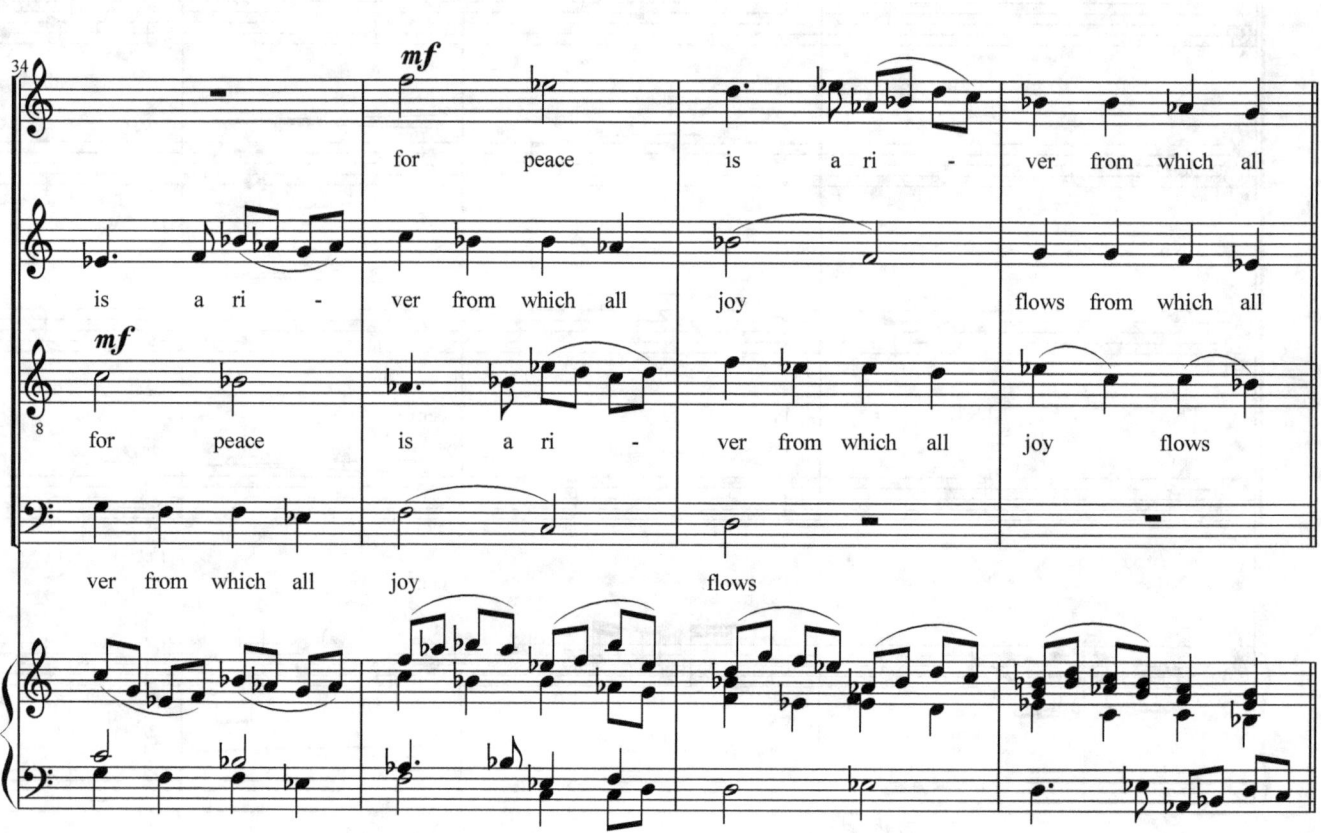

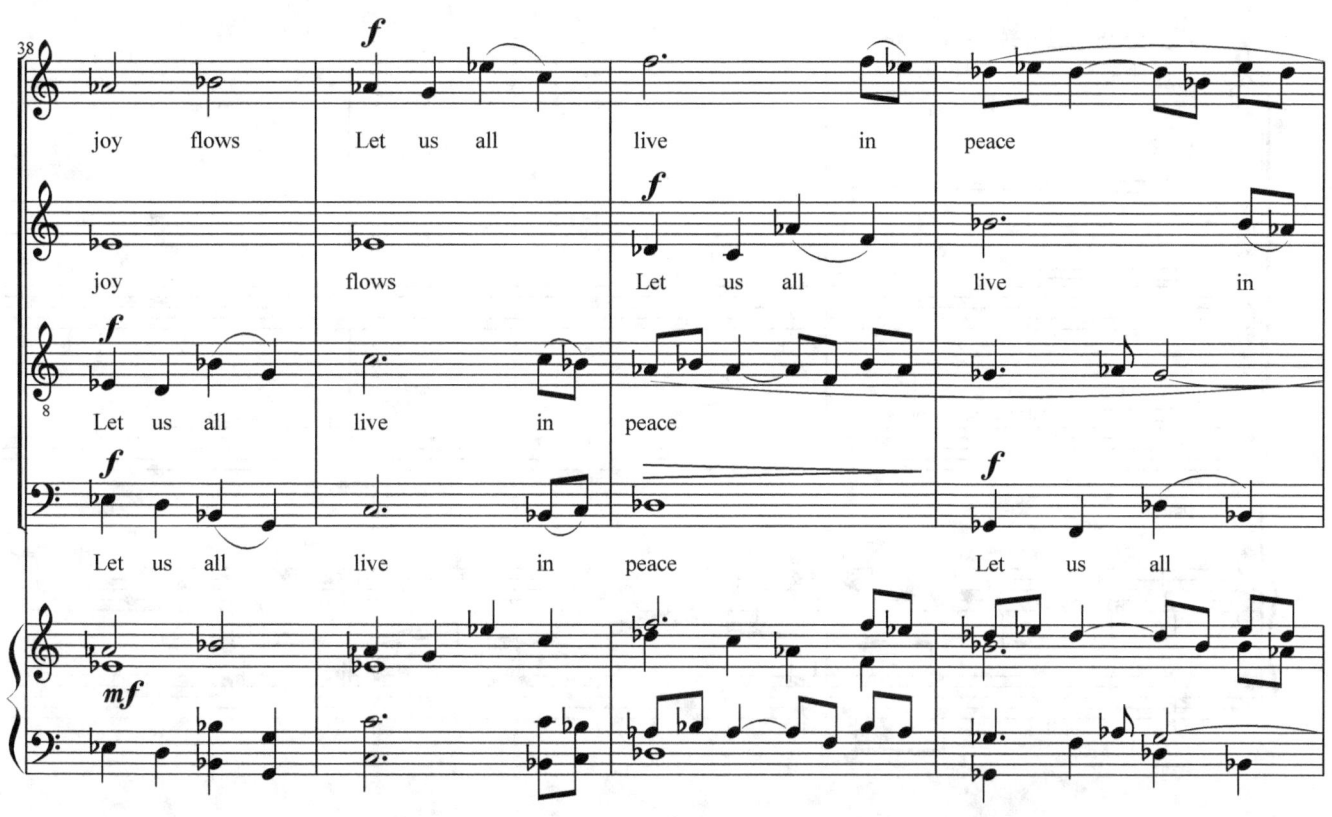

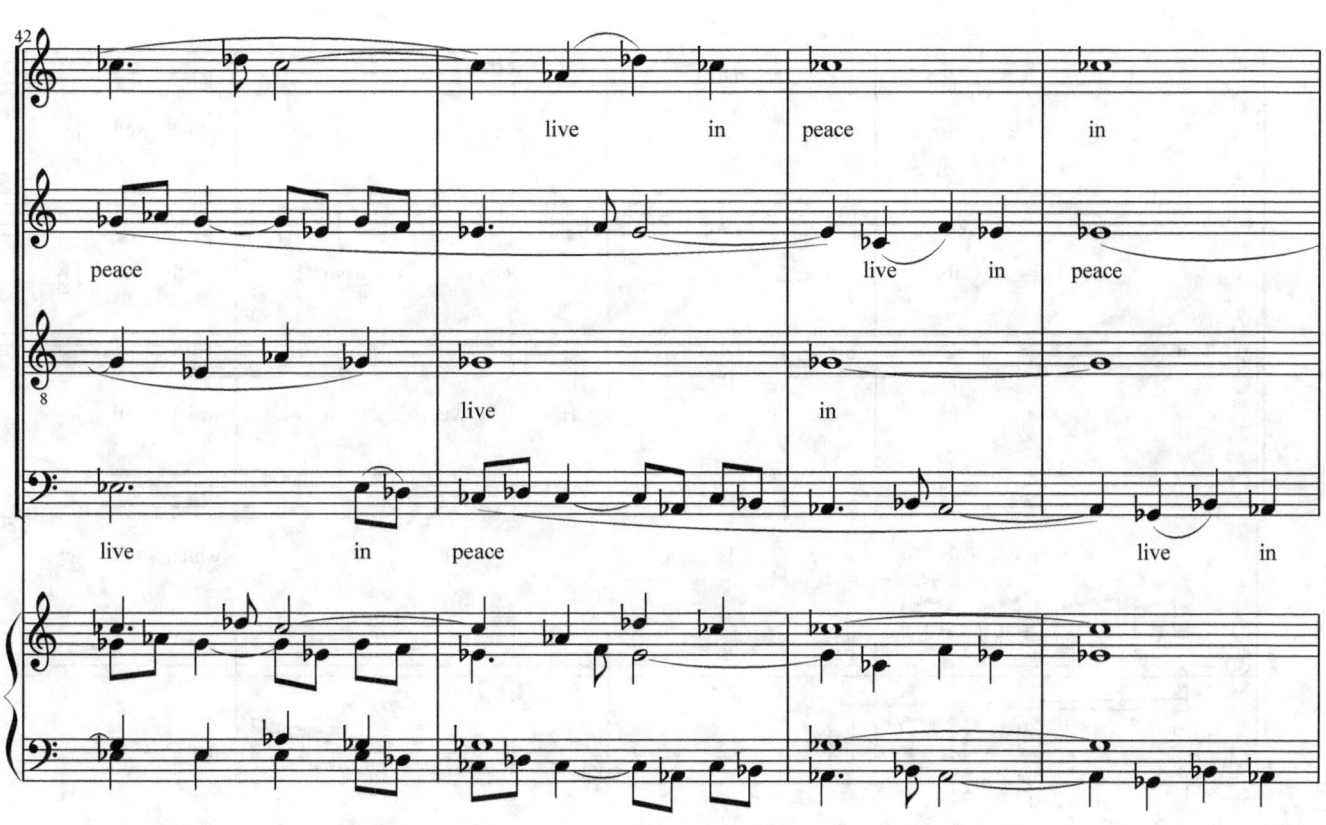

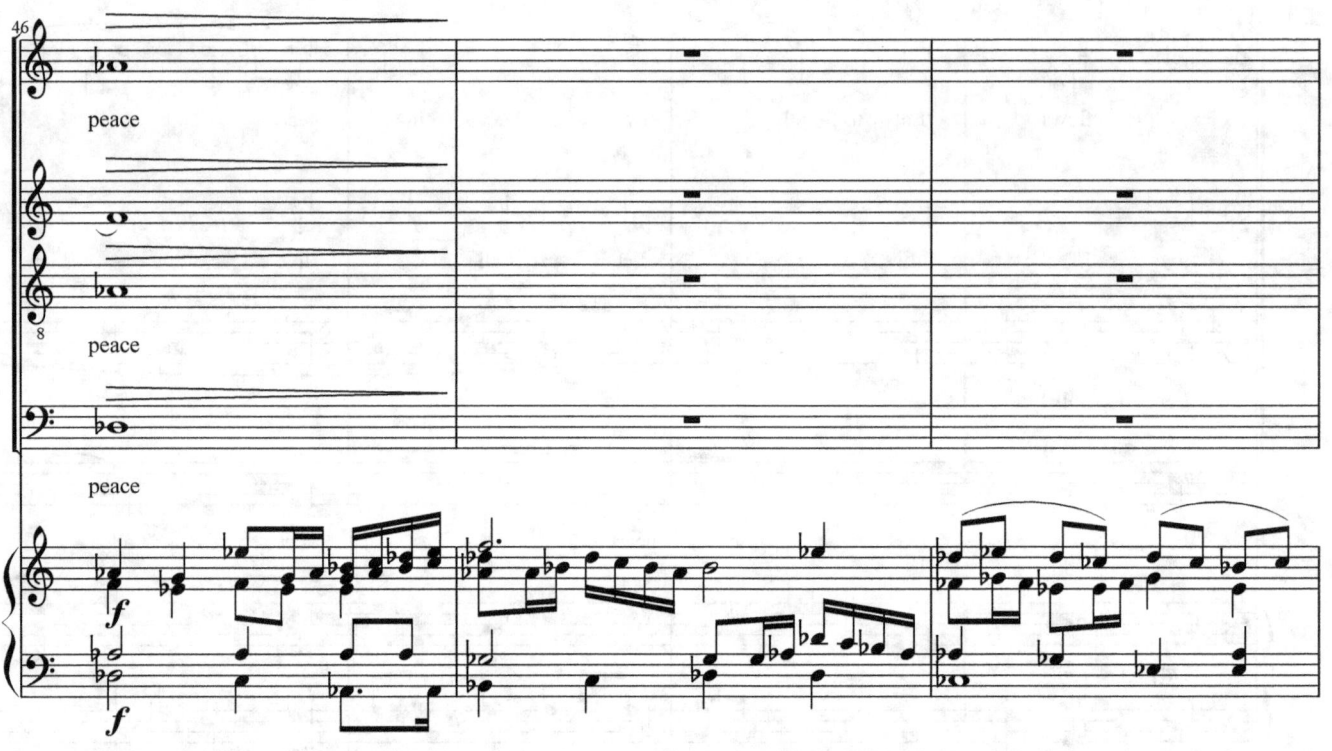

peace

peace

peace

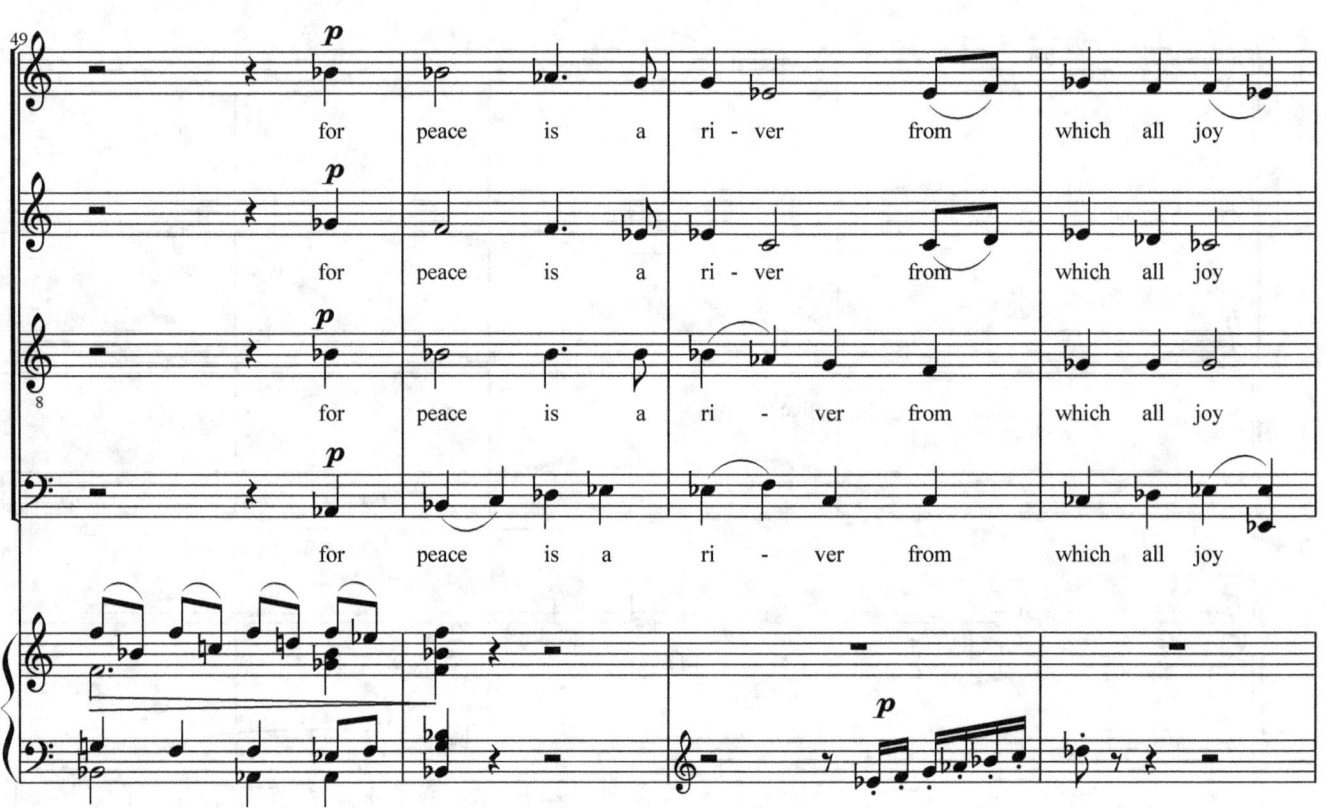

for peace is a ri - ver from which all joy

for peace is a ri - ver from which all joy

for peace is a ri - ver from which all joy

for peace is a ri - ver from which all joy

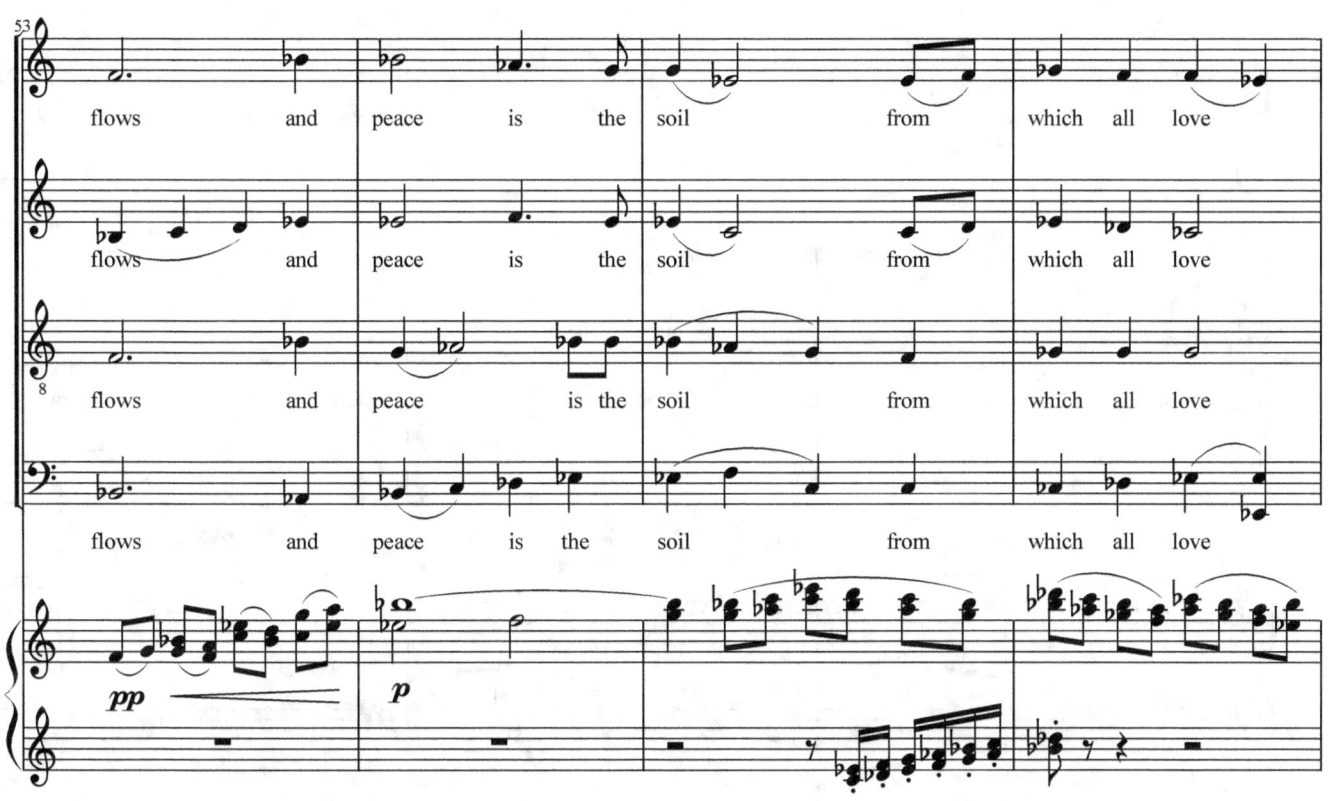

flows and peace is the soil from which all love

flows and peace is the soil from which all love

flows and peace is the soil from which all love

flows and peace is the soil from which all love

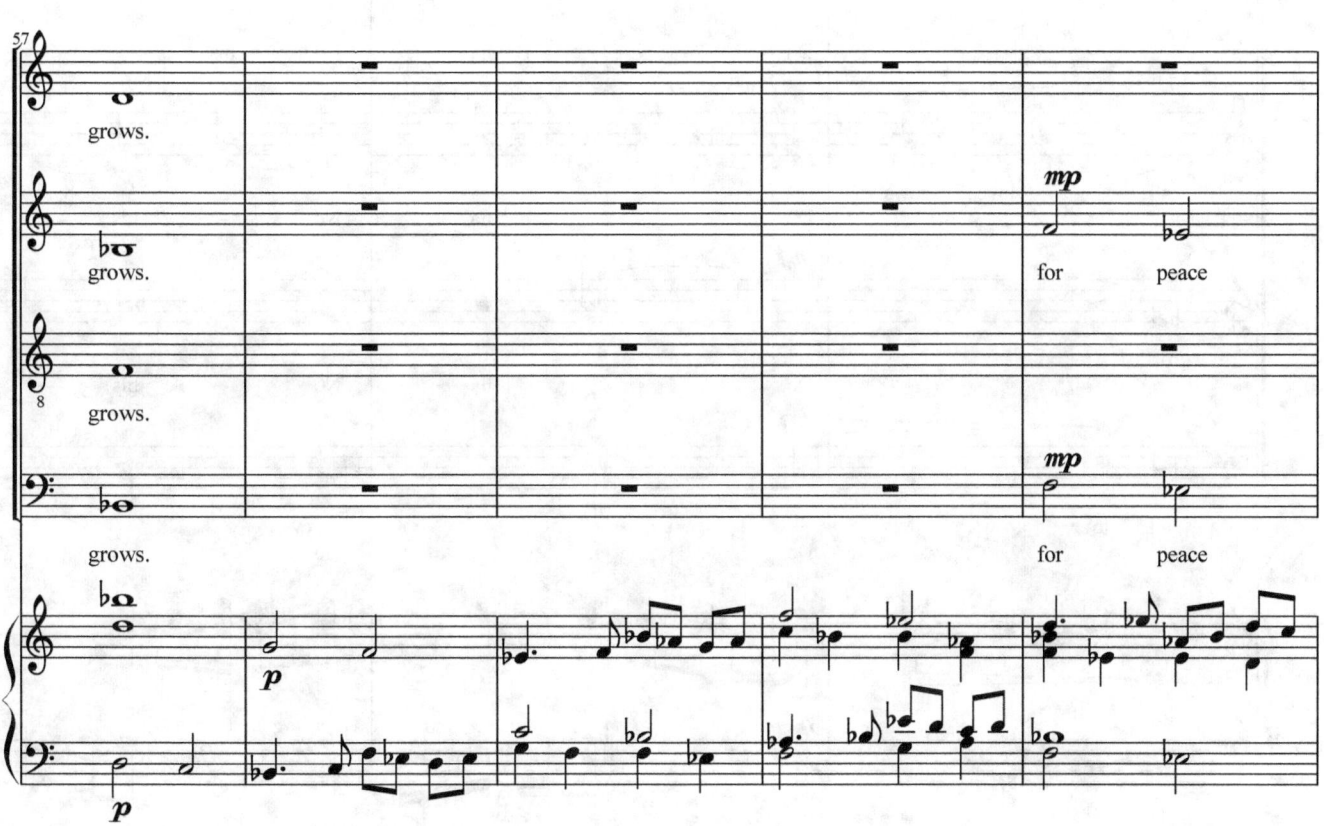

grows.

grows.

grows.

grows.

for peace

for peace

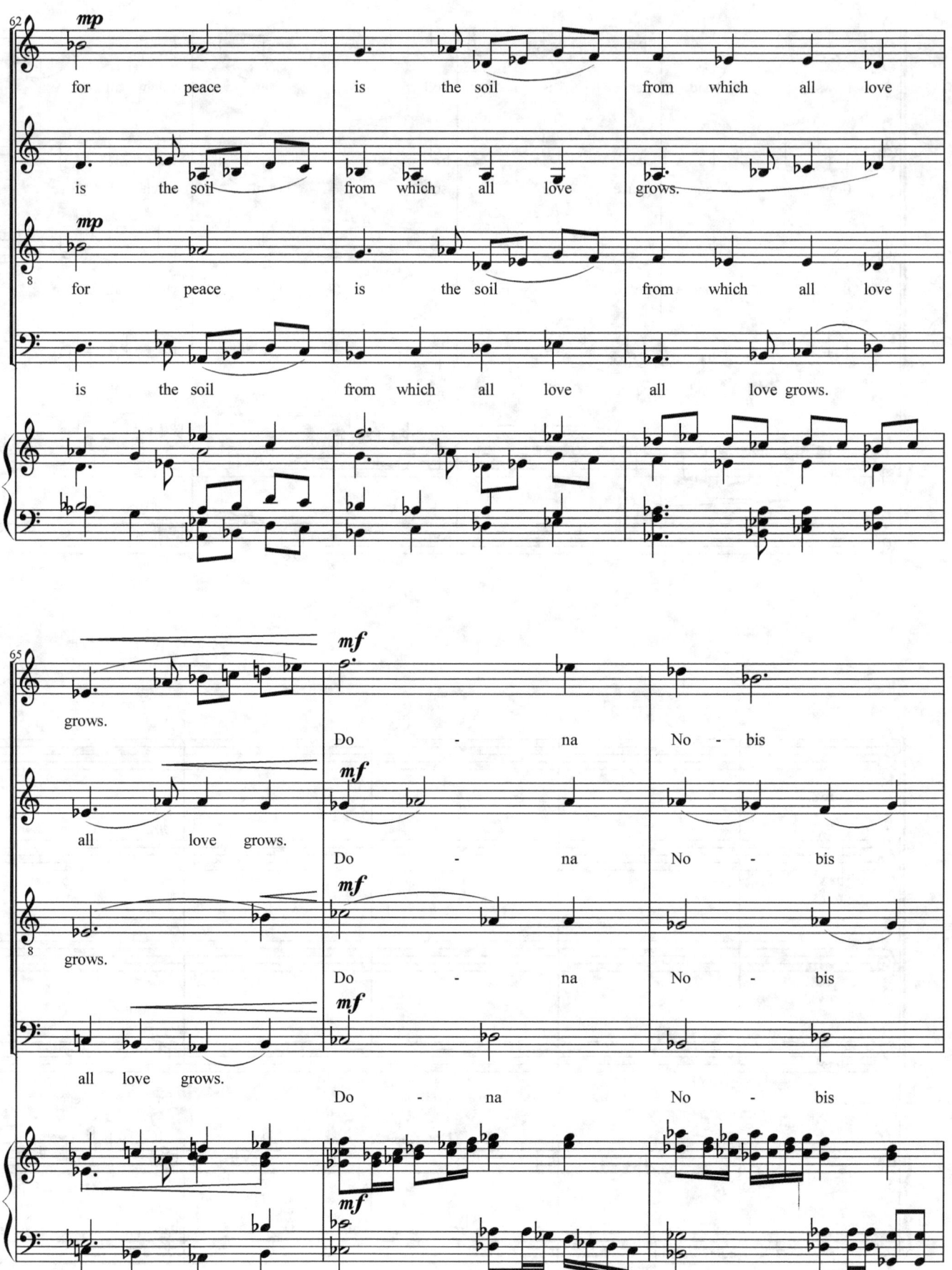

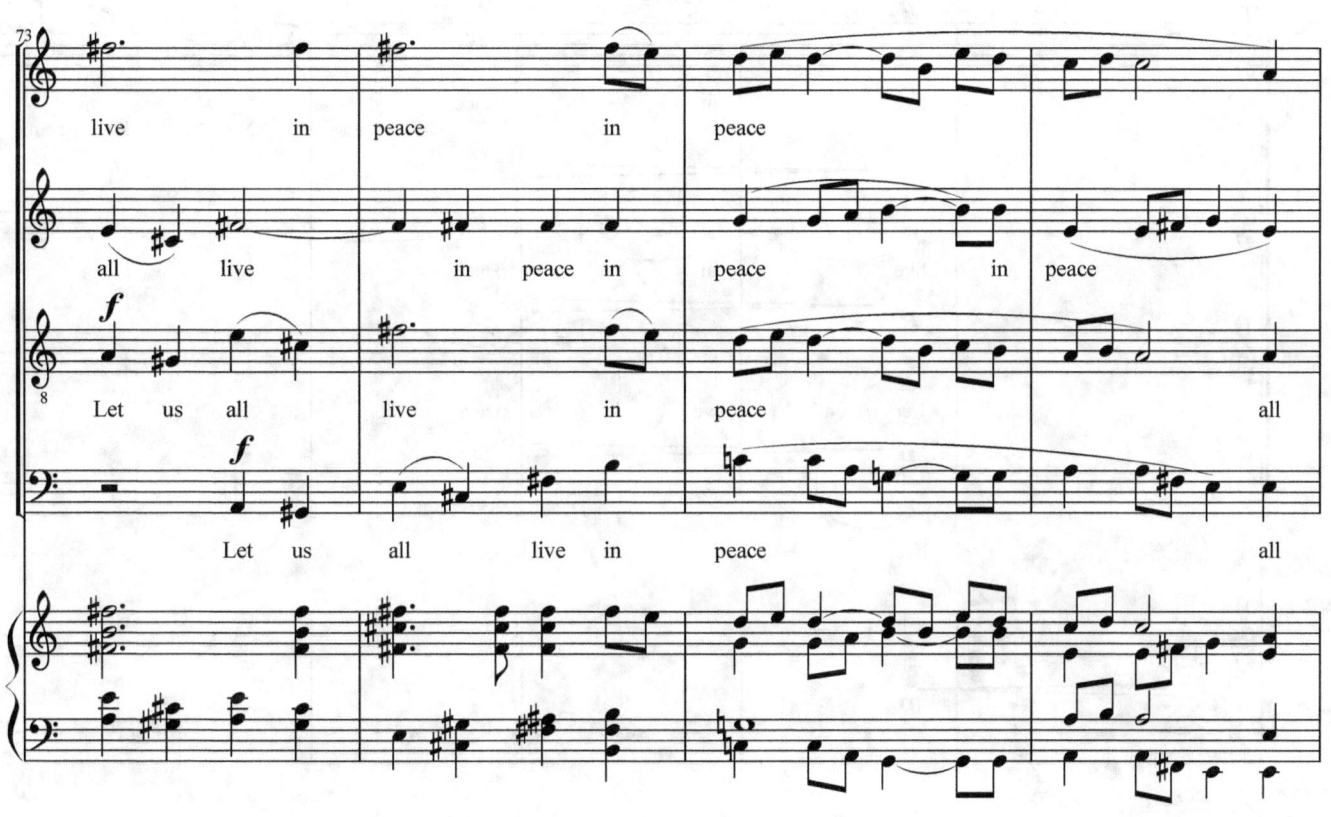

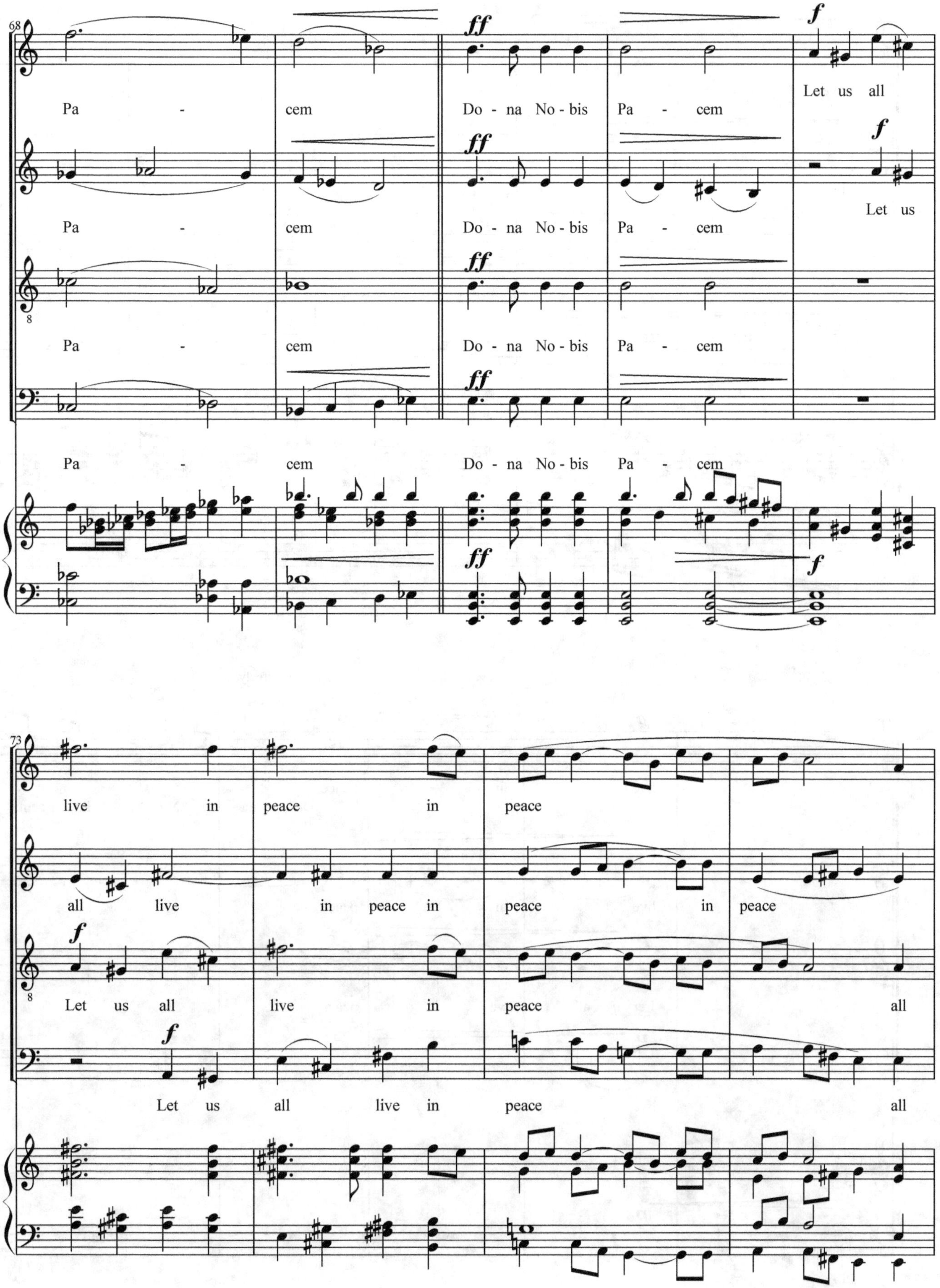

Pa - cem Do - na No - bis Pa - cem Let us all

Pa - cem Do - na No - bis Pa - cem Let us

Pa - cem Do - na No - bis Pa - cem

Pa - cem Do - na No - bis Pa - cem

live   in peace   in   peace

all   live   in peace in   peace   in peace

Let us all   live   in   peace   all

Let us   all   live in   peace   all

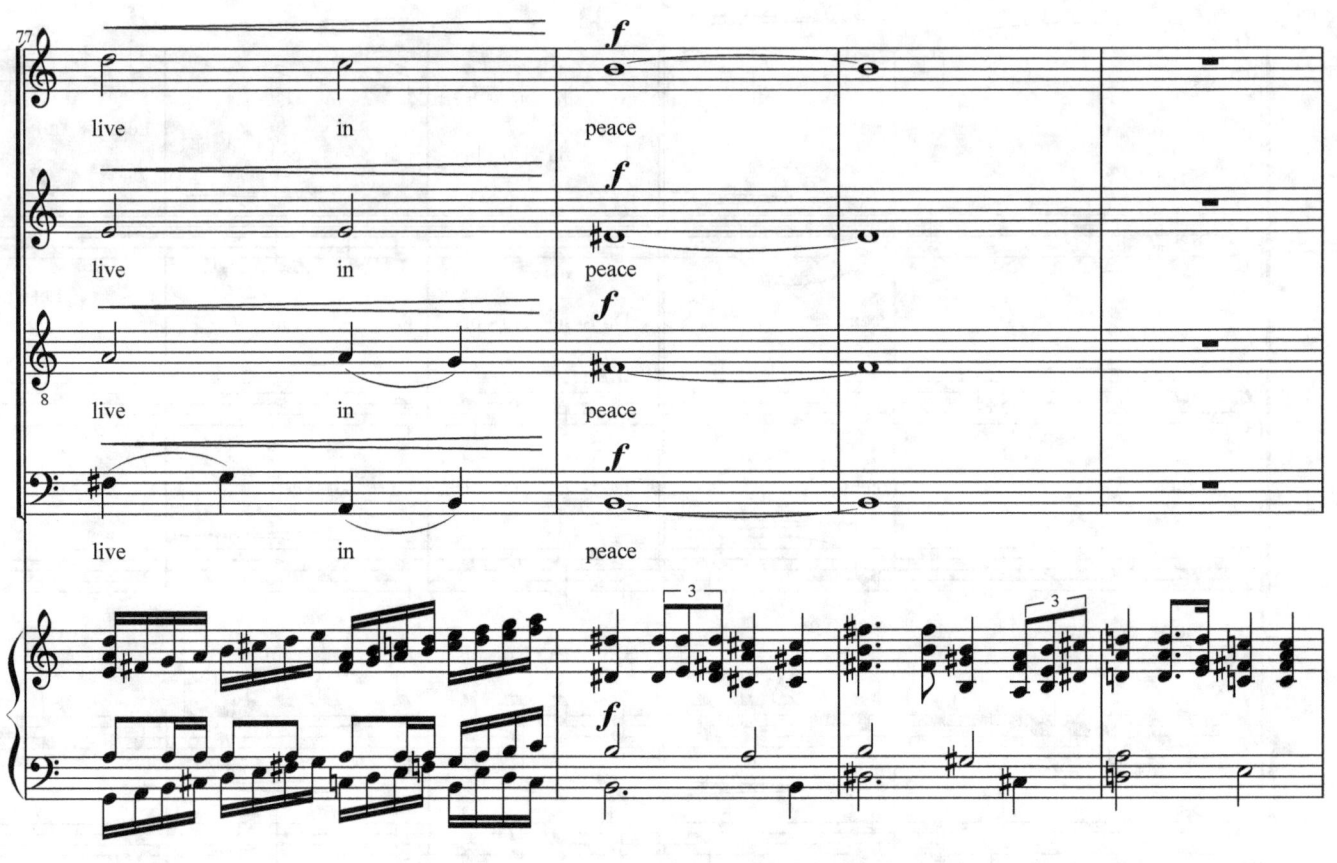

live   in   peace

live   in   peace

live   in   peace

live   in   peace

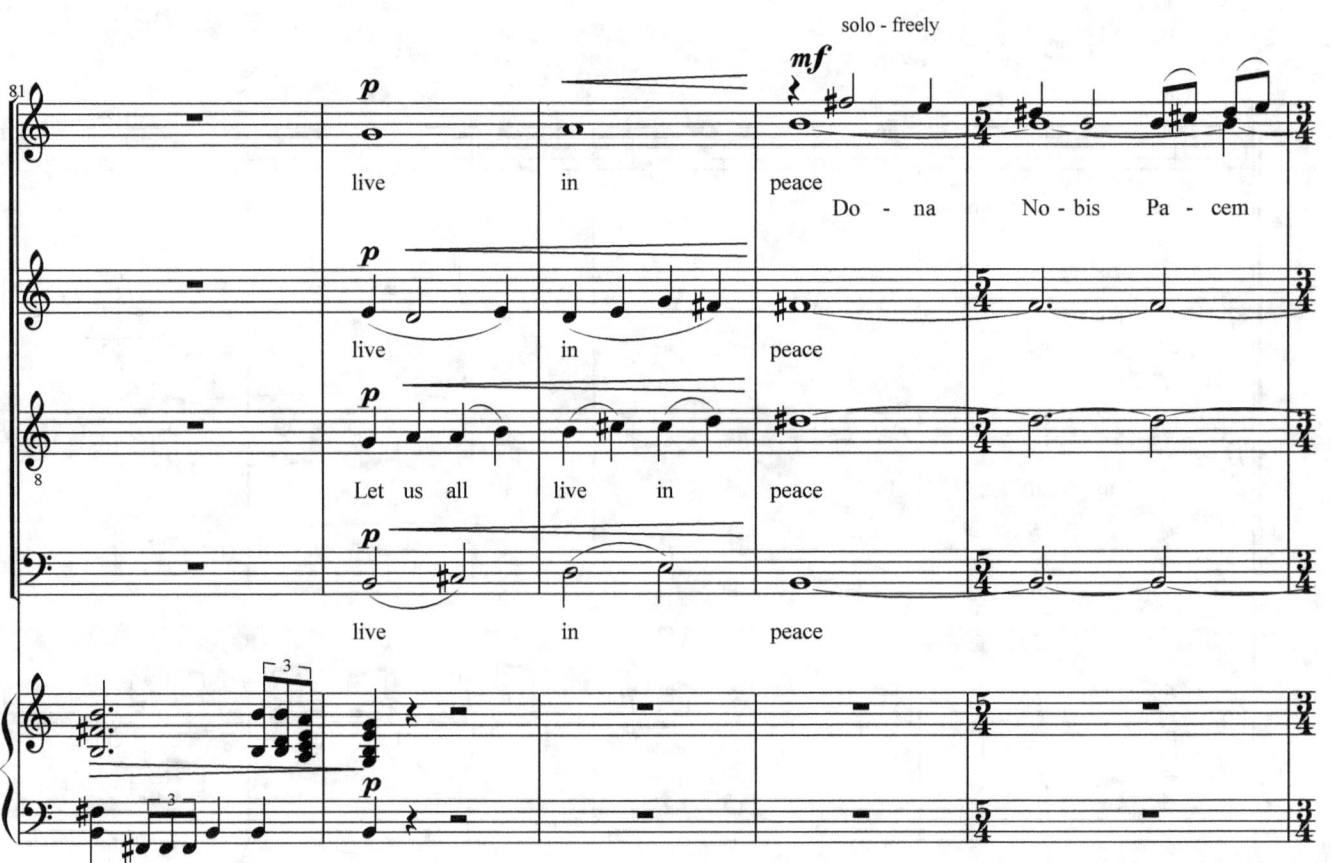

solo - freely

live   in   peace

Do - na   No - bis   Pa - cem

live   in   peace

Let us all   live   in   peace

live   in   peace

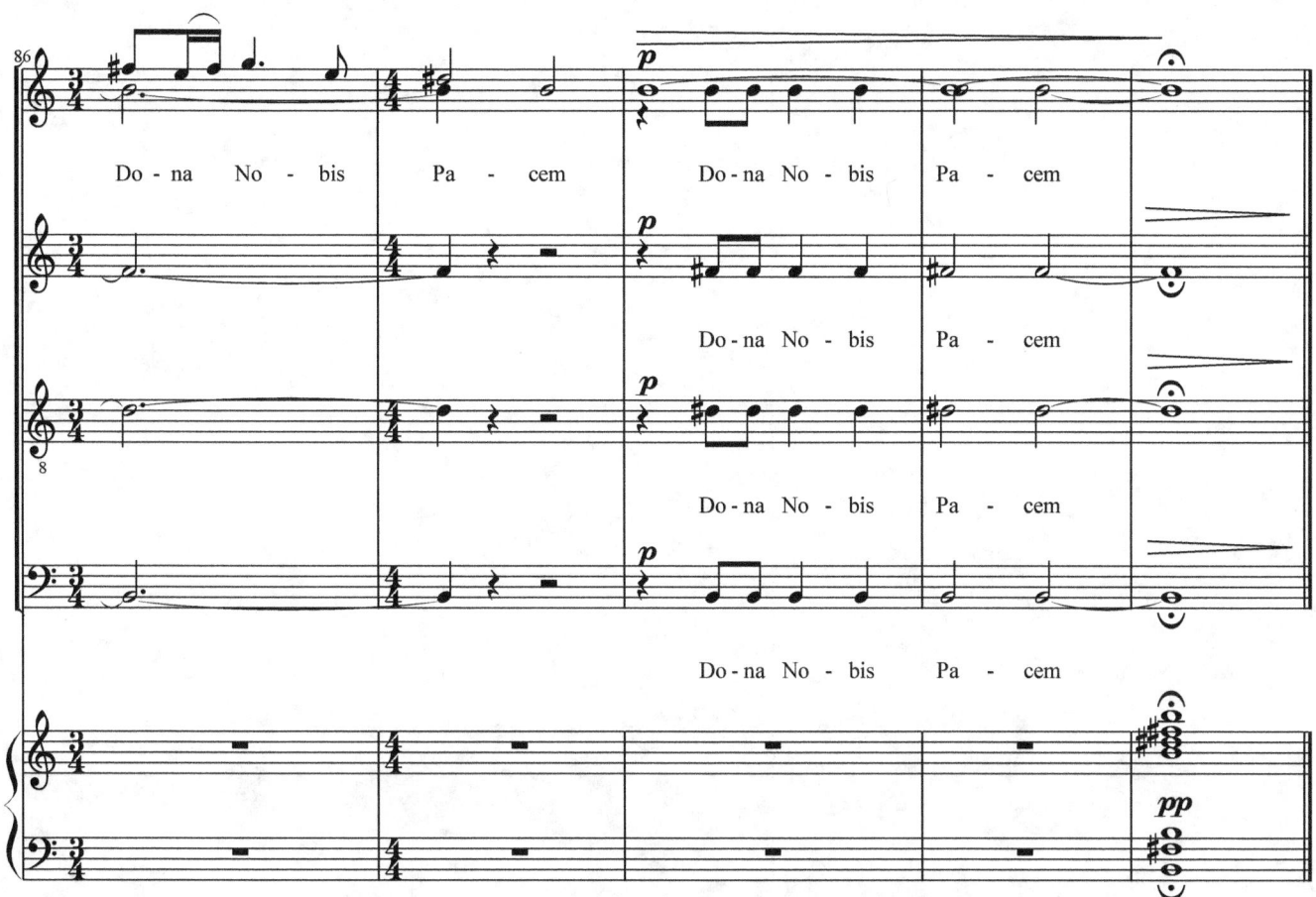

Do - na No - bis   Pa - cem   Do - na No - bis   Pa - cem

Do - na No - bis   Pa - cem

Do - na No - bis   Pa - cem

Do - na No - bis   Pa - cem

Love Is Love

Ken Langer

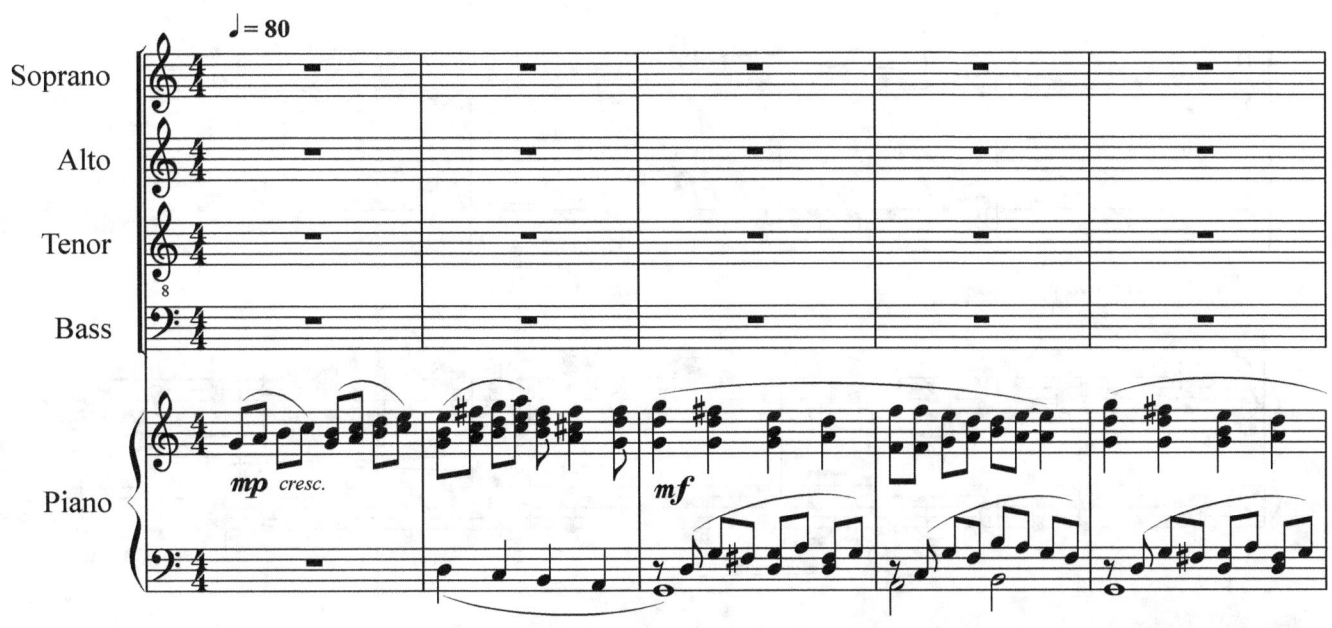

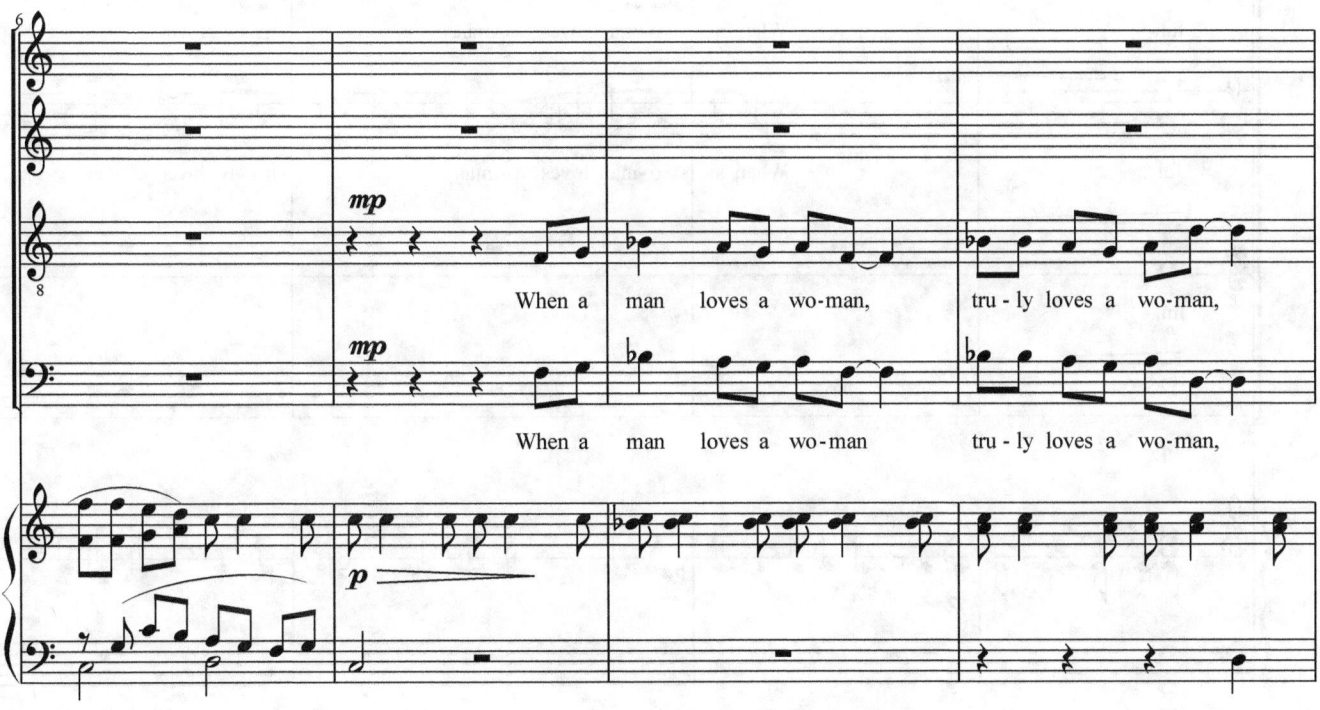

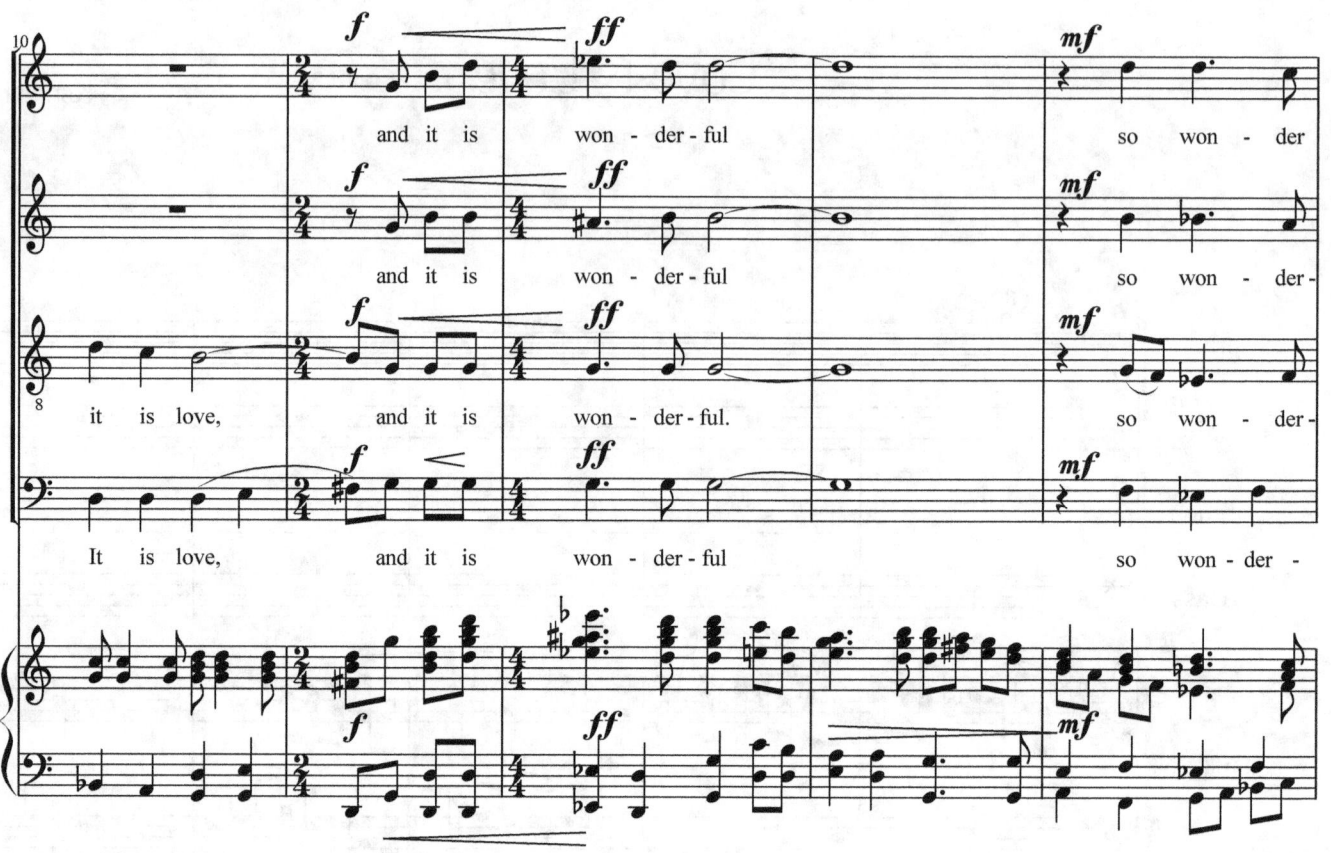

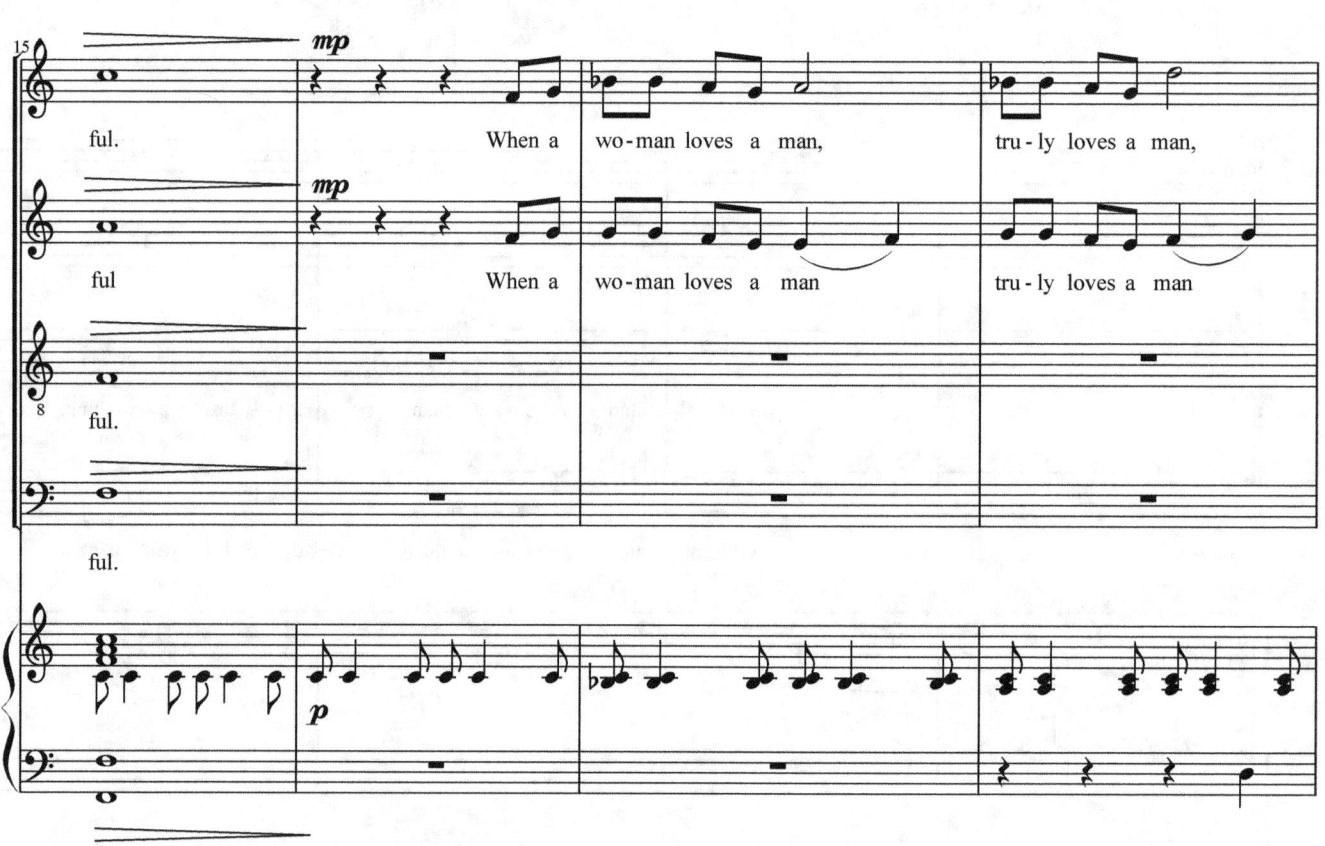

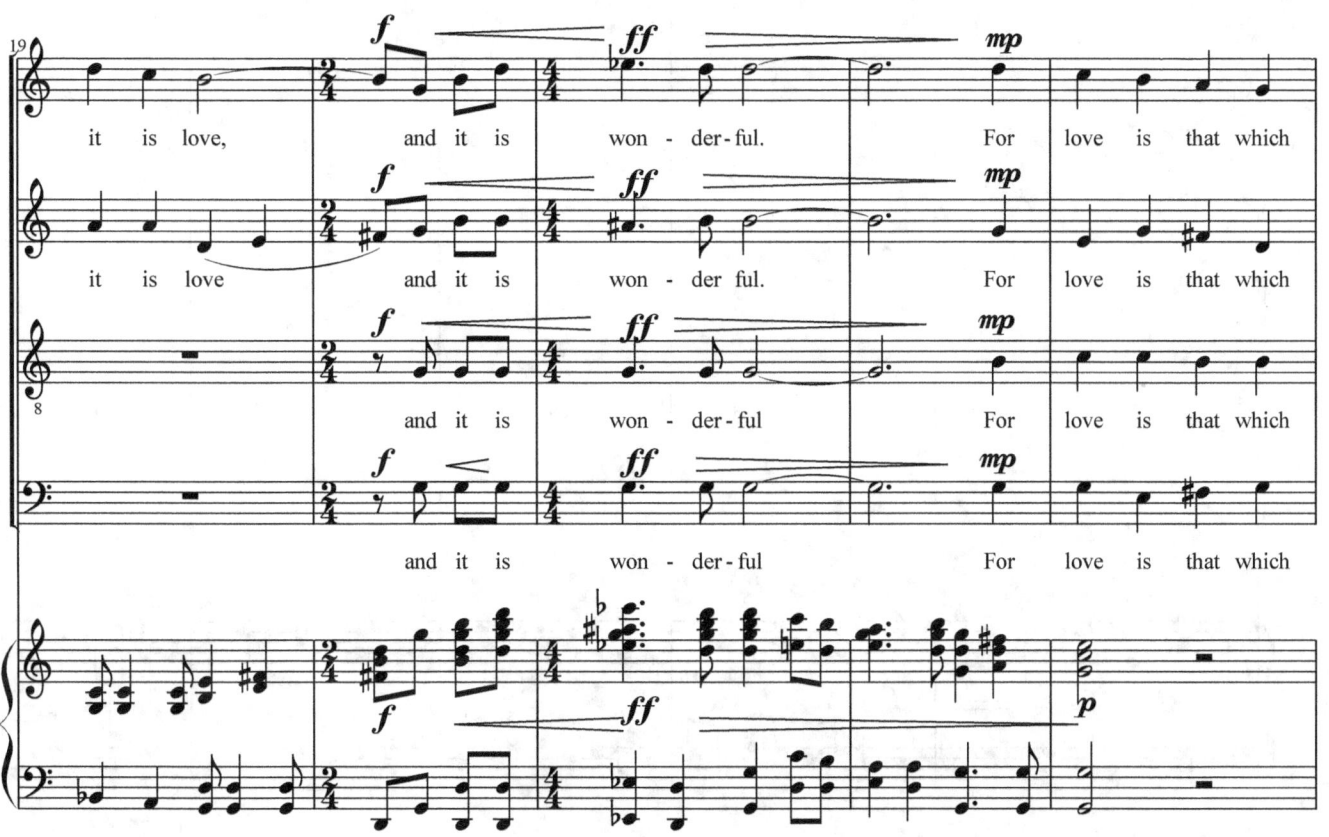

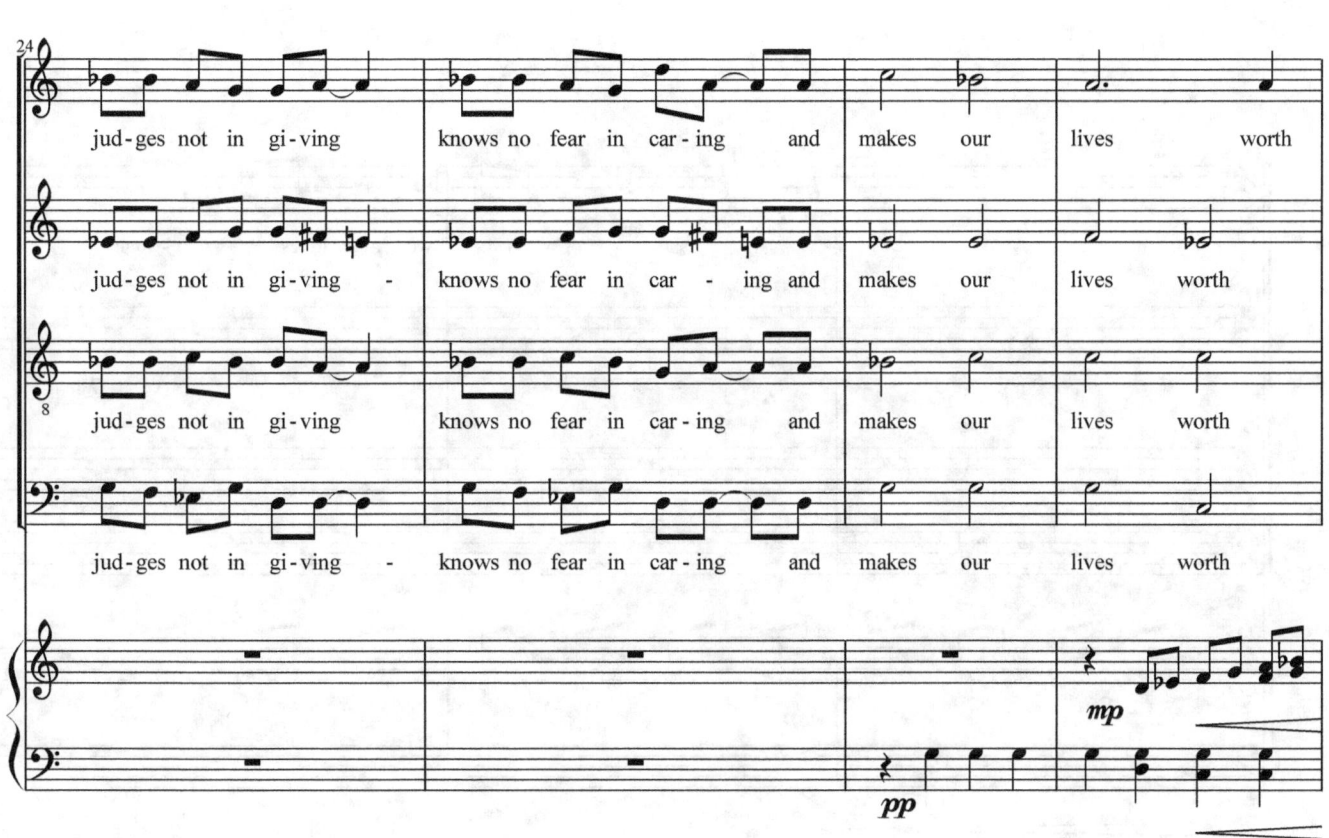

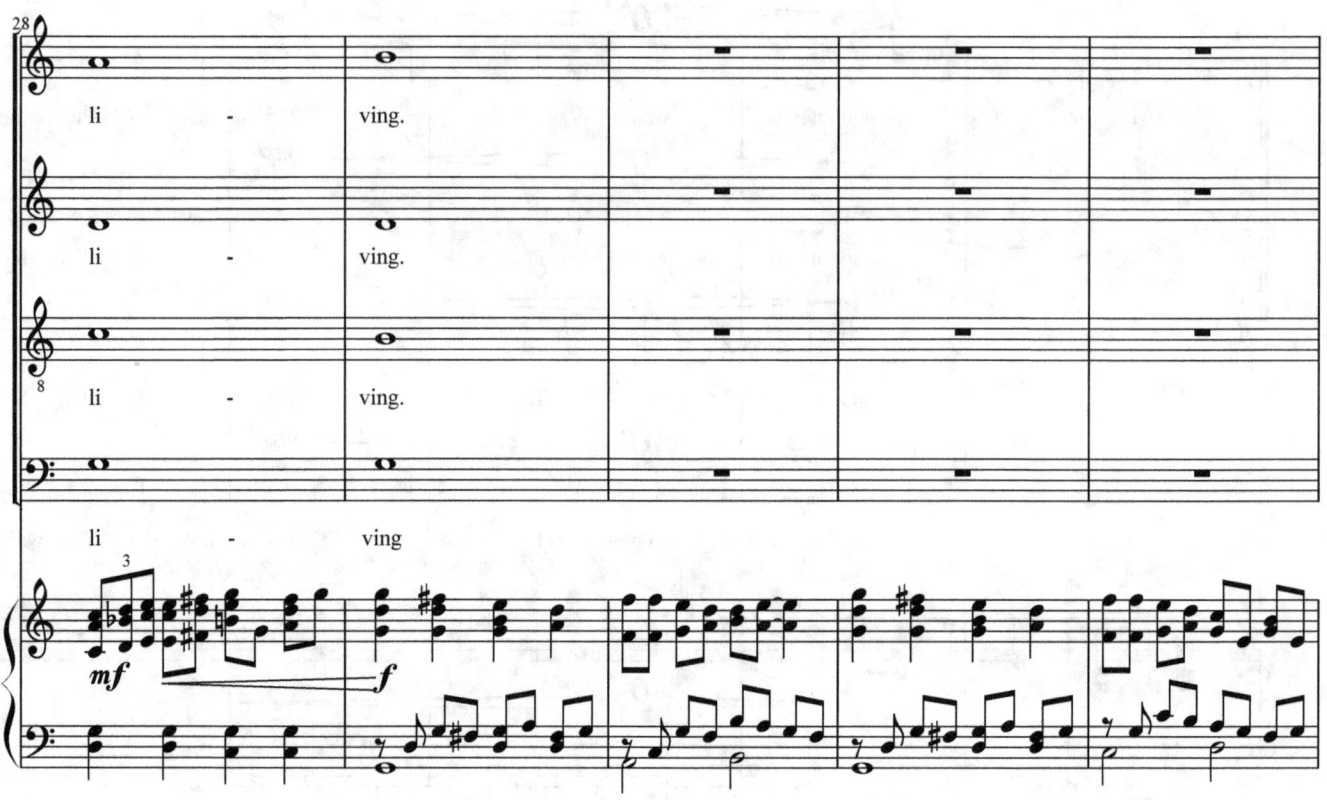

li - ving.

li - ving.

li - ving.

li - ving

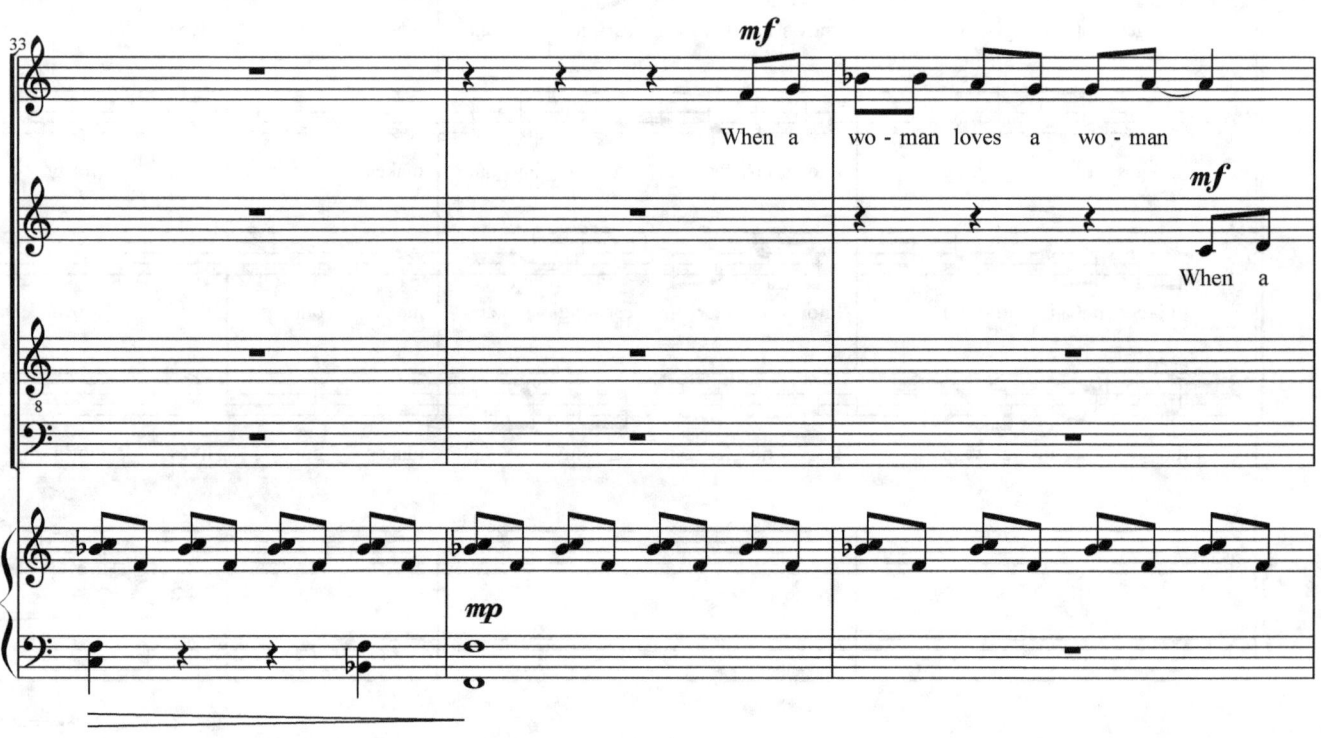

When a wo - man loves a wo - man

When a

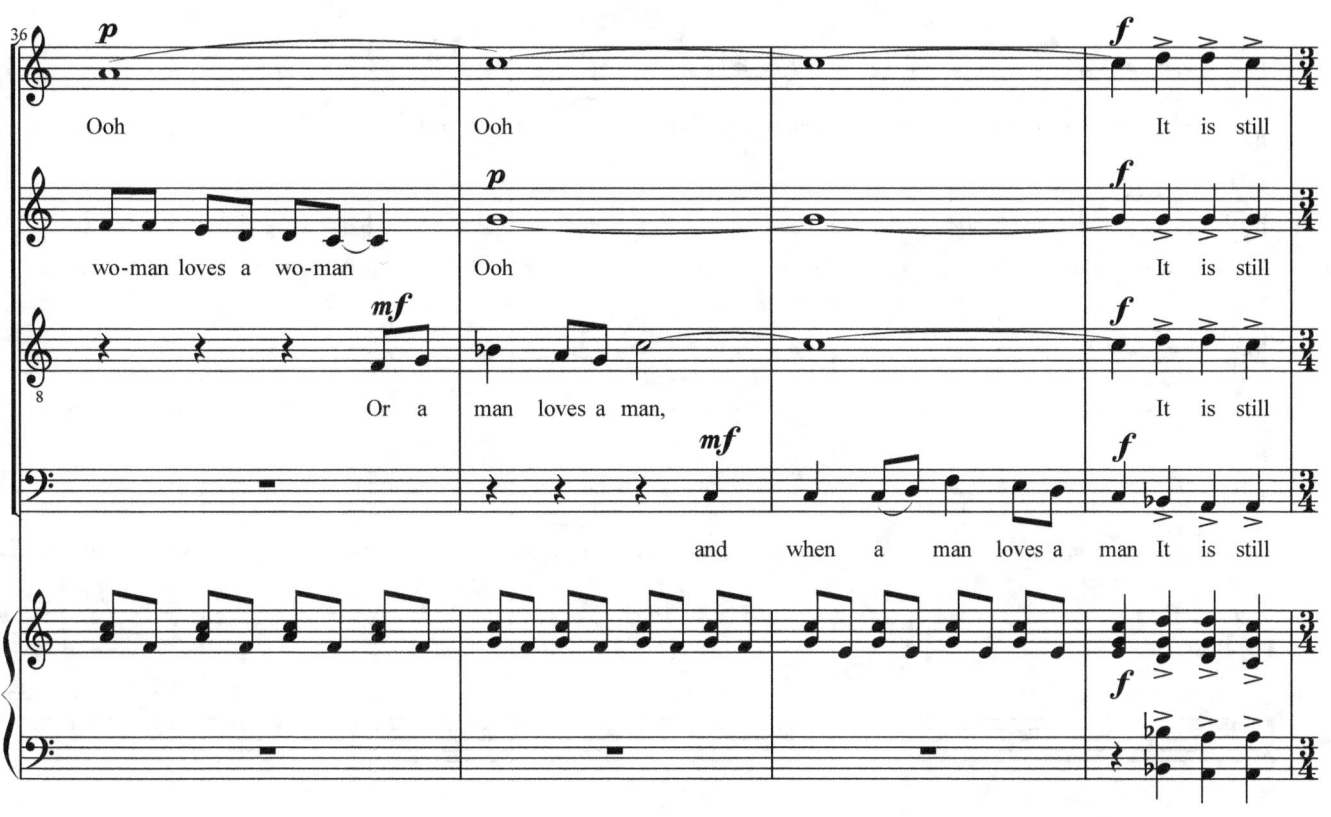

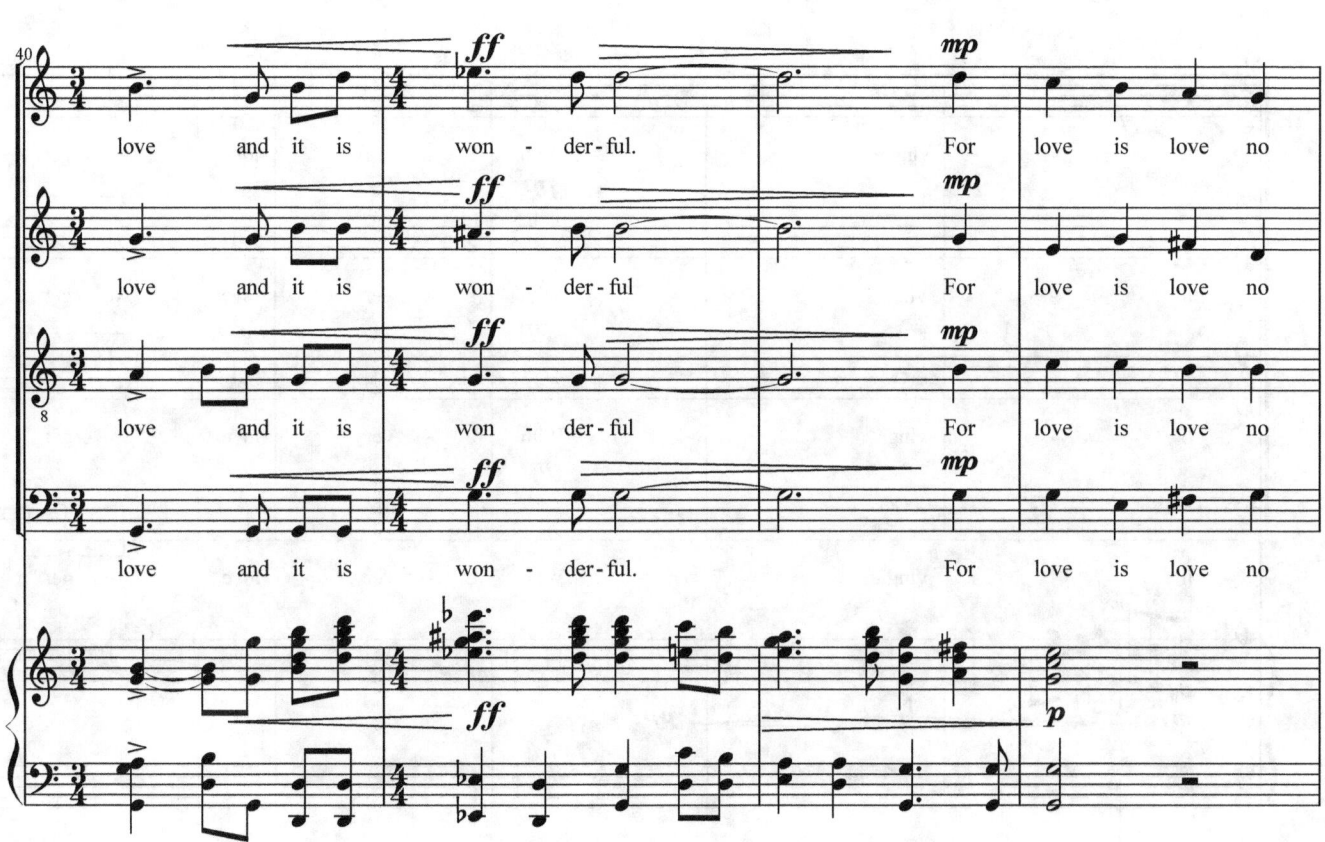

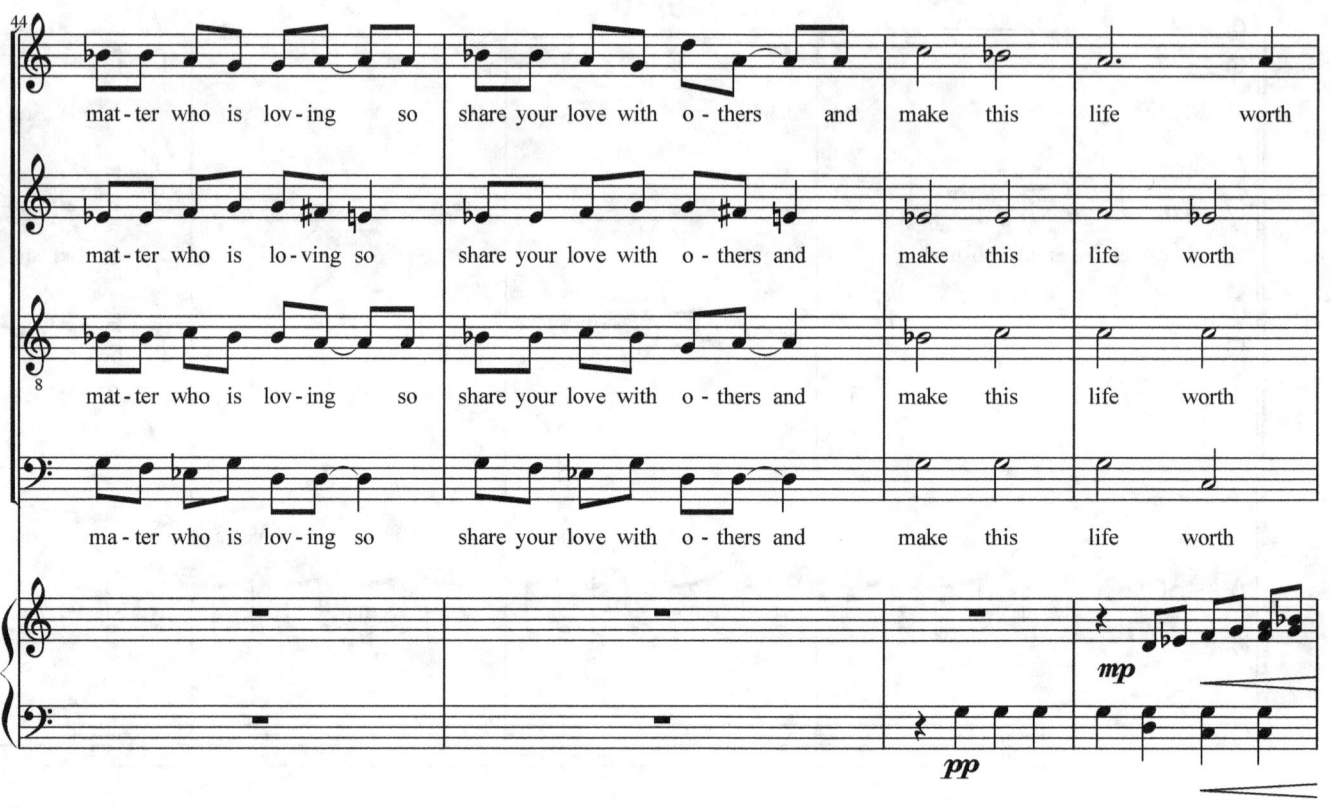

mat - ter who is lov - ing   so   share your love with o - thers and   make this   life   worth

mat - ter who is lo - ving so   share your love with o - thers and   make this   life   worth

mat - ter who is lov - ing   so   share your love with o - thers and   make this   life   worth

ma - ter who is lov - ing so   share your love with o - thers and   make this   life   worth

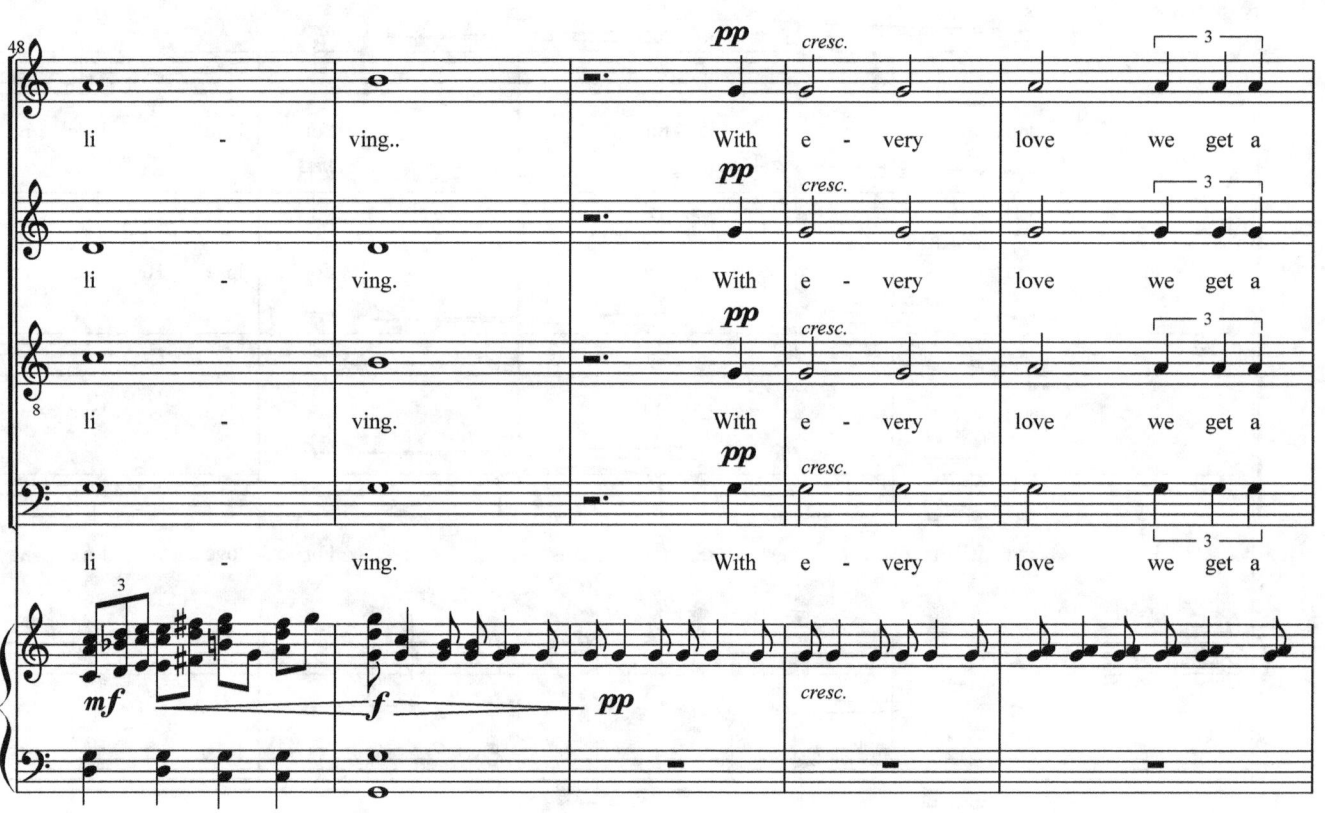

li - ving..   With e - very love we get a

li - ving.   With e - very love we get a

li - ving.   With e - very love we get a

li - ving.   With e - very love we get a

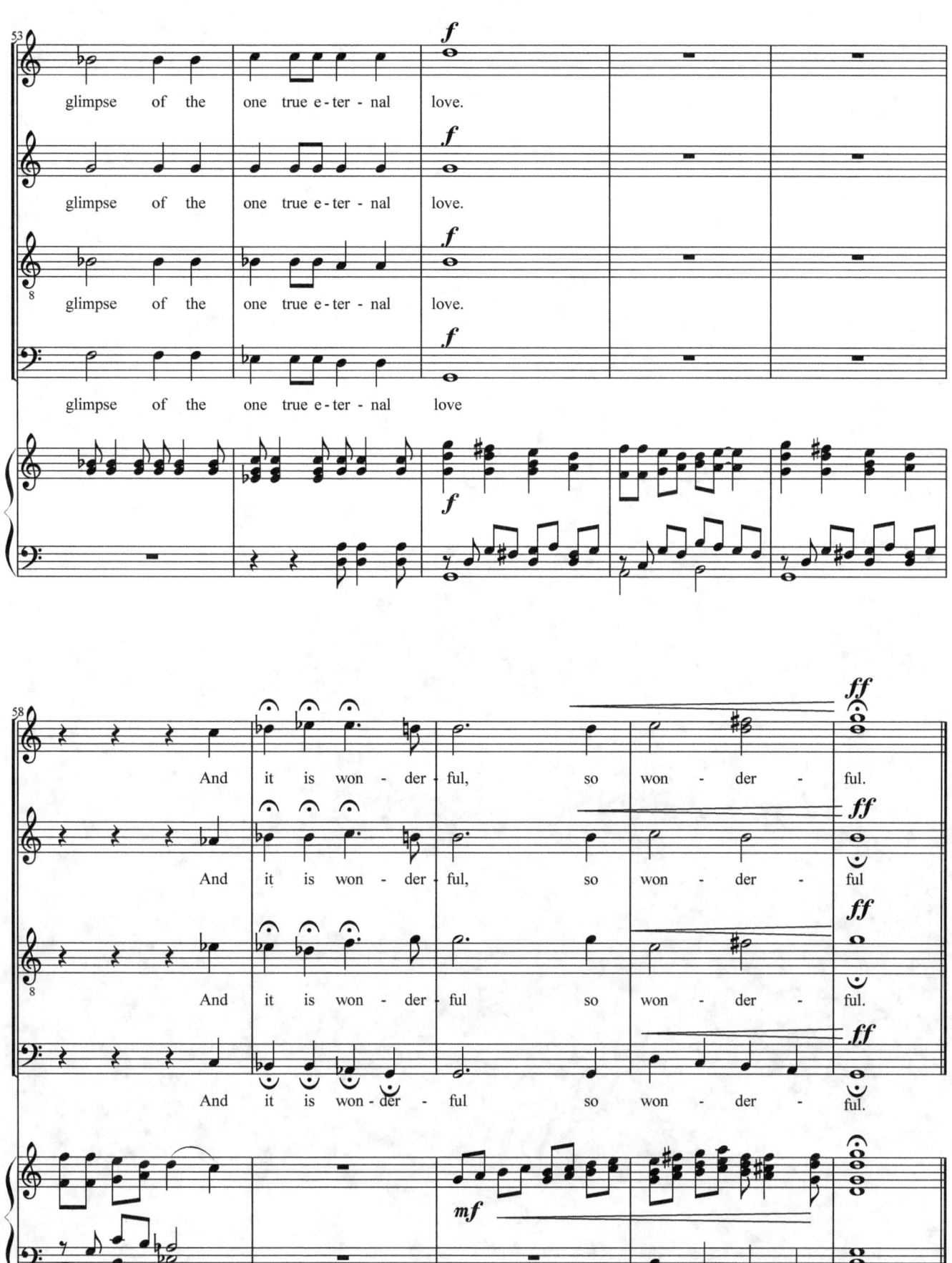

Love's Philosophy
from "Wedding Music"

text by Percy Bysshe Shelley

music by Ken Langer

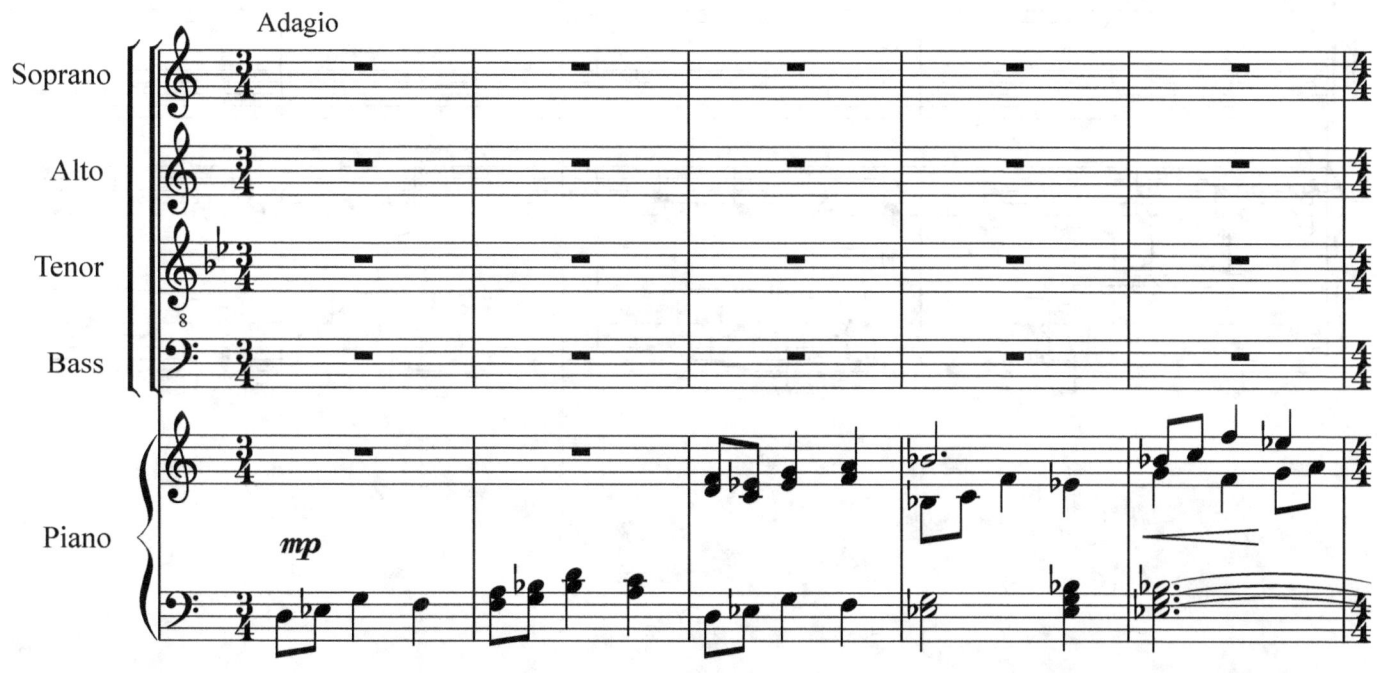

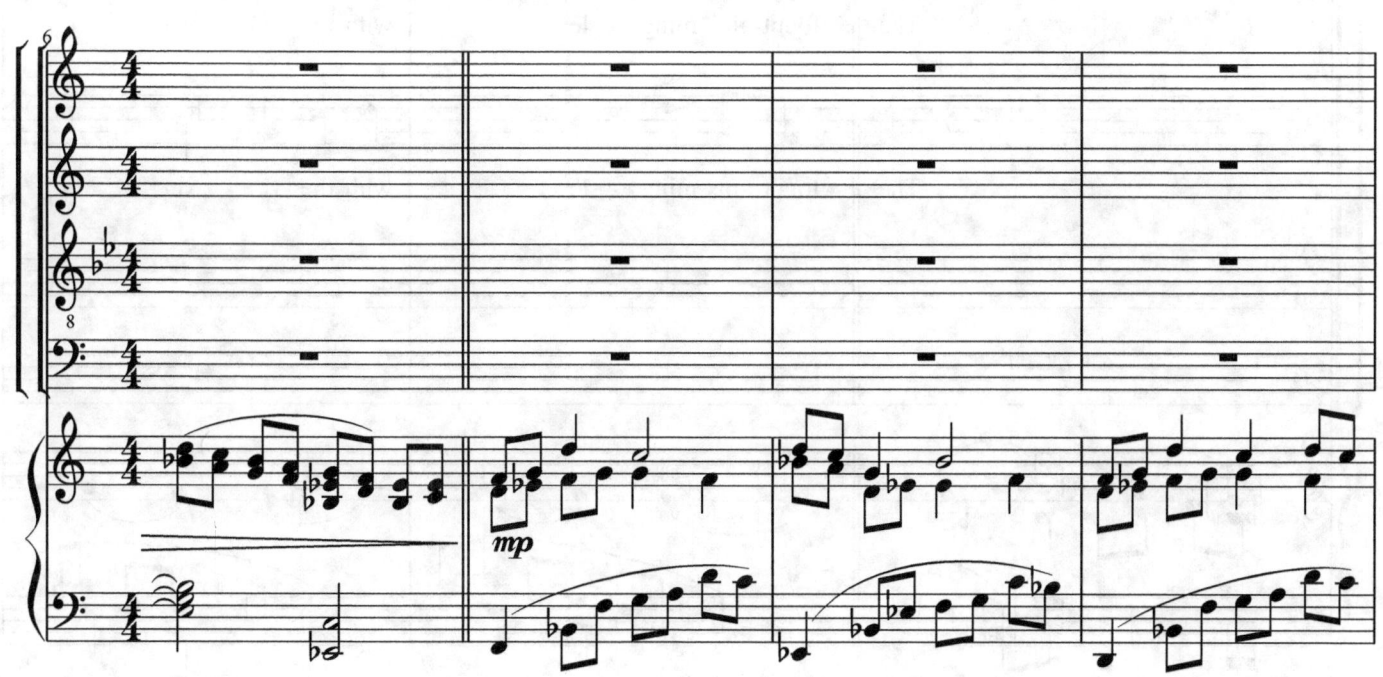

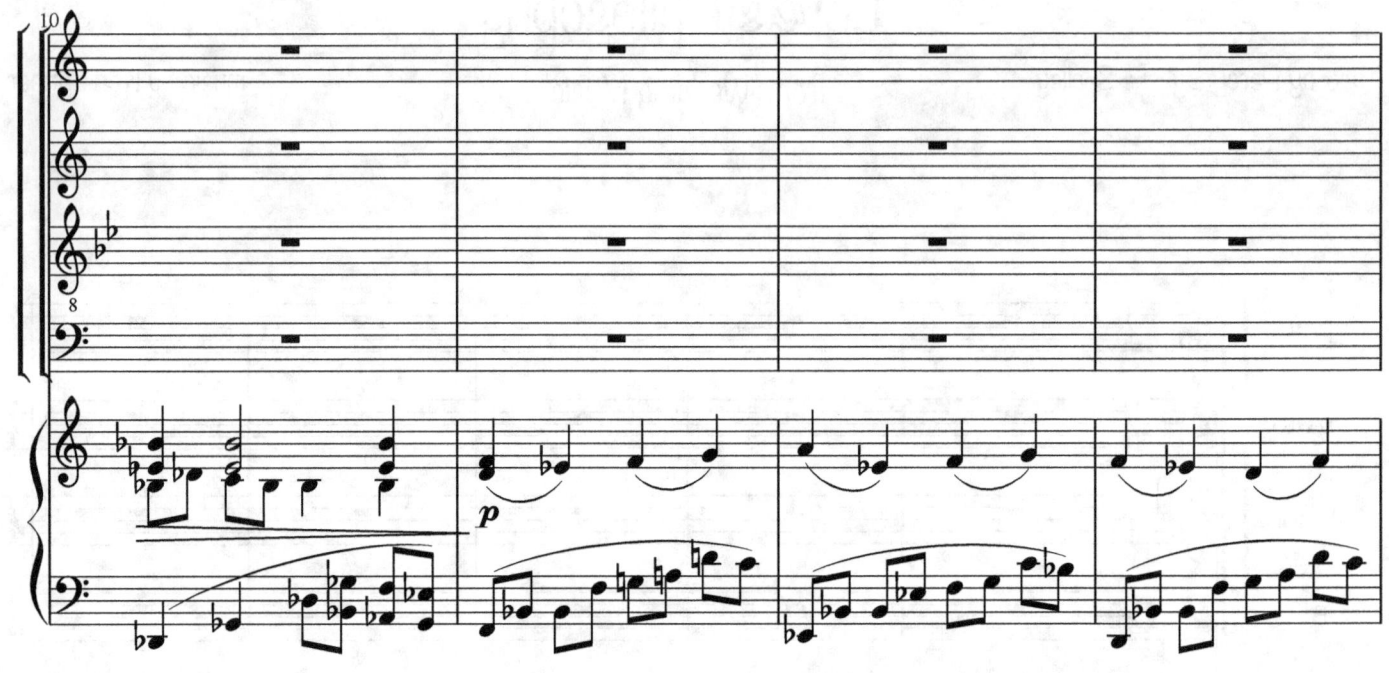

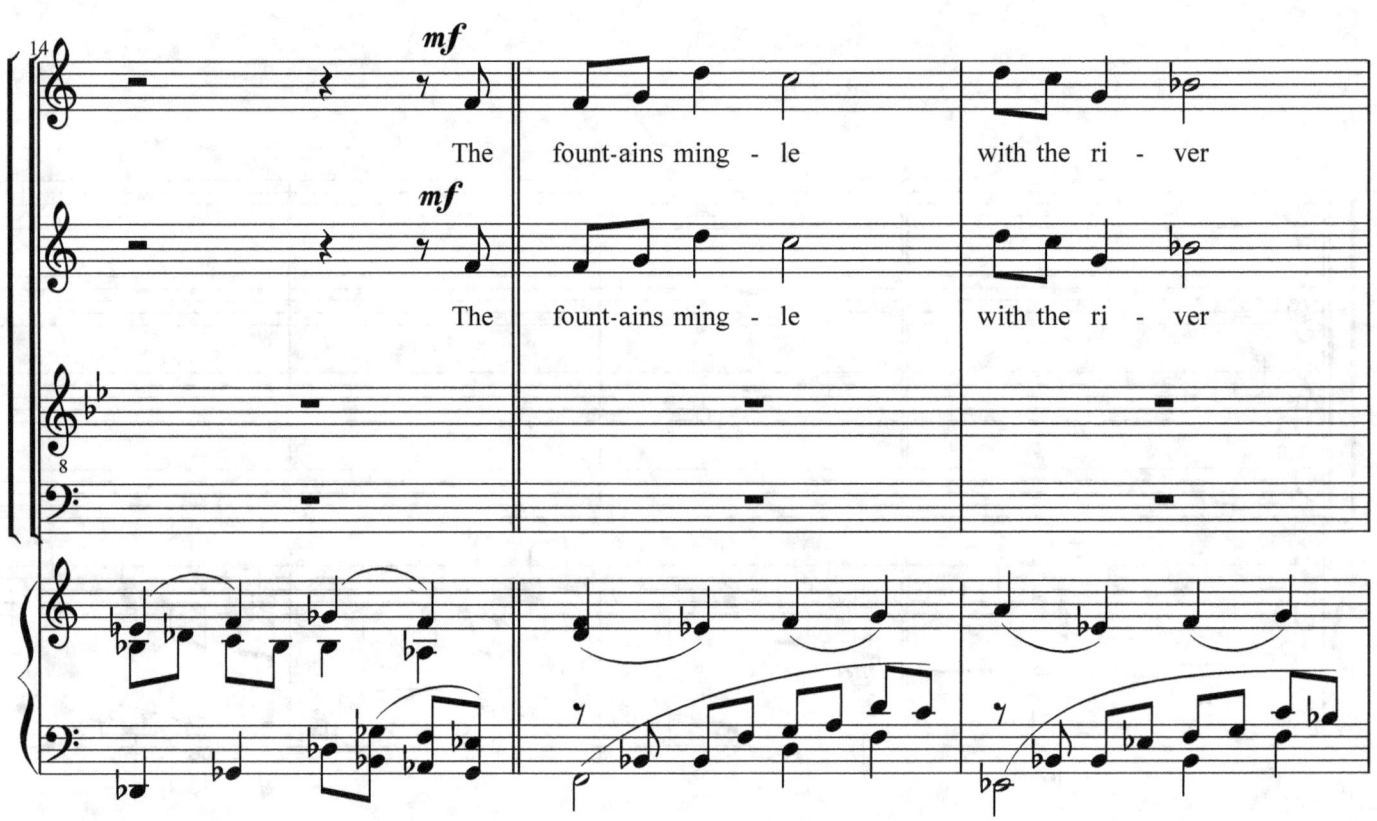

The fount-ains ming - le with the ri - ver

The fount-ains ming - le with the ri - ver

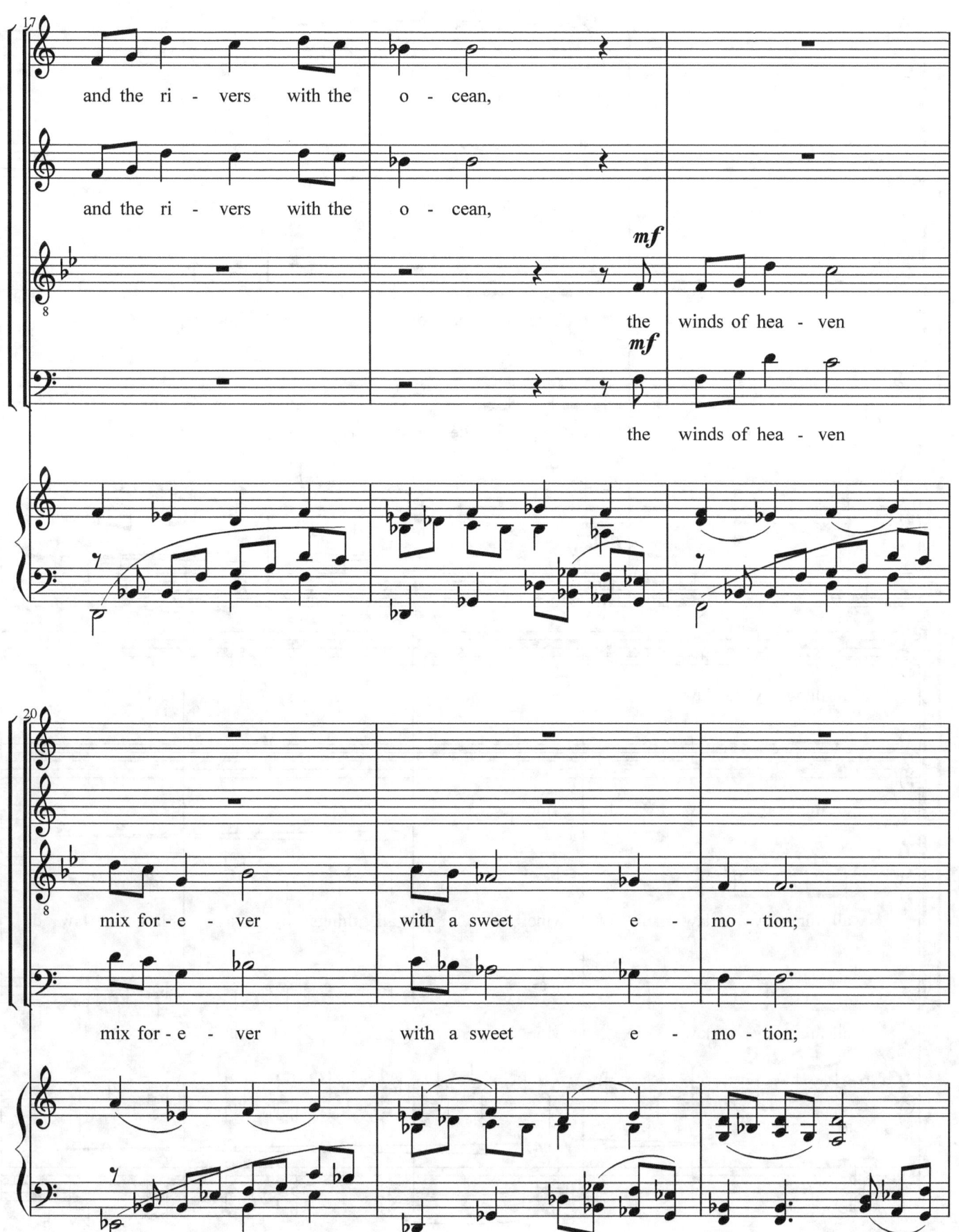

and the ri - vers with the o - cean,

and the ri - vers with the o - cean,

the winds of hea - ven

the winds of hea - ven

mix for-e - ver with a sweet e - mo - tion;

mix for-e - ver with a sweet e - mo - tion;

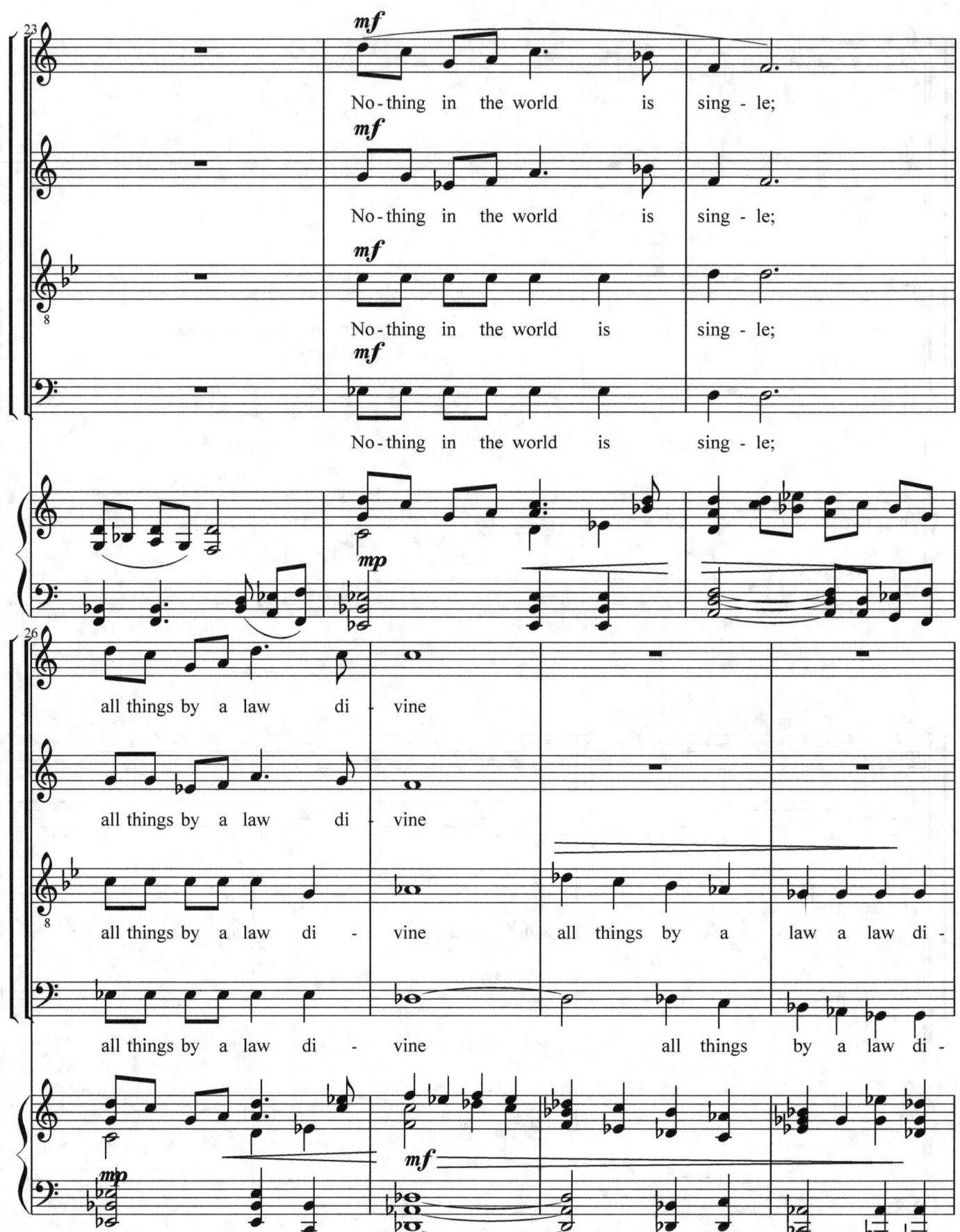

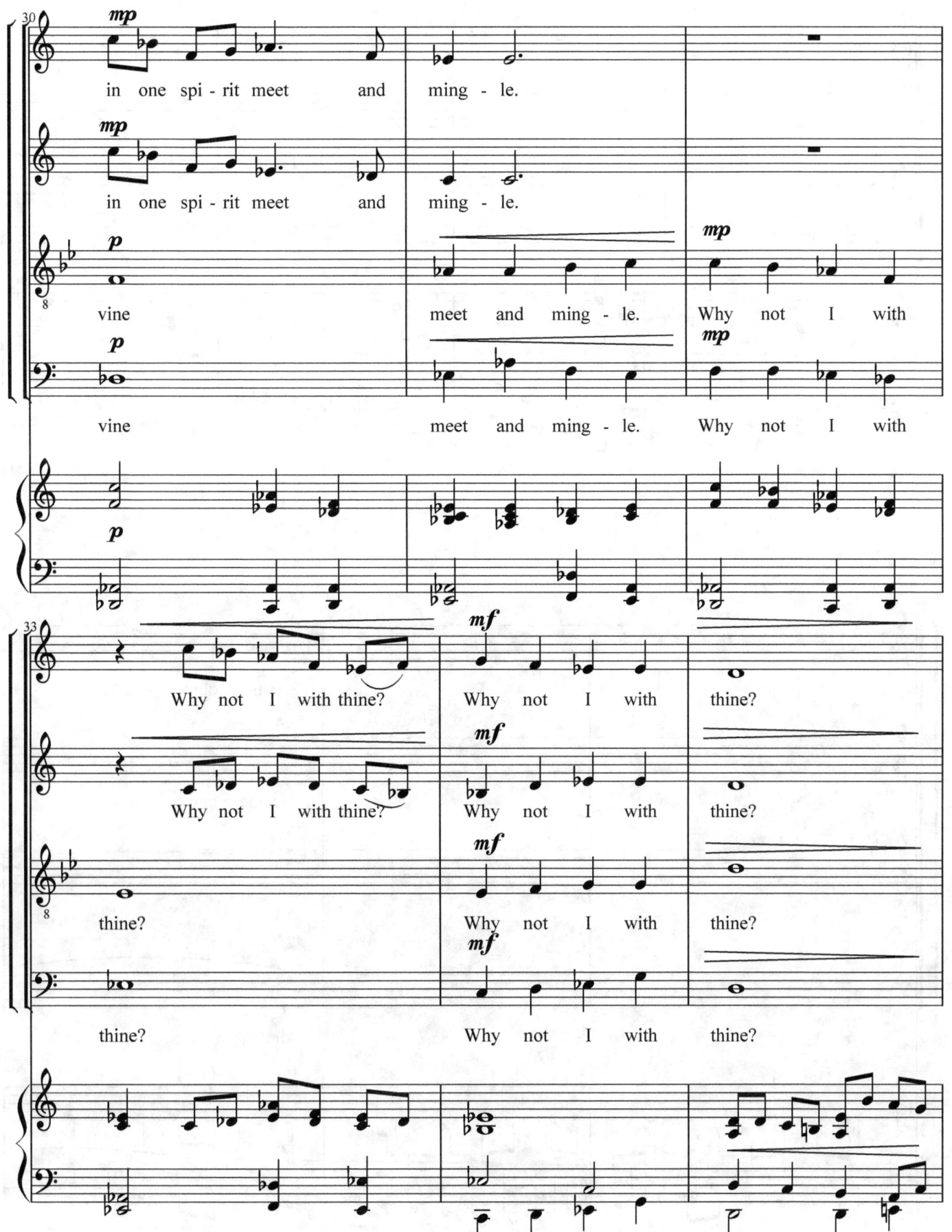

in one spi - rit meet and ming - le.

in one spi - rit meet and ming - le.

vine meet and ming - le. Why not I with

vine meet and ming - le. Why not I with

Why not I with thine? Why not I with thine?

Why not I with thine? Why not I with thine?

thine? Why not I with thine?

thine? Why not I with thine?

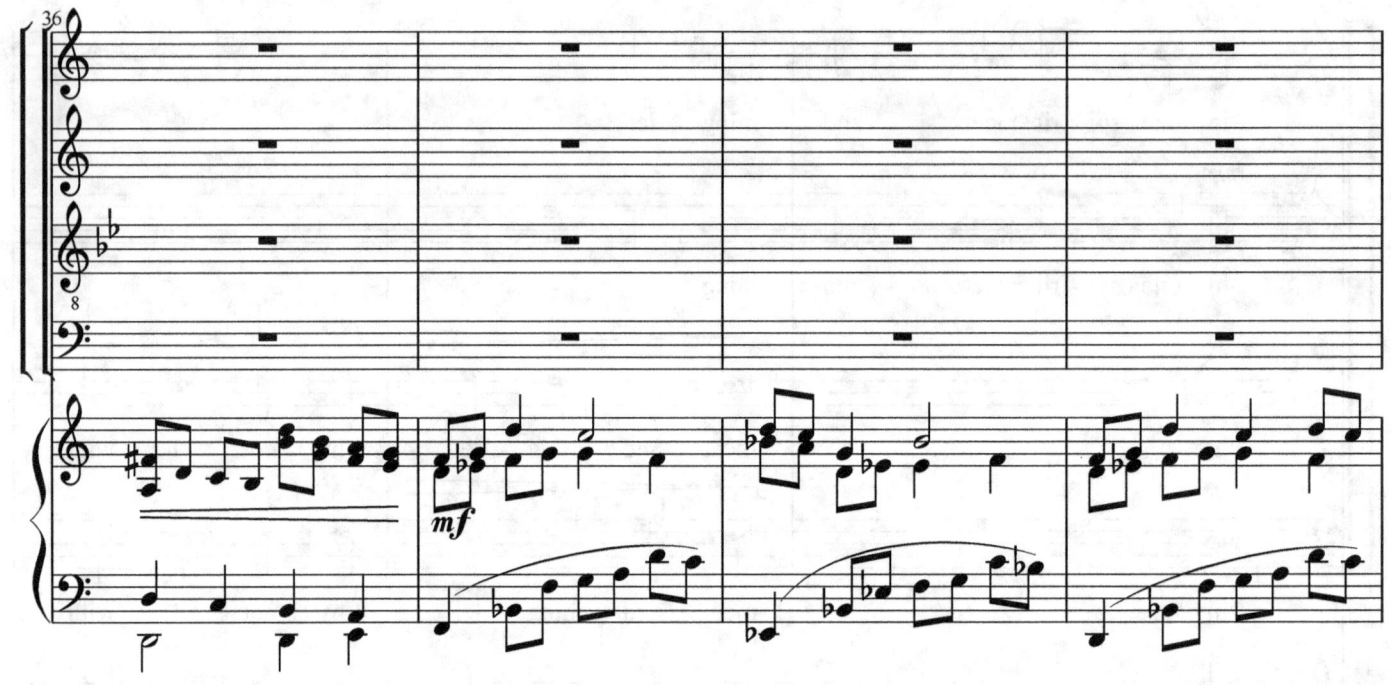

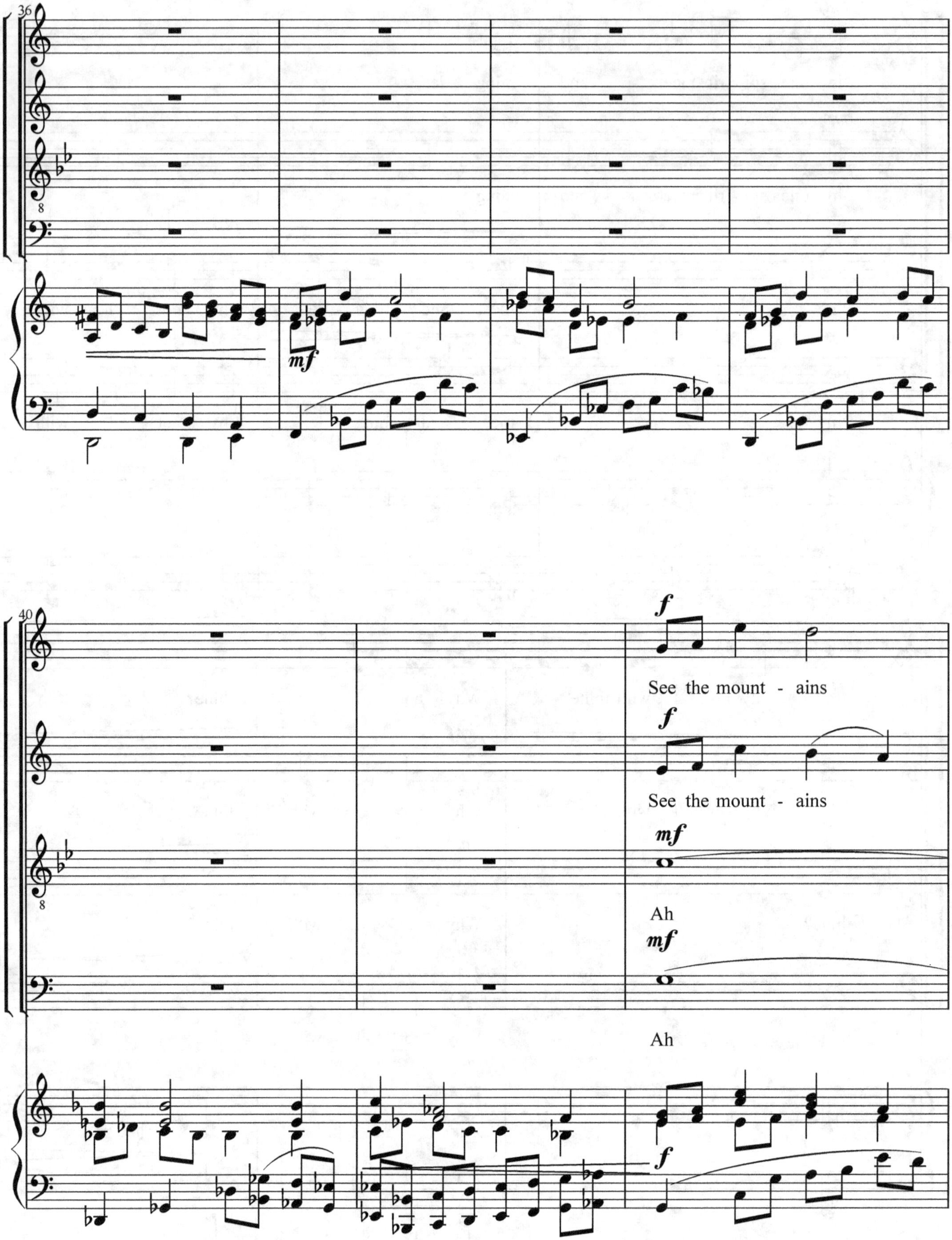

See the mount - ains

See the mount - ains

Ah

Ah

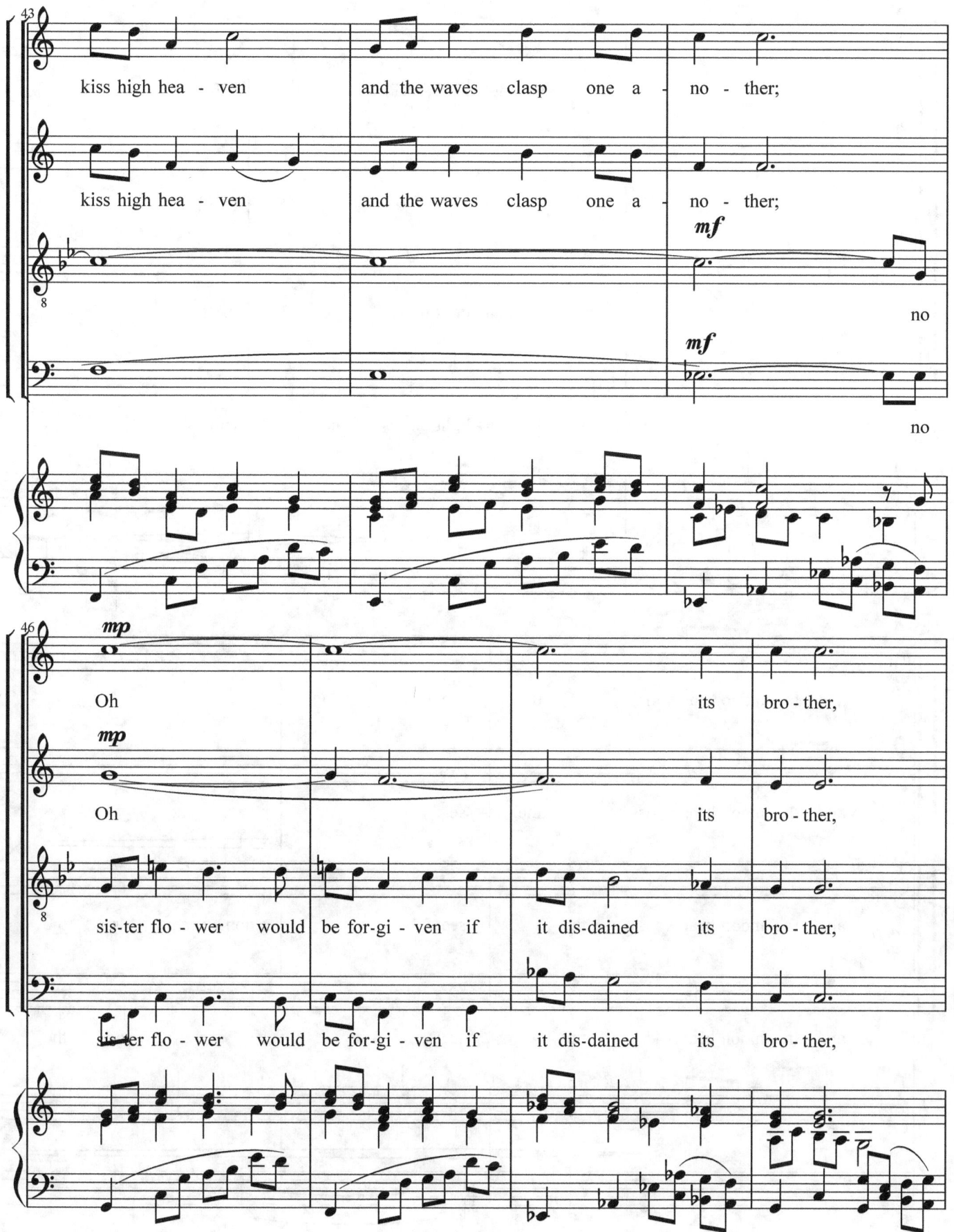

kiss high hea - ven and the waves clasp one a - no - ther;

kiss high hea - ven and the waves clasp one a - no - ther;

no

no

Oh its bro - ther,

Oh its bro - ther,

sis-ter flo - wer would be for-gi - ven if it dis-dained its bro - ther,

sis-ter flo - wer would be for-gi - ven if it dis-dained its bro - ther,

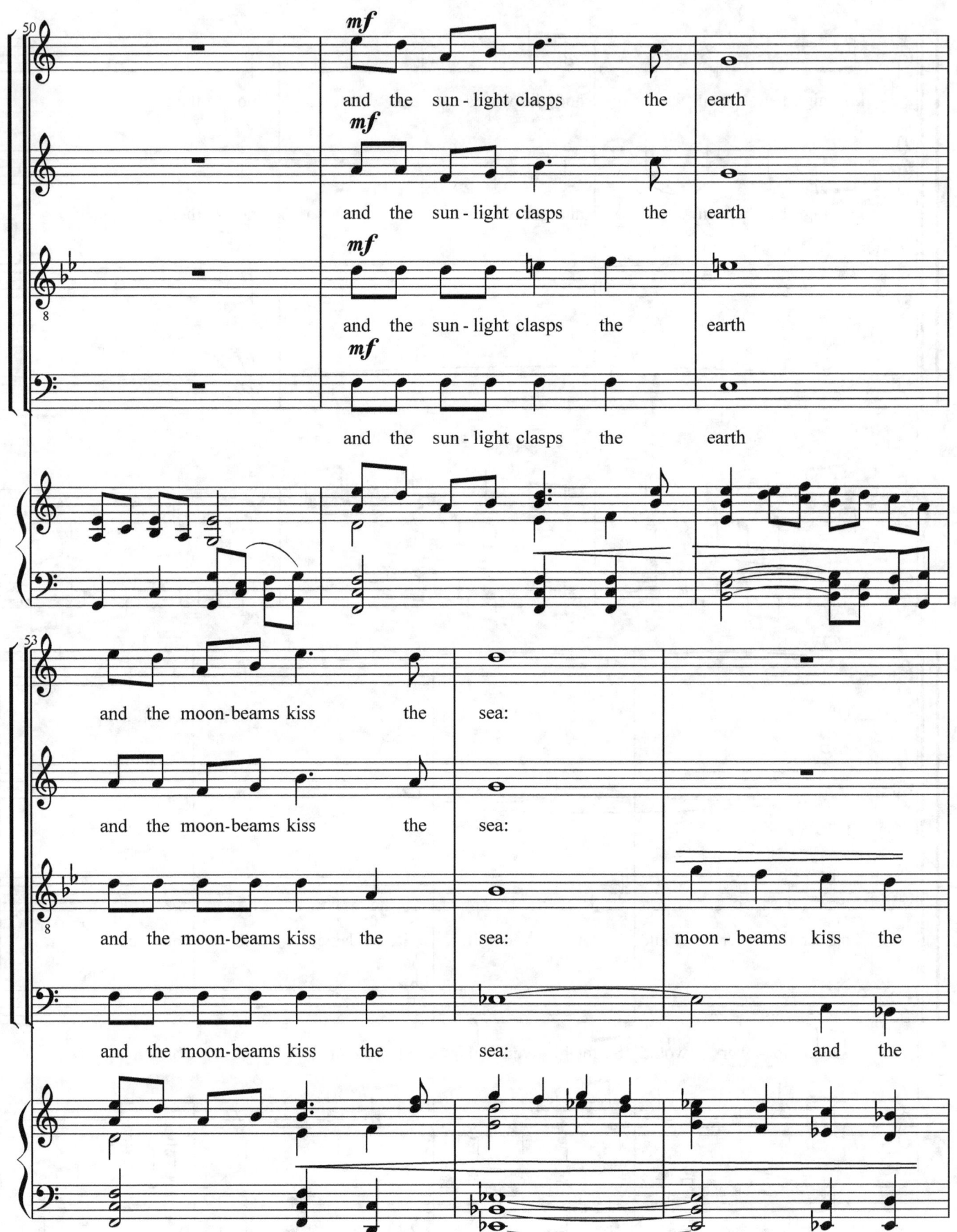

and the sun-light clasps the earth

and the sun-light clasps the earth

and the sun-light clasps the earth

and the sun-light clasps the earth

and the moon-beams kiss the sea:

and the moon-beams kiss the sea:

and the moon-beams kiss the sea: moon-beams kiss the

and the moon-beams kiss the sea: and the

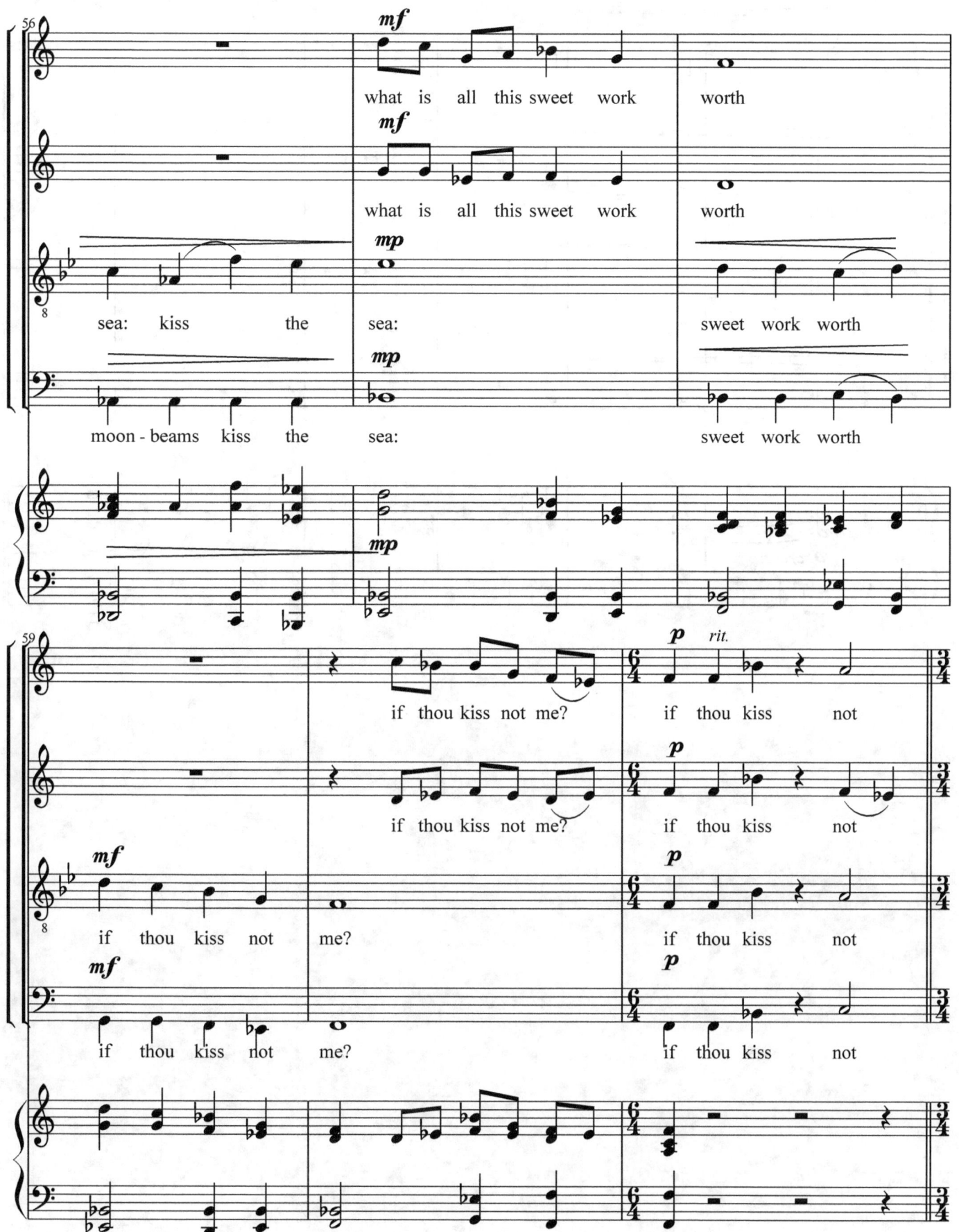

Slower

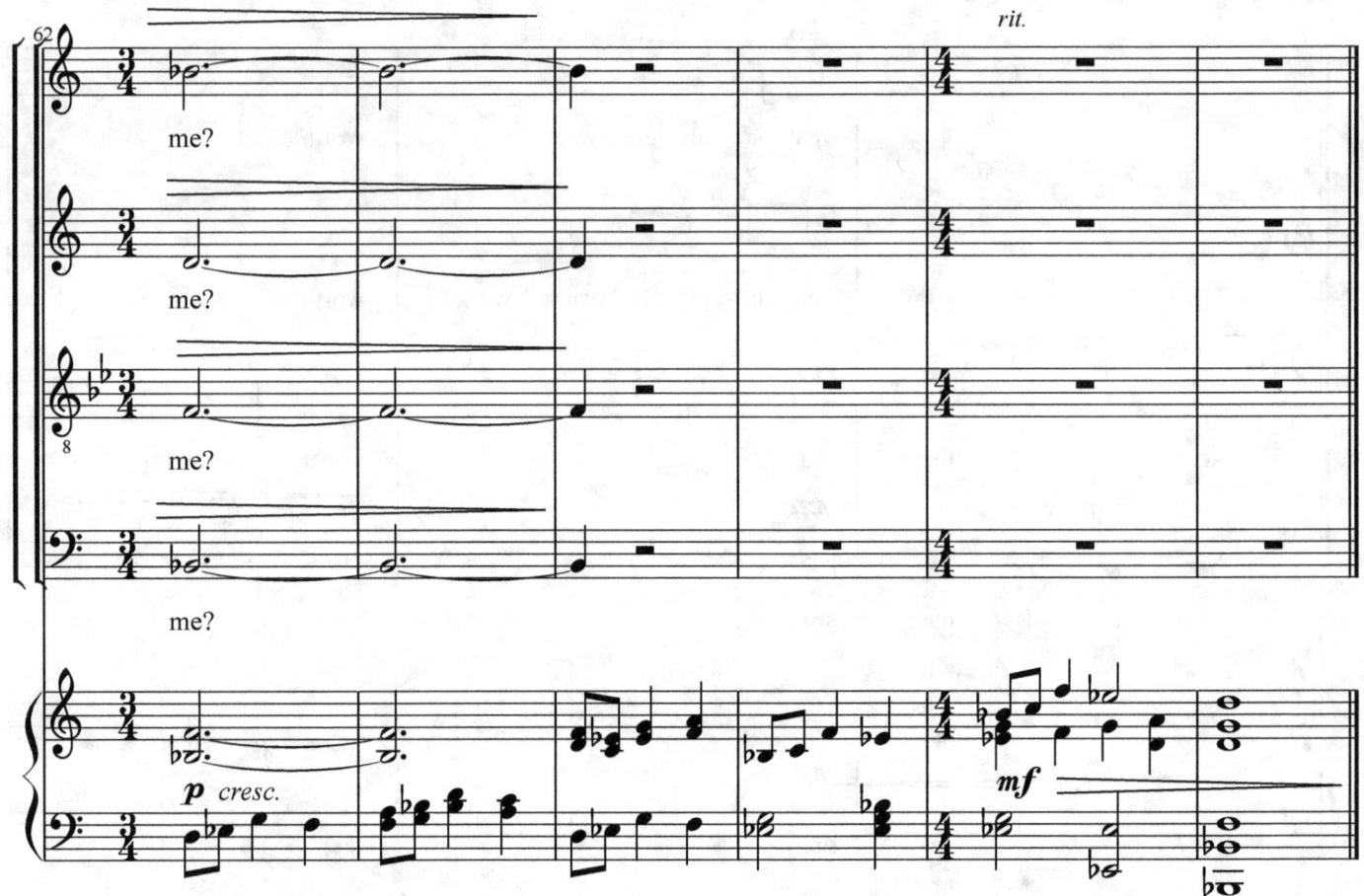

me?

me?

me?

me?

There Are Flowers

Ken Langer

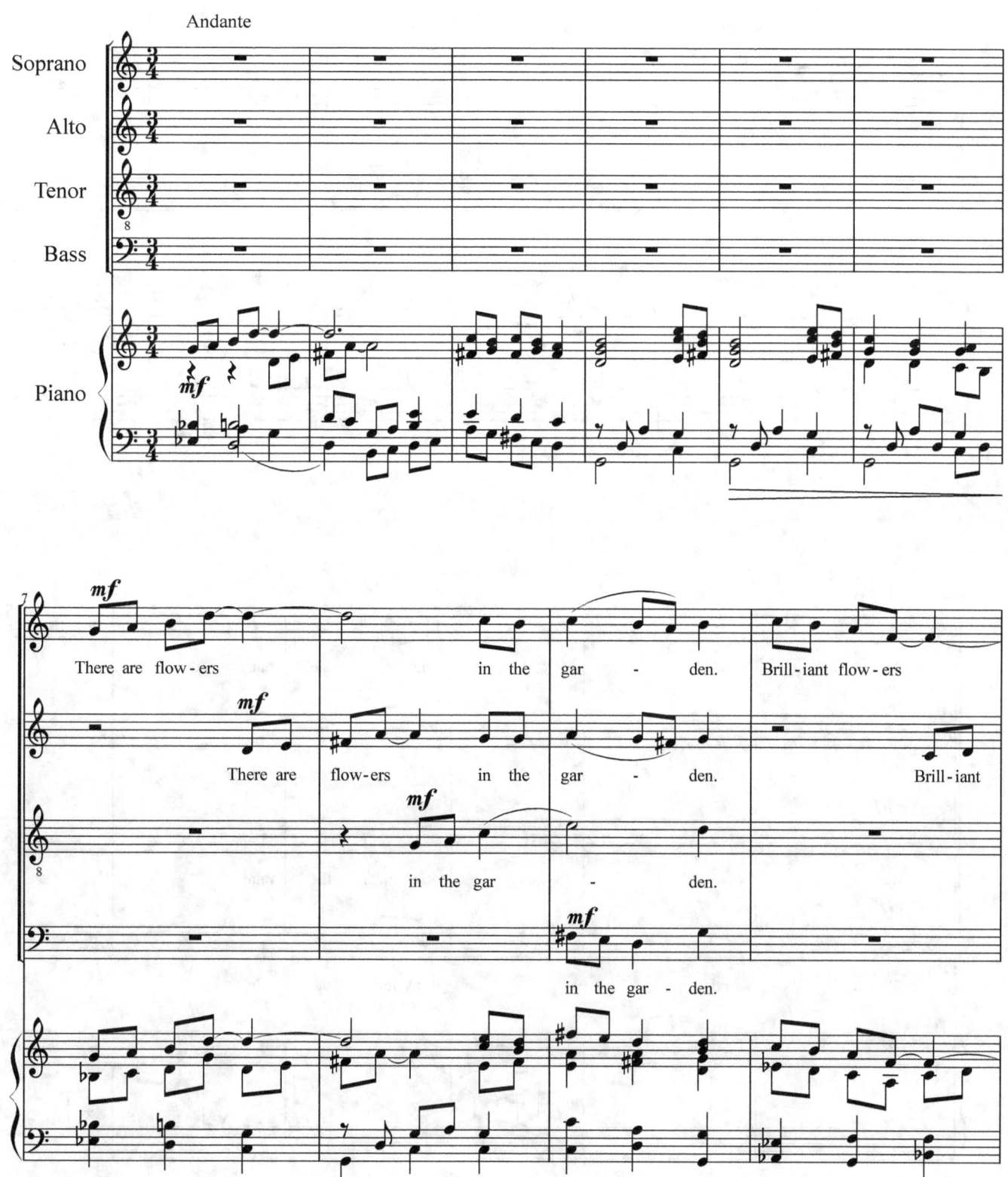

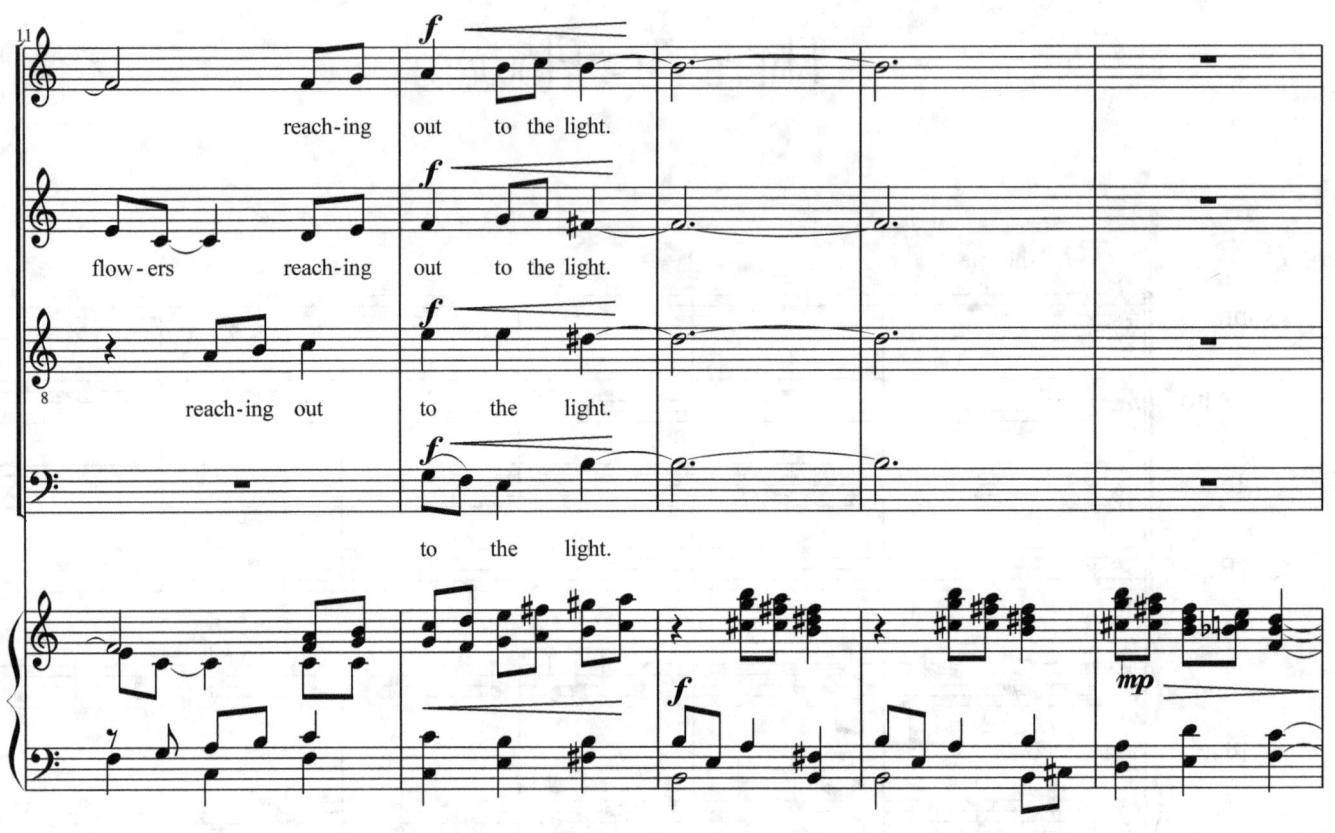

reach-ing out to the light.

flow - ers reach-ing out to the light.

reach-ing out to the light.

to the light.

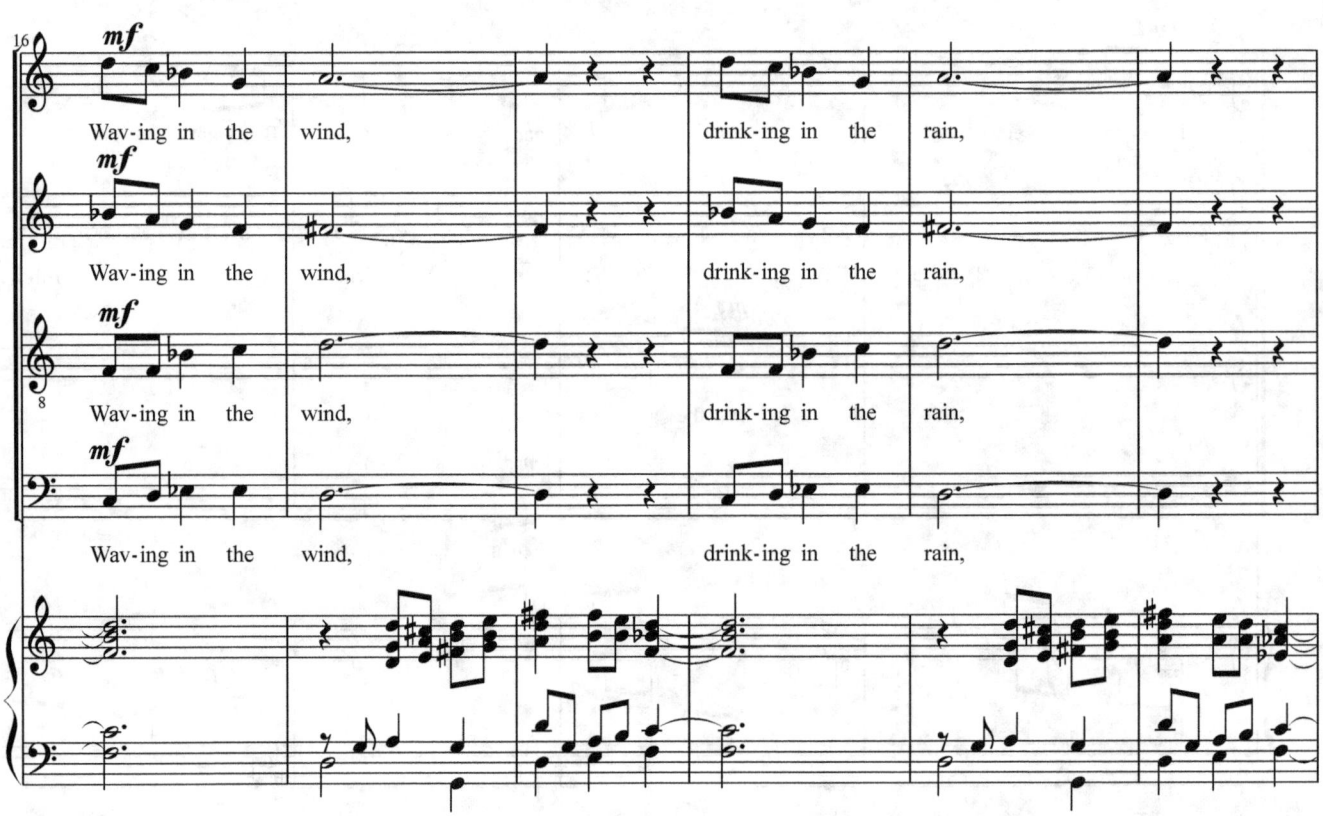

Wav-ing in the wind, drink-ing in the rain,

Wav-ing in the wind, drink-ing in the rain,

Wav-ing in the wind, drink-ing in the rain,

Wav-ing in the wind, drink-ing in the rain,

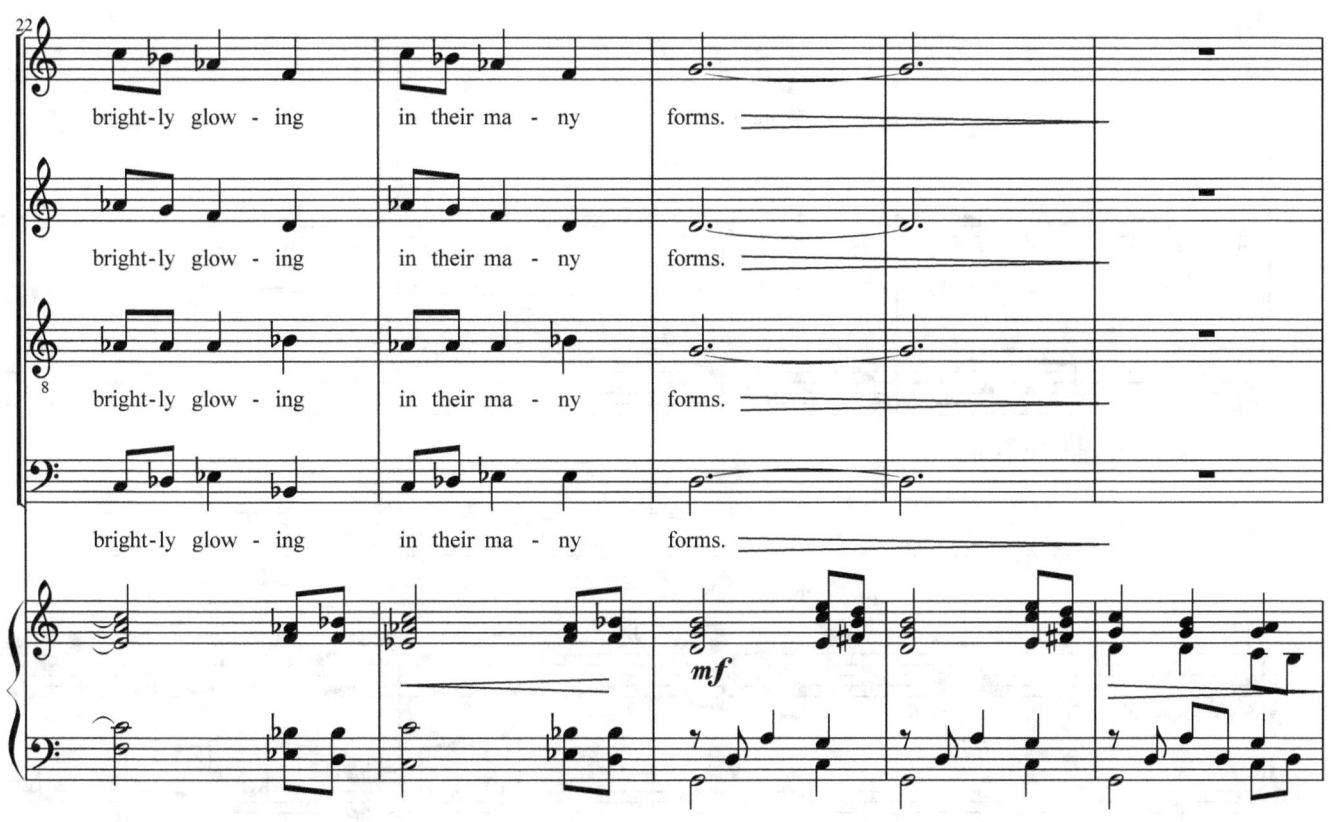

bright-ly glow - ing in their ma - ny forms.

bright-ly glow - ing in their ma - ny forms.

bright-ly glow - ing in their ma - ny forms.

bright-ly glow - ing in their ma - ny forms.

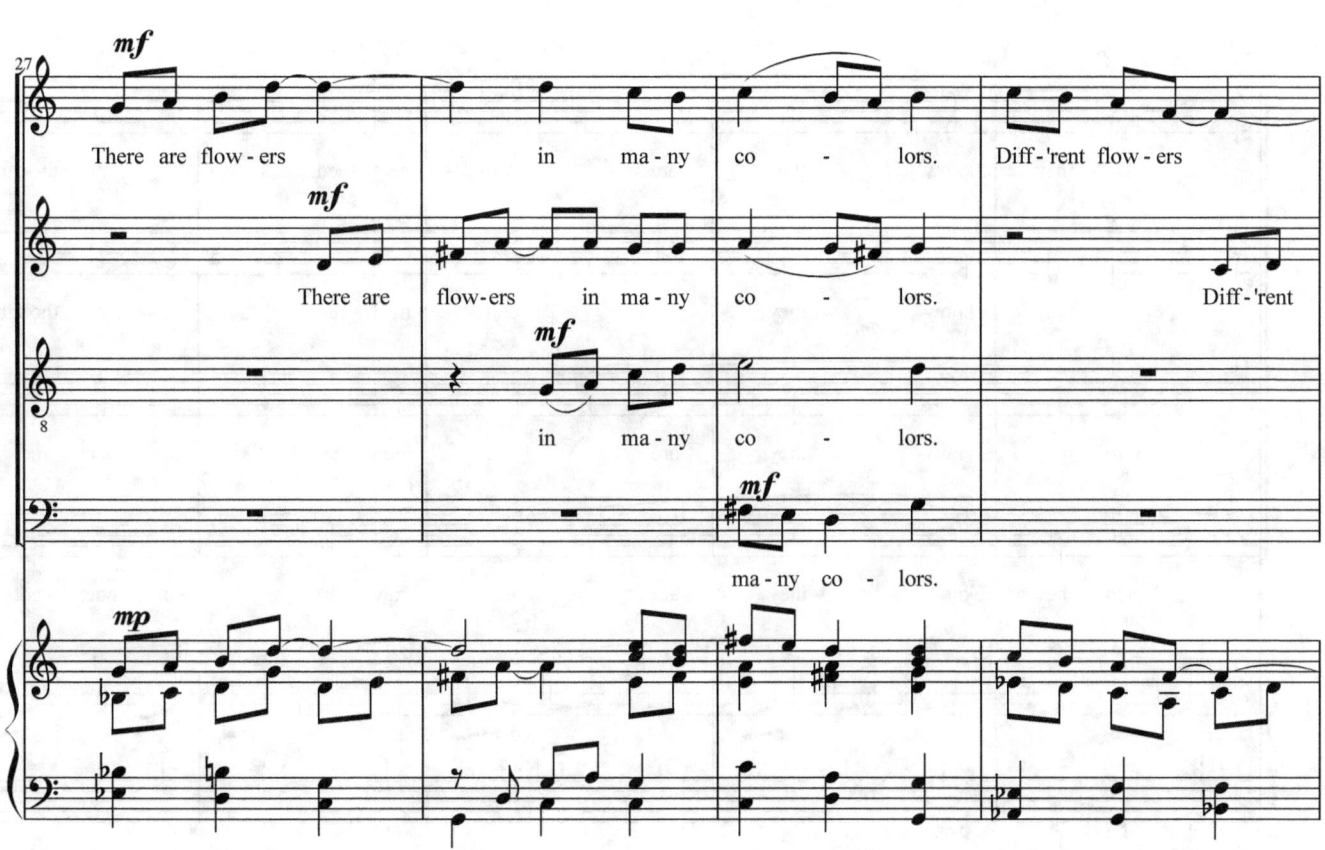

There are flow-ers in ma-ny co - lors. Diff-'rent flow-ers

There are flow-ers in ma-ny co - lors. Diff-'rent

in ma-ny co - lors.

ma-ny co - lors.

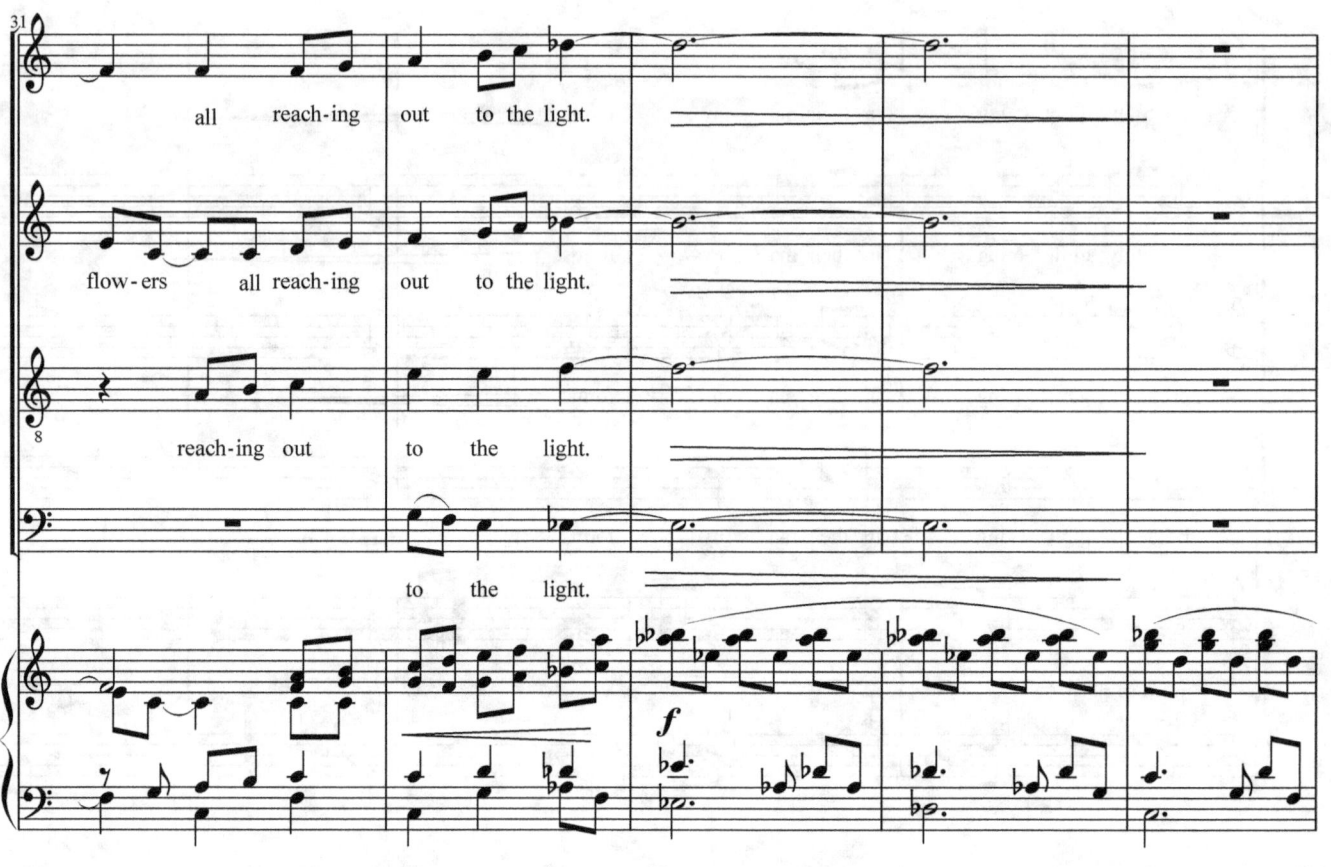

all reach-ing out to the light.

flow-ers all reach-ing out to the light.

reach-ing out to the light.

to the light.

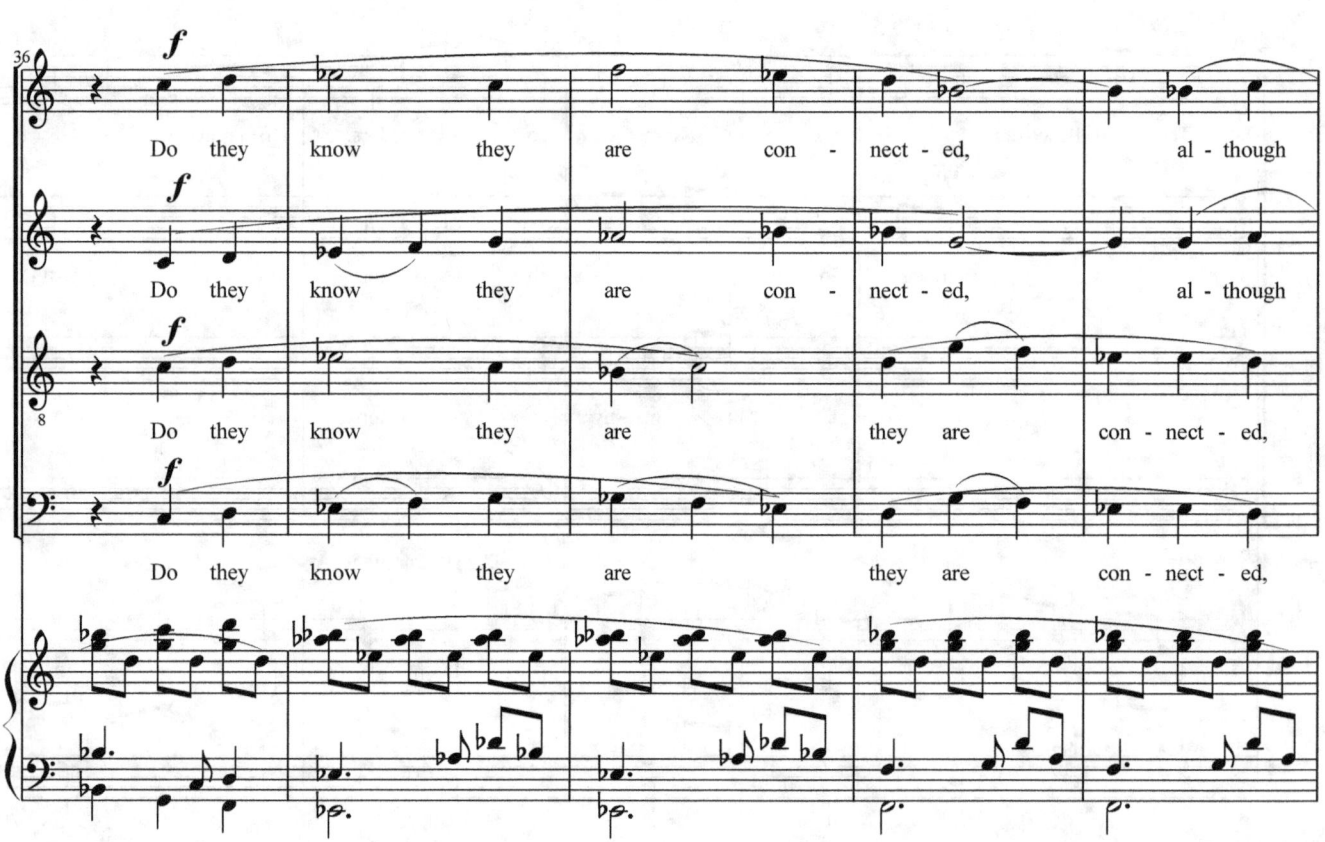

Do they know they are con - nect-ed, al - though

Do they know they are con - nect - ed, al - though

Do they know they are they are con - nect - ed,

Do they know they are they are con - nect - ed,

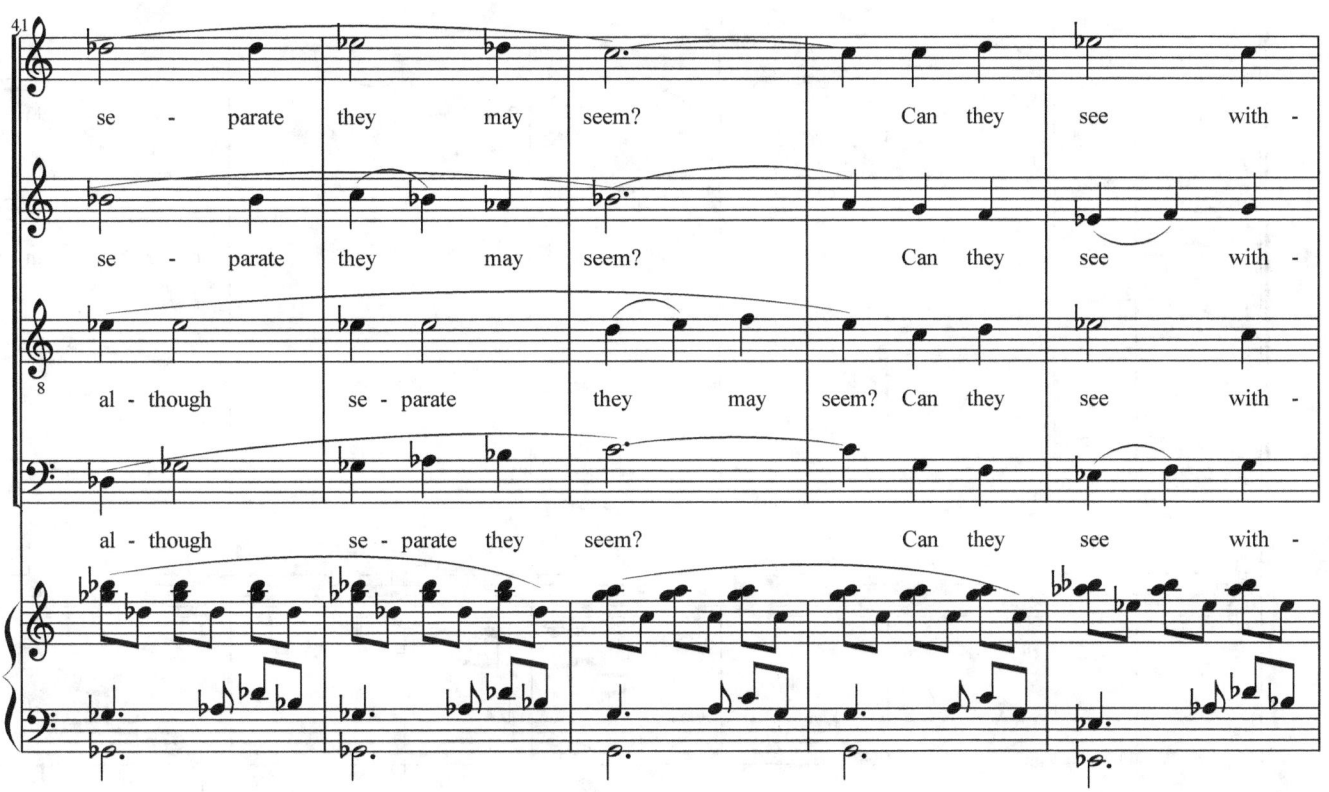

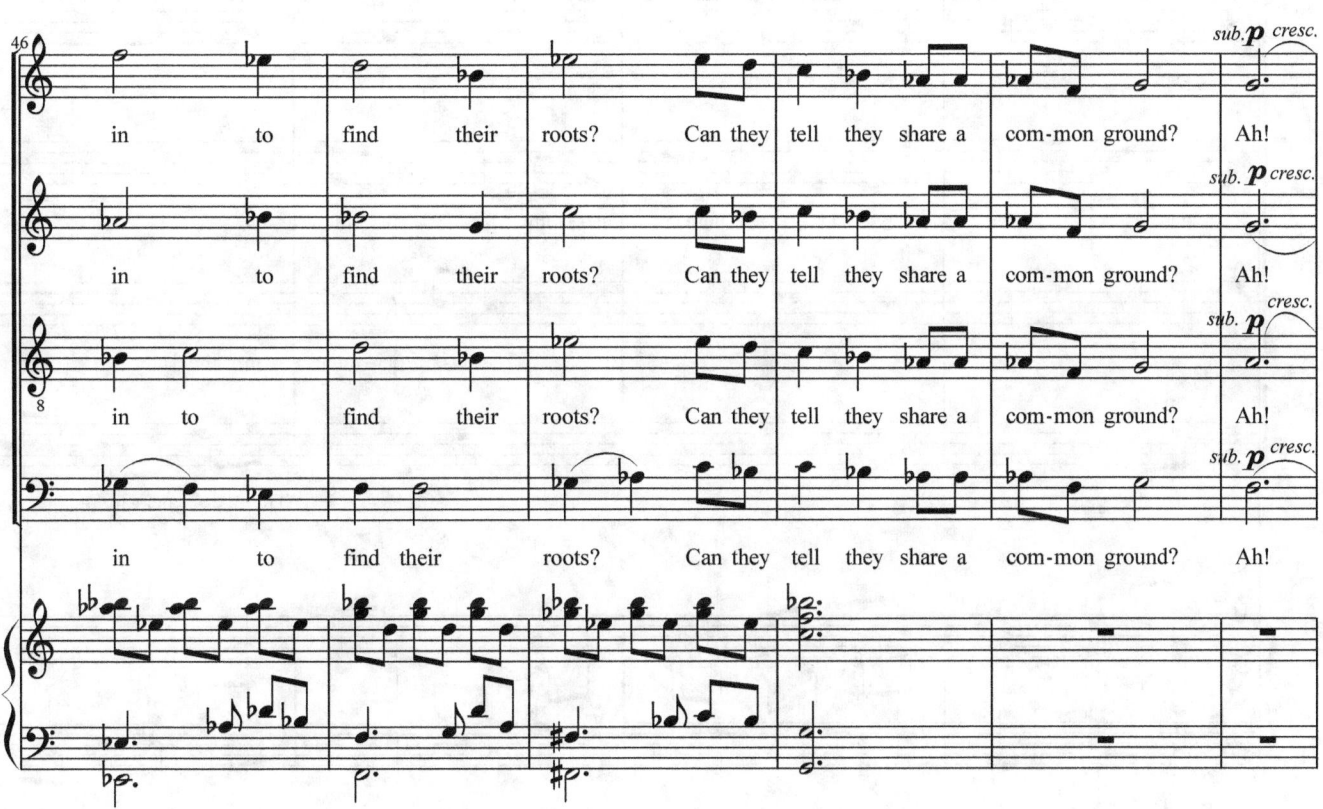

99

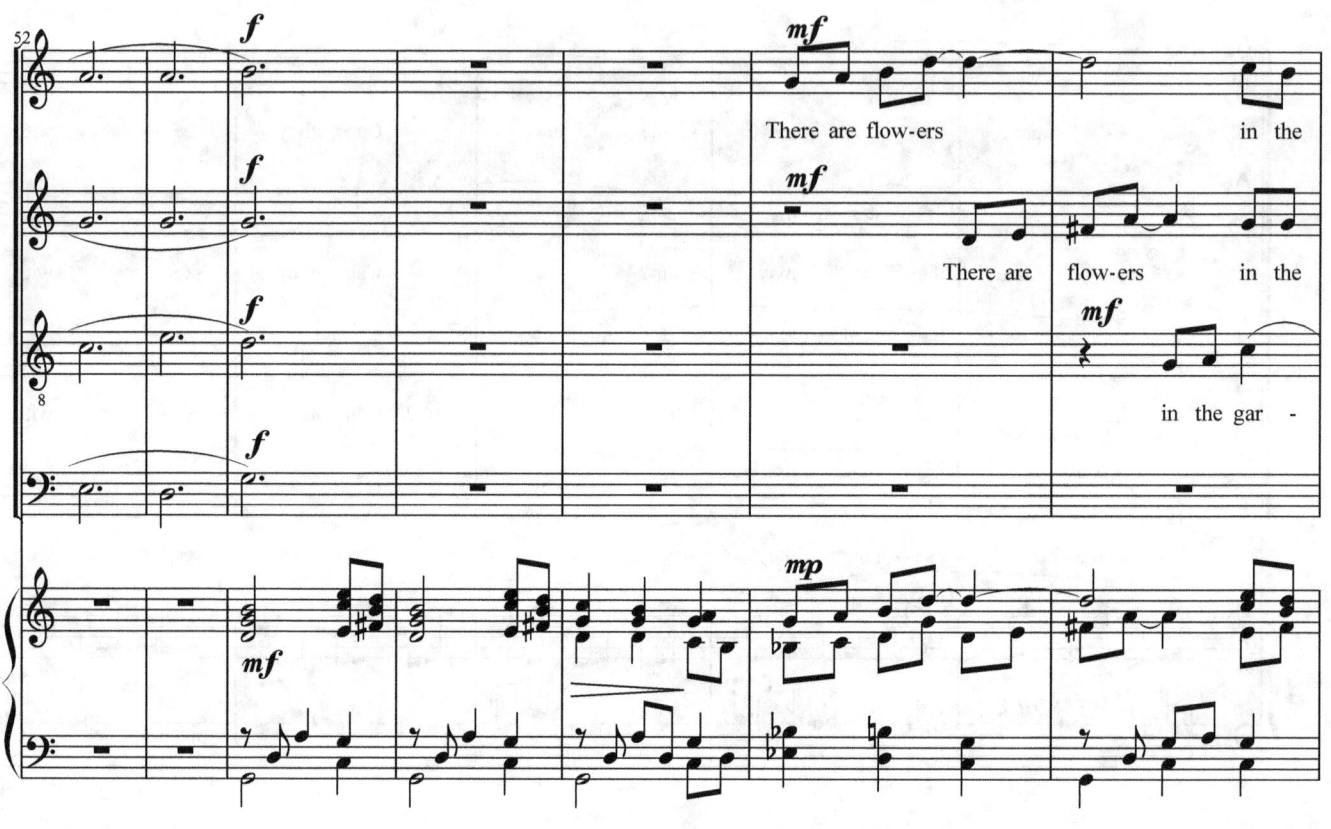

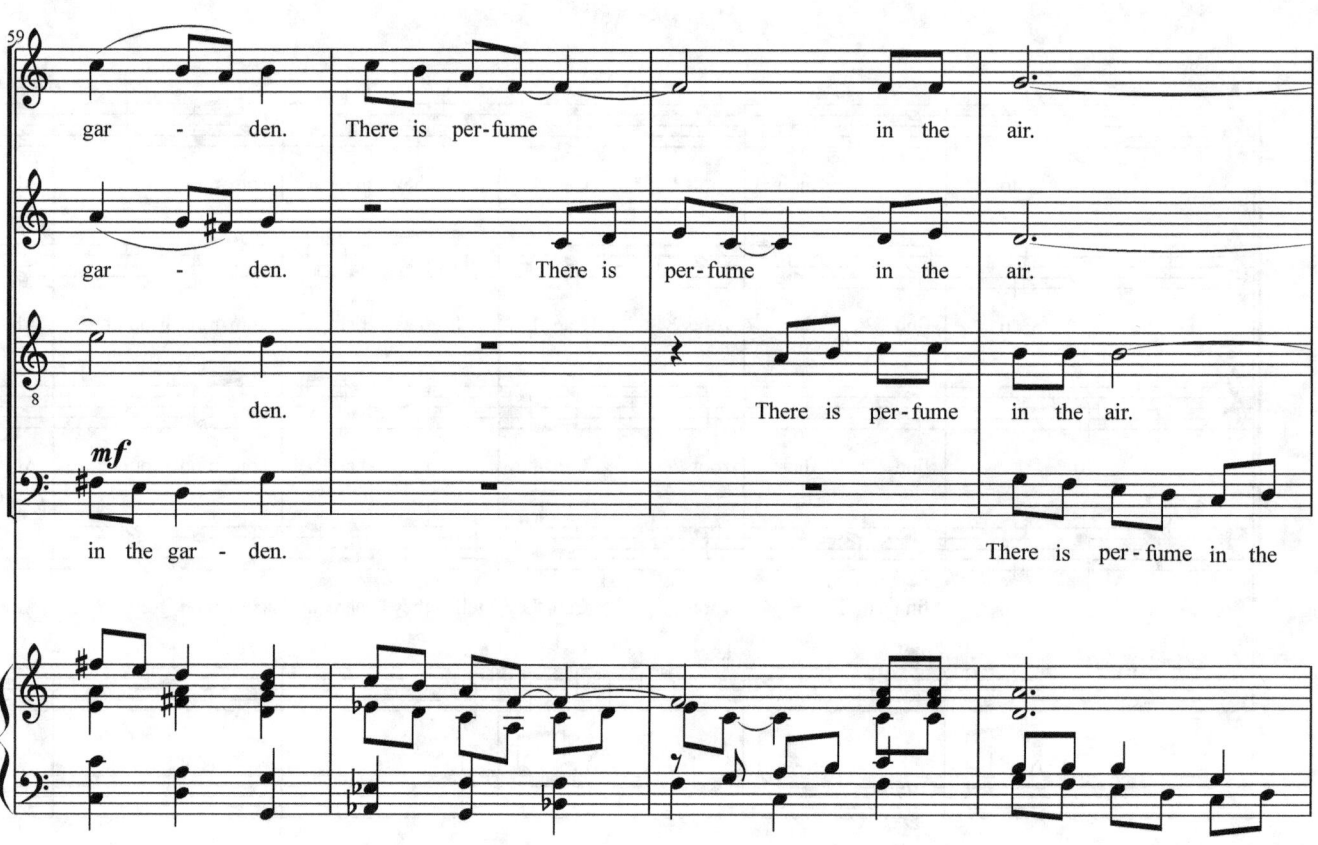

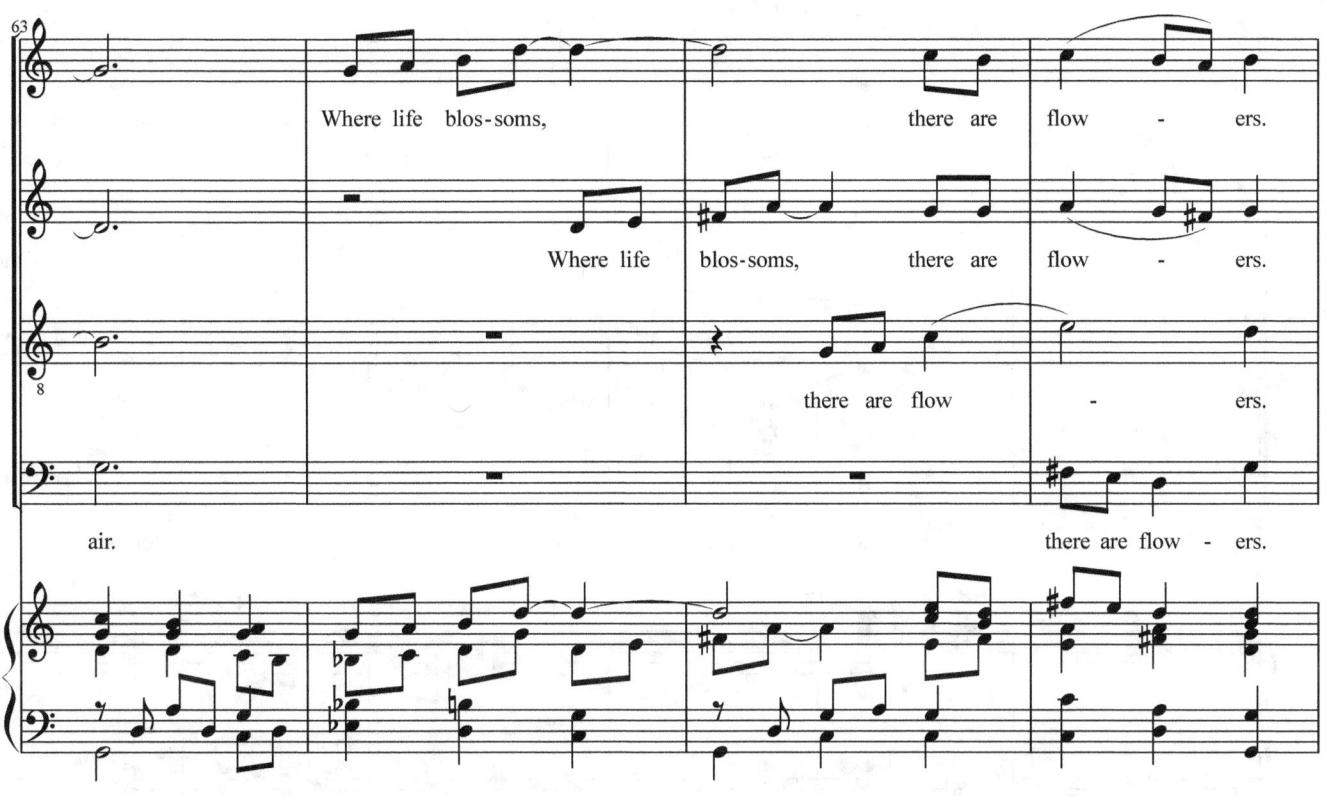

Where life blos-soms, there are flow - ers.

Where life blos-soms, there are flow - ers.

there are flow - ers.

air. there are flow - ers.

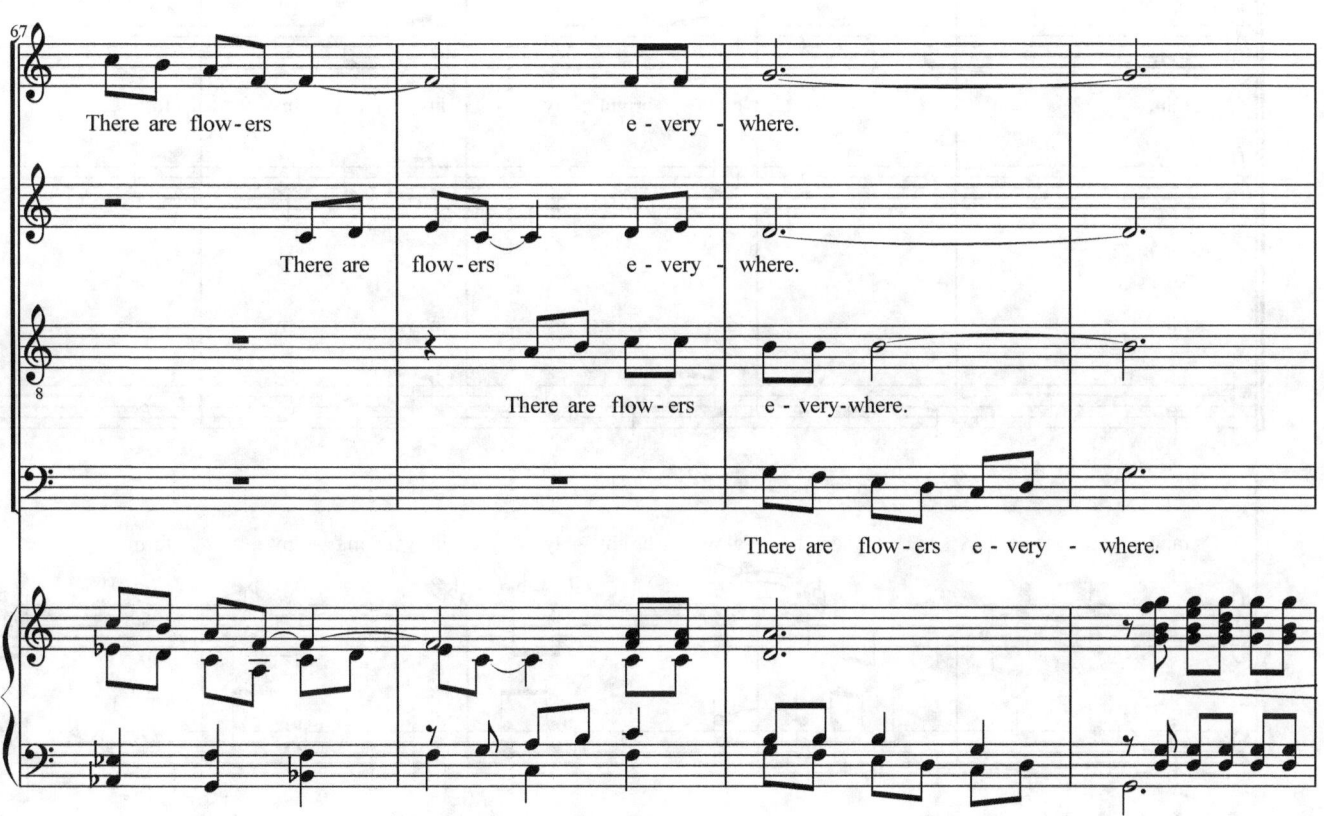

There are flow-ers e - very - where.

There are flow-ers e - very - where.

There are flow-ers e - very-where.

There are flow-ers e - very - where.

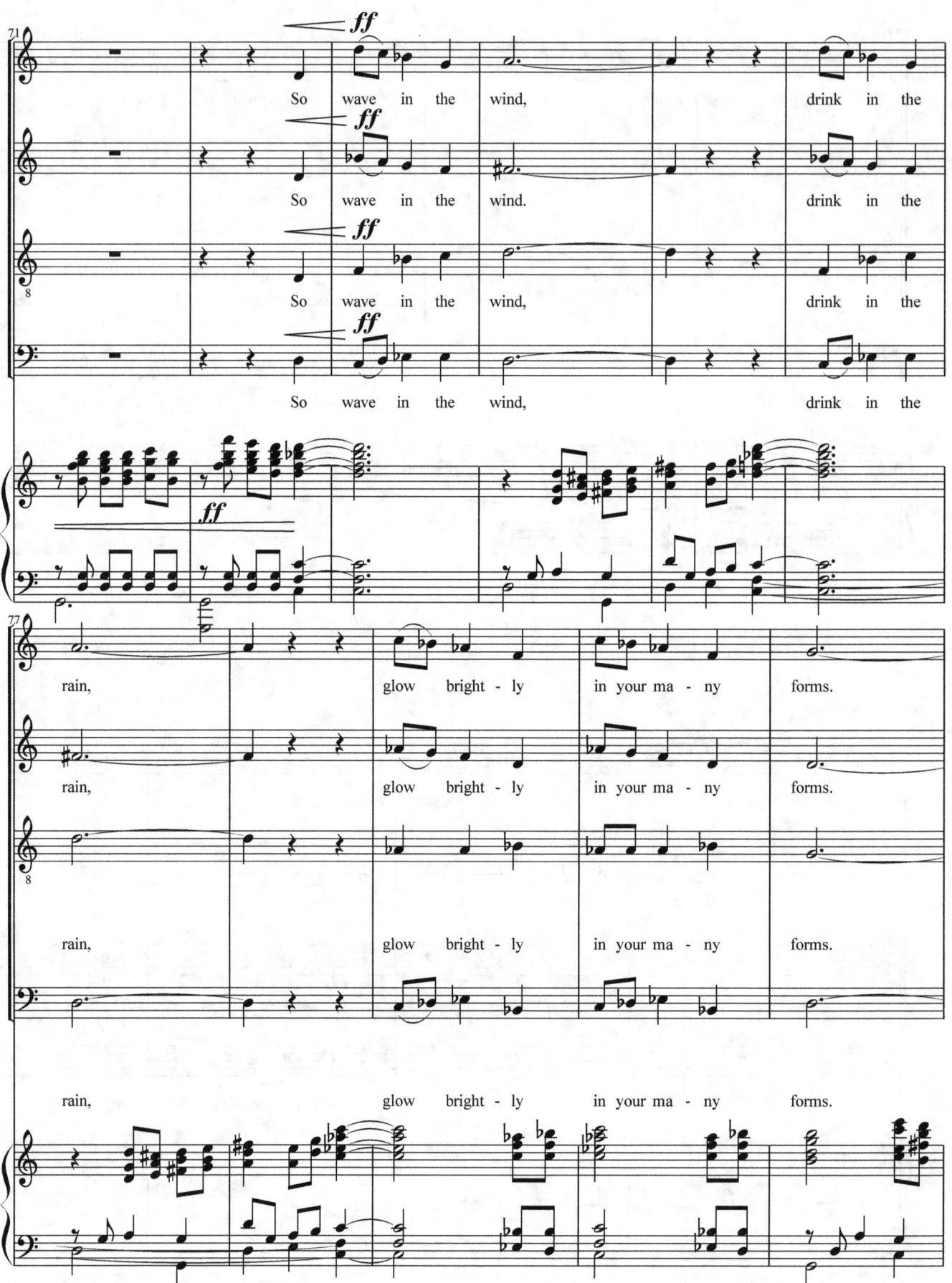

So wave in the wind, drink in the

So wave in the wind. drink in the

So wave in the wind, drink in the

So wave in the wind, drink in the

rain, glow bright - ly in your ma - ny forms.

rain, glow bright - ly in your ma - ny forms.

rain, glow bright - ly in your ma - ny forms.

rain, glow bright - ly in your ma - ny forms.

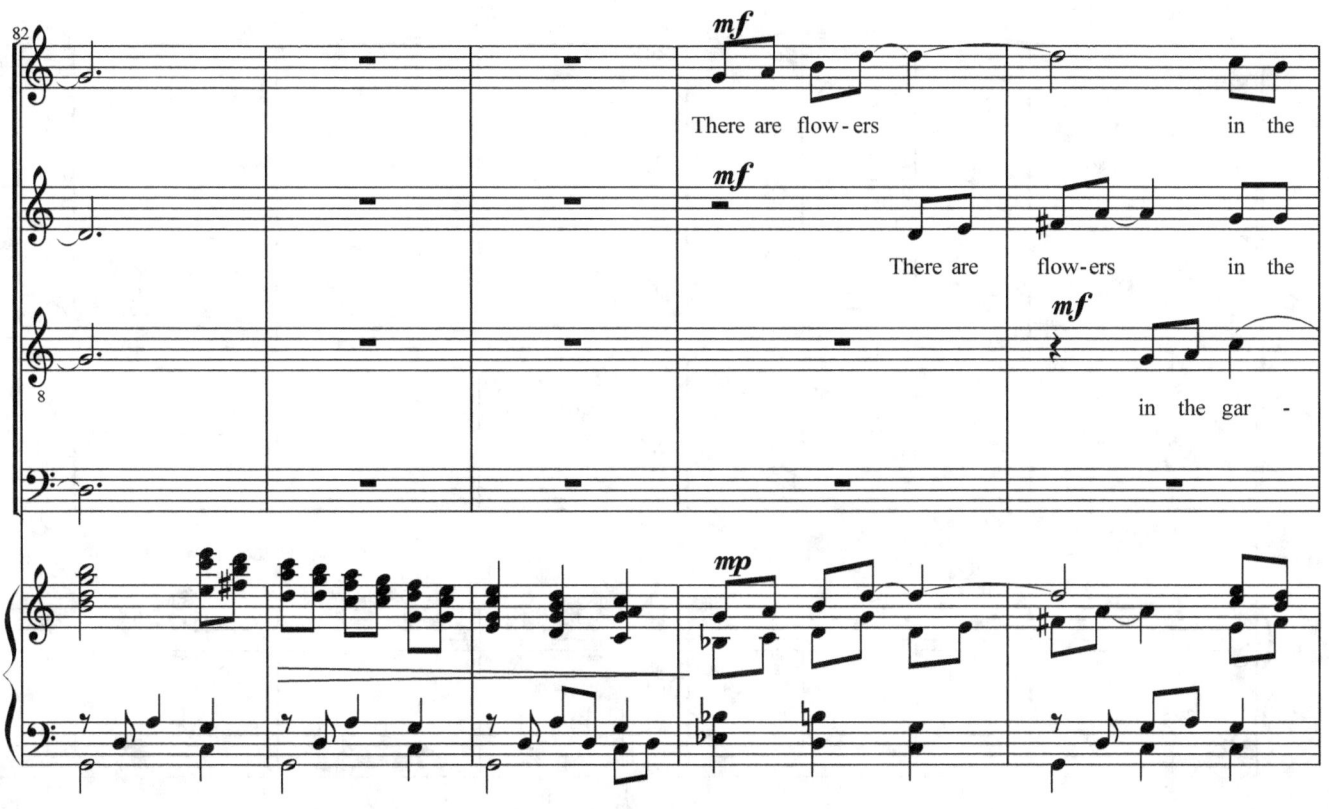

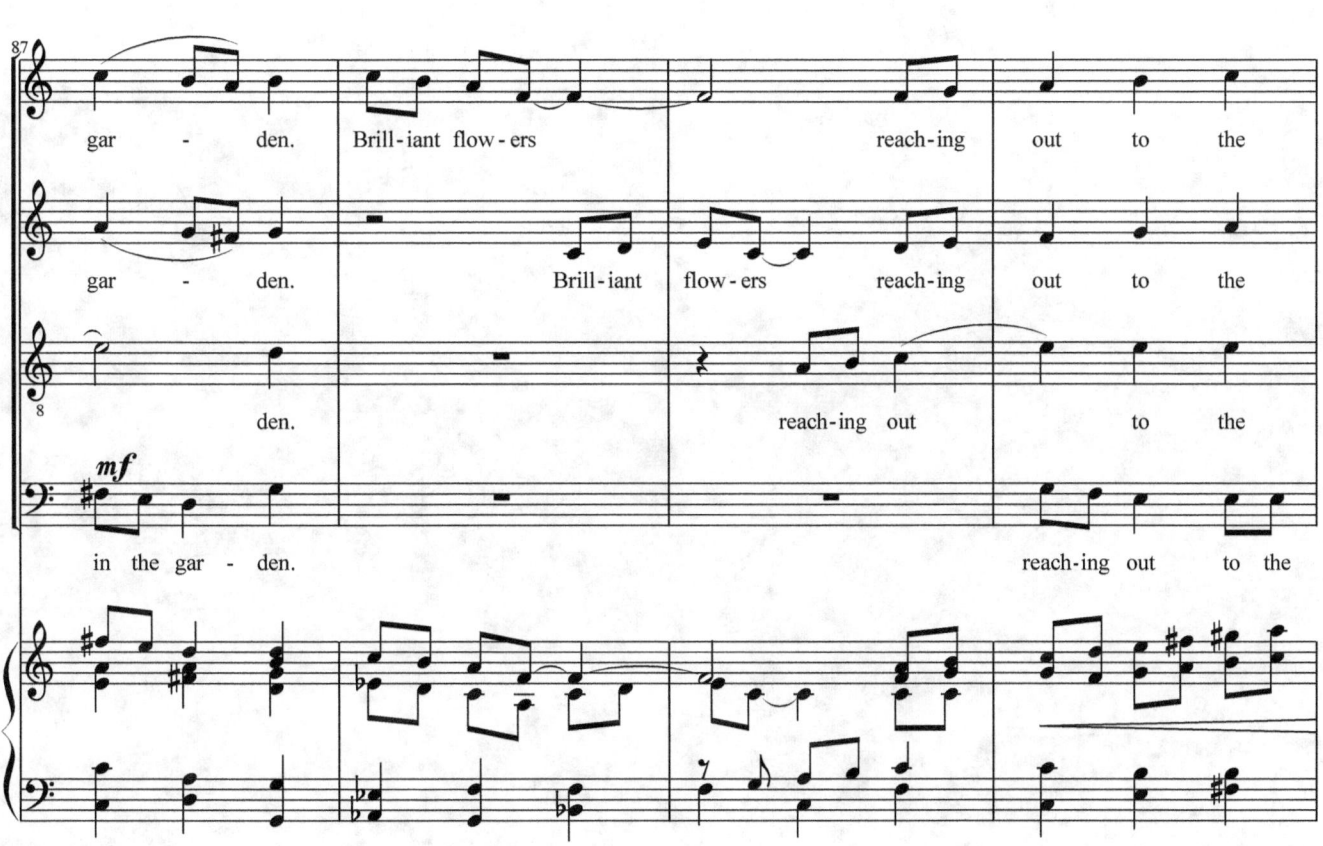

103

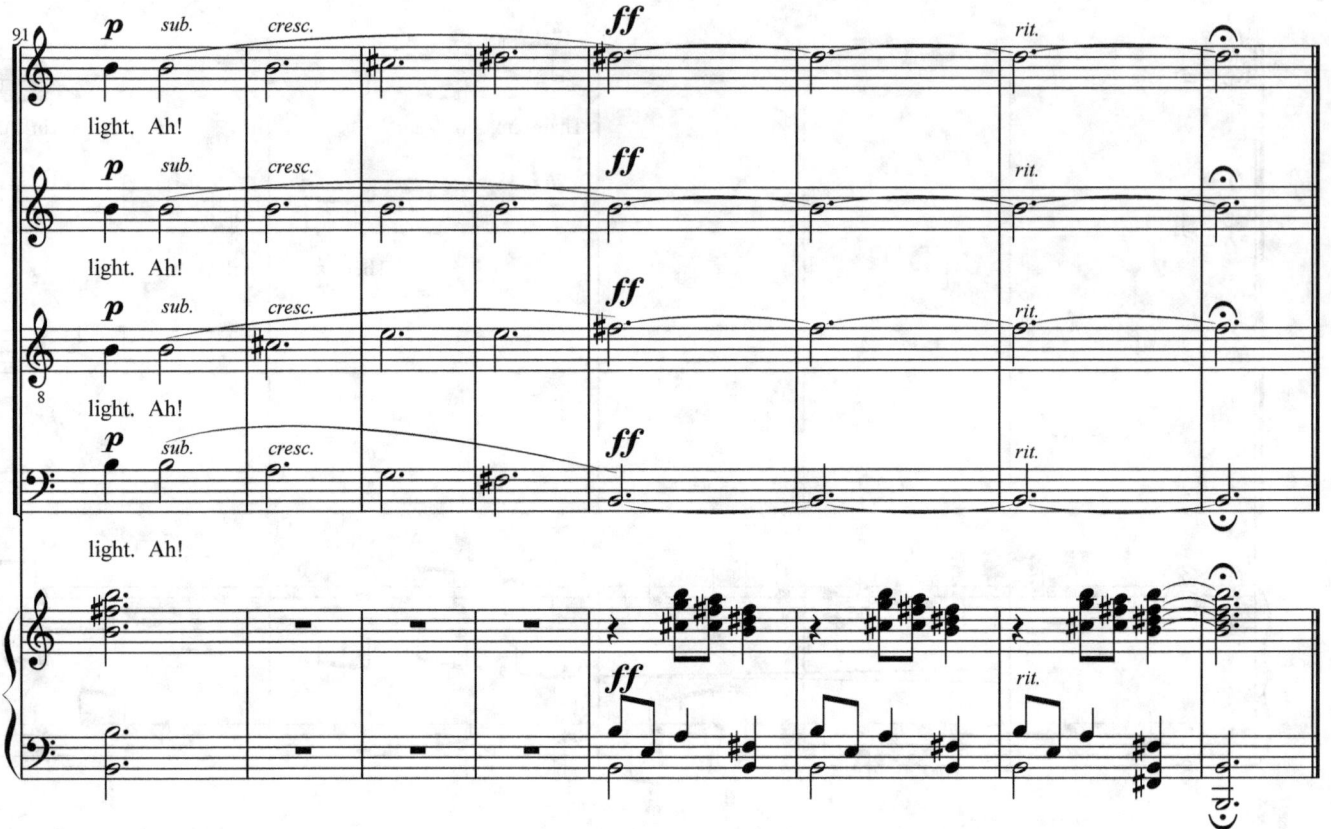

light. Ah!

light. Ah!

light. Ah!

light. Ah!

Vocalise

Ken Langer

For the Whitestone Choir. Emerson Eads, Director

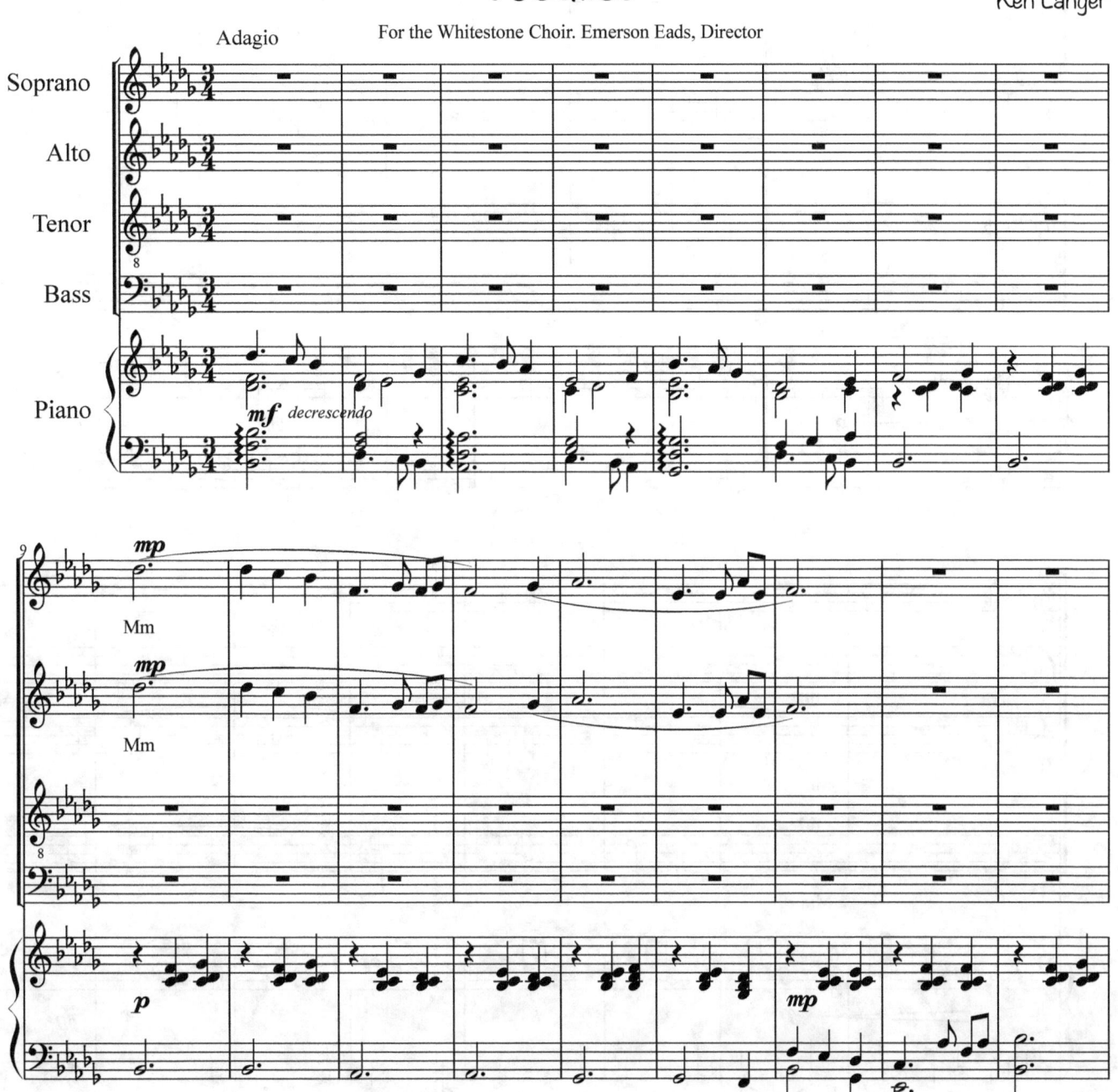

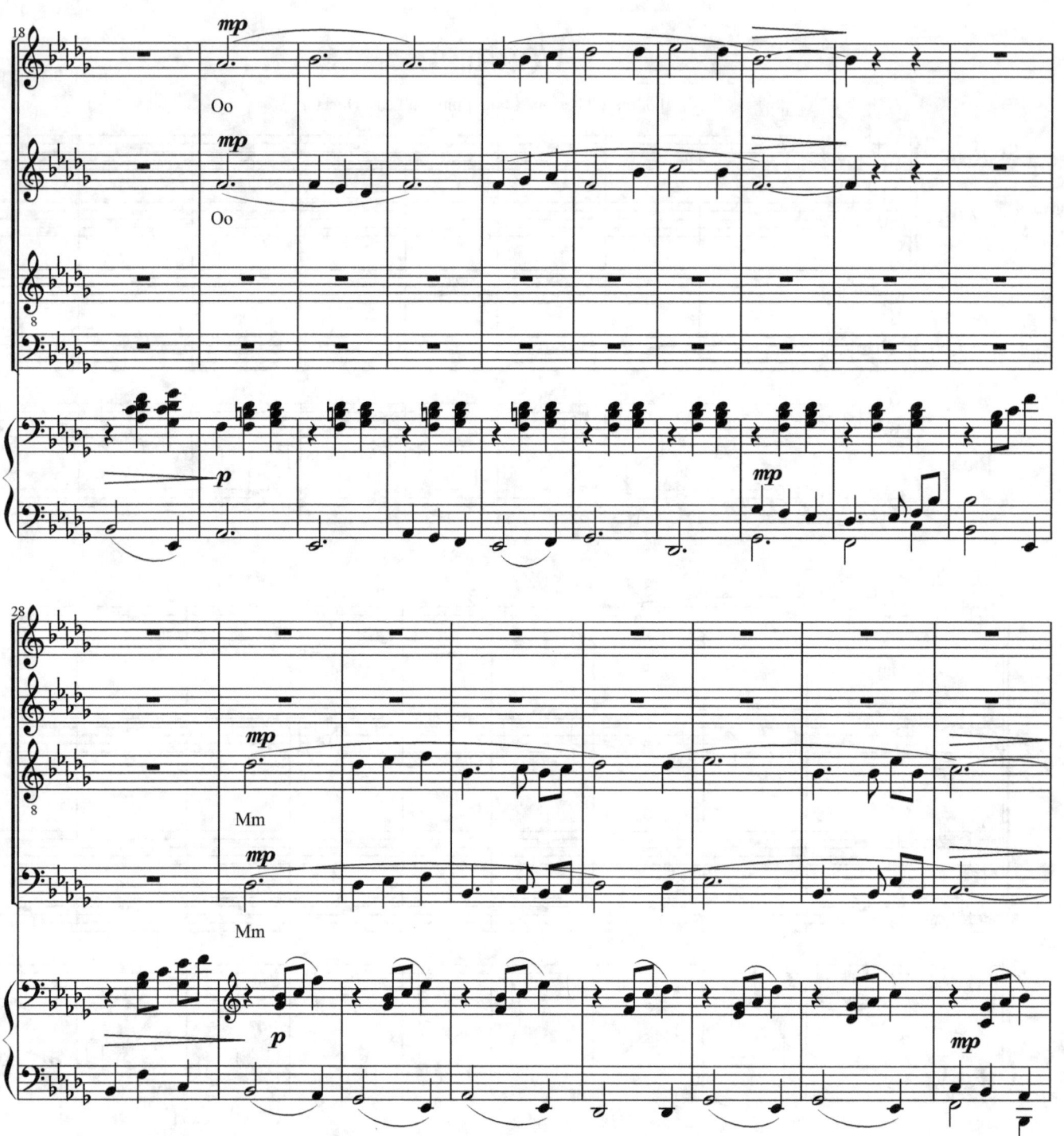

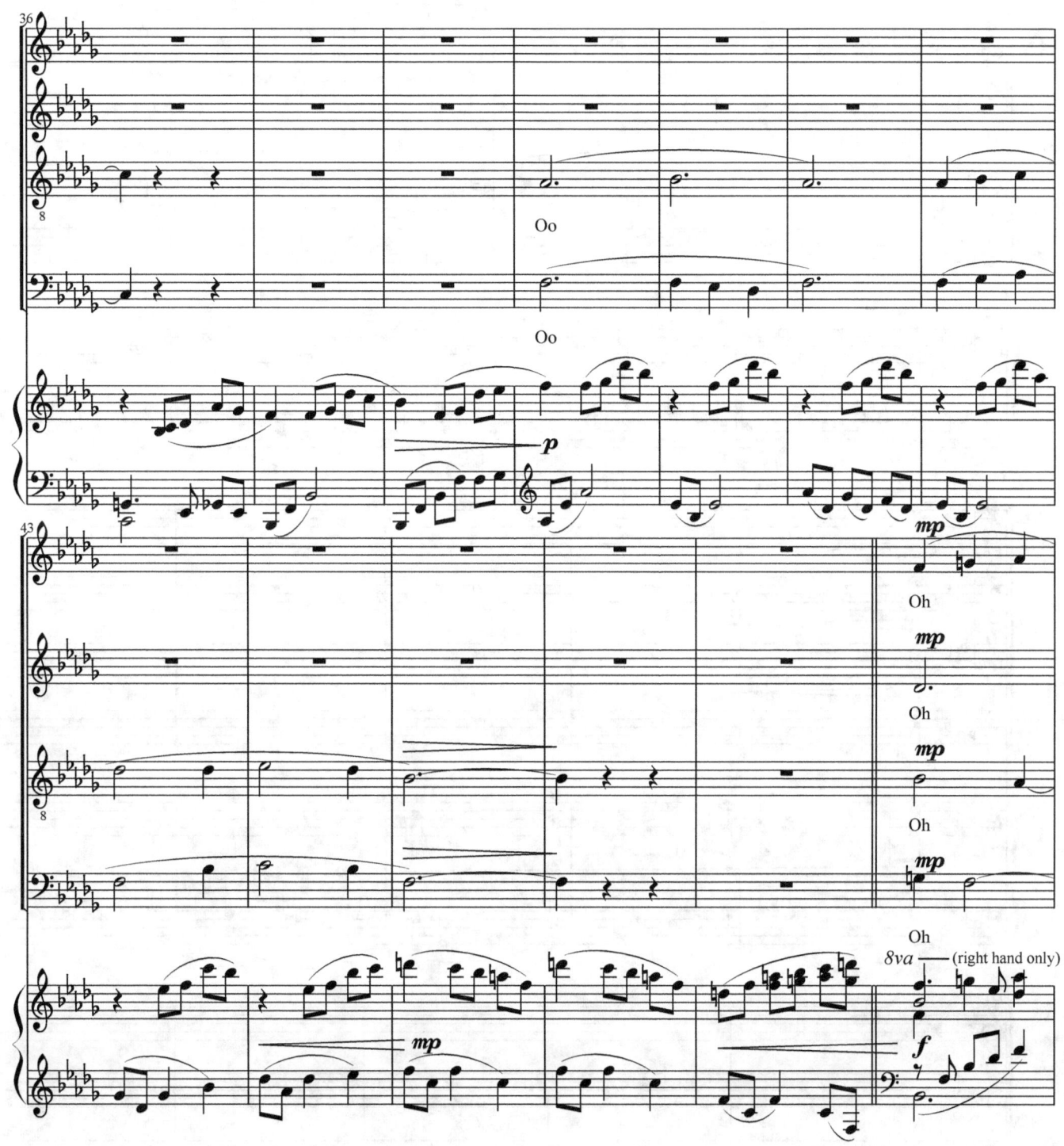

Oo

Oo

Oh

Oh

Oh

Oh

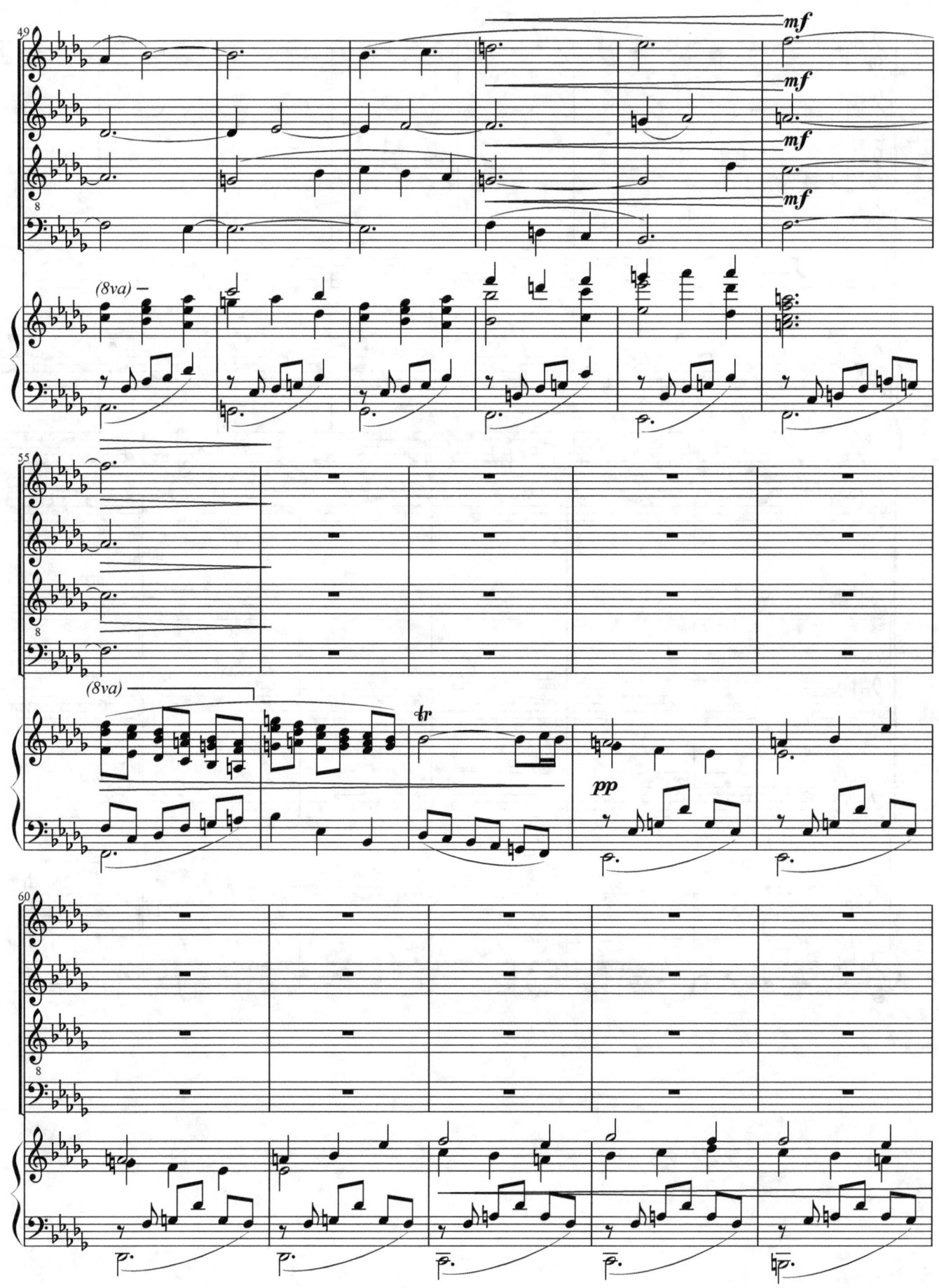

108

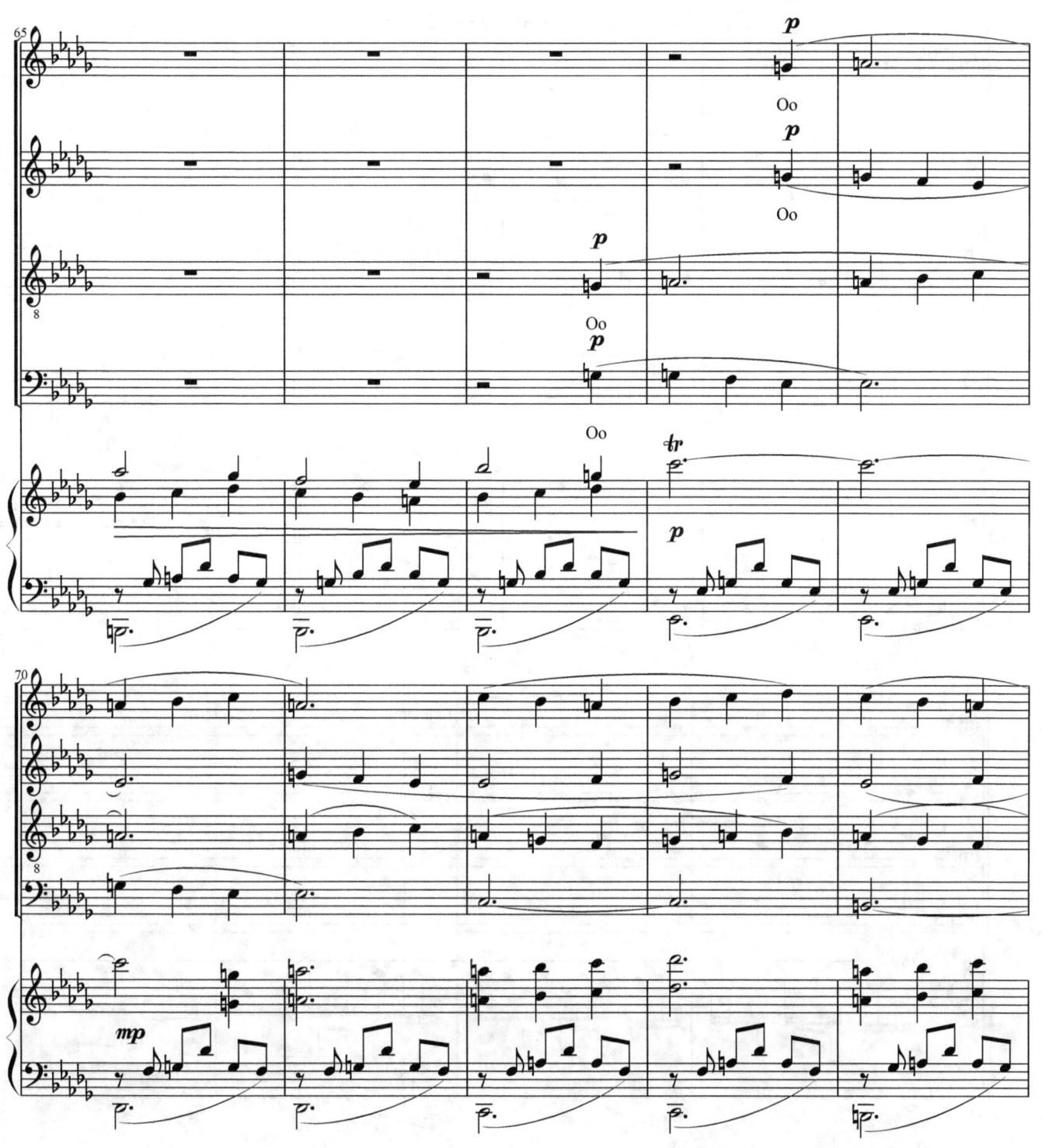

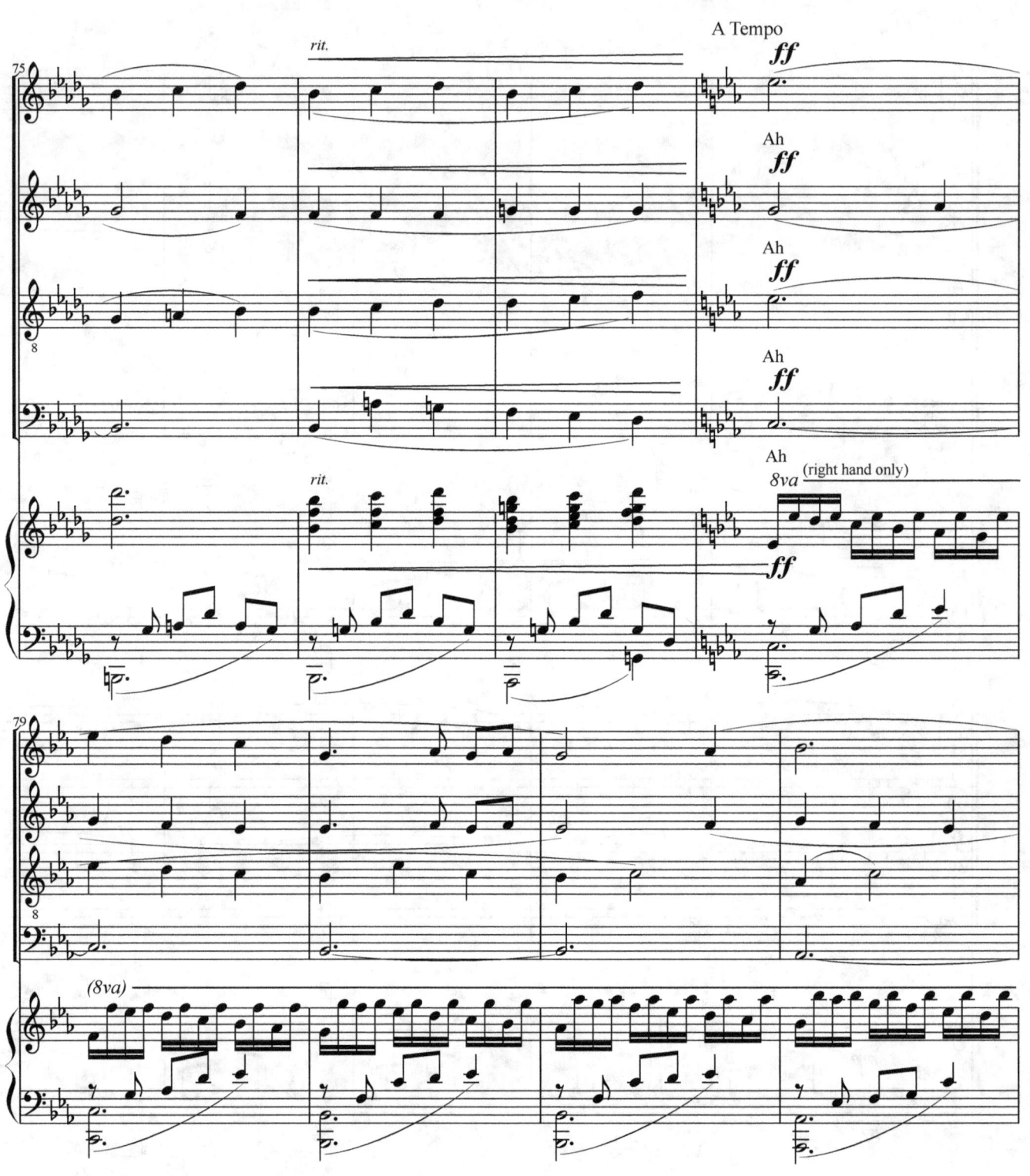

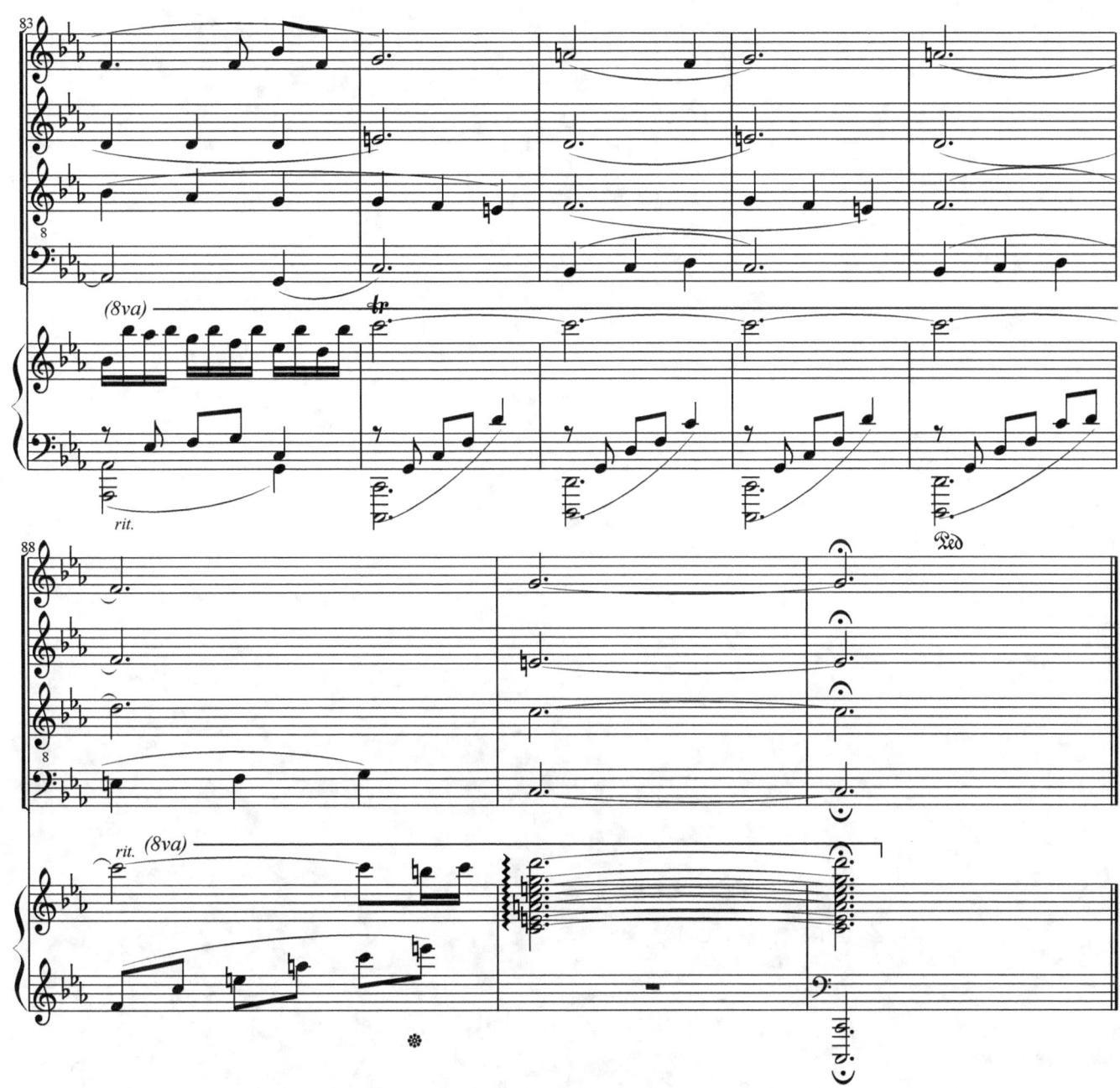

111

Waters of the World

Ken Langer

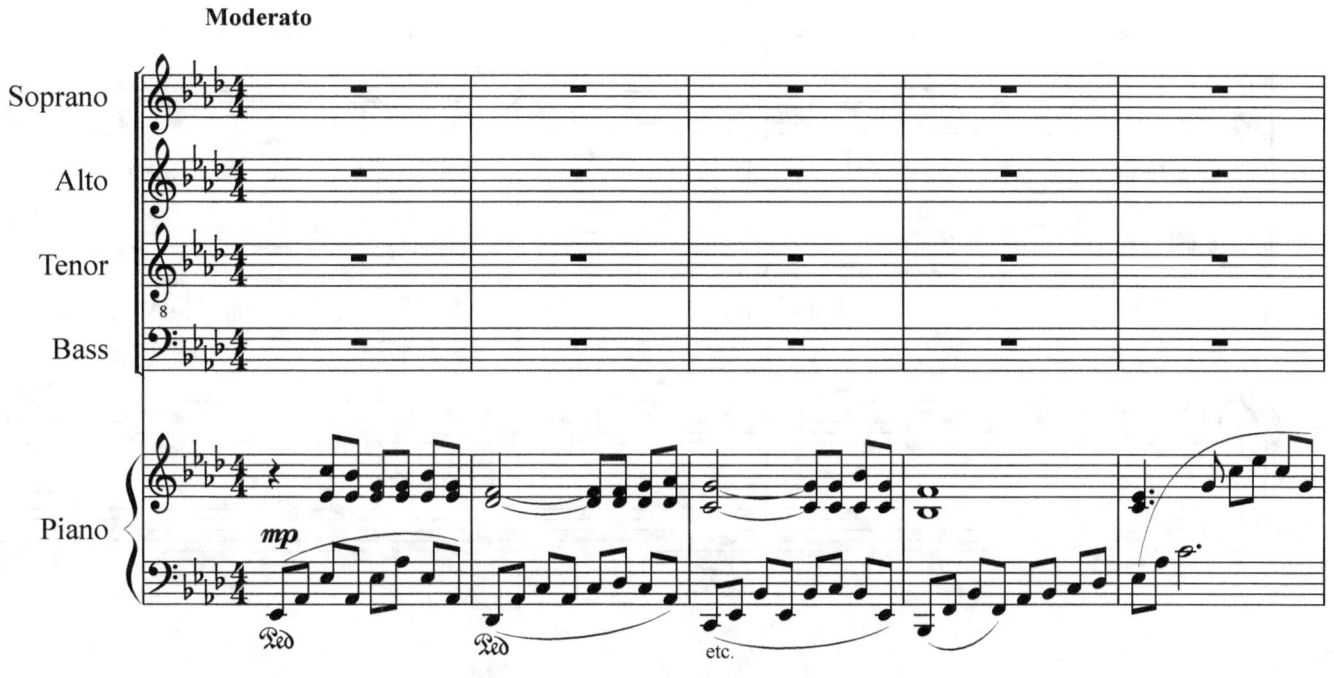

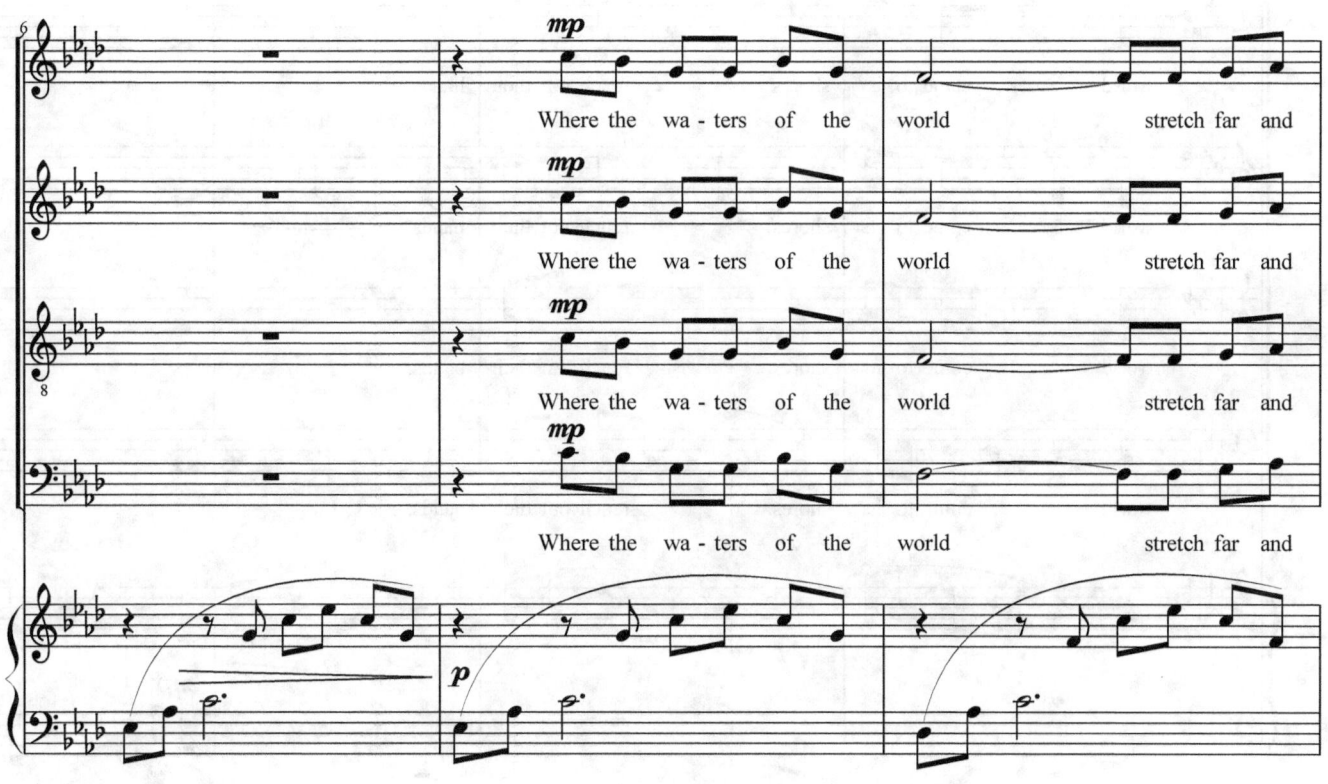

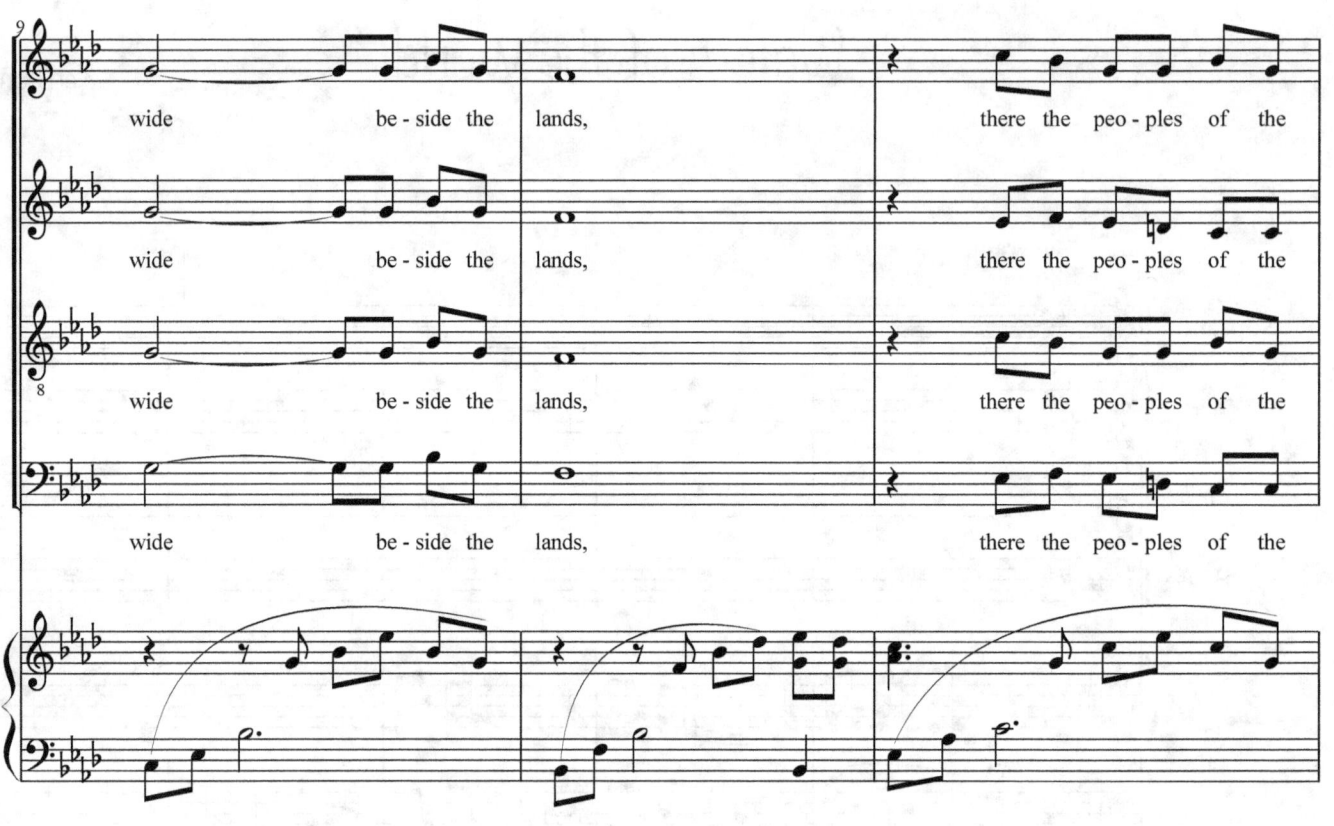

wide   be - side the   lands,   there the peo - ples of the

wide   be - side the   lands,   there the peo - ples of the

wide   be - side the   lands,   there the peo - ples of the

wide   be - side the   lands,   there the peo - ples of the

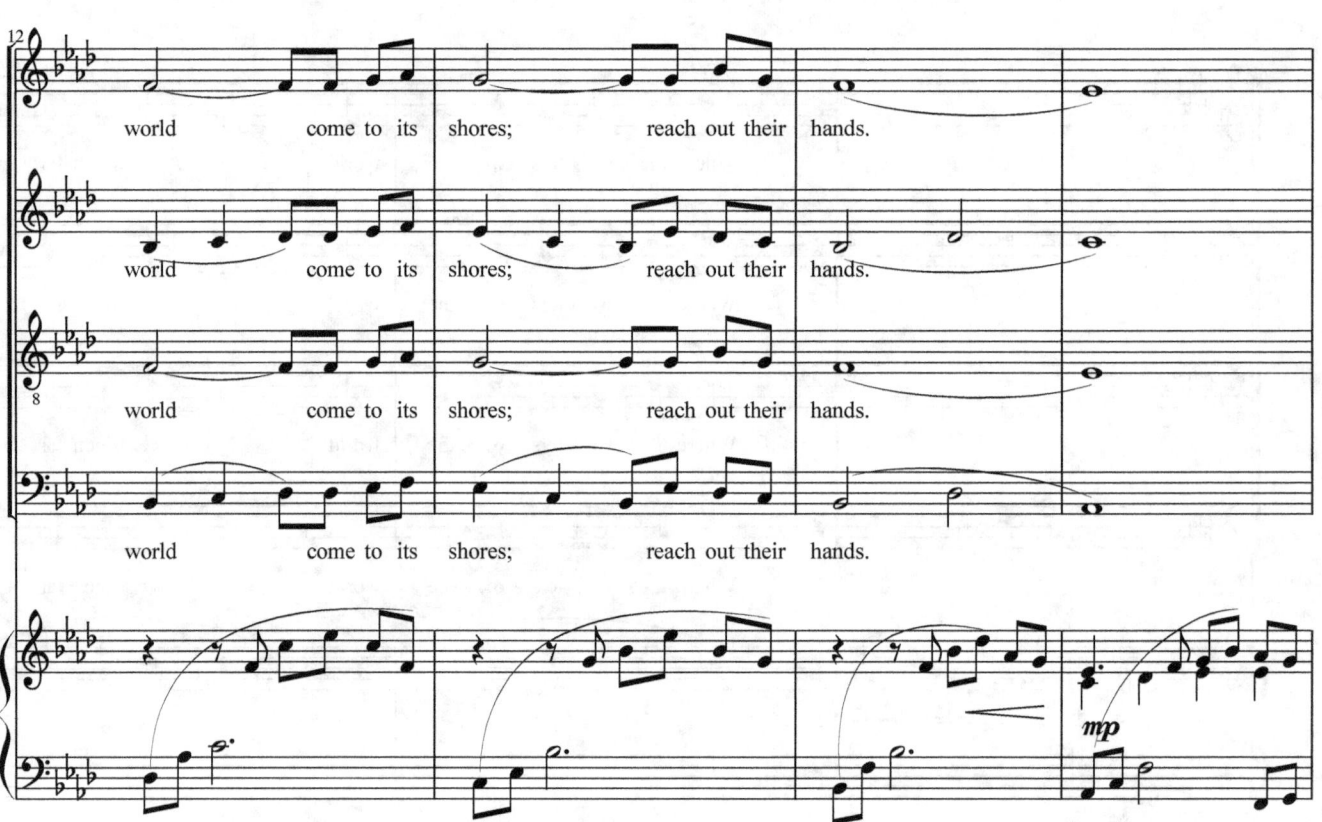

world   come to its   shores;   reach out their   hands.

world   come to its   shores;   reach out their   hands.

world   come to its   shores;   reach out their   hands.

world   come to its   shores;   reach out their   hands.

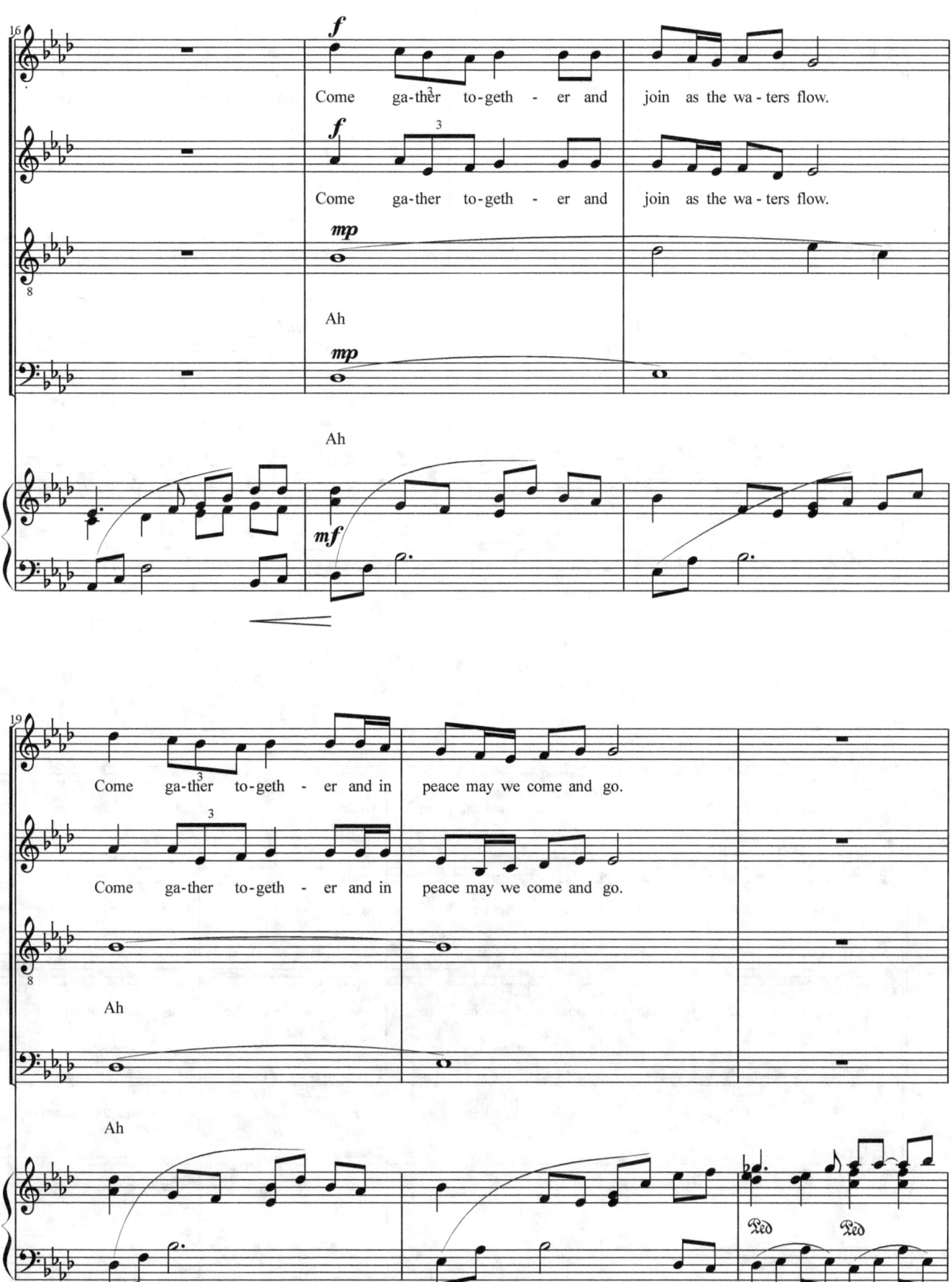

Come ga-ther to-geth - er and join as the wa-ters flow.

Come ga-ther to-geth - er and join as the wa-ters flow.

Ah

Ah

Come ga-ther to-geth - er and in peace may we come and go.

Come ga-ther to-geth - er and in peace may we come and go.

Ah

Ah

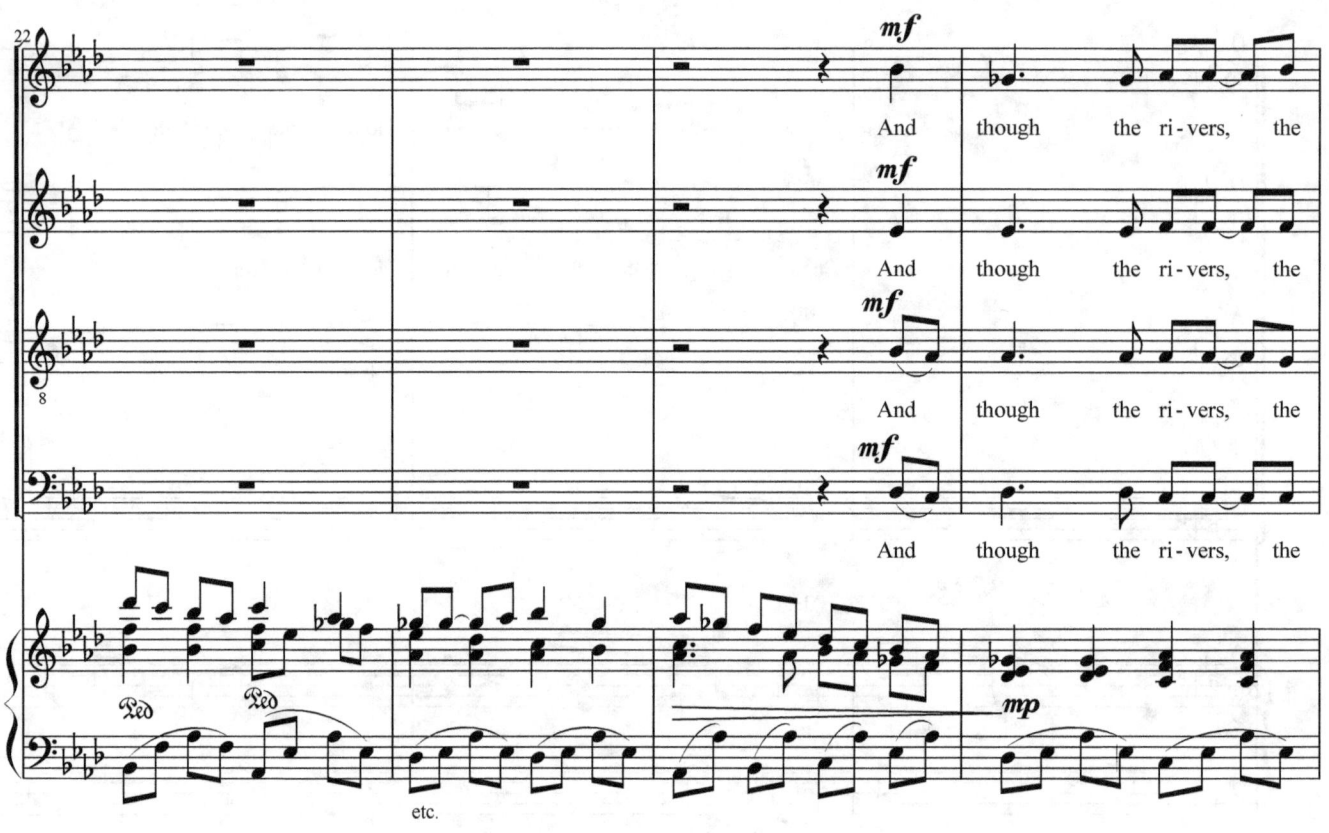

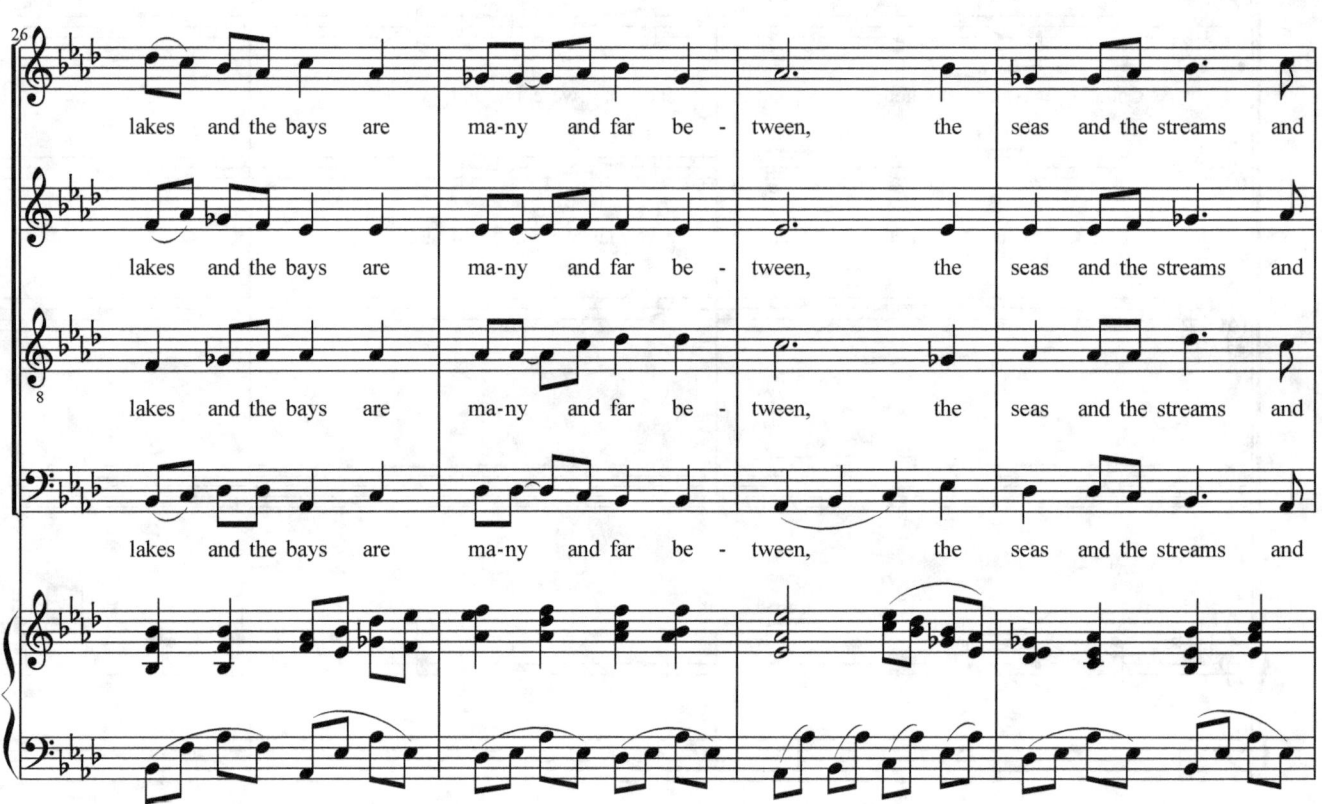

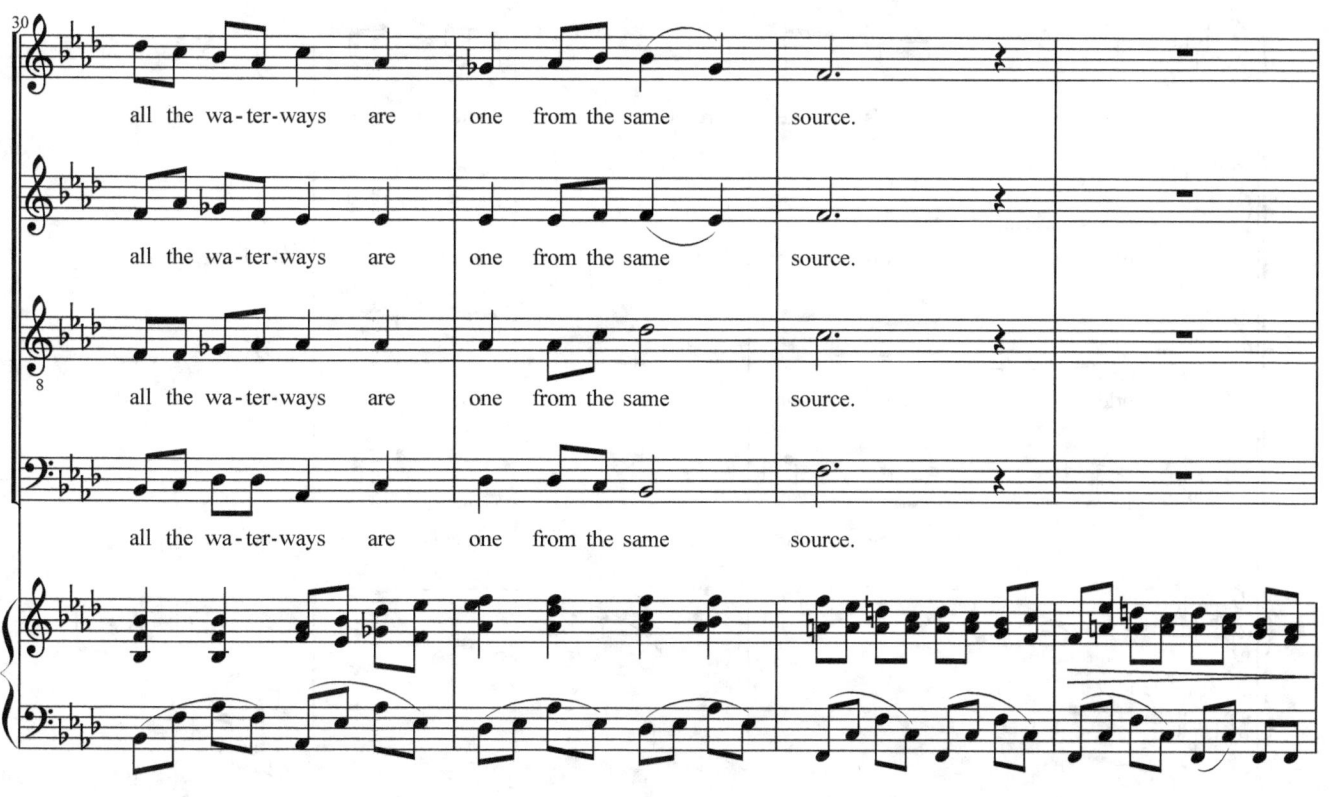

all the wa-ter-ways are one from the same source.

all the wa-ter-ways are one from the same source.

all the wa-ter-ways are one from the same source.

all the wa-ter-ways are one from the same source.

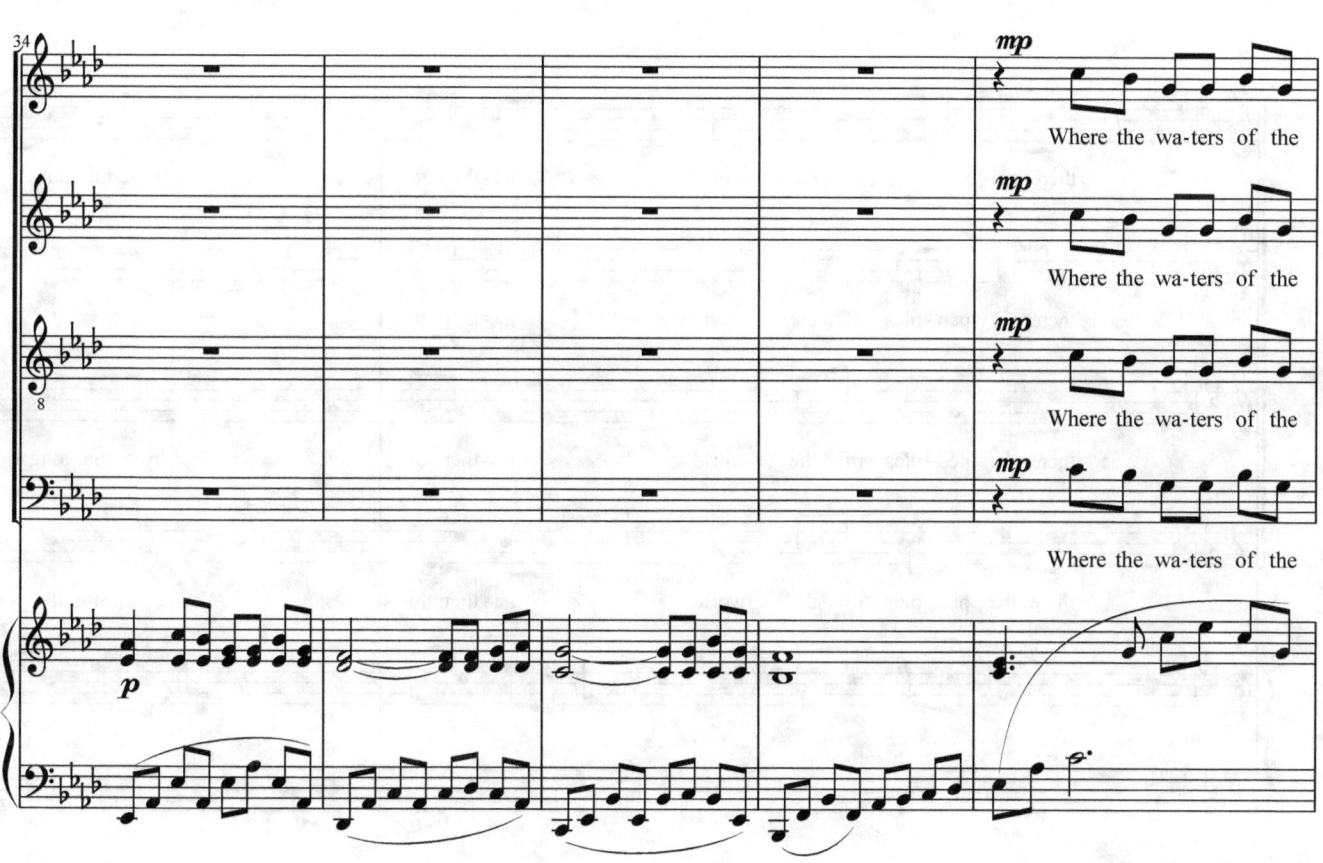

Where the wa-ters of the

Where the wa-ters of the

Where the wa-ters of the

Where the wa-ters of the

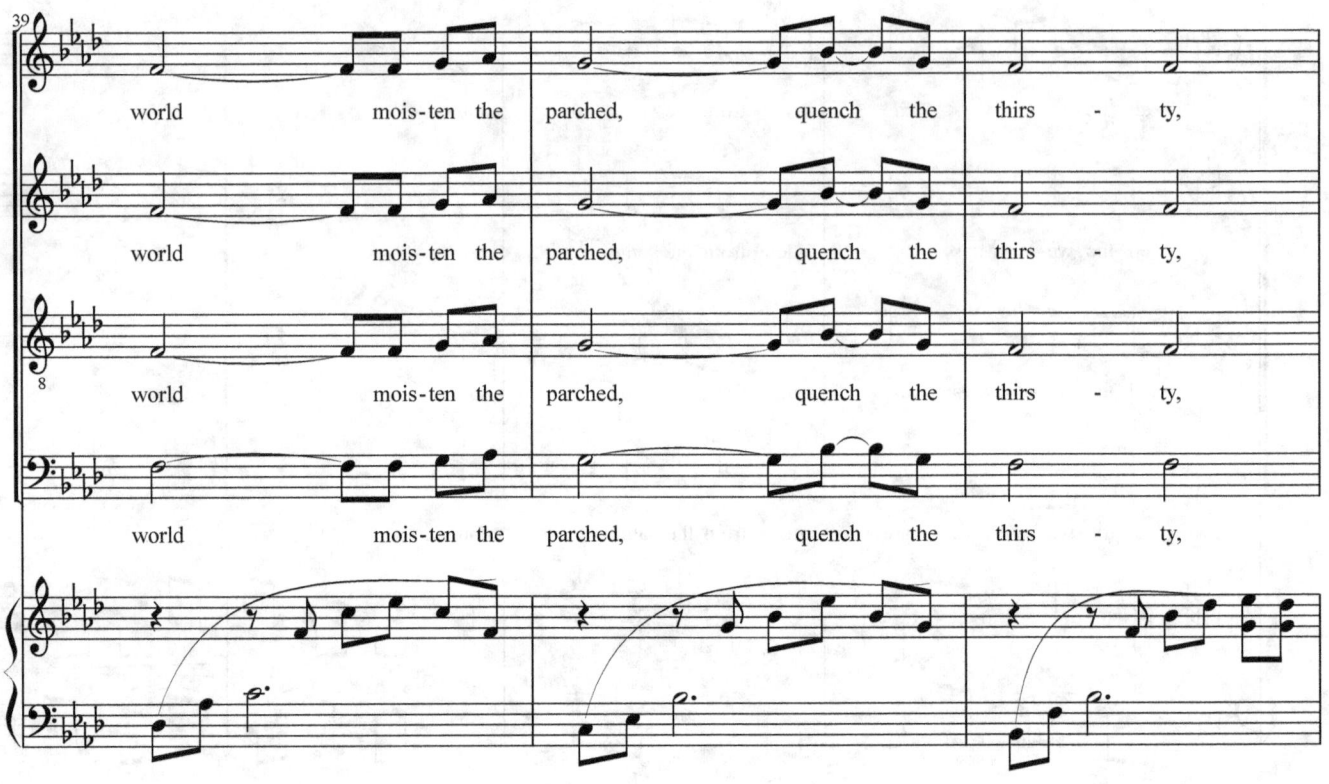

world   mois-ten the   parched,   quench   the   thirs - ty,

world   mois-ten the   parched,   quench   the   thirs - ty,

world   mois-ten the   parched,   quench   the   thirs - ty,

world   mois-ten the   parched,   quench   the   thirs - ty,

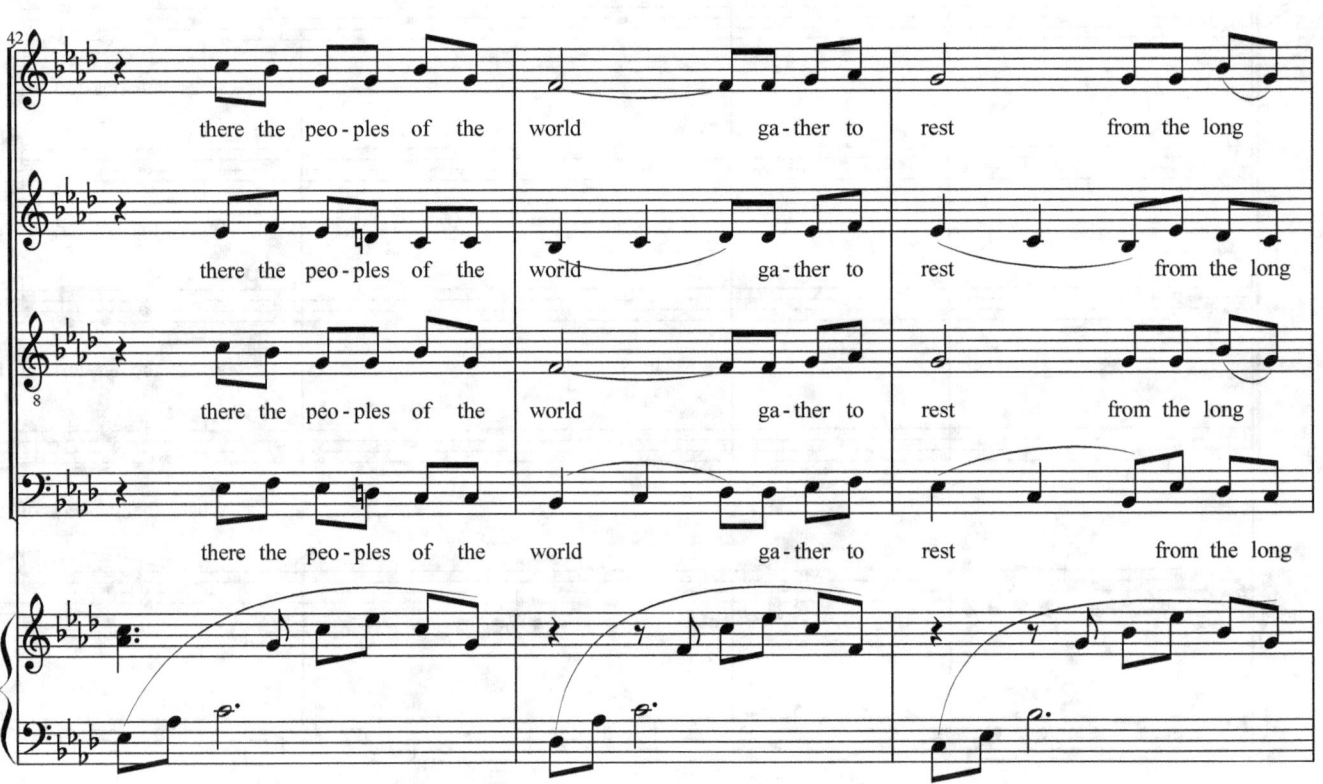

there the peo - ples of the   world   ga - ther to   rest   from the long

there the peo - ples of the   world   ga - ther to   rest   from the long

there the peo - ples of the   world   ga - ther to   rest   from the long

there the peo - ples of the   world   ga - ther to   rest   from the long

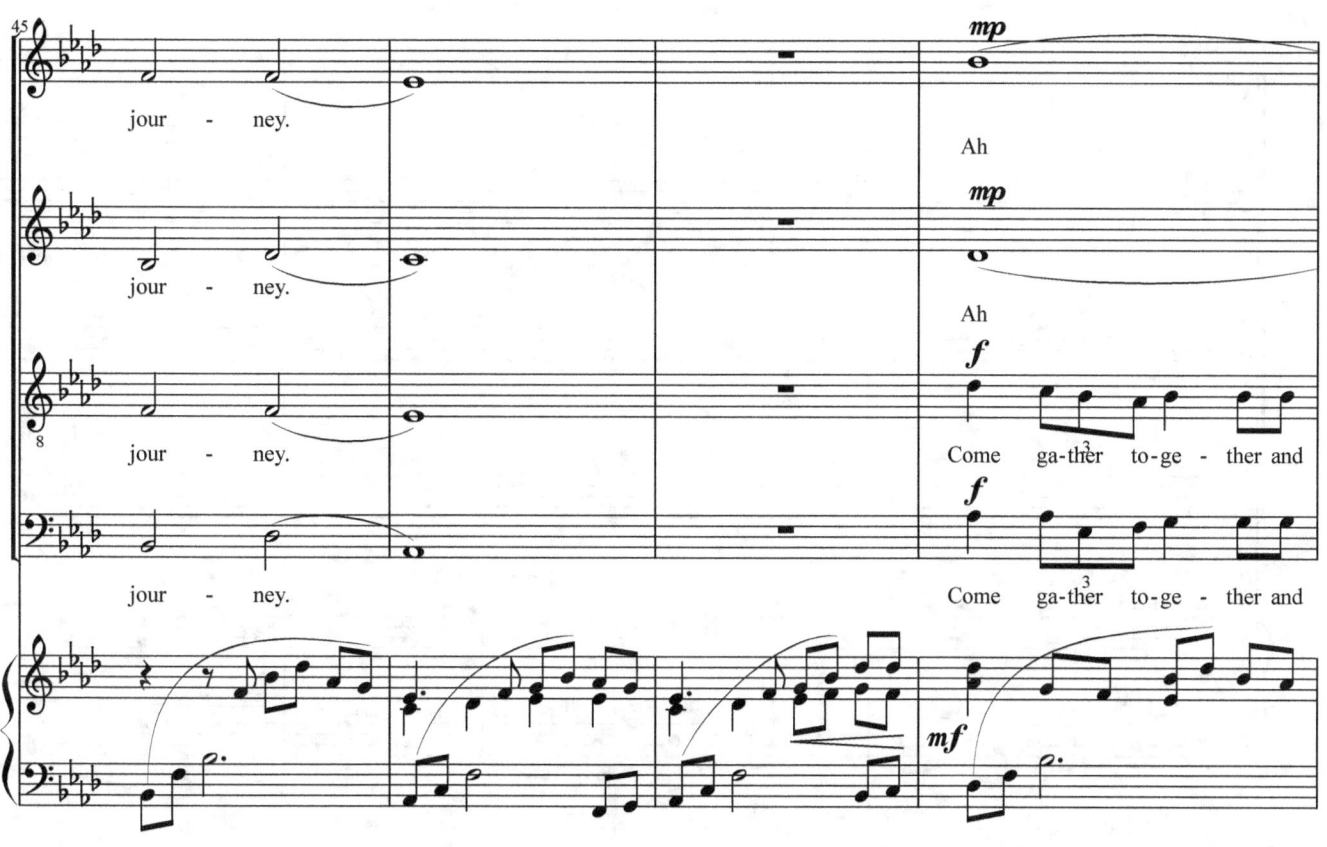

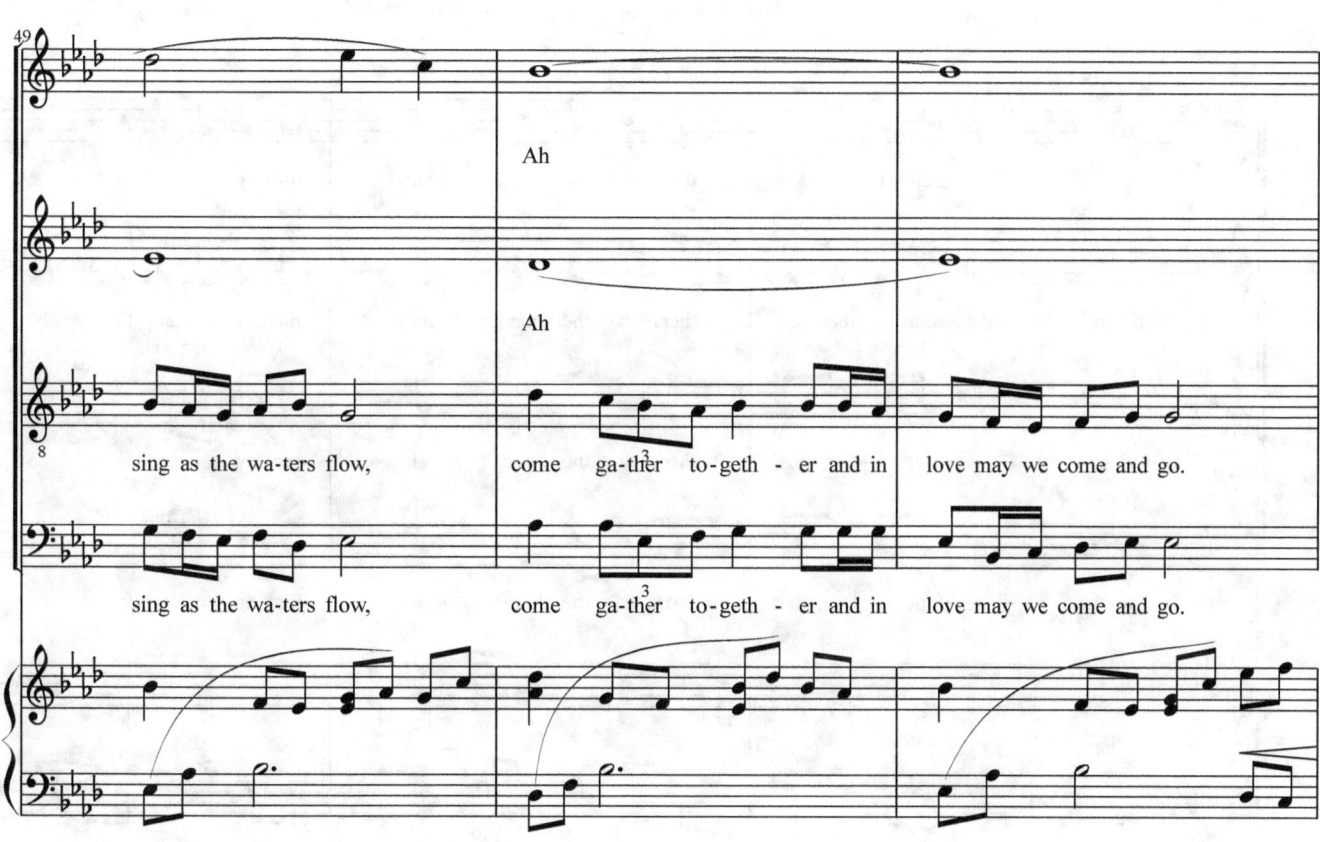

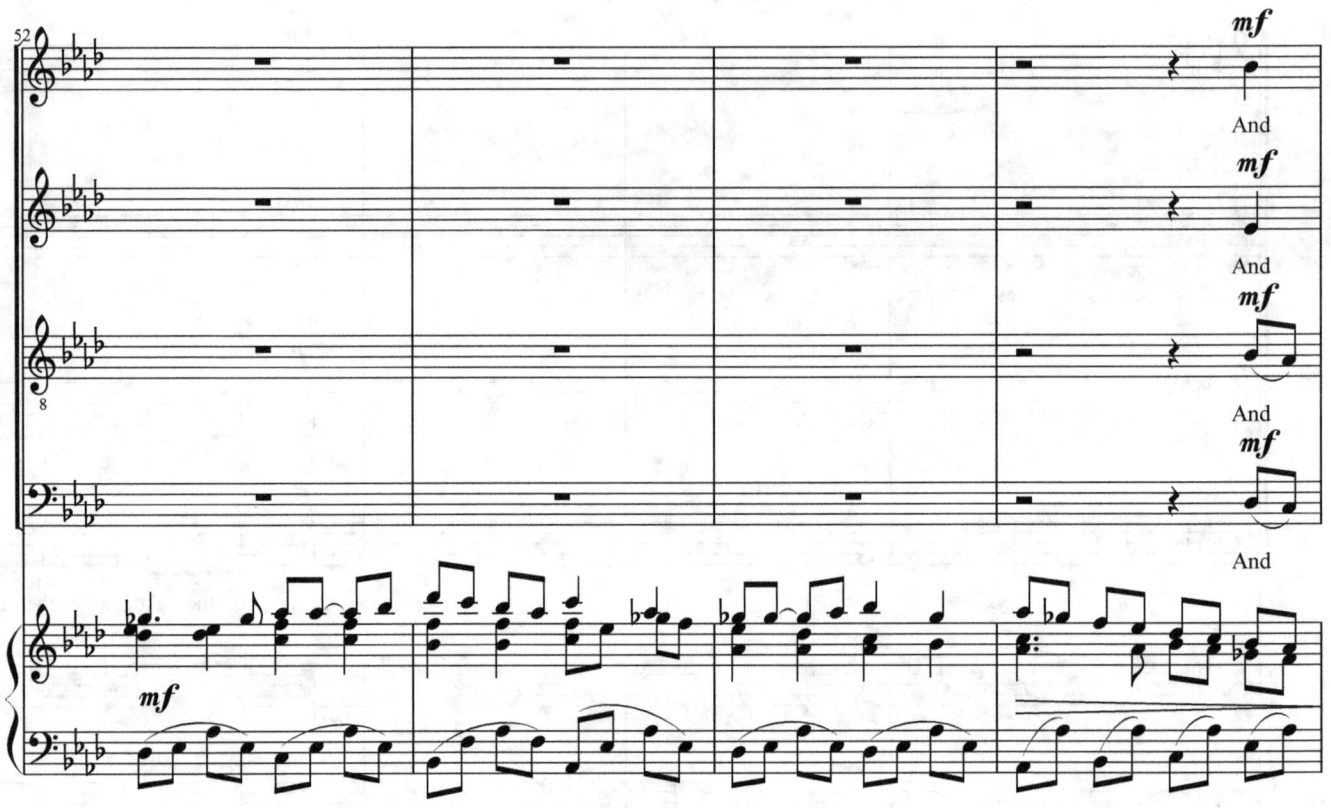

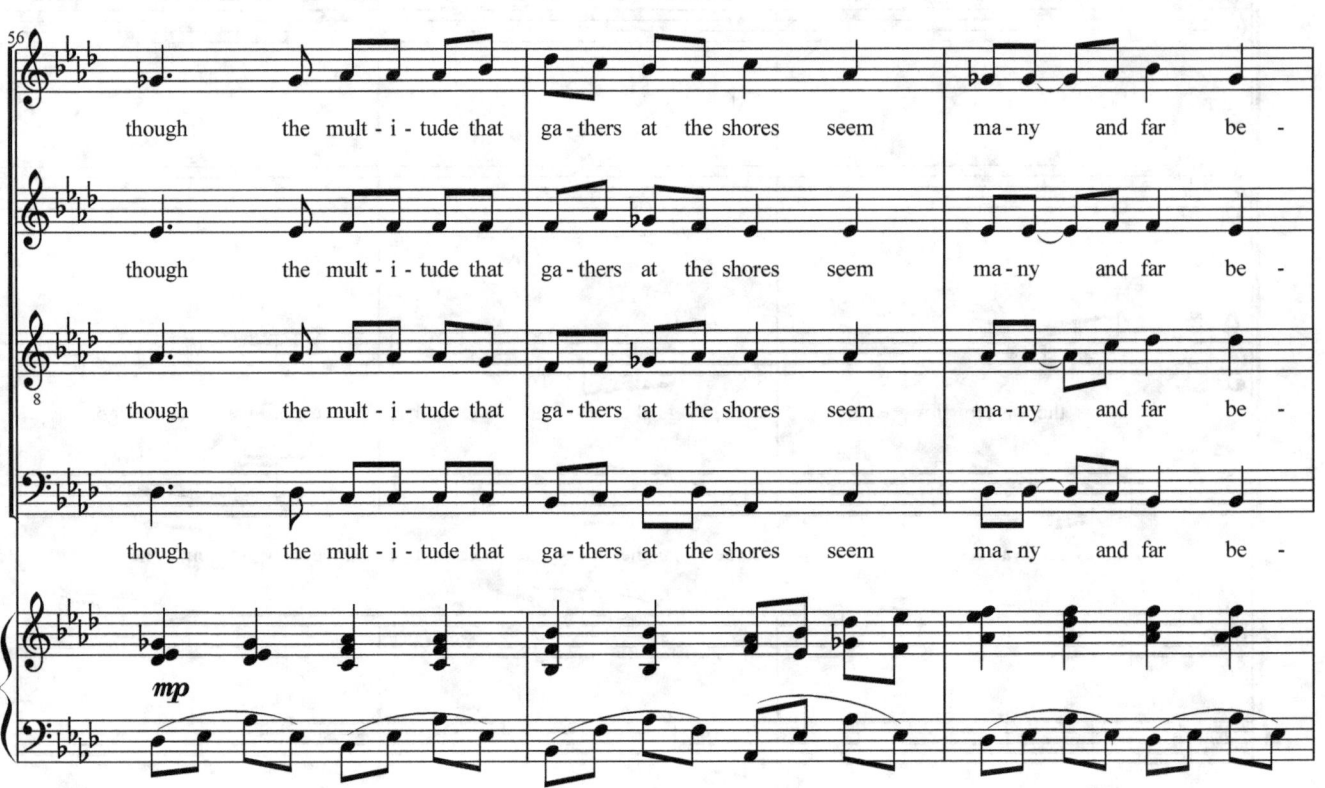

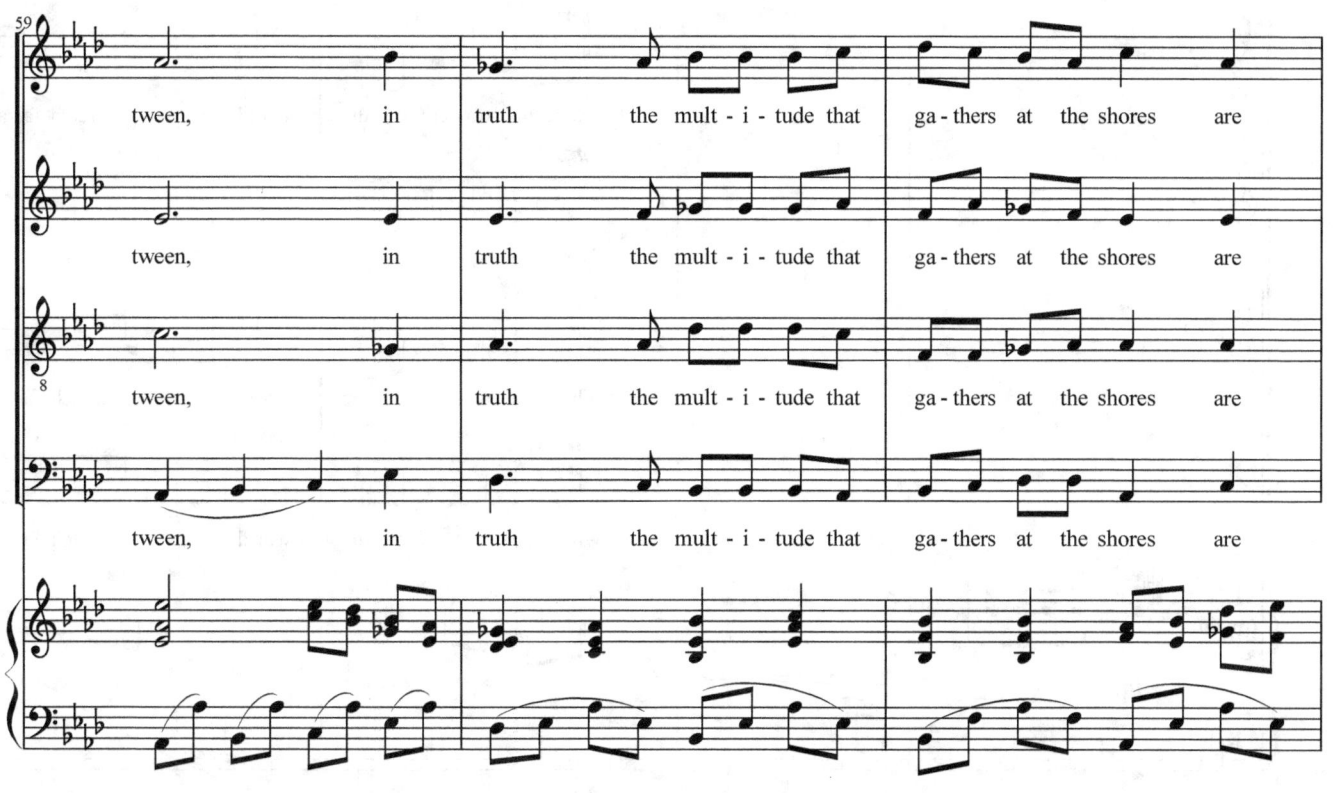

tween,   in   truth   the   mult - i - tude that   ga - thers   at   the shores   are

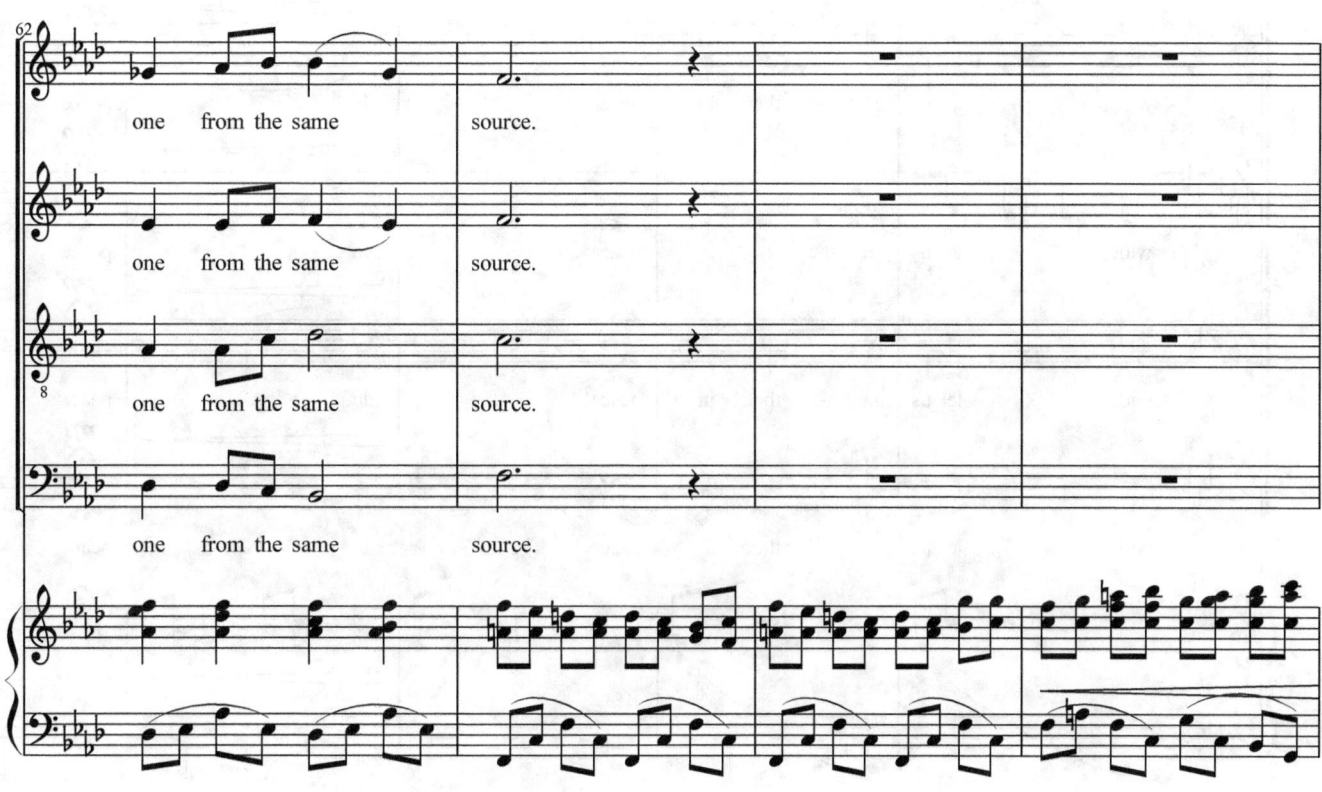

one   from the same   source.

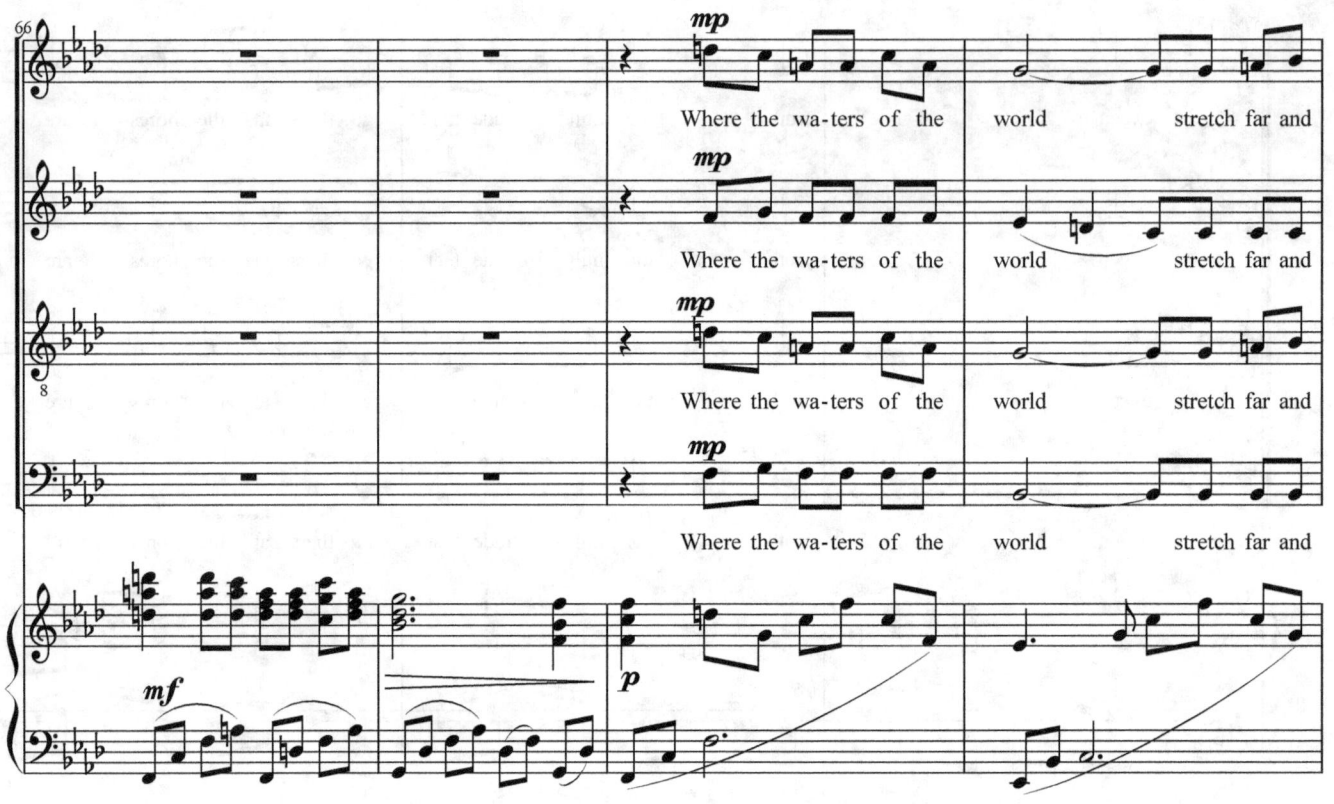

Where the wa-ters of the world stretch far and

Where the wa-ters of the world stretch far and

Where the wa-ters of the world stretch far and

Where the wa-ters of the world stretch far and

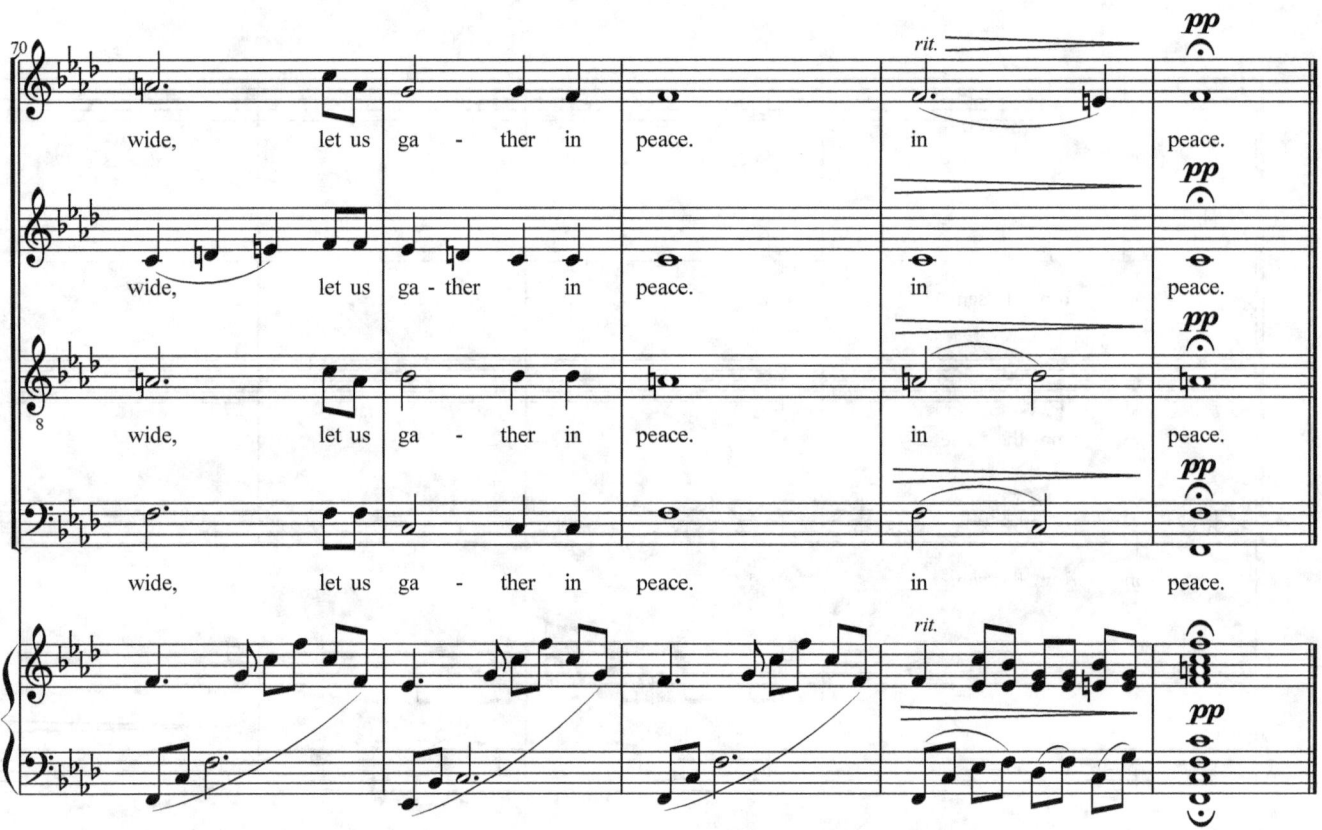

wide, let us ga - ther in peace. in peace.

wide, let us ga - ther in peace. in peace.

wide, let us ga - ther in peace. in peace.

wide, let us ga - ther in peace. in peace.

About The Composer

Dr. Kenneth Langer was born in the Pittsburgh area in 1959. He began playing trumpet in the 5th grade and decided in high school to make music his career.

Dr. Langer earned a Bachelor's Degree in Music Education at James Madison University in Harrisonburg, Virginia; a Master's of Music Degree at Radford University in Radford, Virginia; and a Ph.D. In Music Theory and Composition at Kent State University in Kent, Ohio. He has taught music at several small colleges.

He has also been the Director of Music and Arts at the Eno River Unitarian-Universalist Fellowship in Durham, North Carolina and the Assistant Conductor and Resident Composer at the Montpelier Unitarian-Universalist Church in Montpelier, Vermont.

During his twenty years of writing over 150 original works of music for various genres including brass, chorus, strings, orchestra, wind ensemble, and woodwinds; he has received numerous awards for his compositions including being named Vermont's Composer of the Year in the year 2000 and winning placement in several international composition contests. He has commercially published well over 30 compositions.

Dr. Langer currently lives in the Boston area with his family where he works as the Head of the Music Program at Northern Essex Community College in Haverhill, Massachusetts.

Publishers

Music For Brass

Nichols Music Company (Ensemble Publications)
P.O. Box 32 Ithaca, NY 14851-0032
www.enspub.com

Solid Brass Music
P.O. Box 2277 Rome GA, 30164
www.solidbrassmusic.com

Cimarron Music Press
15 Corrina Lane Salem CT 06420s
www.cimarronmusic.com

Wehr's Music House
www.wehrs-music-house.com

Music For Chorus

Yelton Rhodes Music
1236 N. Sweetzer Avenue #5 West Hollywood CA 90069
www.yrmusic.com

www.ingramcontent.com/pod-product-compliance
Lightning Source LLC
Chambersburg PA
CBHW081238180526
45171CB00005B/466